T0355326

Wilde in the Dream Factory

Wilde in the Dream Factory

Decadence and the American Movies

KATE HEXT

OXFORD
UNIVERSITY PRESS

OXFORD
UNIVERSITY PRESS

Great Clarendon Street, Oxford, OX2 6DP,
United Kingdom

Oxford University Press is a department of the University of Oxford.
It furthers the University's objective of excellence in research, scholarship,
and education by publishing worldwide. Oxford is a registered trade mark of
Oxford University Press in the UK and in certain other countries

Published in the United States of America by Oxford University Press
198 Madison Avenue, New York, NY 10016, United States of America

British Library Cataloguing in Publication Data
Data available

Library of Congress Control Number: 2023945981

ISBN 9780198875376

DOI: 10.1093/9780191987335.001.0001

Printed and bound in the UK by
Clays Ltd, Elcograf S.p.A.

For Rufus

Contents

List of Figures

Preface: The Ghosts of Wildean Decadence

Oscar Wilde died on 30 November 1900 but, had he lived on, he would have gone to Hollywood. He liked the United States when he undertook a year-long lecture tour there in 1882. And he always needed large sums of money, of the kind offered by the movie industry.

Wilde's most famous works—*The Picture of Dorian Gray* (1891), *Lady Windermere's Fan* (1892), and *The Importance of Being Earnest* (1895)—had put him at the centre of literary London. However, soon after *Earnest* opened, he seemed to be finished, both personally and professionally: bankrupt, legally separated from his wife and barred from even contacting his children, his beloved mother dead, and his plays closed.[1] His hubristic decision to sue Lord Queensberry for libel in spring 1895 had ended with Wilde himself in the dock and, after two further trials reported around the world, he was sentenced to two years' hard labour in Reading Gaol for 'acts of gross indecency'. There was hope, though. As he moved around Europe in penury and self-imposed exile after his release in 1897, he was editing his social-comedy plays for publication, adding new jokes to improve on the performance texts. He began to imagine a future where he'd write more plays and make a fresh start.[2]

We don't know whether these fantasies had formed into plans when Wilde began to grow more unwell with the middle-ear infection that would lead to his death.[3] We do know that he was attracted to the money he might make in the United States. In autumn 1897, he wrote with glee to his publisher Leonard Smithers that the *New York Journal* 'have millions, and like what is calculated to make a stir of some kind, or any kind'.[4] Whatever would he have made of Hollywood's largesse? After all, this was a man who could resist everything except temptation.

For that matter, what would Hollywood have made of Wilde? When the first motion picture studios were erected in Los Angeles, thirteen years after his death, there was still a lingering scandal around his name. Still, Hollywood always liked a bit of scandal and it loved charismatic scoundrels of the kind Wilde might have become. If, as Lord Henry speculates in *Dorian Gray*, ' "everyone who disappears is said to be seen at San Francisco" ', it is not too difficult to imagine Wilde, in the hale old age he never had, being seen there too, before heading south to Los Angeles to look for ' "all the attractions of the next world." '[5]

Hollywood might have offered Wilde the artistic community and opportunities he craved when, in exile, he imagined 'the possibility of my art coming again into touch with life'.[6] He would have been just 60 in July 1915, when the first American feature-film adaptation of *Dorian Gray* was released. He'd have been 68 when Alla Nazimova premiered her outrageous all-gay production of *Salome* on New Year's Eve 1922. We could imagine him heading out West with his loyal friend Frank Harris, who knew Charlie Chaplin; partying at Nazimova's house on Sunset Boulevard with his niece Dolly Wilde, who was one of Nazimova's lovers. Or, when future Hollywood screenwriter Ben Hecht travelled to London to meet Arthur Machen in 1918, he would surely have sought out Wilde, another of his literary idols. They might have dined at the Ritz or taken in a film with Wilde's dear friend Robbie Ross, who lived nearby and frequented the pictures with a young soldier on his arm.[7]

These are fantasies, yet Wilde did go to Hollywood. Not in the flesh but in spirit, taken there by his self-conscious heirs, who were many and various. *Wilde in the Dream Factory* tells this story. It begins with Wilde's 1882 tour and traces his evolving influence up to the mid-1940s, These decades after Wilde's death were the high point of his reputation in the United States; a period in which he and his most famous characters were widely, even (dare one say) wildly, influential. For the journalists of the Chicago Renaissance and Greenwich Village, as for the avid bohemians of the Midwest and the European immigrants who arrived at Staten Island already steeped in decadent writings, Wilde was an icon. These three circles, seemingly so diverse, would converge in Hollywood on a quest. They sought work—lucrative work—as well as artistic opportunities and the hedonistic lifestyle that Los Angeles could offer. They brought Wilde with them because he, his plays and stories, were part of their imaginative fabric.

Wilde also had fantastic box-office potential. For, in Hollywood, he and the decadent movement he represented would not primarily be identified with high culture but with entertainment. His *Salomé* (1891) inspired some of the first short rough-and-ready films in the Nickelodeon days of the 1900s. From the mid-1910s, as multi-reel adaptations came to define the industry, his popularity created demand for adaptations. Today, these movies are of interest primarily for the cultural history they illuminate. It is what happened next that makes Wilde's posthumous Hollywood career especially notable. From the 1920s, as the film industry developed new sophisticated narratives and cinematographic techniques, Wilde's style took on a life of its own that helped to shape the movies forever.

Like a lot of research projects, this book began with a puzzle. Idly watching YouTube clips some years ago, I came across *Ziegfeld Follies* (1946), a movie I hadn't seen since I spent my teens collecting hundreds of musicals on VHS tapes. One of its standout musical numbers is 'This Heart of Mine', performed by Fred Astaire and Lucille Bremer, and directed by Vincente Minnelli. It's a beautifully lavish song-and-dance sequence that tells a love story in miniature. The scene opens with an establishing shot of a masked satyr. As the camera pans to the right, we see that this is just one of ten such satyr statues presiding over the circular ballroom (Fig. 0.1). On rewatching, I found the satyrs surprising and familiar. Immersed in the decadent movement—I was writing a PhD on Wilde's mentor, Walter Pater—I realized that these figures were from half a century earlier. They bear a striking resemblance to Aubrey Beardsley's first cover illustration for the self-styled

Fig. 0.1 Establishing shot for 'This Heart of Mine' in *Ziegfeld Follies* (1946)

organ of the decadent movement, *The Yellow Book*, in 1894 (Fig. 0.2). Indeed, they *are* Beardsley's illustration, realized in 3D.

The question was what the satyrs were doing here in a big-budget MGM number. *Ziegfeld Follies* is a revue movie which takes the slender conceit of Florenz Ziegfeld (William Powell) up in heaven dreaming about producing one more show, to put together a series of musical and comedy sequences featuring MGM'S brightest stars. It was made at the zenith of MGM'S Arthur

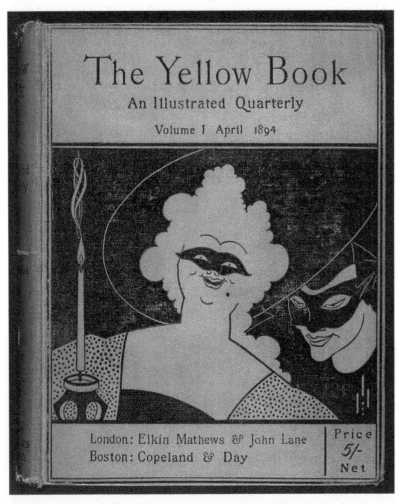

Fig. 0.2 Aubrey Beardsley's cover illustration for *The Yellow Book* 1 (April 1894)

Freed Unit, when the studio's publicity boasted 'more stars than there are in the heavens'. Gene Kelly and Fred Astaire dance together on-screen for the first time in 'The Babbitt and the Bromide'; Judy Garland performs one of her first sophisticated roles in the satirical number 'A Great Lady has an Interview'. It is good family entertainment, formulated to raise spirits during the war, and 'This Heart of Mine' is, at first glance, very much in that vein. However, the Beardsleyesque satyrs bring a ludic eroticism and sexual ambiguity quite antithetical to the ostentatiously domestic values of MGM and the Motion Picture Production Code, which strictly governed what could be said or shown on-screen from 1934. Perhaps they were an incidental allusion without any larger significance, save to a fevered imagination. Perhaps they weren't. The satyrs ironize the romance between Astaire and Bremer and, what's more, this seems too pointed to be accidental. Perhaps—just perhaps—this is a story of lust, not love. At the end of the number, as Bremer glances up to meet Astaire's eyes and they walk together into the night, they are certainly not planning the white-wedding future that the Production Code sanctioned.

After several years of watching classic movies wherever they could be found, sometimes on DVD, occasionally on reel-to-reel in archives, or often streamed via dodgy websites one of which fatally damaged my computer, I came to realize that those satyrs are no random one-off. Only, it isn't Beardsley who mainly haunts Golden Age Hollywood, despite notable guest appearances: it is his sometime friend, collaborator, and fellow decadent Oscar Wilde. Golden Age Hollywood, it turned out, was thoroughly suffused with glimpses of Wilde. Recall *The Greatest Show on Earth* (1952) and its unfolding drama of Buttons (James Stewart), the kindly clown who never removes his make-up. As Buttons's mysterious past catches up with him and we begin to suspect that he might be a killer on the run, he murmurs outside the big top, 'Well, each man kills the thing he loves.'[8]

This unattributed quotation from Wilde's *Ballad of Reading Gaol* (1898) is a very small clue to Wilde's larger presence in American pictures—a presence that was established from the industry's beginning. While direct references like this are rare, multiple adaptations of *Salome* and *Dorian Gray*, and considerable interest in Wilde's social comedies, pronounce his popularity. To this emerging movie world, Wilde's star potential was clear. He had always been a countercultural force and on-screen it would be no different. References to his works were often subtle but they were not benign. Even before pictures moved, he was a household name in the United States and, for those who read the newspapers' culture pages or went to the theatre, that name would forever evoke the homoerotic desires threaded through his works and life story. A reference to Wilde on-screen was thus a subversive gesture, hidden in plain sight. It signified crime, secrecy, and sexual indiscretion. As the American movie industry took shape, with feature-length productions and the start of censorship, Wilde's style and characters suggested ways to put sex in the air. Some of the industry's biggest names—Roscoe 'Fatty' Arbuckle, Nazimova, Mae West, Ernst Lubitsch, Ben Hecht, Samuel Hoffenstein, William Faulkner, and Alfred Hitchcock amongst them—translated Wilde's characters, motifs, and wit into original screenplays across a range of genres from the first gangster films, B-movie horrors, and films noirs, to screwball comedies and big-budget musicals. As they did so, they helped create the image of Wilde we have today: as naughty, audacious, modern.

If Wildean influences, allusions, and rewritings mostly went unremarked in the early twentieth century, it's because they occurred in a culture that was tacitly familiar with his works in a way that today we neither remember nor expect. The story of Wilde and the American film industry doesn't fit on to our map of early twentieth-century cultural history as we think we know it. Hollywood and Wilde have seemed to be different countries, the latter, along with the entire and decadent movement, swept away by the First World War, before the golden age of cinema. While the institutionalization of Wilde on university courses has tended to emphasize his more highbrow and serious aspects, it has distanced him further from the mass entertainment industry. At the same time, with a few exceptions, critical studies of influence between literature and film have pivoted closely around the more legible issues of adaptation. Often the maps we need to navigate culture are oversimplified to impose a semblance of order on the messy realities of how trends and influences really operate. None of these distinctions would have been made a hundred years ago. Despite several notable attempts to rethink Wilde's place in twentieth-century literature and a few mentions of his work in relation to movies, a full understanding of how their shared place in American cultural life remains a significant absence.

Wilde in the Dream Factory aims to provide such an account. In doing so, it shows that, when Wilde and his decadent contemporaries go to the movies, their crimes and immoral doings become fun. On the big screen, decadent figures show their true colours as extravagant counterpoints to high modernism with the desire for entertainment at their core. The decadent movement comes out as a tradition in which criminality abounds, with drug-taking, theft, and even murder, all an inherent part of the amoral fabric of a life lived for pleasure alone. As in Wilde's writings, such shenanigans on film revolve around the figure of the decadent or dandy. His most compelling characters—Salome, Dorian Gray, Lord Darlington,

Mrs Erlynne, Jack and Algernon—helped to create the blueprint for the bon-vivant dandy-cum-charismatic-misfit on-screen. Over the first decades of the film industry, Wilde's plays and novel were adapted and sampled; his characters inspired new writers too, offering lightly coded subversions within the conservative values of the Production Code. All this played out against a backdrop in which 'art for art's sake', the famous dictum of the decadent movement, was brought to life as never before, helping to create not only American cinema but also Oscar, for ever.[9] Wilde may never have gone to Hollywood himself. If we look again though, and more closely, in the studios and on the big screen, we see that he was there from the start.

1

Wilde in the American Imagination

The United States' relationship with Oscar Wilde began in 1882. It was then, during his twelve-month tour, packed with over 140 lectures and at least ninety-eight interviews, that the foundations were laid for his posthumous film career.[1] In Great Britain, Wilde's fledgling fame was as a scholar and poet. In America it would be different. While on the tour he met two of its great literary figures: Walt Whitman, with whom he got on, and Henry James, with whom he most certainly did not.[2] However, he'd published very little in 1882 and his public persona was, first and foremost, that of a flamboyant dandy and sage of art and fashion.[3]

Developing his witty repartee on the road with the express purpose of reaching beyond the cultural elite, Wilde hectored, counselled, and seduced his audiences—pioneers in the Midwest as well as metropolitan society types—on subjects ranging from art, fashion, and interior design to the literary celebrities he knew. Whatever the subject, the guiding principle was always 'art for art's sake', the deceptively simple kernel of the decadent movement. Taking the secular gospel of art, pleasure, and beauty, which this adage encapsulated, Wilde packaged it in a celebration of the individual. 'Bad art', he told audiences, 'is a great deal worse than no art at all';[4] 'one should never talk of a moral or an immoral poem—poems are either well written or badly written, that is all';[5] 'The supreme object of life is to live. Few people live. It is true life only to realize one's own perfection, to make one's every dream a reality'.[6] Such epigrammatic views anticipated a fast-moving twentieth century that would have no time for long languid Victorian sentences.

The tour itself was far from an unmitigated success but it left an indelible impression of Wilde on the American imagination. What precisely that impression was varied: Wilde was a curiosity to many, a freak show to others, and an inspiration to a few. But no matter where he went he made headline news in a blaze of bons mots and good tailoring. 'I have nothing to declare', he announced on his arrival in New York, 'except my genius.' Only he probably didn't say that. Like much about Wilde it became part of his myth after the tour ended.[7]

Wilde in the Dream Factory. Kate Hext, Oxford University Press. © Kate Hext (2024).
DOI: 10.1093/9780191987335.003.0001

In the public consciousness Wilde's wit blended with his famous publicity photographs, shot in New York by Napoleon Sarony (Fig. 1.1). The audacious overall effect was reinforced by a multitude of stage parodies. Gilbert and Sullivan's operetta *Patience* toured America at the same time as Wilde, like him, promoted by Richard D'Oyly Carte. Featuring Reginald Bunthorne as an irrepressible aesthete, with many similarities to the real thing, it made for good publicity.[8] Local touring companies got in on the act too, ironically, often doing better business than Wilde himself. One such was *Patience Wilde; or Ten Sisters of Oscar Wilde*, a burlesque featuring 'Wilde' played in drag by Francis Patrick Glassey.[9] If imitation is the most sincere form of flattery, then parody may be the most insincere form of criticism. Only it didn't really matter. In a newly emerging era where there was no such thing as bad publicity, these parodies did as much as Wilde's lectures and interviews to create his persona and shape his brand of decadence in America.[10]

Wilde would return to the United States himself only briefly in 1883.[11] Over the decades that followed, though, Wildean decadence took root there and flourished despite, and sometimes because of, his notoriety for 'the love that dare not speak its name'.[12] In 1895, Wilde's three trials and subsequent imprisonment were widely reported on the front pages of the same New York newspapers that months earlier anticipated Broadway productions of his new plays, *An Ideal Husband* and *The Importance of Being Earnest*. The facts were these: Wilde had sued the Marquess of Queensberry for libel after what *The Evening World* euphemistically called Queensberry's 'disgraceful epithet'.[13] His redacted accusation was that Wilde was 'posing as a ——'.[14] It was evidently too incendiary to print the fact that Queensberry had accused Wilde of being a sodomite.[15] When, after a torrid time in the witness box, Wilde withdrew the charge, the effective Not Guilty verdict paved the way for another trial—this time with Wilde in the dock. On 5 April 1895, the first front-page reports appeared in New York's evening papers that Wilde had been arrested at the Cadogan Hotel and charged with 'acts of gross indecency' that very day. Like Queensberry's accusation, the details of exactly what he had done wrong were very few.[16] In the trial by media the verdict was, though, clear. 'The career of Oscar Wilde ended to-day in blackest infamy', the New York-based *Sun* reported the day after his arrest.[17] The unfolding courtroom drama was narrated in the press with all the suspense and scene-setting of a soap opera.[18] When Wilde took the stand he gave a defiant performance that would secure his stardom, defending his homoerotic love. Some American papers omitted his shocking defence.[19]

Fig. 1.1 Napoleon Sarony's portrait photograph of Oscar Wilde in New York (1882)

However, others published his exchange with lead prosecutor Charles Gill in all its glory. They recognized Wilde's star power.[20]

Like the parodies of Wilde during his tour, in America the trials became rolled into his legend. Their sinful glow was essential to his wickedness, and his wickedness was part of his charm; wickedness being, as Wilde had written in his 'Phrases and Philosophies for the Young', 'a myth invented by good people to account for the curious attractiveness of others'.[21] In America, his cultural presence became integral to a larger general interest in the nexus of ideas and figures associated with pleasure and beauty for its own sake. While in the Old World, fine lines distinguished Pre-Raphaelitism, aestheticism, decadence, and symbolism from each other as they evolved successively in the late nineteenth century, these movements arrived together in America and blurred in its cultural imagination. The priority they all gave to beauty, art, and pleasure was a response—a riposte even—to William Dean Howells and his morality-driven naturalism.[22] Their main influence would be not on criticism but on fiction and the arts, where the whole idea of living for beauty, art, and pleasure was embodied in the flâneur, the dandy, and the decadent, who shaded into each other as misfits against the grain, whose aesthetic experience in various forms was to be the fulcrum of their lives.

Little Magazines and Newspapers

Today we tend to see Wilde and the decadent movement as literary phenomena. In truth, across Europe, decadence influenced fine art and music, making its biggest impact on public consciousness through Wilde's plays and Beardsley's scandalous illustrations. Wilde's career as a playwright was even more prominent in the United States where his agent was the legendary Elizabeth 'Bessie' Marbury. From the 1890s, she handled the rights for his plays and ensured that his social comedies opened in New York soon after their London premieres.[23] It's partly as a result of her dynamism and connections that Wilde's and Beardsley's styles came to influence American theatre, commercial publishing, photography, illustration, and journalism—as well as highbrow literature—in ways undreamt of by the Old World aesthetes.

Wilde's American tour created other influential Wildeans too. The enigmatic and largely forgotten Fred Holland Day is a case in point. As a teenager he met Wilde on tour and they became regular correspondents.[24] A decade later his Boston-based publishing house Copeland & Day distributed *The Yellow Book* stateside and produced the illustrated first American edition of

Wilde's play *Salome* (1894) alongside editions of other decadent works.[25] In the late 1890s Day took up photography, which he was among the first to champion as an art form in its own right. His pictures were suffused with the motifs and styles of the wider decadent movement, with his spectral images of nymphs and satyrs, ancient Greek boys, and crucifixion scenes overturning the commonplace idea that photography was a byword for realism. One of the most striking is titled *Hypnos* (*c*.1896) (Fig. 1.2). The young man personifies the desire for beauty for its own sake, shot in soft focus with his eyes closed as his lips touch a stylized poppy. His state of (un)dress, coupled with his feathered chaplet headdress, idealizes ancient Greek homoeroticism in a way common in fin-de-siècle decadent writing.[26] Beyond its provocatively risqué subject, Day's image suggests the potential for translating decadent aesthetics into mechanically reproduced art. Decadence could be germinal, adaptive to new forms.

Fred Holland Day may not show us the America we expect to see. In the 1890s, the American Dream as we know it was being born.[27] This was a decade that prized the frontier spirit, even as it was evolving in new directions defined by industrial entrepreneurialism and fledgling Progressivism.[28] Day was not alone, though, in seeking a different kind of American Dream. His was the dream of 'art for art's sake' and of the sexual freedom, delicious languor, and myth-making that followed (theoretically at least) in its wake, in place of hard work and Puritan ethics. The main advocates of this philosophy in the 1890s were the little magazines, notably *The Chap-Book* (1894–8) and *M'lle New York* (1895–8). Both very chichi, with high production values, self-consciously modelled on *The Yellow Book*, these magazines started a trend. Shirley Everton Johnson characterizes it in *The Cult of the Purple Rose* (1902), writing how 'scarcely a day passed that did not witness the birth of a new publication of this character'.[29] Johnson's novel is the story of Harvard undergraduates who are inspired by *The Yellow Book* to found their own little magazine. Entitled *The Pink Mule*, it would exist for the sole purpose of cultivating 'art for art's sake', issued in just one prohibitively expensive edition.[30] As an affectionate parody, *The Cult of the Purple Rose* captures the aesthetic posturing fashionable on the East Coast at the time.

While Ivy League decadents could seem cultish and self-satisfied—and often they were—their interests presage a wider flowering of decadence that carried on unabated by Wilde's ignominy in London and sections of the US press. In 1905 New York-based poet George Sylvester Viereck famously reported the rumour that Wilde was not in fact dead but living under a pseudonym in New York until the world was ready for his spectacular

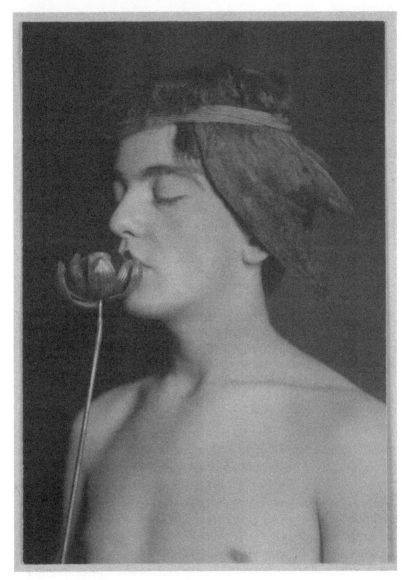

Fig. 1.2 Fred Holland Day's *Hypnos* (c.1896)

return.[31] Reports of Wilde's reincarnation were greatly exaggerated. However, when Viereck wrote a novel titled *The House of the Vampire* (1907),
with a Wildean protagonist, he was on to something. As in Viereck's mad
and irresistible novel, Wilde *was* coming back to life, not in person but via

his imaginative influences. Future songwriter Howard Dietz, for instance, read Wilde as a student at Columbia University. Soon after, in 1917, as publicity director for the newly founded Goldwyn Pictures, he appropriated 'art for art's sake' to create the studio's motto: *ars gratia artis*. He translated it into Latin for greater gravitas and added the lion from the crest of his alma mater.[32] In 1924, when Goldwyn Pictures merged with Metro Pictures and Louis B. Mayer Pictures, this became the logo of MGM, emblazoned forever on the reel of film above Leo the Lion's head. During the heyday of Mayer's reign at MGM it stood as an ironic anathema to his imperative for family values in the studio's movies. While much else has changed about MGM since its glory days it remains the logo today, its origin in the decadent movement long since forgotten.

By the 1910s the tendrils of Wilde and the decadent movement had spread further into magazine and newspaper offices. It was there that many of the best Hollywood writers started out as critics, writers, and reporters.[33] *The Little Review* was the most famous of the little magazines. When its editor Margaret Anderson declared that 'Art for art's sake is merely the sensible statement of the most self-evident fact in the world', she was consciously using the decadents' rallying call to boast of the magazine's modernity and liberal values.[34] Her Wildean vision of art jostled with and evolved into what we would now call literary modernism on the magazine's pages. It also facilitated modernism: 'art for art's sake' underlies Anderson's incredulity towards the moral opprobrium of political and religious leaders. This was nowhere more apparent than in its defiant serial publication of James Joyce's *Ulysses* (1918–20), for which Anderson and co-editor Jane Heap were convicted of obscenity in 1921 and forced to cease publication of the novel.[35] Today we bracket *Ulysses* as a modernist novel—perhaps the ultimate modernist novel—but it appeared between the very same covers as a new essay by Arthur Symons, author of the definitive article 'The Decadent Movement in Literature' (1893), and short stories by Ben Hecht that were saturated in the decadent motifs of *The Yellow Book*.[36] The publication of *Ulysses* also began just a month before a new production of *The Importance of Being Earnest* marked the opening of Joyce's own theatre company at Theatre zur Kaufleuten, in Zurich. A coincidence, no doubt. The point is this: decadence was not some Victorian moment left behind in the last century—far from it. Anderson and *The Little Review*, like Joyce and his production of *Earnest*, showed that it was modern and radical, ushering in a countercultural assertion that art might reject morally improving political or social uses.

There was, though, never anything as definite as a decadent *movement* in the United States. Instead, that principle of 'art for art's sake', and the styles it suggested, flourished in pockets as a countercultural spirit over the first decades of the new century. I've noted above that America's relationship with Wilde began in 1882 but it was only gradually that his influence became apparent, coming together in the literary world with the rich culture of the United States that long predated Wilde, interacting with the legacy of Edgar Allen Poe, and culminating with the phenomenon that newspapers called 'the new decadence' in the late 1910s and 1920s.[37] Beyond *The Little Review* there were various other examples of 'the new decadence', some of which we'll come back to in Chapters 4 and 5. The Claire Marie Press, founded by irrepressible dandy Donald Evans, was rooted in decadent styles and motifs even as these were reimagined into foundational works of modernism, including Gertrude Stein's poetic masterpiece, *Tender Buttons* (1914).[38] For all that American decadence looked back to the established figures of the European original, the experimentation shows that it was far more than a tribute act.

However, this is already a story taking a wrong turn. Anderson, Evans, and Stein were, like Day, part of a cultural elite for whom decadence suggested a deliciously perverse twist on a lifestyle already their own: that of the wealthy cosmopolite. They were, as many of the European decadents had been, the leisured offspring of hard-working and high-principled families, with inherited wealth they could splash on funding artistic endeavours. Their story is far from the full story. Wilde himself came from a wealthy family and he flirted with high culture. At the same time, the fact that he was greeted in America as a showman in training was definitive. As his plays and stories appeared over the next fifteen years, their reception was imbued with this kind of showmanship.[39] In the 1910s and 1920s, as during his year-long tour and indeed as today, he had broad popular appeal. While his works and those of European decadence were influencing the independently wealthy literati and arty, they were also a force in the newspaper offices of Chicago, in little off-Broadway theatres and repertory theatres, am-dram, one-reel Nickelodeon films, and among small-town readers who devoured reprinted decadent books.

Wilde and other figures from the decadent movement—including Walter Pater, Aubrey Beardsley, and Arthur Symons—were prominent in the vibrant bohemianism of regional centres—*la vie bohème* as it was known—from the late 1890s.[40] Magazines such as *The New Bohemian: A Modern Monthly*, based in Cincinnati, illustrated outposts of regional decadence in

America's smaller cities, alongside the far more storied decadence-inspired *Chap-Book* and *M'lle New York*.[41] As these currents developed in the first years of the twentieth century, a proliferation of cheap editions of fin-de-siècle books brought new audiences to Wilde and his decadent contemporaries. The most enduring was the Modern Library of the World's Best Books, known today as the Modern Library. It was founded in 1917 by Boni and Liveright to provide affordable books at 60 cents each. With an eye to the market, its debut list of twelve titles began with Wilde's *The Picture of Dorian Gray*.[42]

Moreover, Wilde directly inspired the era's biggest and most successful bid to deliver affordable literature to the masses. Emanuel Haldeman-Julius was the self-educated son of Jewish immigrants from Russia. In 1904, aged 15, in Philadelphia he bought a 10-cent edition of *The Ballad of Reading Gaol*. Decades later he recalled the moment:

> It was winter, and I was cold, but I sat down on a bench and read that booklet straight through, without a halt, and never did I so much as notice that my hands were blue, that my wet nose was numb, and that my ears felt as hard as glass. Never until then, or since, did any piece of printed matter move me more deeply ... I'd been lifted out of this world—and by a 10¢ booklet. I thought, at that moment, how wonderful it would be if thousands of such booklets could be made available.[43]

He found a way to do just that, creating the Little Blue Book series in 1919 in the tiny town of Girard, Kansas. Wilde's *Ballad* was one of his two first titles. Issued in pamphlet form and stapled together, Little Blue Books sold in their millions for 5 cents apiece. Titles ranged widely, including literary classics, but the list never played safe. An ardent socialist and atheist, Haldeman-Julius was keen to push radical and unconventional viewpoints, and Wilde featured prominently.

Haldeman-Julius was a regional bohemian and so were many of his readers. In his novel *Our House* (1919), Henry Seidel Canby, later a founding editor of the *Saturday Review of Literature*, dramatized two of them. Set in his home town of Wilmington, Delaware (lightly disguised as 'Millington'), *Our House* features a protagonist not unlike Canby himself, who spends his time reading *Dorian Gray* and other decadent literature while making ends meet writing press ads, and dreaming of making it as a writer. He is frustrated by his prospects when he meets a local girl who seems to share his interests, and she ventures a question close to her heart:

'Do you read Pater?'

'That's what I mean—to live with a perfect appreciation of beauty and thought—to burn with a gem-like flame?'

She turned her eyes afire with intellectual passion upon him. 'It's difficult,' she said—'here in Millington.'[44]

The intellectual world of *Our House* is quite different to the one we inhabit today; one in which the reader is reasonably expected to know the reference here to Walter Pater's (in)famous Conclusion to *Studies in the History of the Renaissance* (1873): 'To burn always with this hard gem-like flame, to maintain this ecstasy, is success in life.'[45] This hedonistic flourish inspired Wilde. 'It is my golden book,' he told W. B. Yeats of *The Renaissance*; 'it is the very flower of decadence: the last trumpet should have sounded the moment it was written.'[46] Such decadent aspirations are part of a forgotten America now. The loss is not to intellectual history alone. We forget at our peril how rich and various the American Dream once was. Today that phrase evokes narrow narratives of self-made materialism, but a century ago many ordinary Americans dreamed larger. As Jonathan Freedman has shown, far from being seen as elite or effete, decadence and aestheticism were enthusiastically embraced by the upwardly mobile in the West and Midwest, who seized on 'art for art's sake' as a subversion of gentry high culture and its values.[47] In places like Omaha and Fort Worth, as well as in small cities and university towns, Wilde and his contemporaries were integral to the culture boom that began in the 1890s. Their essays and stories validated and inspired local versions of aestheticism in Middle America.[48]

Take, for example, two of golden-age cinema's biggest names, who we'll discuss more later. Vincente Minnelli, who directed 'This Heart of Mine' with its Beardsley satyrs in *Ziegfeld Follies*, had a long interest in decadent style. By the time he was nominated for the Best Director Oscar in 1952, he was fully fledged as 'the Oscar Wilde of the camera', 'the aesthete in the factory'.[49] He was the ultimate director of musical films at the pinnacle of this genre, working in the flashiest studio during the golden age of Hollywood. Minnelli grew up in Delaware, Ohio, where, reading his father's books, his 'flights of fantasy were boundless'.[50] From 1919, working as a window dresser and a photographer in Chicago, he became enthralled by Wilde and James Abbott McNeill Whistler.[51] Over the next decade, his self-education in fin-de-siècle art, literature, and culture became an important part of his self-transformation from 'a timid boy from Ohio who liked to draw and who hid in the background' to 'an aesthete and man of the world'.[52] From Whistler and decadent writers like Wilde and Firbank, new imaginative vistas opened to him. 'I was', he later remembered,

> eager to read more. And since neither friends nor family had any such books in their collections, I explored the world of Brentano's. Even the process of selecting a book dazzled me. I saw customers come in and go directly to the book they wanted. How did one develop this homing instinct? What were all those worlds they were seeking?[53]

He was seeking a world made for art and entertainment, and he found it in Brentano's in Greenwich Village. While living in the village he illustrated *Casanova's Memoirs* (1930) in the style of Beardsley.[54] The high point of Beardsleyism had passed, but it had formed Minnelli and many others. By the time he relocated to Hollywood in 1940, he was fashioning himself as a dandy with a yellow sports jacket in a homage to Whistler and the Yellow Nineties.[55] Like Minnelli, the man who was to become Hollywood's ultimate screenwriter, Ben Hecht, discovered decadent novels in Chicago when he arrived as an apprentice reporter from Racine, Wisconsin, in 1914. Wilde and the decadent tradition were the dream of the small-town, working-class boy who never went to university and desperately wanted to be a sophisticated cosmopolitan. From their modest backgrounds, the fantasy of endless leisure and sexual liberalism, owning beautiful objects and making witty remarks in spacious drawing rooms, had an obvious aspirational appeal.

Starting out as a reporter makes Hecht typical in another way too. For it was in the newspaper offices at least as much as in the bijou publishing houses of New York and Chicago that decadence was first packaged to meet the demands of America's mass market. Journalists were saturated in the literary influences of the 'belated cosmopolitan decadence' that had gained popularity in America.[56] Mostly they were not college graduates but autodidacts, as Minnelli and Hecht were. When the latter fictionalized the office of the *Chicago Daily News*, where he worked from 1914 to 1923, he evoked how his hard-living telegraph editor lived in 'a 'bacchanal of words' reading Joris-Karl Huysmans, Gustave Flaubert, Théophile Gautier, Symons, and Pater, while waiting for news stories to break.[57] Even decades later, Hecht's dominant memory of the *Daily News* office was of 'crack reporters hunched over first editions of Arthur Symons and George Moore'.[58] His accounts remind us that the appeal of decadence was broader and deeper than Wilde and Beardsley. If all this seems counter-intuitive—it's hard to imagine that hacks on today's *New York Post* have similar reading lists—that is a salutary warning against reading the past, even the fairly recent past, through the lens of the present.

Little magazines and newspapers were not separate worlds. Journalists like Hecht moved between the two. At the same time the version of decadence fostered in the newspapers was distinct in an important way: it was populist. In contrast to the pricey little magazines that introduced modernism to the world, or rather to a highbrow elite, newspapers and affordable magazines had a broad readership who wanted to be entertained.[59] Turning away from abstract discussions of 'art for art's sake', they focused on the commitment to sensation that this phrase encapsulates and which its adherents pursued. Out went ponderous classical references and Pater's hesitating gloom. Decadence became racier and more sensational, with all the wit and brevity of Wilde's epigrams now given an American twist. There was even an advertisement for the Westminster Bank in South Carolina that counselled people of 'The Importance of Being Earnest' with their savings.[60] When Burton Rascoe introduced Huysmans's À rebours (1884), in the *New York Tribune*, as 'the book that launched a thousand quips and burnt the topless towers of tedium', this was one of numerous enthusiastic profiles of fin-de-siècle decadent writing.[61] Not only that, but Rascoe's distinctly American idiom closed the space between nineteenth-century Paris or London and the United States in the 1920s, rendering decadence more engaging to modern Americans.

Not everyone was impressed. What some commentators praised as the new decadence, others condemned as a travesty. Richard Le Gallienne— minor British fin-de-siècle poet and one of Wilde's lovers, who had emigrated to the United States—published an article titled 'The Coming Back of Oscar Wilde' in 1919. His judgement was severe: 'it has not been the least of Wilde's misfortunes that he has been posthumously appropriated for their own by an unpleasant rag-tag and bobtail of literary and artistic failures and poseurs, would-be "decadents" and "degenerates".'[62] Is Le Gallienne's remarkable slight directed at the Hechts and Rascoes who championed decadent writing in the popular press? It might well be. There is in his dismissal more than a whiff of social prejudice. These new decadents were diverse and differently educated, and they were not to Le Gallienne's taste.

Whether Le Gallienne liked it or not, the language of decadence began to change after its Atlantic crossing. Its cultural significance was altering considerably too. In Europe, decadence had symbolized declining imperial power and could sometimes be imperious. By contrast, America drew out its naughtiness and eroticism, using these qualities to poke fun at Puritanism. That is one of the reasons why America also loved Beardsley. His style first made a mark in the original illustrations included in Copeland & Day's *Salome*.[63] It grew into a trend via the little magazines. By

Fig. 1.3 Front cover of *Bruno's Weekly* (16 December 1916)

the 1910s America's newspapers and magazines were awash with grotesque and whimsical characters that were clearly Beardsley's children: drawn in economical black lines, with an ironic hauteur and a hint of perversity, characteristics considered decidedly modern. In 1918 Frank Pease declared that the United States was in the grip of 'The Vogue of Beardsley'.[64] His reputation peaked with major exhibitions in Chicago and New York in 1919, which were the first retrospectives of his work. And this was even before the furore caused by H. S. Nichols's *Fifty Drawings by Aubrey Beardsley* (1920), containing previously unknown works selected, the frontispiece declared, from Nichols's own personal collection. The truth soon came out: they were forged.[65] The covers of *Bruno's Weekly* (1915–16) featured images of imperious Beardsleyesque dancers and artists (Fig. 1.3), while Ralph Barton drew in Beardsley style for *Vanity Fair*, the *New Yorker*, and, later, Anita Loos's *Gentlemen Prefer Blondes* (1925).[66] 'The Vogue of Beardsley' went on and on.

The scent of decadence in the air precipitated impassioned calls to rehabilitate Wilde's reputation. It was part of his myth to be the comeback kid, always in need of rediscovery by a new acolyte to explain him to the world. Again and again, during the first decades of the twentieth century, as they did so, articles tried to reposition him as a serious intellectual. He was and always had been. However, that aspect was not of interest to the American mainstream, where his real appeal was as a bringer of fun, general naughtiness, and aspiration. Such qualities somehow didn't count for the gatekeepers of high culture but those people didn't matter really. Underground and in popular culture a different and far wider influence had begun.

Onstage

Before the movies, Wildean decadence proved its popularity with the American public in the theatres.

Ever since Wilde's tour and the lively parodies it inspired, his presence in American culture had been defined by its theatricality. *Salome* first put Wilde in vogue on the American stage. Or, at least, his play was frequently onstage, if not in vogue, sometimes provoking outrage. We all know the story of Salome, the young woman who would perform the Dance of the Seven Veils for the lascivious Herod in return for her wish to kiss the severed head of John the Baptist (Jokanaan in the play). It came from the Bible, giving it a fig leaf of respectability. Wilde had made it into a modern drama, drawing out the erotic, forbidden sadomasochistic desire and voyeurism of its central figure. When he wrote the play in Paris among the Symbolist poets he had hoped that it would realize his long-held ambitions as a serious dramatist.[67] Banned from public performance in Great Britain by the Lord Chamberlain's Office in 1892, Wilde did not live to see it onstage. His words gave Salome an interior life absent from earlier depictions. His heroine is, though, also a femme fatale who weaponizes her sexuality to fulfil her desires. By the 1900s it was this aspect that made the play and its title figure popular—Salome was a forerunner of the flapper.

The Copeland & Day edition of the play was just the start of a phenomenon termed 'Salomania', that saw Wilde's heroine revered by some and reviled by others. If the first major American production of *Salome* in 1906 was controversial—and it was—that was nothing compared to what was to follow.[68] Richard Strauss's opera, based on Wilde's play, caused such a scandal that it closed after a single performance at the Metropolitan Opera House on 22 January 1907. It was, wrote one conservative reviewer, 'sinister, compelling, disgusting'.[69] Some of the capacity audience walked out, and the end was marked by scattered applause and a sense of disbelief.[70]

Too scandalous for the Met, versions of *Salome* nonetheless became an underground sensation. Away from the Upper East Side and Broadway, Wilde's play and sections from it were performed frequently—so frequently, in fact, that the young Irving Berlin wrote a song about it. His 'Sadie Salome, Go Home!' (1909), sung by Fanny Brice, was a comedy number about a girl who'd gone onstage as Salome and her suitor, Moses, who begs her to come back home. It was Berlin's breakthrough into the big time, featuring such wonderful rhymes as 'I'm your loving Mose' and 'Where is your clothes?', and

> Who put in your head such notions?
> You look sweet but jiggle with your feet
> Who put in your back such funny motions?[71]

Despite such heartfelt appeals, Sadie seems to prefer her new life in vaudeville and there she remains at the end of the number. Berlin's song puts Salome into an American context, reflecting the play's popular appeal in music hall performances. It is an early illustration of how Wilde's strong, independent, and sexually liberated female characters would be taken up by, and absorbed into, American culture as they helped to shape it.

Sex was inevitably key. Between 1910 and 1915 Maud Allan toured America with her show, *The Vision of Salome* (Fig. 1.4). Her self-choreographed Dance of the Seven Veils was set to a score by Marcel Rémy and it combined 'horror, desire, wildness and ecstasy' with 'undisguised eroticism'.[72] It was the last in particular that captured the public's imagination. Allan's show launched a frenzy of imitators, parodies, and merchandise.[73] The New York Theatre even ran a 'School for Salomes' to train aspiring performers for the vaudeville circuit.[74] Most of these spin-offs were ephemeral entertainments that contributed in minor ways to the Salome phenomenon. Others were more significant. Aida Overton Walker, an African American impresario known as the 'Queen of the Cake Walk', toured nationwide between 1908 and 1912 with her raunchy vaudeville version of Salome's dance (Fig. 1.5). The sensational element of Wilde was still very much alive. It wasn't respectable, but it was popular.

Or again, Edwards Davis was 'a Los Angeles minister who gave up the pulpit to go on the stage' with his own very successful theatrical adaptation of *The Picture of Dorian Gray*.[75] Between 1909 and 1912 he toured the US vaudeville circuit, almost topping the bill just below Annette Kellerman, 'The Famous Diving Venus', before heading out to Hollywood to take supporting roles in over a dozen short films.[76]

There were also full productions of *Salome* in New York's immigrant and ethnic minority communities. In 1913 the Sicilian actress Mimi Aguglia impressed Carl Van Vechten with her 'compelling power' in the role, at the tiny Gotham Theatre in Harlem.[77] In 1923, in Chicago, the Ethiopian Art Theatre opened their debut season with a double bill of *Salome* and *The Chip Woman's Fortune* by African American playwright Willis Richardson, complete with spirituals sung by a gospel choir in the interval. It was, the *Chicago Evening Post* suggested, 'the artistic event of the season' with an acclaimed performance by Evelyn Preer (Fig. 1.6).[78] The company played to packed mixed-race audiences for two weeks before transferring to New York.[79] In July 1929 Wilde's tragedy was performed by an African American cast at the Cherry Lane Theatre in the West Village. It was led by pioneering dancer and impresario Hemsley Winfield, who sensationally cross-dressed as Salome in the title role, reminding us of Wilde's crossed-dressed imitators during the 1882 tour: outrageous and hugely popular.[80]

These various American *Salome*s, wholly forgotten today, highlight two important distinctions between Wilde's US influence and that in Europe. The first is how his works appealed to African American audiences and performers. Though anathema to snobbish self-appointed keepers of the

Fig. 1.4 Publicity photo of Maud Allan for *The Vision of Salome* (1908)

Fig. 1.5 Publicity photo of Aida Overton Walker for *Salome* (*c*.1911)

THE NEGRO IN DRAMATIC ART

 RAYMOND O'NEIL

EVELYN PREER, THE GIFTED NEGRO ACTRESS, IN "SALOME"

Fig. 1.6 Publicity photo of Evelyn Preer in the Ethiopian Art Theatre production of *Salome* (1923)

Wildean flame like Le Gallienne, this was actually nothing new. Wilde had long been linked with the oppressed and repressed. During his American tour, as Michèle Mendelsohn shows, his identity as an Irishman and his effeminate self-presentation meant that he was portrayed—or rather parodied—in the press and onstage both as a black man and a woman.[81] These depictions visually highlighted what was *other* about Wilde. Adaptations of *Salome* a generation later by Walker and Winfield picked up on this identification of Wilde with African Americans, as well as questions over his gender identity, and brought them together with the empowering figure of Salome, as a strong Jewish woman. Their performances recognized, as Wilde himself recognized, that he and his works offered a voice for marginalized people.

The second distinction of *Salome* in the United States is the refreshing lack of reverence with which it was staged. Wilde's theatrical afterlife in continental Europe very much centred on earnest renditions of *Salome*.[82] That may be why, when it has been told, the history of Wilde's theatrical influence in the decades after 1895 has emphasized tragedy and repression.[83] In common with America's fresh take on Wilde, productions played fast and loose with *Salome* and its title character to make both more modern and exciting. Wilde's appeal beyond the drawing rooms of Gramercy Park was not as a totem of high culture, or at least that was not the main thing. What appealed was the malleability of his work: its adaptability to the demands of vaudeville audiences and iconoclastic performances. In that setting, audiences responded with whoops, whistles, and cheers.[84] *Salome* performed in drag or in a vaudeville context is hardly a straightforward tragedy anymore.

It is little wonder that at the height of Salomania Wilde's greatest heroine became an early cinema star. The Nickelodeon film *Salome; or, The Dance of the Seven Veils* (1908) was the most famous of numerous one-reel films that capitalized on the publicity around Strauss's *Salome* at the Met and the beginning of Allan's world tour in *The Vision of Salome*. In the Nickelodeon film, as in Allan's show and others, her Dance of the Seven Veils was excerpted from the wider story to present Salome as a screen spectacle. Such was Salome's popular appeal to Nickelodeon audiences that there were even several comedy spin-offs—*If You Had a Wife Like This* (c.1908), *The Saloon Dance* (c.1908), and *Salome Craze* (1909). All are now lost.[85] Still, these Nickelodeon Salomes were prescient: Wilde's presence in the movies was to be based around spectacle and excess, at least at first.

Meanwhile Manhattan preferred Wilde's social comedies. In 1916, the *New-York Tribune* hailed the first major revival of *A Woman of No Importance* (1893): 'it cannot be claimed that it has aged. Wilde, like Shaw, wrote not for the moment but for the century.'[86] Several high-profile revivals followed, with *The Importance of Being Earnest* a particular favourite. *The New Yorker*'s theatre critic, Charles Brackett, was impressed; reviewing the 1926 revival, he called *Earnest* 'the most sparkling play produced in the nineteenth century.'[87] Fast-forward two decades, and the same Charles Brackett was Billy Wilder's screenwriting partner in Hollywood. Their original screenplay for *Sunset Boulevard* (1950) is haunted by Wilde. Its story of Norma Desmond, faded star of the silent screen, unfolds with references to *Salome*, offset by a playful nod to *Earnest* when Joe's 'Bunburying' is discovered, like Jack Worthing's, through the inscription on a cigarette case.[88] These Wildean allusions could be the work of either Brackett or Wilder: the latter was himself a former reporter, who interviewed Strauss about *Salome* in Vienna.[89] Most likely it was both. For they are typical examples of newspapermen-turned-screenwriters, and their enduring knowledge of Wilde's plays is a testament to the ubiquity of these plays.

The 1910s and 1920s ushered in an unprecedented seriousness and urgency in addressing contemporary events onstage, with the melodramas of Eugene O'Neill, revivals of George Bernard Shaw's pacifist plays, and a new breed of war drama that reached its apotheosis in *What Price Glory?* (1924) by Maxwell Anderson and Laurence Stallings. At the same time, comedies, especially farces, were popular and an appetite for escapism favoured Wildean comedy.[90] *The Convolvulus* (1914) by Allen Norton reworked the farce of society manners that Wilde had created, exploiting the public's receptivity to queering reality with its camp humour.[91] A few years earlier Preston Gibson hit the headlines when he plagiarized numerous epigrams from *A Woman of No Importance* and *An Ideal Husband* in his own play *The Turning Point* (1910).[92] Later, drawing on the public's seemingly inexhaustible desire for Wildean wit, there would even be a musical version of *Earnest*, called *Oh, Earnest!* (1927), though it wasn't a success.[93]

As in publishing, so in the theatre, there was life beyond New York. Wilde enjoyed a vivid afterlife in regional and touring productions which were integral to *la vie bohème* beyond the cultural centres. His social comedies were frequently staged in towns and cities across America. *Earnest* and *Lady Windermere* were particularly beloved: there were over a hundred separate productions of *Earnest* and over fifty of *Lady Windermere* outside New York between 1900 and 1920.[94] Some were tours, such as the acclaimed *Lady Windermere* starring Margaret Anglin, which opened at the Hudson Theatre, New York, in 1914, and played nationwide.[95] A high proportion of the others were university productions from the expanding state universities, performed for the public.[96] Even more were amateur dramatic productions. Is it too disparaging to say that they were considered dependable productions, requiring little staging and not much in the way of acting to succeed? This seems unfair, though it was often remarked in reviews that Wilde's wit was the real star of the show.[97] To further recommend them, Wilde's drawing-room comedies conveniently sidestepped a number of problems faced by live theatre from the 1910s onwards. The failures of representation that marred war dramas and the relative lack of spectacle in theatrical productions in comparison to silent feature films, were simply not an issue here. As a reliable crowd-pleaser, *Earnest* was often put on by amateur groups for charity benefits.[98] In January 1911, 'well-known Baltimore amateurs' even performed it in aid of the House of Mercy, an Episcopalian charity for 'fallen women', with President William H. Taft and his wife among those who had taken a box for the show.[99]

Far from Washington, *Earnest* was a popular choice for college and school productions. In 1917, in the town of Mount Sterling, Kentucky, it was the annual high school play. Its tickets went on general sale with an advert promising that it was 'A Sure Cure for the Blues'.[100] In October 1920, the Drama Club of Moscow's production of *Earnest* was so successful that it went on a state tour of Idaho.[101] All but a few of these productions are now untraceable, marked only as ads or by short reviews in the local papers. The remarkable thing is that there were so many—innumerable productions of Wilde's social comedies, across America. By 1913 am-dram stagings of *Earnest* were so familiar that they had become a cliché. An unsigned short story in the *El Paso Herald* is based around one such fictitious production in which the fastidious young woman cast as Cecily must watch on helplessly as her unrequited real-life love, the young man playing Algernon, reunites with an ex-girlfriend.[102]

The success of Wilde's social comedies may, once again, have its roots in his 1882 tour. We most often think of Wilde as a maverick and he was in many ways. His plays became a phenomenon at almost the same time as Henrik Ibsen was beginning to have an impact on the rather staid Victorian stage.[103] He was not, though, without precedent. Most obviously he drew on the conventions of Victorian melodrama that he elsewhere mocked.[104] More surprising is his possible debt to blackface minstrelsy in the United States.[105] Mendelssohn suggests that as a playwright he looked for inspiration in the forms and techniques of the minstrel acts he had seen on the road in 1882. Several contemporary newspapers commented on the fact that *A Woman of No Importance*, his second play, opens with one of minstrelsy's signature tropes: the stock set-up of a witty back-and-forth between three key characters seated in a row onstage. When the curtain opened on a trio seated thus, it was a visual cue to audiences familiar with minstrel shows that wit and farce were to follow.[106] The link to minstrelsy makes Wilde's social comedies about the British upper classes altogether less remote from the twentieth-century America, where live minstrel shows remained popular through the 1910s and transferred to radio and cinema in the 1920s.

We will never know exactly what regional am-dram productions saw in Wilde. It is reasonable to assume—as Freedman says of little magazines— that they played down the 'subversive power' of Wilde's plays so that they might be allowed into 'the canon of the "cultural"'.[107] Some part of the public's appetite for Wilde's comedies may even have been a conservative move, the longing for tradition, or—as Ronald H. Wainscott qualifies it—'what was assumed to be traditional' in the face of a difficult present.[108] Certainly,

Wilde's social comedies had become acceptable in some polite circles even while *Salome* remained illicit. The fact that Wilde's most subversive comedy, *Earnest*, was performed in aid of an Anglican charity with the President, no less, in the audience, illustrates the point. Likewise, *Dorian Gray* had been banned from W. H. Smith in 1891, but by 1921 it was a subject of discussion at local reading groups in provincial America.[109] As with the bohemian journals of a decade or so earlier, it is likely that Wilde's regional acolytes pandered to bourgeois tastes, but then Wilde's comedies always had. After going to see one of the first performances of *Lady Windermere* in 1892, Henry James had complained:

> there is so much drollery—that is, 'cheeky' paradoxical wit of dialogue, and the pit and gallery are so pleased at finding themselves clever enough to 'catch on' to four or five of the ingenious—too ingenious—mots in the dozen, that it makes them feel quite 'décadent' and raffiné and they enjoy the sensation as a change from the stodgy.[110]

James would never understand, or wish to understand, Wilde's appeal. However, he strikes on an important point here. Wildean decadence worked on two levels, keeping the bourgeoisie entertained while tipping a wink to the dissident: the queer, who recognizes the acts of subversion beneath the drawing-room comedy surface. It was no different in Baltimore and it would be no different in the movies.

Starting Out in the Movies

The notion of Wildean decadence journeying from nineteenth-century England to twentieth-century Hollywood becomes inevitable once we fill in the history of the movement's transatlantic crossing and flowering in America's newsrooms, theatres, and Nickelodeons.

Wilde's burgeoning popularity in American theatres and paperback sales dovetailed with the motion picture boom in the 1910s. This was a crucial period in cinema's history which saw it revolutionized from a novelty entertainment into the most popular art form in the world. Audiences grew exponentially while, in just a few years, the length of a moving picture increased from a standard one-reel of 10 minutes to multiple-reel feature films of 20 minutes or more.[111] In 1912 only a handful of feature films were produced in the United States; by 1915 this figure was over 600.[112] It seemed that there was a place for Wilde in this new entertainment industry but what shape would it would take?

Far away from Hollywood, in Mayfair, London, Robbie Ross, the executor of Wilde's literary estate, was pondering this very question.[113] I noted in the Preface that he was himself an enthusiastic filmgoer in the 1910s and he was not oblivious to the seismic change cinema was bringing to cultural life. It's unlikely though that Ross knew much about Wilde's enduring popularity in America. Very few of the US repertory productions sought permissions from the Estate, and Ross's relations with Wilde's US representatives were chilly and confused.[114] Yet he did know that Wilde could be a hit in the movies. In a 1915 letter he wrote,

> It has always occurred to me that many of Wilde's stories would make much better kinema films than the actual plays—I refer, particularly, to 'The Young King' and 'The Birthday of the Infanta', which, as you know, have been made into ballets in Russia and, I think, in Germany. Of course, different terms would have to be arranged if this could be carried out; and I presume some kind of words, however foolish, would have to be composed for the actors who play in front of the camera. At all events there would be required a good deal of construction for arranging the different scenes. I should like to do this myself [...] I really think they would be tremendously popular.[115]

Here, Ross specifically envisages screen adaptations of short stories that present a more socially respectable side of Wilde's literary legacy, filtered through European high culture. It would be a cinematic Wilde that Ross could control—complete with himself as the scenario writer—as he had controlled and rehabilitated Wilde's image on Great Britain's literary scene.[116]

American film wouldn't work like that. Ross knew nothing about the business side of the industry so he sought advice in vain from theatre producers of his acquaintance trying to get an entrée into film-making.[117] The idea went nowhere. In 1917, though, he and his solicitor Martin Holman were again trying to get Wilde into the movie business, this time with their sights set specifically, in Holman's words, on 'some American firm of producers' because 'they pay better and there is less trouble with them'.[118] Ross was equally keen:

> it would be an excellent idea to have libretti to several of Wilde's stories prepared for submission to some of the American Filming Companies if we could only find the right man for the job.[119]

The trouble was that neither had any idea about how to approach the American Filming Companies or how to find a scenario writer. After some brief interest from an American producer, the idea faltered once more.[120]

The ironic twist is that, all the while, Ross and Holman were in close contact with a major player in the growing American movie industry. Daniel Frohman had inherited the US production rights for Wilde's social comedies in 1915 and since 1912 he and Adolph Zukor had been partners in the Famous Players Film Company.[121] In the late 1910s Frohman was in regular contact with Holman and Ross. Only, they were not on the best terms; this was indeed the chilly and confused relationship noted above. There was a long-standing disagreement between them over who owned the worldwide rights to adapt Wilde's social comedies as movies. Frohman claimed that *if* the films were produced in the United States then it was him because he owned the US production rights.[122] However, Ross argued that the rights to cinema adaptations could not be included in theatrical agreements that were made between 1892 and 1895—i.e. before cinema. Neither side would back down or reach a compromise.[123] Did Frohman himself want to adapt Wilde's social comedies to the screen? It is at least possible. He oversaw the screen adaptations of several of his own stage production successes in this period.[124] Another question is whether there is no American adaptation of Wilde's social comedies prior to 1925 because of the dispute with Frohman, but we'll come back to that later.[125]

While Holman, Ross, and Frohman wrote letters about hypothetical terms and conditions for screen adaptations, other US film-makers were making plans without them. Ross was determined not to tolerate any unauthorized film adaptations but the difficulties of keeping track of the American movie industry were too much even for him.[126] Indeed, by the time Ross and Holman corresponded on the matter, not only had the *Salome* Nickelodeon shorts appeared, but *Dorian Gray* had been adapted as a feature film in the United States by the Thanhouser Film Corporation (1915), a point of which Ross seems to be entirely unaware. With film studios struggling to keep up with consumer demand for feature films that had a proper narrative arc and character development, the market in literary adaptations was thriving. Their screen scenarios could be written quickly with the original book as a guide. Author recognition guaranteed audiences and familiar plots enabled them to follow the story with a just few sentences on the intertitles. William Shakespeare's plays and Charles Dickens's novels had an obvious appeal. Besides the kinetic energy of their plots and the potential for awe-inspiring sets, these classics offered well-known stories with the potential to secure the middle-class audiences needed to establish cinema's cultural legitimacy.[127] From D. W. Griffith's groundbreaking adaptation of Dickens's *The Cricket on the Hearth* (1909) to two epic adaptations of *Romeo and Juliet*, released by Fox and Metro respectively, to commemorate the 300th anniversary of Shakespeare's death in 1916, film-makers saw the possibility of realizing their cultural aspirations in these masters of English literature.[128]

On top of the permissions problem, Wilde posed some issues in comparison to titans like Dickens and Shakespeare. He was of course a writer with excellent public recognition. Most immediately, though, with the notable exception of Salome's dance, his plots lacked kinetic energy or epic scale. More critically still, his quintessence is in his language; words that would go unheard in the silent era before synchronous dialogue. These were not insurmountable obstacles. While Wilde's continued popularity and background presence in America's public consciousness laid the foundations for feature-length adaptations of his works, his position in culture may also have helped. His name was ambiguously poised between scandal and legitimacy, depending on how familiar one was. His promise of transgression and danger was exploited on-screen by feature films ostensibly seeking respectability, with these assets hidden in plain sight, under cover of the legitimacy afforded by literary adaptation.

The adaptation or 'picturization' of Wilde's unfinished play *A Florentine Tragedy* (1913) provides an example. Made as part of Warner's Features—a prestigious series of multiple-reel movies, featuring lavish period sets and costumes, and a cast led by the Shakespearean actors Arthur Maude and Constance Crawley—this might appear to be part of the industry's quest for to establish its respectability (Fig. 1.7).[129] However, an astute reviewer in the trade press recognized full well that, underneath, the production was seeing what naughtiness it could get away with. 'There are parts in it which escape the strict laws of the Censorship Board by a narrow margin,' he noted cautiously.[130] Months after the movie's release to excellent reviews, Maude, who also wrote the screen scenario and acquired exclusive US rights for the play, staged a live theatrical version at the Los Angeles Orpheum.[131] Wilde's last play has never been so loved; it would never again be given a major adaptation.

It was *Salome* and *Dorian Gray* that were to define Wilde's legacy on-screen for the first quarter of the twentieth century. In the context of American cinema, with Kinetoscope peepshows and Nickelodeons as predecessors, Wilde's most obvious appeal was to sensation and naughtiness. A 1913 advertisement sought distributors for an as-yet unproduced two-reel

Fig. 1.7 Still of Arthur Maude and Constance Crawley with an unknown actor in *The Florentine Tragedy* (1913)

adaptation of *Dorian Grey* [*sic*]. Placed alongside forgotten titles including *Shadows of the Night*, *Condemned for Witchcraft*, and *Triumph of Death*, this was headlined as 'THRILLING SENSATIONAL SPECTACULAR'.[132] American movie companies frequently sought to entice audiences like this:

targeting those who wanted to watch exciting escapades on-screen, as in the one-reel pictures and peep show entertainments of a few years earlier. A mere 14 per cent of American silent films have survived. The *Salome* shorts, the 1913 *Dorian Grey*, and *A Florentine Tragedy* adaptations are not among them.[133] There is no evidence that the 1913 *Dorian Grey* was actually produced.[134] Internationally, there are more losses, films that now exist only as ads or grainy stills: *Dorian Grays Portræt* made in Denmark (1910); a Russian *Portret Doriana Greia* (1915); a four-reel British *Dorian Gray* (1916); a German adaptation, Das *Bildnis des Dorian Gray* (1917); and a Hungarian version, retitled *The Royal Life* (*Az élet királya*; 1917). Their spectral existence evidences the international interest in Wilde's novel, though we have only vague clues as to how these adaptations looked. The loss of these films came about in several ways. Some were simply thrown away like the ephemeral entertainments they seemed to be. Others were misplaced during multiple studio mergers and acquisitions, destroyed in studio fires, or have deteriorated beyond recognition. A number may still be in storage somewhere, waiting to be rediscovered. This does happen, if rarely; we discuss one such glorious find in Chapter 2.

Tracing Wilde's journey through the American imagination in the first decades or so of the twentieth century shows us that he had a presence—an important presence—in America's cultural life as the cinema age was coming into being. This presence was distinct from the afterlife Ross was defining for Wilde in Great Britain, and from the literary Wilde of America's middle-class drawing rooms and Ivy League universities. This Wilde was one that resonated with America's popular forms and vernacular. He was modern, the star advocate of 'art for art's sake' at a time when that dictum was gaining new adherents across the social spectrum. He represented a queer and aspirational kind of American Dream. It was one of the main reasons why America loved him and it was how, as the flickers developed into feature films, his works would take on a singular role.

2
Naughty, Decadent, Silent Moving Pictures

In 1915 the blockbuster film-maker D. W. Griffith published a polemic enti-tled 'The Rise and Fall of Free Speech in America'. Issued in pamphlet form, its pithy and trenchant views on the film industry were illustrated with cartoons. Its main argument was that industry censorship threatened the educational imperatives of cinema, based on Griffith's belief that '[t]he mov-ing picture is a powerful and growing factor in the uplift of humanity'.[1] Film-makers must be allowed to depict the wages of sin, he stormed, not only in the interests of free speech but also in order to provide moral lessons to their audiences.[2] As a film-maker and as a polemicist, Griffith 'infused Victorianism with moral passion' or sought to.[3] It was more an aspiration than a reality. As movies expanded to fill the centre of American popular culture in the mid-1910s, a tension emerged between their entertainment imperative from vaudeville and their Victorian impulse to educate.[4] Exactly what and who the movies were for was uncertain.

This tension was to remain for some time but the balance between education and entertainment was changing. While Griffith imagined 'the uplift of humanity' there was a subtle but unmistakable new trend for movie plots that focused on lead characters who succumbed to sin—not for the moral education of their audience but for pure entertainment.[5] The eponymous stars of *Dorian Gray* and *Salome* embodied this shift whereby Victorian standards were not to be upheld but transgressed on-screen.[6] Wilde's anti-heroes stand alongside Mr Hyde, Camille, and a host of other arch-transgressors who captured the imagination of a movie-going pub-lic in the process of rejecting Victorian norms for the pursuit of pleasure.[7] The trend undermined Griffith's hopes for cinema but here's the irony: that greater moralizer had himself starred as the Young Syrian in the first major American stage production of *Salome* in 1906.[8]

When early US film-makers looked at Wilde, they didn't focus on his dandyism or even—primarily—his queerness, as a film-maker today would.

Wilde in the Dream Factory. Kate Hext, Oxford University Press. © Kate Hext (2024).
DOI: 10.1093/9780191987335.003.0002

What they saw, rather, was a writer of thrilling and salacious modern criminal characters who transgressed Victorian morality to make great box-office.
The lost Nickelodeon shorts of *Salome*, produced around the same time
as Griffith appeared onstage in Wilde's play, set the tone for what Wilde's
influence on the American screen would be: sensational, naughty, and very
modern. In the atmosphere of the mid-1910s, Wilde and the American
film industry shared a proclivity for exciting and sometimes even criminal
goings-on that resisted the ambitions of figures like Griffith. It would mean
that these adaptations often came perilously close to the limits of moral
acceptability.

Film-makers wanted visually exciting and strongly-plotted stories for the
mass market. On film, Wilde's afterlife would then be quite different from
his books' reception in private libraries and literary circles. There became
two Wildes: one for the elites and one for the masses. The very same cities
of New York, Chicago, and San Francisco were home to the fledgling film
industry and the more elite decadent scene indicated by Fred Holland Day,
Gertrude Stein, Donald Evans, and *The Little Review*. While the cognoscenti
responded to the subtle and more philosophical dimensions of Wilde and
the decadent movement, moviemakers focused on the sensationalism of
Wilde's more shocking plots, in *Salome* and *The Picture of Dorian Gray*.
Both were adapted several times in the 1910s and they resonated with the
American film industry's most lucrative subject: thrilling crimes. The so-
called transitional era of American cinema, between 1908 and 1915, was
awash in criminal activity—on-screen and off-. Crime films like Griffith's
An Unseen Enemy (1912), Lois Weber's *Suspense* (1913), and two adaptations of *Dr Jekyll and Mr Hyde* (1912 and 1913) were among the most
significant releases, with their sensational plots providing the impetus for
new camera techniques and special effects. Meanwhile, off-screen, piracy,
theft, and physical violence were rife in the industry as civil war broke
out between independent film-makers and the all-powerful Motion Picture
Patents Company. In Chicago and New York, film-makers were in hock to
Mob-run protection rackets and getting away from the mobsters became one
of many reasons to move out West.[9]

In this fever of crime and rapid expansion, the movie industry looked to
Dorian Gray and *Salome*. What film-makers found were not historical texts
for adaptation but works that were edgy and already modern. Their eponymous anti-heroes are charismatic criminals. It helped that the translation
of Wilde's works on to film was punctuated by the still-unfolding sequels of

the scandal around his life. Every new headline, each fresh salacious outrage, confirmed Wilde as a man custom-made for this moment: both for the cinema and for an era that liked its stars to come with equal measures of panache and scandal. If film-makers could only find a way to harness the illicit excitement of Wilde's plots for the screen, they could make Dorian and Salome into movie stars too. And so they did.

Decadent Criminals

American film-makers drew out from Wilde a criminal heart that had always been there. For understandable reasons it is his imprisonment for 'acts of gross indecency' in May 1895 that symbolizes the long association between decadence and criminality. This is far from the only crime which weaves its wicked way through the decadent movement.

Theft, burglary, and murder abound in a long history of crime in the pursuit of decadent pleasure. This began in what could be called the first decadent novel, Théophile Gautier's *Mademoiselle du Maupin* (1835), in which the despotic emperors of Rome inspire the protagonist d'Albert to boast that he can outdo their criminal acts in his pursuit of beauty.[10] Admiration for criminal activity also features in Charles Baudelaire's essay, 'The Painter of Modern Life' (1863), as the flâneur, the pinnacle of modern individualism, is twinned with the criminal by the way he hurtles through the crowd, motivated by 'a fatal, irresistible passion'.[11] The atmosphere of moral mayhem inaugurated in the literary world by Gautier and Baudelaire influenced Wilde directly.[12] It expands far beyond him too, out to the very corners of decadence, as when Mrs Gereth attempts to steal the precious 'things' in Henry James's *The Spoils of Poynton* (1896) and we realize that Jay Gatsby has built his fortune on a bootlegging empire in F. Scott Fitzgerald's *Great Gatsby* (1925). Later on, when Graham Greene conceived the ultimate punk gangster Pinkie, star of *Brighton Rock* (1938), as 'a working-class Baudelaire', what he recognized is that the mind of the decadent is a criminal mind.[13]

The decadent movement's principle of living purely for sensual moments and pleasure really couldn't recognize the rule of law. In its wholesale revision of moral values, social rules, as Arthur Symons wrote, are 'made by normal people for normal people, and the man of genius is fundamentally abnormal'.[14] The decadent would live by his own rules, in theory, if not always in practice. Living was to become an art as well as a means to afford endless pleasure. A poor buttonhole is an unforgivable crime against taste and taste is the only measure of value. Beyond that, anything goes.

An analogy between the well-dressed man of ostentatious good taste and criminality predated the decadent movement. In the early nineteenth century, British popular culture bracketed thieves together with dandy-flâneurs and men-desiring-men. These figures mingled in the urban backstreets at night and there too, by the mid-nineteenth century, they shared an argot or 'flash' in which the language of thieving and the emerging language of sexual deviance overlapped: 'queer money' was counterfeited money, and a 'queer cove' meant a rogue. The commingling of these social misfits precipitated an uncomplimentary affinity between them in the public imagination, rooted in their perceived duplicity.[15] For, all of them were wicked creatures of the night, whose unspeakable and deceptive deeds seemed to threaten 'respectable' people.

An especially cheeky cartoon from 1818, entitled 'Dandy Pickpockets Diving', makes the point (Fig. 2.1). The key figure is the dandy-cum-thief on the centre left. In a fairly crude visual double entendre for sodomy, one

Fig. 2.1 Isaac Robert Cruikshank's 'Dandy Pickpockets Diving' in *Caricature Magazine* (1818)

of his hands is in the victim's back pocket, stealing his wallet. His other hand meets suggestively with that of his accomplice in front of the second one's crotch, which also draws our eyes to their feminized, hourglass figures.[16] The message is clear—thieves and sexual deviants are cut from the same cloth. They are defined by secrecy and transgression, walking the streets alongside respectable people, their true devices unseen.

The British decadent movement brought together the duality of the criminal and dandy. Then they turned this figure around, celebrating him—for in the beginning at least it was always *him*—and seeing his duplicity not as fearful but fabulous. The disregard for rules and frisson that Gautier and Baudelaire saw in transgressing them became part of the fabric of the British decadent movement. Crime—or 'fantastic crime', as Walter Pater breathlessly called it—offers a singular kind of thrill to tireless hedonists.[17] Pater's sneaky valorization of crime is to be found in his late essay on 'Raphael' (1892). At the beginning of the essay Pater asserts that the defining characteristic of Umbria in Raphael's time is the 'enthusiastic acquisition of knowledge for its own sake'.[18] As the essay unfolds, Pater's imaginative eye follows Raphael to Perugia and this idea of knowledge for its own sake mischievously shifts:

> The Baglioni who ruled there had brought certain tendencies of that age to a typical completeness of expression, veiling crime—crime, it might seem, for its own sake, a whole octave of fantastic crime—not merely under brilliant fashions and comely persons, but under fashions and persons, an outward presentment of life and of themselves, which had a kind of immaculate grace and discretion about them, as if Raphael himself had already brought his unerring gift of selection to bear upon it all for motives of art.[19]

Like much of Pater's writing, the passage has to be reread before its sensational implications can be properly understood. In its typically Paterian structure, the sense of this long single sentence gets carried away with its cadences, so it is easy to miss the shocking comparison that is its subject. But here, using the same familiar idea of 'art for its own sake', from his Conclusion to *The Renaissance*, and 'knowledge for its own sake', discussed earlier in the essay, Pater now admires 'crime . . . for its own sake'. Is he suggesting an analogy between art, knowledge, and crime? The form of words seems to suggest so, and Pater's own excitement is palpable. These are such 'fantastic crimes' in part because their clandestine nature does not disturb the appearance of social grace, permitting Pater to imagine crime as fashionable, sexy, and glamorous. The implied analogy with 'art for art's sake' is reinforced by the metaphor of the octave, which not only suggests the range of crimes but alludes back to one of Pater's most famous lines: 'all art aspires to the condition of music.'[20]

The decadent movement's playful celebration of criminality reaches its apotheosis in *Dorian Gray*. Here, Pater's acolyte Wilde draws explicitly on the idea of crime for its own sake while sensationalizing the principle of art for its own sake in the figure of Dorian. The basic tenets of the plot are almost too familiar. When Dorian sees the portrait Basil Hallward has painted of him, he fully realizes his youth and beauty for the first time. Influenced by the charismatic Lord Henry, he makes a Faustian wish that his portrait would show the signs of ageing while he himself remains forever young. As he embarks on a life governed by pleasure and seeking new experiences, his painting becomes a magic picture; it bears the marks of his decay and moral turpitude, while he retains eternal youth. It's a secret he'll have to guard with his life and which he will even murder Basil to protect. I say that the plot is too familiar because, extraordinary as it is, this familiarity tends to obscure one very important fact: *Dorian Gray* is the story of a career criminal. In it, Wilde reprises the topics of poisoning and murder which he had used to farcical effect in his short story, 'Lord Arthur Savile's Crime' (1887).[21] 'All crime is vulgar, just as all vulgarity is crime', Lord Henry comments to Dorian.[22] Dorian hates vulgarity too but make no mistake: his life of pleasure is wrought through crime. Only, Dorian is an altogether more prolific criminal than Arthur Savile. As he wonders at 'sin so marvellous, and evil so full of subtlety', he turns, like Gautier, to the decadent emperors of Rome: Tiberius, Caligula, Domitian, Nero, Elagabalus.[23]

Dorian is a blackmailer, a drug user, a kerb-crawler, a bugger, and a thief, long before he becomes a first-degree murderer. His thefts in particular, if in a way his least obvious or serious crimes, position him as a Janus-faced decadent: at once the inheritor of the queer history of thieving and the harbinger of a genre yet to be born—the cinematic crime thriller. Like Pater, Wilde makes us dig down into his prose to recover and interpret the clues to these crimes. We must piece them together like a detective to work out what Dorian is really up to. In the novel's experimental chapter 11, Dorian's years-long devotion to art and beauty is charted as a sensual odyssey immersing the reader in his successive obsessions. How exactly does Dorian acquire all the tapestries, perfumes, jewels, and gowns with which he fills his home and his life for years on end? Wilde tells us that he has 'collected', 'procured', 'accumulate[d]' these objects, motivated by his 'curiosity'—a word repeated throughout the chapter.[24] No doubt some are legitimately bought. There is also more going on. Despite the euphemisms, elaborate descriptions of Dorian's beautiful, sensual objects are framed by the suggestion that at least some were procured by underhand means. Careful readers should notice that Wilde's extensive—indeed, exhaustive and exhausting—descriptions of Dorian's collections are followed by a hint that their true provenance may be criminal:

> it was rumoured that [. . .] he consorted with thieves and coiners and knew the mysteries of their trade [. . .] There were times when he looked on evil simply as a mode through which he could realize his conception of the beautiful.[25]

Wilde gives us pause here to reconsider how Dorian has collected his beautiful things. He inhabits the backstreets of the East End alongside the 'thieves and coiners', the very same milieu that created the 'flash' argot shared by thieves and sodomites in the early nineteenth century. As in 'Dandy Pickpockets Diving', his familiarity with this world suggests sexual transgression. It also indicates that Dorian is a pilferer, a robber, a crook, a suggestion half secreted in Wilde's narrative, as crimes are secreted in Dorian's life. Perhaps acts of theft thrill Dorian's just as much as the sensual objects themselves.

In his pointed review of *Dorian Gray*, Pater criticized the fact that Dorian loses 'the sense of sin and righteousness', concluding that the ultimate moral of the novel is that 'vice and crime make people coarse and ugly'.[26] Pater's criticism raises more questions than it answers. Quite apart from the irony that Wilde's novel takes Pater's own principles to their ultimate conclusion, we might well ask whether crime is only criminal when it makes a person coarse and ugly. To the aesthete, whose judgement of right and wrong is made on purely aesthetic grounds, perhaps so. Is that why the frenzied, bloody, vulgar murder of Basil marks the beginning of the end for Dorian? Because he loses his cool. Before that fatal misstep Dorian is the perfect criminal: discreet, dashing, and without compunction.

Raffles, Early Film Star

A few years later, E. W. Hornung's *Raffles* (1898–1909) channelled sensational crimes à la *Dorian Gray* into a series of rollicking adventure stories. Today A. J. Raffles is all but forgotten, eclipsed in the cultural memory by his contemporary Sherlock Holmes, whose creator, Arthur Conan Doyle, was Hornung's brother-in-law. At the fin de siècle, Raffles was a transatlantic phenomenon as the first fictional character to really show what potential the decadent criminal had to become a movie star. In retrospect the reasons are clear. Raffles is handsome and charismatic, aristocratic and witty. He is also—undercover—a daring criminal, scaling walls and donning disguises to carry off audacious burglaries of diamonds, pearls, and much else.

The popularity of *Raffles* in Great Britain and America riffed on popular images of the English aristocratic criminal. The Whitechapel murders in 1888 had caused a media sensation of speculation over the identity of Jack the Ripper, feeding the public's appetite for serial crime drama.[27] However, when Hornung conceived the characters for his stories, he based Raffles 'the gentleman thief' and his accomplice Bunny not on anything as gritty as the Ripper but, rather, on Oscar Wilde and Alfred 'Bosie' Douglas.[28] Notwithstanding the fact that Hornung had known Wilde a little, and allusions to him and Douglas appear throughout the *Raffles* stories, what did Wilde as a character have to bring to the crime-thriller genre?[29]

The idea of Wilde and Bosie becoming models for a pair of upper-class cat burglars is less fantastical in context of the links between theft and homo-eroticism. Wilde suggests a very singular kind of heroic villain. For Raffles is an aesthete as Wilde was. His conception of Good and Evil is based on his hedonistic pursuit of pleasure. He spurns married life for the company of men, bases his personal identity on sartorial style, and adopts a variety of masks to disguise himself.[30] Raffles is courageous like the heroes of Victorian *Boys Own* fiction, but he entirely lacks the Christian moral compass that those stories held sacred. He performs fearless rescues and tackles dastardly villains, all in the interest of hedonism. Such a hero was a bold innovation in the emerging genre of the crime thriller.

Raffles also takes its view of crime from Wilde and Pater. Raffles and Bunny commit burglaries that are spectacles of cunning, raising—Raffles contends—theft to the realms of 'art for its own sake'. He is even a crime snob, squaring up against others he dismisses as criminal thugs and disdaining how their vulgar attempts to steal contrast with his own elegant endeavours. In 'A Costume Piece' (1899) he explains to Bunny that a burglar like him does not mainly steal for want of money:

'Does the writer only write when the wolf is at the door? Does the painter paint for bread alone? Must you and I be driven to crime like Tom of Bow and Dick of Whitechapel? You pain me, my dear chap; you needn't laugh, because you do. Art for art's sake is a vile catchword, but I confess it appeals to me.'[31]

Raffles's aesthetic view of crime as an art is certainly outrageous. The principle is the same as Pater's suggestion in 'Raphael', only now stated unabashedly. To wit, crime can be perpetrated for its own sake, with an artistry that makes it compelling and fantastic. The big difference between Pater and Hornung is that the latter realizes the thrilling plot potential in the concept of crime for its own sake. For the first time he makes a deca-dent criminal into a fully fledged hero. 'A Costume Piece' is typical. In its short and action-packed story, Raffles is affronted by the brutish manner of a diamond magnate and plans to steal his rarest diamonds to teach him a lesson. Disguised as a vagabond, he watches the man's house for days before launching the burglary, only to realize that the target has rumbled him. Get-ting away—just—but with Bunny held captive and the police being called, Raffles must find a way to perform the theft elaborately and perfectly before it's too late, and free Bunny along the way.

In contrast to *Dorian Gray*, then, sin in *Raffles* is writ large. This sin is not restricted to an enthusiasm for 'fantastic crime'. The stories draw on the affinities between thieving and homosexuality embedded in British culture, and we see that burglary stands as a metaphor for buggery. This is a bold move within 'the generic language of adventure fiction', a genre strongly associated with heteronormative masculinity.[32] *Raffles* thoroughly subverts all that. As the eponymous gentleman-thief and his accomplice pass secretively in and out of each other's rooms at night, unseen by respectable people, hatching plots, their criminal conspiracy becomes an intimate, secret pleasure.[33]

Such pace and drama were new to the decadent tradition. Hitherto, deca-dent characters had adapted poorly to the demands of plot. The most famous are defined by turgid introspection and torpid self-indulgence by the pacey standards of Raffles and his kind. Joris-Karl Huysmans's *À rebours* is a circular journey through the immersive sensual experiences of its main protagonist who has retreated alone to his chateau. Pater's experimen-tal novel *Marius the Epicurean* (1885) charts the aesthetic and emotional development of its title figure. Action is in short supply. Wilde began the change, realizing that to be marketable the decadent novel must jettison ennui, at least sometimes. He injected sensation and horror into *Dorian Gray*. Still, Dorian's languid sensual self-indulgence and drawing-room con-versations feature more prominently than his exploits, which are implied with minimalist touches. Defending his novel in the *Scots Observer*, Wilde famously wrote, 'Each man sees his own sin in Dorian Gray. What Dorian Gray's sins are no one knows. He who finds them has brought them.'[34] Of course this statement was an attempt to deny responsibility for what critics called immoral. To an extent it is true, though, insofar as Dorian's 'sins' are conjured up in the reader's imagination rather than being detailed in the narrative. Mass market appeal would require a different kind of page-turning writing, one that did indeed show wrongdoing as the basis for an action-packed plot.

Raffles realized this for the first time. With his combination of pleasure-seeking, high living, and taste for derring-do, Raffles became a prototype for the decadent-thief-turned-desirable-anti-hero on film. His blending of thrilling criminality and decadent values, plus the public's familiarity with Hornung's original stories, made *Raffles* a popular choice for early adaptation: first on the West End and Broadway stages, and then on film at the burgeoning Nickelodeon theatres.[35] America took to him from the very first stories, which were published in the high-profile *Collier's Weekly Magazine* from 1898. Homages or rip-offs accompanied the official stories, raising their profile further. These included a *Raffles* comic strip and a spoof short-story collection, *Mrs Raffles, Being the Adventures of an Amateur Crackswoman* by John Kendrick Bangs (1905) in which Raffles's widow (as if he were the marrying kind) moves to America and takes up with his old chum Bunny to begin a burgling spree in New York and Newport, Rhode Island.

Hornung's later *Raffles* stories were published in America contemporaneously with the production of one-reel films based on the title character. When the New York-based company Vitagraph released their short, *Raffles* (1905), audiences loved the protagonist's combination of good breeding and criminality without punishment. As in fiction so in film, these characteristics made him a singular hero, outraging the emerging conventions of the criminal on-screen with his charisma and irascible humour.[36] The first *Raffles* film was so successful that it helped to establish Vitagraph as a major producer.[37] Such was its protagonist's fame—and the inadequacy of copyright legislation—that his name and character were used in numerous early shorts, from *The Society Raffles* (1905) to *Raffles the Dog* (1905), and even a Keystone comedy called *Baffles, Gentleman Burglar* (1914). In this fast-growing market with its appetite for criminal capers, Raffles also found himself cast alongside another Nickelodeon favourite, Sherlock Holmes, in *The Burglar and the Lady* (1914; lost).

Raffles outraged sections of the print media even as he delighted audiences. His exploits contributed to a general sense that cinema was immoral and when the fledgling industry turned in earnest to securing cultural legitimacy Raffles's cheerful immorality had to go. A surviving fragment from *The Society Raffles* shows us how a sanitization of his immorality began to take effect. The scene opens on an expensively furnished drawing room. Raffles, in evening dress, passionately kisses a woman in front of an open window while he reaches behind her head, removes her tiara, and passes it out of the window to Bunny. The audacity, aestheticism, and thieving are still there but the suggestion of homoeroticism has gone. No sneaking into Bunny's rooms at night anymore; Raffles the film star is resolutely heterosexual. Later Raffles's use of his ill-gotten gains also became problematic on-screen. In two versions of *Raffles, the Amateur Cracksman*, starring John Barrymore (1917) and House Peters (1925) respectively, and the first sound version, *Raffles* (1930), with Ronald Colman, our hero is recast from a self-interested aesthete into a Robin Hood figure, robbing from the rich to give to the poor. These politic rewritings begin a long vacillation in American cinema between desire for the decadent screen hero and fear of his immoral influence. That pendulum would continue to swing back and forth throughout the film industry's first decades.

Feature-length *Dorian Gray*

When *Dorian Gray* was first adapted for the American screen in 1915, it was palpably influenced by the *Raffles* phenomenon.[38] It wasn't just that *Raffles's* success paved the way for *Dorian*, though that helped. If Wilde had taught Hornung about the character of the aesthete, now Raffles could teach Dorian something about how to be a modern cinematic criminal. Produced by the Thanhouser Film Corporation, with Harris Gordon in the title role, *Dorian Gray* focuses on Dorian's crimes and fully exploits the cinematic potential of his secret in the attic. After all, Wilde's plea that 'What Dorian Gray's sins are no one knows' would not transfer well to the screen. On the contrary, everyone should know what Dorian's sins were because action sequences and shocking images were good box office. The publicity poster promised 'An epic of the pace that kills!'—and it was.[39] As a two-reel film of just 20 minutes long, action and sensation were prioritized, banishing all the ennui of the source novel.

Making *Dorian Gray* into a thrilling crime adventure began with restructuring and editing Wilde's plot. The novel opens with Basil presenting Dorian with the portrait, and Lord Henry verbally seducing him. In the film, Basil and Lord Henry are reduced to walk-on parts with no trace of Henry's epigrams on the brief title cards. It starts instead with an episode that occurs later in the novel, wherein Dorian falls in love with Sybil Vane (Helen Fulton) while she plays various Shakespearean heroines onstage. This visually seductive opening capitalizes on the popularity of Shakespeare adaptations with the movie-going public, as well as dramatizing the film's preoccupation with watching and being watched. Moreover, it establishes Dorian's 'perverse' criminal inclinations. In the opening minutes, Dorian pants with desire as he watches Sybil playing Rosalind in drag as Ganymede and then kisses her (still dressed as him) passionately backstage (Fig. 2.2). This is at once subtle and shocking. In the mostly-lost contemporary European adaptations of *Dorian Gray*, homoerotic touches 'helped to construct a very definite image of the monstrous male homosexual'.[40] The German adaptation *Das Bildnis des Dorian Gray* (1917), for instance, pictured Dorian in

Fig. 2.2 Dorian Gray (Gordon) and Sybil Vane (Fulton) in a cross-dressed embrace in *The Picture of Dorian Gray* (1915)

make-up and feminine poses, an expression of boredom and bemusement.[41] Homoerotic scenes in mainstream American cinema, though, were very rare, apart from some comedic cross-dressing episodes, and quite absent from adaptations of Shakespeare.[42] So this gesture to the homoeroticism of Wilde's novel is daring. It shows how Wilde's by-then partly submerged history of sexual deviance could be exploited to go beyond what could be shown overtly in mainstream cinemas.

Perhaps the director Eugene Moore was seeing what he could get away with in a society at once morally judgemental and covertly interested in illicit sexuality. In 1915 the tension between these was in play more than ever. Closely connected with the debate about cinema's future, the industry was on the cusp of a new era of censorship after the landmark case of *Mutual Film Corporation* v. *Industrial Commission of Ohio*. Several months before *Dorian Gray*'s release the court ruled that the First Amendment could not be applied to films and that, as a business, the film industry had the potential to do harm. In effect, this gave state and local censorship boards the legal right to censor and ban films.[43] During the cautious period around the ruling the studio head Edwin Thanhouser asserted that he was 'strongly opposed to producing any picture that contains brutal and uncalled-for crimes, or anything with a suggestive nature.'[44] Just how sincere Thanhouser was we cannot know but *Dorian Gray* suggests that his moral stance wasn't shared by everyone who worked for his studio.

On the screen Dorian's downfall is as thrillingly subversive as the cross-dressed kiss. New sequences in the film inject pace into the catalogue of sensations and sluggish drawing-room discussions characteristic of Wilde's novel, translating Dorian's aesthetic reflections into the stuff of movies. In one such scene we see him dancing and drinking maniacally at a party, while in another he visits a cocaine den in disguise. A series of short pacey shots show him paying the dealer, snorting the cocaine, and exiting the building— looking around to check he has not been spotted. Then, in a way which recalls Raffles's escapades, under cover of darkness, he climbs up to a first-floor window and breaks into his own house to avoid detection. As noted above, in the original novel Dorian's crimes, audacious though they are, appear half secreted in Wilde's prose, making hardly a ripple in the routines of his life until the murder of Basil. On film, by contrast, these crimes would be foregrounded to make the plot more exciting.

In Wilde's novel, Dorian is addicted not to cocaine but to opium. He visits 'opium-dens, where one could buy oblivion, dens of horror where the memory of old sins could be destroyed by the madness of sins that were new'.[45] Cocaine was a more modern substitute, which for US audiences in 1915 evoked the Harrison Narcotics Act that came into force a few months before the film's release.[46] This Act marked the beginning of drug control in the United States, effectively banning opiates and cocaine alike. It was cocaine in particular that was publicly linked to sexual violence and the breakdown in social order in 1910s.[47] In a typical account from 1914 the *New York Medical Journal* explained that its effects

> are more terrible than those of any other drug—the power of decision goes, morality is dead; and, long before the stage of madness has been reached, with its morbid suspicions, its sense of persecution ending so often in acts of violence and murder, the man is sunk below the level of his follow creatures, unspeakably degraded, perverted, lost.[48]

Dorian's cocaine addiction in Thanhouser's adaptation thus embodies the immorality, paranoia, and potential for violence which he increasingly displays in Wilde's novel. It also renews the analogy between drug addiction and homosexuality established by the original novel at a time when new legal classifications rendered each as criminal and unnatural addictions.[49] The depiction of drug use in *Dorian Gray* 'is both a camouflage and an expression for the dynamics of same-sex desire and its prohibition'.[50] Indeed, in the extract from the *New York Medical Journal*, note that the cocaine addict is described as 'degraded, perverted, lost'—terms very similar to those used to moralize against gay men in the period. In effect, it extended the suggestion of sexual deviance in the film's opening scenes to give the film a modern subversive edge.

Suspense-filled sequences like Dorian's coke binge were congruent with Thanhouser's established reputation for thrilling literary adaptations. The studio's first big successes had been multi-reel literary adaptations, including *David Copperfield* (1911) and *Dr Jekyll and Mr Hyde* (1912). Film-making was increasingly sophisticated in the mid-1910s and *Dorian Gray* borrowed new camera techniques from the studio's growing body of crime dramas to energize the plot. Tracking shots and close-ups, similar to those in Thanhouser's watershed crime thriller *Crossed Wires* (1915), follow a Dorian who is always on the move. The camera tracks him in medium close-up as he runs and walks to the secret portrait locked in his attic, pausing only to theatrically lock a door or peer around to check that no one is watching. The action shots reach their climax in the revised ending, which sees Basil confront Dorian in the attic. Instead of the discussion which precipitates Basil's murder in the novel, the men brawl before Dorian stabs the painting in an ill-fated attempt to escape his conscience. This action-packed sequence had, as the publicity promised, 'the pace that kills!'—and as such it is a stark contrast with Wilde's novel. For critic Jeff Nunokawa the only secret left about *Dorian Gray* is that 'the book is boring: for all the thrill . . . long stretches of the story are almost unbearably uninteresting'.[51] Is this sacrilege? The definitive recovery of Wilde's reputation in recent decades has seen a canonization of Oscar as a writer who can do no wrong. As Nunokawa notes, the ennui of Wilde's prose and the reader's in reading it, realizes the avowed boredom of *Dorian Gray*'s characters at the level of narrative.[52] In the movie, by contrast, Dorian doesn't sit down; he barely has a chance to catch his breath.

Wilde's novel did offer new and exciting opportunities for special effects on-screen. It had pioneered cinematic images before there was a cinema, with the spectral animation of Dorian's portrait anticipating the stop-start motion of early special effects. The portrait is nothing less than an autonomously altering image that thrills Dorian, its own private audience, like a Nickelodeon show.[53] Likewise, his eternal youth anticipates cinematic preservation: holding him still in time while those around him grow old. Although the first short film was not made till 1895, it was predated by magic lanterns and Praxinoscopes, both of which used lights, mirrors, and shadows to create the illusion of moving pictures. The vivid, horrifying images of the portrait in Wilde's novel evoke these elements of early cinema machines. We do not know for sure that Wilde was familiar with early cinematic technologies but the imagery in *Dorian Gray* makes it a distinct possibility.[54]

The cinematic quality of the Picture is essential to the drama of the novel. Remember the halting moment in Wilde's novel, when Dorian first sees that the Picture has altered:

As he was turning the handle of the door, his eye fell upon the portrait Basil Hallward had painted of him. He started back as if in surprise. Then he went on into his own room, looking somewhat puzzled. After he had taken the buttonhole out of his coat, he seemed to hesitate. Finally, he came back, went over to the picture and examined it. In the dim arrested light that struggled through the cream-coloured silk blinds, the face appeared to him to be a little changed. The expression looked different. One would have said that there was a touch of cruelty in the mouth. It was certainly strange.[55]

(a)

(b)

Fig. 2.3 In *The Picture of Dorian Gray* (1915)
(a) Dorian (Gordon) looks at his portrait after Sybil's death;
(b) As he leans forward to examine it, the Picture's mouth
contorts into a grimace.

Later, as the portrait captures Dorian's crimes and misdemeanours—'in
the mouth the curved wrinkle of the hypocrite', 'cunning' eyes, the 'scarlet
dew' that spots the hands 'like blood newly spilt'—it sensationally becomes
the closest thing we have to Exhibit A for the prosecution as evidence

of Dorian's misdeeds.[56] The Picture's indelible evidence of Dorian's transgressions appears before him like a horror film and he comes to take 'a monstrous and terrible delight' in watching it.[57]

For a film industry that was from its very inception self-reflexive, the spectacle of Dorian's portrait in the novel was especially resonant. The link between moving pictures and criminal evidence had already featured in *The Evidence of the Film* (1913), in which a fraudster is caught when he is accidentally filmed committing his crime. Perhaps it was this film, with its shocking animated evidence, that inspired another important innovation on Wilde's novel in Thanhouser's film: its animation of the Picture's changes. As Wilde wrote it, Dorian never actually sees his portrait degenerating. However, Thanhouser's film shows the expression contort from a smile to a grimace before our very eyes and Dorian's (Figs. 2.3 (a) and 2.3 (b)). The effect conjures up the memory of cinema's origins as an exciting technological spectacle: '"a theatre of attractions".[58] At the same time it reminds us how Wilde was aspiring to the movies before there was any such thing.

Dr Jekyll and Mr Hyde . . . Starring Lord Henry

Thanhouser's innovations showed beyond any doubt that Wilde's characters and plots could be adapted to provide the spectacle of a peep show within a gripping narrative arc. Dorian's dangerous charisma and shocking exploits, piqued by hints of queer desire, were thrills that might have been made for cinema. Their potential is brought into focus by Paramount's 1920 feature-length adaptation of Robert Louis Stevenson's *The Strange Case of Dr Jekyll and Mr Hyde* (1886).

It had been announced in 1919 that John Barrymore would star in Paramount's new adaptation, not of *Dr Jekyll and Mr Hyde*, but of *Dorian Gray*. Barrymore's role as Raffles in 1917 made him an apt choice. Playing a Wildean hero he would also follow in his father's footsteps: in the 1890s, Maurice Barrymore had starred in the New York premieres of *Lady Windermere* (as Lord Darlington) and *A Woman of No Importance* (as Lord Illingworth), at the insistence of his friend Wilde.[59] Ethel Barrymore later recalled how Wilde used to come to tea at their house in St John's Wood in the 1880s, when she and her brother John were small children.[60] Returning to the 1910s, it was a testament to Wilde's fame that the enthusiastic notice in *Variety* passed over Barrymore Jr.—then at the height of his career—to suggest who would be the real star of *Dorian Gray*: 'All Paramount will have to do is to bill Oscar Wilde's name in large letters to draw a horde of curiosity seekers in addition to the average picture public.'[61] Mysteriously though the production didn't go ahead. In its place, Barrymore starred in *Dr Jekyll and Mr Hyde*. At least it was *Jekyll and Hyde* in name, but not as readers knew it from Stevenson's novella, or audiences from Thomas Russell Sullivan's influential 1887 stage adaptation, or indeed from earlier short film adaptations of which there had been several. Instead, this adaptation, written by pioneering screenwriter Clara Beranger, was filtered through the story of *Dorian Gray*. It became a box-office smash and created a watershed in the look of American crime film.[62]

In it, a new 'Lord Henry' figure called Sir George (Brandon Hurst) influences Dr Jekyll into becoming Mr Hyde. Dominating the film's opening scenes, Sir George acts as a counterpoint to Dr Lanyon, recreating the Basil–Lord Henry dynamic of good and evil influences doing battle for the soul of a naïve young man. This radical addition to the scenario is directly linked to Wilde's novel via Sir George's dialogue, as he incites Jekyll that 'The only way to get rid of a temptation is to yield to it' and 'With your youth, you should live—as I have lived!' Of course these words are Lord Henry's, lifted from the opening scene of *Dorian Gray*.[63] Their use here, without screen credit to Wilde, rings out in striking contrast to silent adaptations of Wilde's own novel and plays in which his words did not appear till 1922.[64] Thematically, the fusion of these fin-de-siècle novels makes perfect sense. First published in 1888, *Dorian Gray* was compared to *Jekyll and Hyde* on its first publication in 1890, and they are twinned by their treatment of a young man who lives a double life and the visually horrific transformations that follow.[65] Transplanting a Lord Henry-type into *Jekyll and Hyde* repivots Stevenson's scenario away from unravelling the mystery of Hyde and his relationship with Dr Jekyll that is central to the original novel. Lord Henry brings a homoerotic aura, with his seductive influence over Jekyll drawing out the latent homoeroticism of Stevenson's novel.

Lord Henry/Sir George is only the most obvious debt to *Dorian Gray* in the 1920 adaptation. All told, this influence is both larger and more subtle. Many of the film's spectral moments are indebted to the visual effects of *Dorian Gray*. In another departure from Stevenson's novel and from earlier adaptations, which traded on the violent thrill of Jekyll's crimes without much attention to atmosphere, this film broods on the screen. Jekyll places a long mirror in his laboratory and it later reflects the spectacle of Jekyll/Hyde's transformation, as Dorian's portrait does for his sins. Elsewhere, the film's chiaroscuro lighting effects recall Wilde's descriptions in

Dorian Gray far more than the brief visual cues in Stevenson's novel. For, there, Wilde anticipated how the movie camera would play with light and dark, inspired by the magic lantern shows and Praxinoscope projections of early cinema. The elongated shadow of a cane knocking on Jekyll's street door and the repeated image of lamplight diffused by fog create a sense of impending horror, even anticipating the celebrated visual effects of German expressionist cinema.

The most shocking of these visual effects comes in a scene with no parallel whatsoever in Stevenson's story. In the latter stages of his double life, Jekyll awakens to imagine a giant spider-like creature in the shadows. Backlighting through a window casts a wan light over his bedchamber, putting the bed and his waking figure into shadow. Next, a double-exposure shot creates a giant translucent spider which crawls out from underneath the bed and, as Jekyll holds up his hand in horror and collapses back on to the pillow, crawls over his body and disappears into him as he spontaneously transforms into Hyde (Fig. 2.4). Where could this fantastical horror, this visual manifestation of Jekyll's debasement, come from? The scene is drawn from *Dorian Gray*. As Dorian descends into a reclusive life, Wilde's narrator reflects that

Fig. 2.4 A giant imaginary spider appears to Jekyll (Barrymore) in *Dr Jekyll and Mr Hyde* (1920)

There are few of us who have not sometimes wakened before dawn, either after one of those dreamless nights that make us almost enamoured of death, or one of those nights of horror and misshapen joy, when through the chambers of the brain sweep phantoms more terrible than reality itself . . . In black fantastic shapes, dumb shadows crawl into the corners of the room, and crouch there.[66]

Wilde's visual imagination in *Dorian Gray* is commonly identified as gothic and this is a classic example. But what would happen if we reframed the effect not as gothic but as cinematic? Wilde is not only looking back to the gothic but forward to cinema. On-screen in *Jekyll and Hyde*, this scene realizes the artificial chiaroscuro images—stark contrasts of black and white—conjured up by Wilde's words. Borrowing the image of 'black fantastic shapes' and bringing these to life on-screen, this *Jekyll and Hyde* becomes far more cinematic than Stevenson's novel ever was.

Salome and Friends

In the late 1910s *Salome* moved centre stage in Wilde's American cinematic legacy. As we know, Wilde's play was both familiar and sensational: banned from public performance in Great Britain since 1892 (a ban that would continue till 1931) and identified with risqué performances of the Dance of the Seven Veils across North America thanks to Maud Allan and the Nickelodeon shorts. As the movie industry developed in the late 1910s, the play had more to offer: a compelling and familiar story, a strong female lead at a time when female audience figures were high and the flapper was emerging, as well as a sensational depiction of crime. The only surprise is that it took until 1918 for there to be a feature-length adaptation. When *Salome* finally reached the big screen, bribery, illicit sex, and murder scandals were making Wilde headline news once more. Only these were not the scandals contained in the play, but fresh ones that engulfed its stars.

Allan's stage *Vision of Salome* was still famous when she was cast in the title role of *The Rug Maker's Daughter* (1915; lost). It was the exoticized love story, set in Constantinople, of Demetra (Allan) and an American suitor, and their adventures in trying to escape the clutches of her father to go to New York together. Its box-office draw was the dances woven into this flimsy plot. For Allan's three dances reproduced those featured in her

Salome show and posters billed her as 'The International Danseuse', capitalizing on her most famous role, while remaining coy about what the role was.[67] There was also a new commercial reason for bringing the ultimate 'Salome Dancer' to Hollywood: Allan's star power.[68] Formerly, the main factor attracting distributors and audiences was the reputation of a film company, but by 1915 it was increasingly stars who got crowds through the turnstiles.[69] *The Rug Maker's Daughter* was basically a vehicle for a strong female lead, with Allan a tried-and-tested star. It hardly took Hollywood by storm, insufficiently innovative in the new medium to make an impression. If Salome was to become a female screen icon, it would be necessary to capitalize on her modernity and the cinematic potential of Wilde's play.

In a bizarre turn of events, Allan reinvigorated the connection between Wilde and transgression in ways no one could have foreseen when *The Rug Maker's Daughter* was released. Back in England in February 1918, Noel Pemberton Billing, the maverick MP for Hertford, published an article in the *Vigilante*, accusing Allan of involvement in a German plot. Sensationally titled 'The Cult of the Clitoris'—a euphemism for lesbianism and moral degeneracy—this article was the latest and oddest episode in Billing's wild conspiracy theory.[70] It alleged that the Germans had the names of 47,000 British men and women, including cabinet ministers and newspaper editors, whom they had coerced into homosexuality and paedophilia, and then blackmailed to undermine Britain's war effort.[71] Luridly homophobic and fantastically implausible, this remains one of the ultimate conspiracy theories: developed over the course of several months in Billing's articles and interventions in Parliament, and feeding on an atmosphere of moral panic and suspicion as the war ground on.[72] The introduction of Allan as one of the so-called cult's ringleaders added some showbiz pizzazz to allegations which were patently outrageous.[73] Echoing Wilde's response to Queensberry, Allan sued Billing for libel. The consequences for her, as for Wilde, were devastating. The trial turned the tables: Billing defended himself and often it seemed as if Allan was the one in the dock. Associations between Wilde's friends and pro-German sympathizers, rumours that Allan was a lesbian (as indeed she was), and the fact that she had been due to return to the stage as Salome in a private London production in March 1918, rendered Billing's mad allegations somehow credible to a public whipped up into a paranoid frenzy. Conflating the actress with her most famous role, Salome's sexual 'perversity' was read into Allan's life as if it were her own. Worse, a dark family secret was uncovered as Billing brandished details of a double murder committed by Allan's brother Theo Durrant in 1895, for which he was executed at San Quentin, as if it was evidence of Allan's own criminality. She lost the case.[74]

The Billing trial reconnected Wilde, *Salome*, and the same-sex desire associated with their names, to audacious crimes with far-reaching public consequences. In those fevered times, Wilde was imagined reaching out from beyond the grave through his acolytes as an enemy of the State and all that it represented.[75] The trial was a sensation in the British press but the lurid details were barely reported by the American press for reasons of propriety. In a comment piece accompanied by a large photograph of Billing, the *New York Sun* opined:

> If ever there was an occasion for newspapers to observe a discreet reserve if not complete silence it was in connection with the Pemberton–Billing–Maud Allan trial. Considerations of patriotism, of national interest, of ordinary justice and even of common decency required this.[76]

It seems unlikely that articles like this did anything to dampen the flames of gossip about a star who was famous across the United States.

Still, it was probably a coincidence that the first full Hollywood adaptation of *Salome* (1918; lost), starring Theda Bara in the title role, went into production at Paramount within a few months of the Billing trial. That this film was made in Hollywood is noteworthy. By 1918 over 75 per cent of American film production had migrated to Los Angeles, abandoning cities elsewhere.[77] Far from the bloody patents wars, this new city offered cheap labour, sunshine, and space to build film studios on an unprecedented scale.[78] Together with the purpose-built picture palaces that appeared across American cities from 1913 and the innovation of multi-reel feature films, this heralded a vogue for biblical epics. *Salome* was a showcase for the scale that Hollywood's sound stages could offer, with large, elaborate sets[79]—quite the opposite of the minimalist designs which Wilde approved from Charles Ricketts for his own production that never was.[80]

The 1918 adaptation of *Salome* exuded sex appeal. True to her own screen persona, Bara played her part as the original 'Vamp'—as the studio publicity called her—with new subplots to emphasize her murderous inclinations (Fig. 2.5). Bara once had loftier ambitions for the role, writing that '[a]s *Salome* I tried to absorb the poetic impulse of Oscar Wilde. I tried to interpret the extraordinary, the hopeless moral disintegration of a woman's soul.'[81] On the evidence we have, it doesn't look as though these ambitions were realized. Bara's image as an orientalized femme fatale combined with

Fig. 2.5 Publicity photograph of Theda Bara in costume for *Salome* (1918; lost)

the lavish and sensational production to limit what poetic soul she could bring to the role.

She did, however, modernize Salome. Her heavy kohl eyeliner and art nouveau costuming lifted Wilde's heroine out of biblical antiquity into a contemporary cosmopolitan America, ready for the jazz age. Bara's Salome was a modern male fantasy: assertive and sexually available and her allure endured. In 1966 the designer Nigel Waymouth reproduced a large publicity shot of Bara's Salome as the centrepiece of the window display at his iconic outfitters, Granny Takes A Trip, on the King's Road, Chelsea. 'She's a Beardsleyesque character—Salome, a vamp,' Waymouth told me fifty years later. 'A woman who's in power, and that's very attractive. That look she's giving you; it's coy and camp, but also screw you.'[82] He isn't wrong. The manner in which Bara reworked Beardsley's image of Salome anticipates where Waymouth would take Wildean decadence decades later, as a now resolutely heterosexual symbol of hedonism in Swinging Sixties' London.

That isn't the whole story of the women who played her. Bara's *Salome*, like Allan's, is also the story of a strong independent female. Allan was a 'financially, legally, and sexually independent woman' and her aspirations beyond the Vamp image were part of a trend shaping the film industry.[83] In the years from 1920 to 1927, between 60 and 83 per cent of filmgoers were women. A revolution was on the horizon, going hand in hand with other new freedoms, and film-makers needed to be mindful of their pitch to this audience. 'Remember the 83 per cent!' was the screenwriter Beth Brown's cry to the overwhelmingly male studio executives as she reminded them to cater to female audiences.[84] Seen from this perspective, the screen's *Salome* was not constructed for the male gaze alone. Her independence, assertiveness, and unabashed desire appealed to female audiences too. She showed another way to be a woman, taking up the assertive sexual energy of the dancers who created Salomania onstage.

There would be more Salomes in this period, some in rather different registers, many that took up her vampy modern makeover. The lost six-reel film *A Modern Salome* (1920; lost) is one of the latter. Also set in contemporary America, it starred Hope Hampton as a young woman in high society, who has an extended nightmare in which she lives out the story of Salome.[85] The film's poster showed Hampton's fashionably bobbed hair made out of the tail of an Aubrey Beardsley-style peacock, with the caption 'A Modern Salome'.[86] Yet it is a very different American Salome, lost for eighty years, who today stands out as especially modern, bringing 'her' back full circle to audacious crime and queer desire. This comedy version was written by and starred an unlikely champion of Wilde: Roscoe Arbuckle. *The Cook* (1918;

rediscovered in 1998), parodies Salome's dance in an extended 4.5-minute sequence.

Like most two-reel slapstick comedies, *The Cook* is based not around plot but successive scenarios, focusing first on a Cook (Arbuckle) and a Waiter (Buster Keaton) as they work in a busy restaurant and the scrapes they get into. The film opens with the sort of sight gags that were standard in silent slapstick, but then the floor show begins. There is a dancer and she is dressed as Salome. Inevitably, the Waiter is inspired to mirror her seductive moves, which parody the orientalized dancing of Allan's Salome. As he takes the dance into the kitchen, the Cook joins in and begins the Dance of the Seven Veils, shimmying in front of the stove as he makes a 'Salome' costume—frying pans as makeshift breastplates, a headdress fashioned from a colander and a washing-up brush—and takes a string of sausages as his veil (Fig. 2.6).

Who and what exactly is being sent up here? The Cook's sultry, heavy-lidded eye make-up suggests that it is Bara's Salome performance. Both films date from autumn 1918. One problem with this thesis: *The Cook* was released a month before Bara's film. Another problem: the Cook's makeshift costume bears no resemblance to Bara's flowing gowns. His parodic kitchen-utensil costume more clearly references Allan's Salome costume, which had

Fig. 2.6 Roscoe Arbuckle does the Dance of the Seven Veils in *The Cook* (1918)

shocked the conservative press a decade earlier. The Cook's dance of death is in fact a homage that blends Allan's Salome with an earlier Bara outing as Cleopatra (1917; partly lost), while anticipating the latter's role as Wilde's heroine. It may even have been a bit of a teaser when it was released as both were Paramount productions.

To grasp that Arbuckle is responding not to Bara's Salome but Allan's puts his Dance of the Seven Veils in a new light. Billing's scabrous allegations against Allan and the libel trial were very fresh in the public memory in autumn 1918. The case had ended just a few months earlier in June. Gender-bending and irreverent, Arbuckle's Dance of the Seven Veils comes closer to the spirit of the comedic Wilde than all the previous 'straight' incarnations of Salome on-screen. It irreverently re-queers her at a time when such queerness was under fierce attack from Billing as sinister and threatening. Arbuckle was a trained dancer and, like Beardsley's ballet dancers, part of the humour of his Salome dance comes from the incongruity between his 275-pound frame and the delicacy of his dainty tiptoe steps: these are captured with a largely static, medium shot that allows his movements to take centre stage, with minimal close-ups and no tracking. The sequence is punctuated by classic slapstick moments—sight gags—but these occur *around* Arbuckle, almost as if he's transcended whatever film Keaton is in to arrive in his own sweet queer world. Gender ambiguity had been a part of Arbuckle's screen persona since *Miss Fatty's Seaside Lovers* (1915). He often appeared in cross-dress, presented in sexual terms, 'even as that sexuality is ironically denied'.[87] Only, before *The Cook*, Arbuckle's cross-dressing act parodied matinee idols and his own masculinity. Now, as Salome, his roundness and baby face are feminized by black-rimmed baby-doll eyes as he dances with mock-seductiveness around the kitchen with Keaton's Waiter, while looking doe-eyed towards the cinema audience. So much is in play here, and that's the right word: the transgressions of Allan's Salome are overlaid with the recent Billing trial and the oddness of Bara's hyper-heterosexualized performance.

Arbuckle's Salome would not have been possible in a commercial release were it not under the cover of farce. As noted above, the politics around the acceptable face of Wilde would always be vexed. The US movie industry's penchant for a discreet whiff of prurient scandal—great box office—was tempered by fear of alienating audiences or even invoking censorship in some states. Arbuckle deftly sidesteps all that with a slapstick routine which embodies and reinstates Wilde's characteristic irreverence. He translates Wilde's knowing, suggestive wit into coded visual cues: a now-you-see-it, now-you-don't game in which the viewer might suspect, but no censor could prove, just what is going on. This is radical on many levels. Not only does the Cook's come-hither look wink defiantly in the face of earnest moral panic but his redefinition of Salome as comic rather than tragic serves also to puncture the seriousness and reverential realism of some stage performances.

As the dance reaches its ever-more chaotic climax, the kitchen hand brings an iceberg lettuce on a silver platter: the head of John the Baptist. There had long been heated debate over the realistic prop heads featured in many productions of *Salome*.[88] If Wilde's play is a rejection of naturalism in theatre, as Ellis Hansen argues, then Arbuckle's skit equally rebuffs realism on the screen.[89] The lettuce's supreme absurdity seems to mock both the outrage over Salome's sexuality and opprobrium in adaptations of the play. Suddenly scared by the lettuce/head he holds and is ready to kiss, the Cook throws it to the ground and picks up the veil of sausages—which becomes an asp and bites him below the breast, before he eats the sausages and leaps up to take his bow. This blending of Salome with Cleopatra in the final moments of the sequence alludes to Bara's playing both, while also recovering the characters' twinship as decadent heroines, alike in their queer homicidal-suicidal lusts.[90] Afeared perhaps of its own implications, the skit then veers back on to safe ground by ending with the tired joke of Arbuckle stuffing his face with the sausages.

* * *

Arbuckle's inspired Salome sketch has a dark coda. By the 1920s, the seamy side of Hollywood was scandalizing America with high-profile tales of debauchery, drug abuse, and death. None was more shocking than the downfall of Arbuckle, who in 1921 went on trial for the rape and manslaughter of actress Virginia Rappe.

On a hot September night Arbuckle drove a group to party at the St Francis Hotel in San Francisco. In a top-floor suite with lots of Hollywood starlets and plenty of bootlegged liquor, it was a standard movie party—until screams were heard coming from a bedroom. Rappe was found with fatal injuries and a panicked Arbuckle. She died of peritonitis a few days later.[91] In a gruesome coincidence, the alleged crime bore an uncanny resemblance to the most infamous scene in *Teleny* (1893), the pornographic novel which Wilde was rumoured to have helped write.[92] The murder trials that followed with Arbuckle in the dock were sensational. The Hearst press predictably turned the tragedy into a tale of 'Beauty and the Beast', told in multiple instalments.[93] After two hung juries, a third trial finally acquitted Arbuckle, but his health and career would never recover. A verdict of Innocent cut no ice; trial by newspaper was what really counted. In the press, Arbuckle's gender ambiguity and physical size—two of his comedic assets—now counted against him as proof of his monstrosity, included in the unfounded allegation that he had crushed Rappe with his weight.[94] On the steps of the courthouse after the acquittal, Rappe's bereaved fiancé gave a public statement: 'Some people don't know how to get a kick out of life, except in a beastly way. They are the ones who participate in orgies that surpass the orgies of degenerate Rome.'[95] Gautier and Wilde had taken up Roman decadence as an inspiration, a boast, even. That now rebounded, as it was bound to, in fierce censure of the excess and deviance they had celebrated. Wilde and decadence had nothing directly to do with Arbuckle's defenestration, but the heady scent and tragic trajectory of fame, indulgence, and downfall bring them into parallel. The decadent movement's irreverence towards law and propriety, and its pursuit of pleasure above all else, anticipated Hollywood in its most hedonistic moments. What the Billing trial and Arbuckle's fate alike showed was that the fun side of Wilde's legacy could quickly turn sour, curdling into deep, barely suppressed, fear of its dangerous underside.

As ever, America was divided. Few thought Arbuckle was really a killer but his role in a raucous and illegal party could not be seen to go unpunished. The exposés that followed his arrest made him a symbol of everything the conservative press and public feared about the movie business. On-screen epics like *Manslaughter* (1922), *The Ten Commandments* (1923), and *King of Kings* (1927), all directed by Cecil B. DeMille, or Fred Niblo's *Ben-Hur* (1925), did nothing to assuage such fears, featuring as they did the immersive debauchery of civilizations grown over-luxurious. Even if there was a moral reckoning before the end credits this was pro forma, overshadowed by the exhilaration of excess, captured by tracking shots across expanses of indulging, scantily clad bodies. For the first time in history, the very 'sins' that hitherto could only be read about or imagined—be it in Dorian Gray, ancient Rome, or even the Bible—were on display and larger than life. Sin could now be seen by everyone in lavish picture palaces across the United States.

The first silent adaptations of *Dorian Gray* and *Salome* had drawn out the modern pleasure-seeking and criminal elements of their source texts at the very same time as real-life decadence saturated the culture of American movies, picked for adaptation because their themes suited the industry and the times, and helping to shape the fledgling art of cinema. The charismatic screen criminal; the aesthete as anti-hero; the spectacular femme fatale; the subversion of normative sexuality for audience members 'in the know': all of these elements were to become core Hollywood motifs. As the fates of Allan and Arbuckle showed, they would be far from uncontroversial.

3

Salome on Sunset Boulevard

On New Year's Eve 1922 a most unusual film was screened publicly for the first time. Outside the Criterion Theatre on Broadway there was no red carpet but perhaps a sense of expectation ran through the damp December air. The Criterion was a regular venue for movie premieres: a hangover from the recent past before the movie industry's centre of gravity shifted to Los Angeles and a sign of new times because the concept of the film premiere was still novel. Just months before, *Robin Hood* (1922) appeared there, starring Douglas Fairbanks, and became a blockbuster.[1]

The title of this new film was *Salome* but it was very different to any *Salome* seen in America before. Posters used an acute accent on the e, as in Wilde's French version, and showed its star, Alla Nazimova, drawn in the moon (Fig. 3.1). Many would have known that the image alluded to Aubrey Beardsley's first illustration for Wilde's play, 'The Woman in the Moon', in which the author's face appears gazing at two androgynous figures from inside the moon (Fig. 3.2). Wilde hated Beardsley's caricature but by 1922 that didn't matter: it had become part of his legend. Nazimova's poster audaciously affiliated her with Wilde's notoriety as a sexual pariah.[2]

We don't know for certain that Nazimova—so famous she only used her surname—was at the Criterion that night, but how could she stay away? She had overseen every aspect of this film and fought for it at every turn. Of all the great women Nazimova had played on screen—Marguerite in *Camille* (1921), Nora in *A Doll's House* (1922)—and stage this was her most personal role. And who would her companions have been that night? Nazimova always kept interesting company. Her closest friends at that time included Charles Bryant, her loyal show-husband, and Natacha Rambova with her boyfriend Rudolph Valentino. Wilde's American agent Bessie Marbury—the very person to whom Oscar entrusted the rights of his plays stateside—was also Nazimova's confidante.[3]

Inside, the 600-seater movie theatre was at capacity.[4] When the curtains parted and Nazimova's name appeared on-screen, the Wurlitzer organ stopped playing. This silent picture was to be played in a completely silent auditorium.[5] Or at least it probably did. We don't know for sure because

Wilde in the Dream Factory. Kate Hext, Oxford University Press. © Kate Hext (2024).
DOI: 10.1093/9780191987335.003.0003

Fig. 3.1 Poster for *Salome* (1923) with Alla Nazimova pictured as 'The Woman in the Moon'

Fig. 3.2 Aubrey Beardsley's 'The Woman in the Moon' for the first English publication of Oscar Wilde's *Salome* (1893)

there's no detailed record of the Criterion screening. However, Nazimova recalls how, in a private preview, she had the music stopped at the moment her name appeared. '"We wanted the bare picture itself [. . .] No aid, you know. Just the picture,"' she explained to an interviewer.[6] Earlier adaptations had given Salome a makeover into a good-time gal who would be equally at home in a bar or a vaudeville act. She had been Americanized. Nazimova had other ideas. Her audiences gasped at a *Salome*[7] that was bold, queer, and European. The most ostentatious signs of these ideas are the sets and costumes, based on Beardsley's illustrations, and title cards which were the first to use Wilde's own words in an American adaptation of his work. Astonishingly for the time, the cast was multiracial, some cross-dressed, and reportedly all gay.[8]

And then there was Nazimova herself as Salome. At the age of 43, Nazimova was far too old to play the teenager. It was, though, a spellbinding performance. For the Dance of the Seven Veils she wore a tight white miniskirt—a screen first—with her hair styled in a modish platinum bob (Fig. 3.3). Jonathan Freedman has traced how the role of Salome was closely identified with Jewishness and 'became a path to glittering stardom for Jewish actresses and dancers', from Sarah Bernhardt to Theda Bara, via Ida Rubinstein. Irving Berlin's music hall song, 'Sadie Salome', noted

Fig. 3.3 Salome (Nazimova) wears a white miniskirt and platinum bobbed wig for the Dance of the Seven Veils

in Chapter 1, was a celebration of this fact.[9] Nazimova marks another turn in this tradition, reworking Salome into gamine modern heroine, a marginalized figure who is a misfit in the tradition of Wilde's greatest American successes.

Was America ready for Nazimova's *Salome*? It seemed that it might have been. The distributor, Allied, a subsidiary of United Artists, delayed its release for nearly a year amid press speculation that it would be censored by the new National Board of Review.[10] But its run at the Criterion was a triumph. The sell-out opening night was followed by four weeks of near-capacity audiences.[11] Reviews praised it as 'one of the outstanding photoplays of the decade' and 'one of the most artistic pictures yet produced for the screen'.[12] If Nazimova had any inkling that her masterpiece would come to be mythologized as the ruination of her career rather than its zenith it didn't show. She gave interviews, organized publicity, and that night, at the height of her powers, looked unstoppable.

Bara might have warned her that it was nigh on impossible to be a strong woman in Hollywood's movie industry. Nazimova was renting her house in 1918 when Bara wrote about misogyny in the emerging studio system.[13] Describing her own experiences as a *Salome* star, Bara asks in unalloyed frustration, 'what is any movie-studio but a chamber of torture to the girl whose imagination is tainted with the flavour of artistic ideals?'[14] Few were more 'tainted' by artistic ideals than Nazimova. There had been signs that the culture was becoming more propitious for female film-makers at a time when the majority of filmgoers were women. *Salome* was the second feature produced by Nazimova Pictures, part of a trend dubbed by *Photoplay* as the ' "her-own company" epidemic'.[15] Notwithstanding this derogatory term, female stars were beginning to gain greater artistic control over their careers and the movies—up to a point.[16] Independent production companies, including the 'her-own companies', were in the main releasing pure and unadulterated entertainment: swashbuckling adventures and dastardly crimes. That kind of box-office appeal wasn't what Nazimova had in mind at all. Certainly she tapped into the 'Salomania' that Maud Allan had brought to America, picked up on the sexual dominance of Bara's vampy Salome and the contemporary angle of *A Modern Salome* a couple of years earlier. 'I collected every picture of Salome that could be found', she told *Picture-Play Magazine* at the time, 'pictures of other actresses and singers, portraits and reproductions of old masters, and sculptured likenesses—anything that stood for *Salome*. I had a scrapbook chock full'. However, she was unimpressed, decrying the fashion for 'prominent busts', beads, and breastplates in those earlier performances with an indignant cry: 'Out!' [...] No! Not for Nazimova!'[17]

Nazimova was both smart and romantic. She believed that Wilde's greatest heroine had the potential to signal a new kind of cinema. In the 1920s, as Hollywood's new studios were in the early stages of becoming 'dream factories' with ever-larger budgets and ambitions to match, the future of the movie industry was a live issue. The spectre of censorship loomed large but it was not the only concern: Hollywood's artistic soul was also at stake. In hindsight, the success of *Robin Hood* points inexorably toward the adventure-driven, big-budget, big-star, blockbuster movies that would come to dominate the US film industry. At the time this future was unclear. Nazimova was one of a number of producers who wanted to do American pictures differently. Cinema in the early 1920s was experimental almost by definition: many commercial movies tried out new cinematography techniques and narrative approaches, artistic risk being greater in a fluctuating industry still working out the proper balance between business and artistry. Moreover, some producers and critics were anxious lest, in the effort to mass-produce movies, they had sacrificed the kind of national artistic identity exemplified by Germany's expressionist masterpieces.[18] In 1922, the prominent art critic S. L. M. Barlow was one of those to call for American cinema to develop its own distinctive visual aesthetic: 'Imagine a Hiroshige, a Beardsley, or a Rackham drawing a series of pictures to be vitalized by the motion picture! Here the camera would be essential; it would produce an authentic movie.'[19]

Hollywood didn't have to go to Europe to see what a distinctive national cinema looked like because Europe was starting to come to Hollywood. As émigrés arrived from the collapsing Russian and Austro-Hungarian empires, they became integral to cinema's evolution, piquing the hope that silent cinema would become a universal language—an 'Esperanto of the Eye' as Griffith called it.[20] Many of Hollywood's most avant-garde films in the early 1920s were conceived and directed by European émigrés, and indeed Nazimova was one: born in Odessa, she spent her early career in Moscow and St Petersburg.[21] By recovering this internationalism we can better understand her vision for *Salome*. Barlow imagined a series of Beardsley pictures vitalized by the motion picture. Released less than a year after his comment, Nazimova's *Salome* was exactly that: one of a handful of films created in the borderlands between the avant-garde and commercial Hollywood at a moment when the artistic future of American cinema seemed to be up for grabs.[22] As Nazimova aspires to Wilde's graceful articulation of female desire, her film looks to Wilde, Beardsley, and the martyrdom of Wilde in her native Russia, to expand the scope of American cinema. This bold artistic endeavour, along with its ultimate failure, tells us much about the American movie industry in the early 1920s and how Wilde could (and could not) find a place therein.

The Garden of Alla and *Aphrodite*

Nazimova arrived at Metro Pictures in July 1917, between Russia's two revolutions, as one of its highest paid stars. A full-page advertisement in *Moving Picture World* announced the news: 'Metro has Signed the Great Nazimova'.[23] She was cast in *The Red Lantern* (1919) and several other now-lost feature films that capitalized on both her gravitas as a stage actress and the generalized exoticism then in fashion. In Hollywood she was making more money than ever before but the dozen or so dramas she starred in were not in the same league as her plays in New York and Moscow with Stanislavski's Moscow Art Theatre. She plotted her next move as a 'her-own company' boss, producing movies to feature strong sensual women very much like herself. Her lush adaptations put a queer spin on the forbidden sensuality consumed voraciously by the public via the movies of Cecil B. DeMille and Erich von Stroheim. Nazimova's movies were visionary, but they put her on a course to being blacklisted in Hollywood.

Nazimova's cinematic ambitions were partly rooted in Los Angeles. She was one of the original members of the Sewing Circle, LA's infamous society of lesbian and bisexual women. By the early 1930s its members included Greta Garbo, Marlene Dietrich, and Joan Crawford, superstars of the silver screen. However, it was in the early 1920s that the circle first established a lesbian scene at Nazimova's palatial home, 8080 Sunset Boulevard, nicknamed the Garden of Alla—without the 'h'.[24] The circle's direct links with fin-de-siècle decadence helped to foster a sense that Los Angeles was bringing their spirit of sexual freedom and artistic experimentalism back to life from the decadent movement. In addition to her friendship with Marbury, Nazimova was close friends with Eva Le Gallienne, daughter of Richard Le Gallienne.[25] Marbury also introduced Nazimova to theactor, would-be decadent poet, and aspiring lover-to-the-stars, Mercedes de Acosta, who became her intimate and a regular at the Sewing Circle.[26] In the mid-1920s, Nazimova even embarked on an affair with Dolly Wilde. The details are sketchy but Nazimova considered Dolly—who gloried in her striking resemblance to her uncle Oscar and commented with a mixture of irony and belief, 'I am more Oscar-like than he was like himself'—to be a magnificent conquest.[27] It seems likely then that Nazimova also delighted in the company of her LA friend Harrison Post, the lover of William Andrews Clark Jr.[28] At the same time as the Sewing Circle was forming around 8080, Clark was beginning his collection of manuscripts with rare editions and letters, and with Wildeana a speciality. Clark had built a large compound, including a library for his burgeoning collection, a few miles south of Nazimova's house, in West Adams.[29] He bought twenty-five letters, written by Wilde to Alfred Douglas and had them transcribed by Post and Arthur Dennison, Lois Weber's publicist.[30] It was, Post's biographer Liz Brown writes, 'an act of devotion—to Harrison and to Wilde's memory—and it was a way for Will to declare his love through someone else's words, ventriloquism as a means to speak freely'.[31]

There were literary ambitions in the Sewing Circle too. Nazimova wrote screenplays and had a passion for the latter-day decadent novels of Carl Van Vechten, whom she knew.[32] De Acosta's debut poetry collection, *Moods* (1919), is woven through with the tropes of fin-de-siècle decadence, featuring theatricality and sometimes discordant musicality, a lone flâneur wandering through the night streets and crowds, and—most definitively—the memories of illicit encounters commingling with a poignantly inadequate present. These examples from 'Memory' and 'Disgust' are typical:

> Do you know I am living tonight in a
> cloud of memory?
> I, who always preach to you of looking
> forward, am sitting here silently looking
> backward and tearing the veil from off
> the dead faces of the past.[33]

> My heart trembled at your careless words and I
> closed my ears and rushed out before you should have
> killed my last illusion and made me hate you.[34]

While de Acosta's poetry isn't all that good, its revival of decadent poetic tropes is typical of the times. Like contemporary poems by T. S. Eliot, Ezra Pound, and Wyndham Lewis, it turns on a sense of the present as an inexorable decline, borrowed from decadent poets like Arthur Symons and Lionel Johnson.[35] Like Eliot in particular, de Acosta's sense of sorrowful nostalgia centres specifically on thwarted desire, a sobering reminder that anxiety and loss were a vivid part of the sexual freedoms represented by the Sewing Circle.

It is those freedoms that we remember because they helped to mythologize Los Angeles. Without the weight of tradition possessed by European cities and even New York, this new city offered the possibility of creating society anew. For some, like Griffith, this was a promise of quasi-religious redemption.[36] For others, like Nazimova, it was a bohemian paradise away from the prying eyes of the authorities. Her Garden of Alla was an extensive Spanish-style villa that epitomized the way that Puritanical morality could be forgotten on the isolated estates of the newly wealthy movie elite. It was to become integral to the legend of Nazimova herself. Inside, it was a pleasure dome filled with lamps, velvet hangings, and divans, all suffused with rich fragrances.[37] Outside, surrounded by terraces and archways, the extensive grounds were cultivated to suggest an Edenic paradise with an orange grove, cedars and palm trees, an aviary, a rose garden, and tropical flowers.[38]

The Sunday afternoon parties were all-female affairs with masquerade games creating an environment in which sexual norms could be more easily transgressed. The pool was designed in the shape of the Black Sea with underwater lighting. Around it, Nazimova drank and chatted with a changing cast of starlets, the brightest of whom included Norma Talmadge, Jean Acker, and Pola Negri, alongside industry friends like scriptwriter Dorothy Arzner and Natacha Rambova. Together these women helped to define the Hollywood lifestyle: a combination of opulence and high-culture pretensions, sunshine and excessive stimulants, not to mention uninhibited sexual conquest.[39]

There is a retrospective tendency to regard this sexually liberal, party-hard Los Angeles as an immaculate conception, brought into being out of nowhere in the Roaring Twenties. Not so. For the theatre stars, writers, and critics who helped create it, both the still-quite-recent fin-de-siècle decadent movement and the decadence of ancient empires offered rich frames of reference through which to conceptualize the pleasures available in Southern California. Chapter 2 ended with the bereaved fiancé of starlet Virginia Rappe, who condemned Hollywood's stars for 'orgies that surpass the orgies of degenerate Rome'.[40] Such analogies were commonplace, and they were as often used to celebrate the excesses of the movie world as to condemn them. In 1922, an anonymously published little book, entitled *The Sins of Hollywood: An Exposé of Move Vice!*, revelled in the parallels with ancient empires, salivating with exclamatory excitement that 'Moviedom's imagination had free play—unfettered, unrestrained it made the scarlet sins of Sodom and Babylon, of Rome and Pompeii fade into a pale yellow!'[41] Less effusively but with a tinge of East Coast envy, Van Vechten commented that 'No one who lived in New York could long remain ignorant of the oft reiterated statement that pictures were growing bigger and better, or of the fact that cinema theatres were being erected of a size to compare favourably with the Colosseum at Rome'.[42] In fact Hollywood was not yet 10 years old: far from a fading empire, it was growing vigorously. Still, historical accuracy wasn't the point. Hollywood's incarnation of art for its own sake and pleasure for pleasure's sake, both rolled into one, on an epic scale, inevitably brought decadence to mind in a culture already steeped in Wilde. It is easy to imagine Beverly Hills as the kind of place to which Dorian Gray would slope off on his unexplained absences. The Cocoanut Grove—night spot of the stars—might have been drawn by Beardsley, full of draperies and satyrs.

As decadence hung heavy in the scented air of Los Angeles, the analogies with ancient empires suggested new ways to expand the artistic potential of cinema too. This was, after all, the first age of the movie epic. Studios exploited their vast new sound-stages, multi-reel productions, and an endless supply of cheap extras, to produce cinematic spectaculars. Bara's *Salome* and *Cleopatra* were two of these. When Griffith's overblown epic *Intolerance* (1916) sank beneath the weight of its pretensions, an excerpted sequence, 'The Fall of Babylon', was released as a stand-alone short (1919) to meet the public appetite for vast and lavish scenes of degeneration.[43] Italian multi-reel features set in decadent empires, *Quo Vadis?* (1913) and *Cabiria* (1914), were also rereleased in 1919 for American audiences. DeMille and von Stroheim did most to make set-piece scenes of sensual indulgence a feature of the American screen. The US-made *Foolish Wives* (1922), directed by von Stroheim, concerns a dashing conman (played by von Stroheim himself) who scams wealthy women. Here, extended and innovative close-up shots of sensual indulgence—from eating caviar to surreptitiously peeping at a woman undressing in a mirror—are interwoven with large-scale events in Monte Carlo to create a new kind of vicarious pleasure on-screen, intensifying the scopophiliac thrills that moving pictures had offered since the Nickelodeon and peep-show days. As the first film to cost a million dollars, *Foolish Wives* almost bankrupted Universal Studios and, after a year of production in which von Stroheim shot sixty hours of material, it was halted and hastily released in a much-reduced form. Such can be the perils of decadence. Freed from all inhibition and restraint, how is it possible to know how much excess is too much? Meanwhile the far more disciplined and ultimately more successful DeMille used his genius for crowd scenes, with thousands of extras, to create extended sequences, showcasing glamour and self-indulgence in *Male and Female* (1919), *Forbidden Fruit* (1921), and *Manslaughter* (1922)—the last featuring the screen's first lesbian kiss, seen fleetingly amid a scene of general debauchery.

Nazimova knew DeMille and von Stroheim personally. She wanted to make a film defined by grand visual spectacles too, only hers must have a strong, independent, and sensual woman at its centre—a woman, that is, very much like herself. In 1920 she started planning it: a film that would bring together LA's atmosphere of possibility with the decadent epic. She would control all aspects of the production. Her first choice was to adapt Pierre Louÿs's novel *Aphrodite* (1896).[44] Set in ancient Alexandria, *Aphrodite* is the story of Chrysis, a beautiful courtesan. After Demetrios becomes besotted with her, she promises to spend the night with him if he brings her three things: the mirror of Bacchis, the High Priestess' ivory comb, and the pearl necklace worn by Aphrodite. After Demetrios has committed theft and murder to acquire these items, Chrysis falls in love with him, but his desire for her has been sated with a vivid dream of making love to her. Now disgusted by his crimes, he looks to find a way to exact revenge. Louÿs's novel offered Nazimova the potential to combine epic scale and the kind of sensual feast seen in 'The Fall of Babylon' with strong female leads. She would star as Chrysis and co-wrote the screenplay with pioneering filmmaker June Mathis, whose other work included the film in which Valentino truly became Valentino: *The Four Horsemen of the Apocalypse* (1921). A century later, the extraordinary screenplay for *Aphrodite* languishes in the archives of the Margaret Herrick Library in Beverly Hills. It was never produced and the screenplay has never been published. So what went wrong?

The first intertitle card with accompanying stage directions provides a clue. It sets the scene for a film that would focus almost entirely on Chrysis and the homoerotic culture of ancient Alexandria:

Super-expose on the following lines:

As for those who knew not this earth-intoxicated youth which we now call antique life, let them be permitted to live again through a fecund illusion in the time when LOVE WAS WITHOUT STAIN, WITHOUT SHAME, AND WITHOUT SIN. May they be permitted to enthusiastically consecrate their enthralled hearts to the sanctuaries of the immortal Aphrodite.

Pierre Louÿs

FADE OUT[45]

Taken from the author's preface, this epigraph pivots the focus of *Aphrodite*—most emphatically with its new block capitals—on to a culture in which same-sex desire and promiscuity are an unabashed part of the social fabric.[46]

With a different focus, *Aphrodite* might have been the kind of historical epic that Hollywood and its audiences loved. It could have trodden the all-important line between acceptable moral content for the censors and racy nudges to audience members in-the-know about same-sex desire. At the outset it looks like the kind of epic that DeMille or von Stroheim might shoot and Nazimova encouraged the association by employing the former Imperial Ballet star Theodore Kosloff because she admired his designs for DeMille's *Forbidden Fruit*.[47] Only it wasn't; Nazimova and Mathis went far beyond what the bosses at Metro Pictures deemed morally acceptable. Reading the unproduced scenario in full, it's not difficult to see how. Nazimova and Mathis excised Louÿs's subplots and distilled the novel's sensual descriptions into meticulously detailed stage directions, defined by the overabundance of rich, sensual, and eroticized objects and images. So long are these passages that the plot is often lost. In the role of Chrysis, Nazimova was to wear the characteristic mien of decadence too: ennui. She first appears 'bored and restless' in an opulent bedroom strewn with rugs, disordered pillows, and 'a few scattered roses—some in garlands, some separate.'[48] She continues to be defined with motifs from Anglo-American decadence, such as her large round fan of peacock plumes, and the stage directions note her 'languid head' and 'expression of a Sphinx.'[49] The overall effect is one of stifling sensual excess, more intense than anything Louÿs had committed to the page.

In the scenario, the destructive hedonism of Louÿs's novel now becomes central. The 'Banquet of Bacchis', a climactic chapter in the novel in which Bacchis discovers the theft of her mirror, becomes a frenzy of destructive excess. The stage directions describe how 'Crushed wreaths strew the floor with flowers. The orgy has developed like a flame.'[50] Lit only by candlelight, it continues: 'The dance is voluptuous, soft and without apparent order [. . .] They throw themselves backward with sudden movements, their bodies tense and their arms forward.'[51] Most of the stage directions here are entirely new, written by Nazimova and Mathis. Their effect is to refocus from the plot and instead on to a spectacle of excess, a bacchanalian carnival of destruction. Frenzied though it all sounds, these directions are carefully crafted as a balance between panoramic images of debauchery and careful attention to detail, a technique that DeMille's direction made into an art form. The scene's gloriously absurd climax comes when a woman has her hair set alight; to put it out, she is dipped upside down in wine.[52] Out-rageous, ridiculous, and exactly what sensation-seeking audiences would love.

Nazimova was an aesthete like DeMille. Each made pleasurable sensa-tions the focus of their movies and dramatized decadent behaviour for the vicarious pleasure of the movie-going public. The difference is this: his films always ended with a moral reckoning, however unconvincing. In *Aphrodite* there was to be no reckoning. The graphic scenes of murder, theft, sensual excesses, and same-sex desire go unpunished. Metro Pictures had no qualms about making pictures about strong and independent women. Coupled with grandiose depictions of sensual excess, it could have been a hit. The fatal problem was that *Aphrodite* was to be a historical epic reimagined through a queer eye, without the good grace to construct a moral ending, and that was unforgivable. Metro Pictures refused to produce it.[53] Next Nazimova adapted Alexander Dumas's *La Dame aux Camélias* as *Camille* (1921)—another story of an independent desirous woman, co-starring Valentino, but one at least in keeping with the narrative and aesthetic conventions of the time. Following its release, Nazimova and Metro acrimoniously parted company.[54]

Salome in Russia

Salome rose out of the ashes of *Aphrodite* and the possibilities suggested by *Camille*. It was to have all the sensuality and ambition of Nazimova's unproduced epic. Only, in *Salome*, Nazimova vetoes the epic scale, histor-ical detail, and glorification of sensual excesses that positioned *Aphrodite* (and for that matter earlier American adaptations of *Salome*) in the US mar-ket for epics. Its style owes more to the nouveau designs of *Camille* but this time Nazimova would be wholly in charge. Made by her own produc-tion company, she would be its auteur: its star, scenario writer (under the pseudonym Peter M. Winters), and producer. Charles Bryant was credited as the director and Rambova as designer once more, both under her guid-ance. Nazimova also worked with the cinematographer Charles J. Van Enger, probably retaining control of the film's edit.[55]

Salome and *Aphrodite* were connected first by Wilde, who dedicated his play, first written in French in 1891, to Louÿs.[56] But Nazimova's *Salome* drew out a quality not apparent in her *Aphrodite*: suffering. This is not dec-orative suffering as in *Aphrodite*—a tokenistic presence, drowned out by insistent images of pleasure—but a deep wellspring where desire and death are fatalistically intertwined. The first title cards set this tone:

The Mystery of Love is greater than the Mystery of Death[57]

This is an especially arresting declaration, bearing in mind the entertaining image of *Salome* in the United States. The line is from Wilde's original play-text, where it appears in Salome's final soliloquy and the way in which Nazimova gives it a new prominence here draws out the play's keynote. Its repetition at the film's end means that its sentiment effectively frames erotic love—or is it sexual desire?—as morbid, inscrutable, and fatalistic.

Wilde's words had been absent from earlier adaptations of *Salome*. They were too seductive or too serious to put on the title cards of films that sought to turn his play into a period circus show. For Nazimova's purposes they were perfect. Not for her, Wilde the sensualist or wit, but Wilde the tragic fatalist. Another of the film's first title cards, written for the screenplay, draws love and death still closer together:

She kills the thing she loves; she loves the thing she kills, yet in her soul there shines a glimmer of the Light and she sets forth gladly into the Unknown to solve the puzzle of her own words — —

The lines allude to Wilde's repeated refrain in *The Ballad of Reading Gaol*:

> Yet each man kills the thing he loves
>   By each let this be heard,
> Some do it with a bitter look,
>   Some with a flattering word,
> The coward does it with a kiss,
>   A brave man with a sword![58]

The paradox of love and murder runs through both. *Salome* features three deaths in consequence of unrequited love and its dialogue is wrought with the fatality of desire. Take, for example, Jokanaan's response to Salome's advances as Wilde writes it:

Art thou not afraid, daughter of Herodias? Did I not tell thee that I had heard in the palace the beating of the wings of the angel of death, and hath he not come, the angel of death?[59]

Evocative though this image is, the paradox of love and death encapsulated in Nazimova's new line is snappier, and cinema title cards demanded snappiness. Having *The Ballad*'s most famous lines echo thus in *Salome* resurrects the ghost of another Wilde: the one American popular culture had tried to forget, the one who published *The Ballad* under prison number C.3.3 after two years in Reading Gaol. It draws attention to the fact that *Salome* is a queer story camouflaged in a heterosexual obsession.

Responses to this different kind of *Salome* were ambivalent. Writing later, Kenneth Anger dismissed Nazimova's film as a failure, criticizing its sluggish pace and morbidity. Even the Dance of the Seven Veils—an opportunity to inject some action into proceedings, in his view—was underwhelming: 'Talk about a disappointment! In Nazimova's version of Salome's Dance old Herod didn't get his money's worth!'[60] Certainly it wasn't what Anger, archmythologizer of silent Hollywood and its sexual mores, wants from Wilde or Beardsley. His genre of triumphalist, out-and-proud retellings of Hollywood's early years has sometimes airbrushed out two things: nuance in the telling and the sorrow of what is being told. Even the tragic deaths featured in glossy black-and-white pictorial histories of Hollywood in this period tend to be melodramatized into a hyperreality, as the dark, seedy side of decadence usually is. And yet de Acosta's poetry illustrates how the fervent and joyous pursuit of sexual freedom at the Garden of Alla coexisted with personal turmoil and despair. She wasn't the only one. During an extended stay there in 1921, Eva Le Gallienne wrote to her mother in desperation: 'who is happy in this chaotic and uncomfortable world?—I know of no-one—least of all myself'.[61] This was the poignant underside of glamorous transgression.

Perhaps Anger's dislike is also a reaction to the way *Salome* looked so different from other contemporary American films that helped to fashion Hollywood as the centre of global entertainment. The fact is that despite the vibrant migrant communities on which Hollywood was built, some of whom nursed avant-garde aspirations, the vast majority of movies looked 'American'—and that wasn't an accident. As Richard Abel has shown, 'America' was imagined into being from its heterogeneous immigrant communities through the movies: Hollywood Americanized the movies, and the movies in turn Americanized America. The new industry provided an image of American community and values, tacitly validating America in contrast to everything *foreign*.[62] Westerns and Civil War films were only the most obvious examples; 'American' values and images were everywhere, including those earlier adaptations of *Salome* and *Dorian Gray*. When Dorian became a coke addict and brawled with Basil in the 1915 adaptation or when Salome became a Vamp via Bara's star persona, these characters were not merely being adapted, they were becoming American. The framing of Nazimova's *Salome* is palpably different. It comes out of a Russian tradition to the point where we cannot understand it by judging it solely against the emerging American mainstream or even in the all-important context of Los Angeles. If we want to grasp its sombre fatalism we must also return to another time and place: fin-de-siècle Russia, the scene of Nazimova's first stage successes during the 'Wildeism' that swept Moscow and St Petersburg.[63]

Wilde in Russia

Wilde's reputation across Europe was based on two things: public interest in his 1895 trials and the popularity of *Salome*. After his death in 1900, knowledge of these spanned out from France and Germany and, as Stefano Evangelista puts it, 'became the main catalyst of the spread of Wilde's literary fame in the rest of Europe'.[64] The way in which the trials and *Salome* came together to define Wilde's presence in Russia is especially singular. In those dying days of the Russian Empire, extensive newspaper reports on Wilde's trials linked self-destruction with same-sex love to create a mythology of redemptive suffering around him.[65] Reflecting the intense interest in Wilde's public downfall, the Russian theatre-director-turned-film-maker Vsevolod Meyerhold framed his acclaimed adaptation of *The Picture of Dorian Gray* (1915; lost) with allusions to Wilde's downfall, an unusual touch in pre-Revolutionary Russian cinema, which tended to use simple plots.[66] Nor was this the most striking aspect of Meyerhold's adaptation. He sensationally cast the female actor Varvara Yanova as Dorian, a move that foregrounded the novel's undertones of same-sex desire.[67]

The fact that Meyerhold was able to draw on at least three Russian translations of *Dorian Gray* for the film's libretto and title cards speaks of its wide circulation.[68] *Salome* was even more popular, with at least half a dozen Russian translations published in the first decade of the new century, at least one of which included Beardsley's drawings.[69] These translations were part of a broader movement. Sergei Diaghilev's journal *The World of Art* (*Mir iskusska*, 1899–1904), *Vesy* (*Libra*, 1904–9), *The Golden Fleece* (*Zolotoe runo*, 1906–9), and *Apollon* (1909–17), edited by Sergei Makovskii, were instrumental in translating, reviewing, promoting, and emulating Wilde and Beardsley. As they did so, they became focal points for a coterie of writers and artists inspired by decadence and the principle of 'art for its own sake'.[70]

In the first issue of *Libra*, for instance, the 'The Poetry of Oscar Wilde' by the poet and translator of Wilde, Konstantin Bal'mont, introduced readers to Wilde's life and works.[71] Diaghilev and his unofficial art editor, Léon Bakst, circulated reproductions of Beardsley's illustrations in *The World of Art*.[72] Makovskii authored an essay on Beardsley's drawings as part of a particularly influential illustrated translation of *Salome*.[73] Meanwhile, Bakst himself was directly influenced by Beardsley's original illustration of 'The Black Cape' for *Salome*, an influence that can be seen in the long black dress of the enigmatic woman seated in his *The Supper* (1902). She is Salome come to back to life to sit on the edge of her chair. waiting expectantly for someone or something in a St Petersburg cafe.[74]

Mostly, though, when Salome came back to life in Russia, she danced. She was a ballerina. Perhaps she always had been: as Narraboth gazes at Salome on her first appearance in Wilde's play, he gushes that 'She is like a princess who has little white doves for feet. One might fancy she was dancing.'[75] Beardsley's theatrically staged scenes also show figures with out-turned feet, toes en pointe, as if captured in the act of performing a battement tendu.[76] These tantalizing suggestions were brought to life in several Russian productions. In December 1908, Ida Rubinstein famously performed *Salome* for one night only, in the Great Hall of the St Petersburg Conservatory, with choreography by Mikhail Fokine. In 1909, a production of *Salome* at the Kommissarzhavskaya's Theater in St Petersburg was to be directed by Nikolai Evreinov, who went on to edit one of the most influential publications of Beardsley's drawings in 1912. His *Salome* was cancelled by the censor, but the private dress rehearsal was attended by major literary figures and became a germinal moment in Russian modernism.[77] Then, in 1913, Diaghilev's Ballets Russes returned to its roots with a production of *La Tragédie de Salome* in Paris, featuring choreography by Boris Romanov and costumes by Serge Sudeikin in the style of Beardsley (Fig. 3.4). By this time Salome's dance was widely considered to be the epitome of erotic transgression and modernity in Russia.[78] It evolved through the Ballets Russes' vision of reality as perverse performance, in which, for the first time a male lead—Vaslav Nijinsky—had danced en pointe, like a ballerina. Did Nazimova see the Ballets Russes production of *Salomé*? It's unlikely, though no doubt she heard about it from Fokine, who became her friend in New York. When it opened she had long since left for the New World.

She surely knew of the way in which *Salome* had become a symbol of sexual and artistic transgression in Russian dance. For it is a much-neglected fact that Nazimova herself asserted that she conceived her film in the style

Fig. 3.4 Publicity photo of Salome (Tamara Karsavina), costumed by Serge Sudeikin for the Ballets Russes production of *La Tragédié de Salomé* (1913)

of Russian ballet.[79] She was already well acquainted with Wilde's *Salome*, having been cast in the title role in a planned 1906 Moscow Art Theatre production.[80] While the play didn't go ahead, she and Wilde were subsequently linked by contemporary reviewers. One suggested that her 'bold and fantastical' acting blended Émile Zola with Oscar Wilde—'a sure way to the hearts of the play-going and reading public' in Moscow.[81] Another wrote that, in the title role of *Hedda Gabler* on Broadway (1918), 'It would seem to be the eradicable Nazimova's idea that the best way to play Ibsen is to play him, from first to last, as if he were a cross between Oscar Wilde's "Salome" and a czardas.'[82] It's difficult to say whether these critics are in earnest (in which case, what would a Wildean style of acting be?), or if they are using Wilde to allude to the well-known fact that Nazimova had relationships with women, or even to indicate her feminist credentials at a time when decadence and the New Women were frequently equated, or to highlight her Jewishness. Whichever way we read the reference, it wasn't a compliment.

The fatalism, same-sex desire, and balletic direction that define Russia's Wilde are integral to Nazimova's *Salome*. It's so obvious that critics couldn't fail to overlook it, as consideration has turned to Hollywood only and not Russia to understand Nazimova's film. Despite Hollywood's drive to Americanize the cinema, Russia—like Eastern Europe—was never far away. By 1930, over 2.5 million people from the former Russian Empire had migrated to the United States, with a boom following the 1917 Revolutions.[83] Los Angeles alone was home to an estimated 1,500–2,000 White Russian immigrants by the late 1920s.[84] In the arts, Russian names had such cultural capital that a young bohemian called Winifred Shaughnessy from Salt Lake City was amongst those who adopted one, becoming Natacha Rambova, Nazimova's close friend and designer of her *Salome*. Former officers and generals in the tsar's army worked in hospitality, opening new venues to cater to the Russian community. An Orthodox church was built. The Russian Film Art Corporation imported films from Russia, promising 'Pictures that are Different'. Russian aristocrats became movie extras.[85] The personal dramas of this last situation even inspired a movie: *The Last Command* (1928), directed by Josef von Sternberg, in which a former commander in the Tsar's army (Emil Jannings), fallen on hard times, is cast in a Hollywood epic about the Russian Revolution, directed by an old civil-war foe who remembers him all too well.[86] This diaspora, 'Little Russia' as it became, was in its infancy during Nazimova's Hollywood glory days. Sergei Prokofiev, a regular visitor to the Garden of Alla in 1921, recalled how the émigré community gathered there to celebrate the Russian New Year, singing 'God Save the Tsar' together at midnight.[87] Theodore Kosloff, Feodor Chaliapin, and Anna Pavlova also visited, while Nazimova socialized with Stanislavski and Mikhail (now Michael) Fokine in Manhattan. A few years later a young designer called Romain de Tirtoff (or Erté as he became known to the world) came to Hollywood at the invitation of Louis B. Mayer. Beardsley was an avowed influence on his art deco sets and costumes. In this Russian micro-cosm, a *Salome* such as Nazimova conceived it through same-sex desire and morbid fatalism, is hardly an artistic bombshell: it seems almost inevitable.

Picturing Beardsley's *Salome*

Nazimova made *Salome* for the kind of people who partied at 8080 Sun-set Boulevard: cosmopolitan artists from Russia and Europe, and Sewing Circle friends. Although—contrary to later accounts—it did find an audi-ence in America's urban centres, Allied Producers and Distributors was not among its fans. The pace and tone disliked by Anger were just the start of the problems. Nazimova's masterpiece was altogether too fatalistic and sexy in the wrong way. When Allied did give it a very limited release, almost all the publicity was organized personally by Nazimova and Bryant.[88]

With the hindsight of a century, it's clear that *Salome* was an outlier in the burgeoning mass entertainment industry. A couple of decades later Fred Astaire would chide Vincente Minnelli, another fan of Wilde, for 'upping the arty' in *Yolanda and the Thief* (1945). Astaire's instinct for entertain-ment over art was quite right when it came to commercial success. In the early 1920s this was not yet clear. The borderlines between avant-garde *cin-ema* and *the movies* were still uncertain. Although from its beginnings the American movie scene was ferociously commercial, there was a small but lively scene of low-budget experimental films at its margins.[89] Early exam-ples, such as *Manhatta* (1921), *The Soul of the Cypress* (1920), and *The Life and Death of 9413—A Hollywood Extra* (1928), were rough and ready, made by small teams of amateur enthusiasts and industry professionals on their weekends.[90] They blended dreamscapes and artistic risk-taking with breaking taboos.

Like other avant-garde films, *Salome* looked to expand the range of Amer-ican cinema. Nazimova had the perfect source material in Wilde's play. Just as *Dorian Gray*'s spectre of an autonomously moving, framed figure gained new significance in the movie age, so *Salome*'s insistent focus on the desiring gaze was given piquancy in an age of cinematic voyeurs. Why not bring this together with illicit lust and self-sacrifice? Nazimova knew there were precedents for that. She was a little disingenuous in telling *Picture-Play Magazine* that she had rejected all of the stock features of earlier *Salome* interpretations. True, she ditched the come-hither performances and historical settings of US adaptations. However, she omitted to mention the Russian *Salomes*. If most American picture-goers didn't know enough to make the connections, others—including those from the Russian immigrant artistic communities—surely would. Diaghilev had put Wilde's heroine and her dance at the centre of a new turn in Russian art and dance. Perhaps Nazimova could do the same for American cinema.

Her *Salome* reinstates Wilde's fascination with destruction and lesbian desire, erased from the loose American adaptations. With this aim, the use of Beardsley's designs is a particular stroke of genius. As Rambova adapts Beardsley's illustrations, she exaggerates and stylizes them into a cohesive and bold design scheme. The flowers intertwined around the back of the main set of *Salome* are simplified versions of Beardsley's bookplate and title-page designs for the play. The intertwined climbing roses of the original have been pruned back; their heads are larger and fewer for a dramatic nouveau effect. Through Beardsley, Nazimova and Rambova could suggest with impunity the very subversions that had condemned *Aphrodite*. These Beardsleyesque designs were fashionable as well as apt. As we know from Chapter 1, in the late 1910s 'The Vogue of Beardsley' brought the fin de siècle into parallel with jazz-age America.[91] A closer look shows that Rambova gives us a distinct Beardsley from that in vogue, just as Nazimova fashions a new kind of *Salome*. Her set and props play up the symbolism of his illustrations, omitted by other US acolytes. At the same time, Beardsley's phallic symbolism—candelabras, swords, erect plant stems and the like—is gone. Rambova's designs remake this into a film about female desire, represented in the most Beardsleyesque fashion: yonic symbols of circles, archways, and veiled entrances. The way into Jokanaan's cistern is the most elaborate, imagined as a gilded, arched cage, over which Salome drapes herself, while at the level of costuming, pearls inscribe eroticism and power on to her body.[92] A contemporary review assured readers that 'Only the highest of the highbrows will perceive the unwholesome aspects of it'.[93] For those highest of highbrows, touches like the arched cage were an artistic coup—a mons Veneris encoded at the centre of the set.

Rambova also takes up the extravagantly theatrical side of Beardsley, focusing on the dramatic and whimsically curved lines of his boldest two-tone patterns.[94] The capacious kimono robe worn by Salome as she kisses the head of Jokanaan is a striking example (Fig. 3.5): it simplifies and enlarges the black-and-white sweeping lines of Beardsley's 'Peacock Skirt' (Fig. 3.6) and 'The Dancer's Reward' while recalling Sudeikin's costuming—almost certainly known by Rambova—for the Ballets Russes *Salome*.[95] After

Fig. 3.5 Salome (Nazimova) wears Natacha Rambova's reimagined Peacock Dress

walking upstage with Jokanaan's head on a silver platter, she kneels, covering herself and the platter with the robe to kiss the severed head. And as the robe aestheticizes the morbid kiss, what could have been a grotesque spectacle becomes a triumph of beautiful style, played out in front of that symbolic cistern cage. Erotically, though, it is an anticlimax. Beneath Salome's cloak, her sadistic pleasure is unseen. Nazimova knows the truth of Wilde's quip in *Lady Windermere's Fan*, the play he finished alongside *Salome*: 'There

Fig. 3.6 'The Peacock Skirt' drawn by Aubrey Beardsley for Wilde's *Salome* (1893)

are only two tragedies. One is not getting what one wants, and the other is getting it.'[96]

But we're getting ahead of ourselves. Long before Salome appears with the severed head, the Beardsleyesque design defines desire in Nazimova's

Salome. Narraboth (Earl Schenck) and the Page (Arthur Jasmine) wear peacock-feathered leggings, heavy eye make-up, canonical pom-pom wigs.[97] Teamed with oversized pearl necklaces on their bare chests and pantomimic gestures, the impression is over the top even for silent film (Fig. 3.7). Touches like these, in theatrically contrasting spaces of black and white, create a self-consciously artificial, ahistorical realm that today looks very camp; it

Fig. 3.7 Salome (Nazimova) and Narraboth (Schenck)

wasn't then—or not straightforwardly. Camp was at most a fledgling category among the literati of New York in the early 1920s. *Salome*'s design does, though, anticipate camp in drawing attention to style for its own sake and theatricalizing gender roles to the point of parody.[98]

The overall effect is an uncanny vision of desire. The pom-pom wigs worn by Narraboth and the Page should be funny and in other hands they would be. Beardsley's impish humour might easily have been rolled into the carnivalesque momentum of a surreal comedy. In another possible universe his satyrs are extras in a Marx Brothers film; Narraboth and the Page would not be out of place at the court of Freedonia in *Duck Soup* (1933). However, Nazimova does not give us comedy for more than a moment. At the heart of her *Salome* there is a tension between the comedic potential of the design and the tone of the scenario. If this is Beardsleyism read through the Ballets Russes, it is also read back through Wilde, with the static quality of his play-text—produced by the repetition of images and phrases, and long rhetorical speeches—evoked on-screen with longer-than-average takes, which made the film appear exceptionally slow-moving.[99] Combined with the morbid title cards and the figure of the Executioner, who remains on-screen throughout, *Salome* is a party emptied of fun.

At the centre is Salome herself. Nazimova brings her title figure to life not as a femme fatale but as a desirous, determined, vulnerable woman. She first appears turning imperiously from Herod's advances in a sparkly minidress before she flounces off. Then, slowly, as she gazes into the distance with kohl-rimmed eyes, something extraordinary begins to happen. Salome becomes a three-dimensional figure, a woman with a mind as well as a body. There are parallels with Ibsen's challenge to bourgeois morality in the figures of Nora and Hedda, both of whom Nazimova had played onstage.[100] Here, though, the challenge is violently rendered, its sexual dimensions writ large. As Salome implores, 'Suffer me to kiss thy lips, Jokanaan', a series of long shots show her and Jokanaan facing close together.[101] They could be two men or two women, mirroring each other, and there is a frisson of same-sex desire in this moment. Nazimova's androgynous beauty contrasts with the voluptuousness of Theda Bara, Maud Allan, and, indeed, Wilde's intended star, Sarah Bernhardt. Like Ida Rubenstein, she has an androgynous figure, hard-won by a combination of strict dieting and clever costuming.[102]

When desire is directed to the opposite sex, it has a grim fatalism. 'You are always looking at her', the Page tells the Young Syrian in Wilde's play. And again, 'You look at her too much. It's dangerous to look at people in such fashion'.[103] With only title cards in the film and without Wilde's spoken words—the first 'talking picture' was *The Jazz Singer* in 1927—the hopeless and ill-fated desiring gaze is brought to vivid life with the movie camera alone. Take the moment when Salome first discovers Jokanaan. In Wilde's play she variously implores, 'I would look on him', 'I would but look at him', 'I would look closer at him', 'I must look at him closer'.[104] The hopeless desire expressed in the conditional tense becomes an imperative, is the catalyst, for cinematographic innovation. In place of these words, a montage shows Salome peering into Jokanaan's cell, while Narraboth watches her and the Page watches him watching her, looking for Jokanaan, with the Executioner presiding over the whole scene. Salome has lost herself in looking; looking towards Jokanaan and towards something else too, something intangible but deeply needed. Narraboth watches her and the Page watches him, each desiring the other in vain. There is a low-key radicalism in these moments. Photographer Charles Van Enger was experimenting with new close-ups and continuity-editing techniques to create the visual grammar of desire on-screen; and not just desire, but unfulfilled desire. His camerawork evokes not mutual recognition, the starting point of reciprocal desire, let alone any erotic pleasure, but unrequited longing that burns at once with eros and pain. Nazimova knew that it is the feelings we cannot articulate that haunt us. Feelings that words cannot touch because we are too close to them. Salome's interior life had never before been explored so tenderly on-screen. It had very rarely been noticed at all among the more obvious visual delights of Salomania. Seen through a lens that attends to Salome's feelings more than to her body, she is transformed. In her close-ups, the signs of ageing around Nazimova's middle-aged eyes are poignant. She is not what she seems to be; hers is a mask that tells us more than the face, as Wilde was wont to write. Thus does this gazing after an idealized love object gain fresh piquancy in an age of cinematic voyeurs.

This pace, androgyny, and sheer hopelessness make for a very unusual Dance of the Seven Veils. It's missing an essential ingredient: eroticism. Anger was right about that but his dreary lament utterly misses the point. Nazimova's dance isn't meant to be sexy enough for Herod to feel he got good value. That's the point. In Wilde's original, Salome's dance could be anything: it is marked simply in his text as '[Salome dances the dance of the seven veils]'.[105] As in Wilde's description of Dorian Gray's portrait, the sparse textual note leaves film-makers and performers to imagine it into being. Predictably, most imagined a performance that made theatre audiences voyeurs of an erotic spectacle like Herod. By contrast, Nazimova asks the cinema audience to feel what Salome feels. When she appears in her tight white miniskirt, she is motionless, holding her translucent veils up over her face. The static camera holds her, still, in the frame and we wonder, as she wonders, what she will do next. Then, slowly, she begins. Eschewing the orientalized gestures of earlier Salomes, Nazimova turns instead to— what else?—ballet: the dance form par excellence of her Russian roots. At the very beginning of Wilde's play, the Page comments that Salome 'is like a woman who is dead. She moves very slowly'.[106] This is exactly how Nazimova performs the dance. Wearing ballet slippers and with toes out-turned gesturing towards pointe, her Salome half chassés self-consciously in a circle before hiding behind her translucent veils (Fig. 3.8). Poised with pointed toe, she looks as if she might begin a ballet sequence—but she doesn't. Like the uncanny presence of Narraboth and the Page, her performance conveys a sense of pleasure and joy curtailed. After an abrupt cut she gathers momentum towards the end of the dance and her movement turns to desperation, as she flings herself from side to side, her eyes wild, before she falls to the ground.

As David Weir comments, 'the whole performance is hard to square with the smirking expressions of various soldiers and courtiers, not to mention the obscenely panting response of Herod (evidently, the tetrarch really gets off on art)'.[107] This disparity between what Nazimova is doing and how

Fig. 3.8 Salome (Nazimova) performs the Dance of the Seven Veils

the men are responding is exactly the point. The male viewers on-screen see what they want to see: a saucy performance. When the camera cuts to Herod, laughing, panting with the satisfaction of desire fulfilled, or perhaps control exerted, he is shown to be ridiculous: a parody of desire measured against Salome's vicissitudes of longing. Meanwhile, the audience sees how Salome really feels during this performance: shy, self-conscious, and desperate. Does this look 'decadent'? It does not. Sensual indulgence for its own sake is not the point here. Mischievously subverting the vicarious indulgences of her cinematic contemporaries, Nazimova's *Salome* is a film about female empowerment, far less equivocal on that score than Wilde's play or Beardsley's illustrations. It is a fitting development of the play in which Wilde was the first writer or artist to give Salome an empathetic interior life.[108]

Sunset Boulevard

In a denouement worthy of an F. Scott Fitzgerald novel, five years later Nazimova was renting a room in the hotel that once had been her own mansion. She had been forced by financial difficulties to run the Garden of Alla as a hotel in the mid-1920s and stayed on as a resident till the venture failed.[109] The (slightly renamed) Garden of Allah's poolside bar became a popular meeting place and temporary residence for writers and stars: Charlie Chaplin, Errol Flynn, Fitzgerald, Ernest Hemingway, Dorothy Parker, and Clara Bow went there for cocktails by the pool and clandestine liaisons. Sergei Rachmaninov and Igor Stravinsky stayed there when they visited Los Angeles. Perhaps they sat with Nazimova out on the terrace talking of the old days and departed friends in Russia. In 1959 the Garden of Allah was demolished to be replaced with a strip mall—a final act that, according to urban legend, inspired Joni Mitchell to write 'Big Yellow Taxi'.

Nazimova had hoped to capitalize on the reach of cinema at a time when Los Angeles seemed to be a cosmopolitan Sapphic utopia with new opportunities for experimental films. It was almost plausible, so why exactly did *Salome* fail? Was it too weird, too queer, too foreign? Certainly its depiction of perverse desire, homoeroticism, necrophilia, and cross-dressing did not accord with the all-American images the distributors wished to purvey. Nazimova deserves much credit for her role in fashioning the Oscar Wilde we know today. She drew out a side of Wilde that English-speaking audiences hadn't seen before, focusing on his queerness and his tragic fatalism. She was right about Wilde too: he is shocking, modern, and artistically daring.

Her mistake was to believe that she could take this as the cue for expanding the artistic scope of American cinema. She had sought to make desire new, recentring its depiction of female subjectivity using symbolism and new cinema technology.

While Hollywood moguls sought the legitimacy and frisson of literary adaptations and half longed for the artistry of European films, they were primarily businessmen not artists. *Salome* squeezed past the censors but her creator could not. Nazimova was not a star suited to the new, more controlling era that was the industry's response to the brouhaha around movies and morals after Arbuckle. When studio heads drew up a list of film stars—117 in all—whose private lives made them morally 'unsafe', the list inevitably included Nazimova.[110] Ultimately, her *Salome* was an outlier in the development of cinema into a mass entertainment industry that had no use for the serious Wilde. It wanted Wilde the entertainer. That understood, his notoriety was a marketable frisson, an unspoken symbol of sexual deviance, so long as it didn't go too far.

It was not, however, the end of Nazimova's star career. Not quite. Billy Wilder's film *Sunset Boulevard* begins with struggling screenwriter Joe Gillis (William Holden) stumbling upon Norma Desmond's decaying mansion. Inside 10,086 Sunset Boulevard, Norma (Gloria Swanson), once the ultimate star of silent cinema, is planning her triumphant return to the screen, indulged by her devoted butler (von Stroheim, no less). She has written the screenplay and intends to star in it. What does she choose? 'It's the story of Salome,' she declares to Joe; 'I think I'll have DeMille direct it.' *Sunset Boulevard* pivots around Norma's vision of her comeback, as she emotionally blackmails Joe to help with her screenplay and become her lover. But the role is too young for her; her era is over and her ambition will destroy both her and Joe.

Sunset Boulevard is not quite, or not only, the story of Nazimova's fate. More broadly it is a celluloid epitaph for the whole lost world of early Hollywood and its forgotten silent stars, who included Nazimova and indeed the stars of Wilder's film—Swanson, von Stroheim, and DeMille, whose associations with the genre of silent epic lend a grandeur to Norma's tragedy. Yet it is partly based on her story, borrowing the Garden of Alla and *Salome* to create a new Hollywood myth. Like Nazimova, Norma is too old to play Salome; like her, she is a pushy woman determined to control all aspects of the production; and like her she lives in a mansion on Sunset Boulevard, though there are no parties anymore. She has been cast aside by an industry that has no use for older women. The score by Franz Waxman quotes from Strauss's Wilde-inspired *Salome*, while Norma's white peacock feathers borrow from Rambova's Beardsleyesque flourishes, and her 'smell of tuberose' connotes eroticism and death—an established trope in decadent literature.[111] Of course, the screenwriters, Wilder and Charles Brackett, knew whereof they wrote. As discussed in Chapter 1, during their respective pre-Hollywood careers—in the 1920s, when Brackett was a reporter in New York, Wilder a critic in Berlin—each had admired Wilde's work and the *Earnest*-style discovery of an engraved cigarette case provides the denouement of *Sunset Boulevard*. Nazimova did not live to see *Sunset Boulevard*. She died of cancer in 1945 and Wilder's movie is an ambivalent tribute— neither a version of her story, nor an accurate mythical substitute. Was she, like Norma, destructive and delusional? She was not.

Today *Sunset Boulevard* is better known through Andrew Lloyd Webber's stage adaptation (1993).[112] It is a rare example of a musical that enlarges the emotional range of its source material, alluding to Nazimova's *Salome* with various light touches in the costumes by Anthony Powell, and Lloyd Webber's music, with lyrics by Christopher Hampton and Don Black. As Glenn Close performed the song 'Salome' onstage in 2016, her movement also incorporated gestures from Nazimova's Dance of the Seven Veils.[113] Crucially, a stage musical can demonstrate Norma's talent in a way that a non-musical drama could not hope to. Wilder's film never shows Norma actually acting, beyond one brief glimpse of a silent movie. Whereas, when Lloyd Webber's Norma sings and dances onstage, we realize that she has been passed over and driven mad, not by lack of talent—she is brilliant— but because she is an artistically ambitious woman in an industry made for and by men. Here, Norma is not delusional about her talent. She is no Sally Bowles. Rather, she is out of time: too old to be a star in a system that craves youth, too assertive for an industry run by men, and too late to resume a career that peaked decades earlier. A brilliantly gifted but deeply thwarted woman. In this way, she is indeed Nazimova.

4

Wilde-ish Spirit Goes West

When Ernst Lubitsch's adaptation of *Lady Windermere's Fan* was released at the end of 1925, it changed Wilde's fortunes in Hollywood. Salomania had defined much of Wilde's success in the United States up to this point, with Alla Nazimova's 1922 adaptation marking both the climax and death knell of the trend. Hollywood wanted European sophistication, but not like that: not too morbid, not too arty, not too sexy. Wilde himself once wrote, 'Personally I like comedy to be intensely modern, and like my tragedy to walk in purple and to be remote.'[1] In the 1920s, as writers, directors, and actors flocked to Hollywood, it remained to be seen whether Lubitsch's comedic, modern Oscar would prevail where the purple and remote one had not.

There were some promising signs, but then there had been promising signs for Nazimova's *Salome* too. As set out in Chapter 1, Wilde's works remained popular into the 1920s, aided by the availability of cheap paperback editions and widespread performances of *Earnest*, *Lady Windermere*, and *Salome*. His literary archive could be lucrative too.[2] In 1920 over 400 of his manuscripts and rare editions were auctioned in Manhattan, fetching a total of $46,866.[3] The following year a figure called Dorian Hope—a persona created by one Brett Holland from North Carolina—forged manuscripts and personal letters by his hero, Wilde.[4] A shrewd operator, Hope targeted the US market because, as he wrote to the auctioneer William Figgis, 'Wilde's popularity in America is astounding [. . .] all the money is now in America.'[5]

It was at this time that interest in Wilde and his decadent contemporaries was giving rise to a new literary current, dubbed by the press 'the new decadence.'[6] This vague group of writers recognized that the milieu of the 1890s was a rich seam to mine in fiction, drawing on readers' familiarity with its characters, ideas, and styles. What they brought into being was a new and a distinctly modern kind of decadent fiction. One of this movement's leading lights, the novelist and critic Carl Van Vechten, best captured its character when he wrote that

> To be 1890 in 1890 might be considered almost normal. To be 1890 in 1922 might be considered almost queer. There is a difference, however.

Wilde in the Dream Factory. Kate Hext, Oxford University Press. © Kate Hext (2024).
DOI: 10.1093/9780191987335.003.0004

The colour is magenta. Oscar's hue was green. The fun is warmer; the vice more léger.[7]

While Van Vechten is ostensibly talking about his friend, the novelist Ronald Firbank here, his appraisal could characterize new decadence more broadly.[8] Its character was decidedly different to the tragic and melodramatic movie adaptations of *Dorian Gray* and *Salome*. Though unmistakably indebted to the 1890s, the new generation of Wildeans rework his styles and concerns into stories that are fun, pacey, and—crucially—naughty, with a nod and a wink to sexual transgressions. Their devil-may-care attitude bespeaks a major cultural shift. According to Edmund Wilson, since these new decadents no longer believed in the evils of sin or its consequences, 'it is possible for the sinner to be amiable again'.[9] Put another way, 1920s' decadence could be fun and it is this spirit that would come to define Wilde's influence in the movies.

How much of this trend was known in London is difficult to say but the Wilde Estate had renewed hopes of the American film industry. Its executor, Robbie Ross, had died in 1918. His successor, Wilde's son Vyvyan Holland, focused less on what film could do for his father's reputation and more on the practicalities of selling the lucrative worldwide film rights. While impressed by Nazimova's star turn in *Salome*,[10] Holland understood that cinema was a commercial industry and he would respond to film studios rather than attempt in vain to control which works they adapted. There had been British film adaptations of *Lady Windermere* and *A Woman of No Importance*, released stateside in 1919 and 1922 respectively.[11] In 1923 the president of the American Play Company met with representatives of the Estate in London to attempt to secure the worldwide film rights to *An Ideal Husband*, *Earnest*, and *Lady Windermere*. There was also correspondence on the matter. Lots of correspondence.[12] These negotiations foundered, however, as the dispute with Daniel Frohman rumbled on. Frohman was still claiming a substantial cut of the payments for any US film adaptations of Wilde's plays; the Estate still demurred, arguing that the 'performance rights' he held for the United States pertained only to stage productions.[13] With Frohman thus necessarily involved, discussions over potential film rights were fraught. Amid suspicion on both sides, lengthy transatlantic written negotiations resulted in an impasse of confusion.

Then there was a breakthrough of sorts. Wilde's first social comedy *Lady Windermere* was sold again—this time to Warner Brothers, to be directed by wunderkind Ernest Lubitsch—via a deal which ingeniously sidestepped both the Estate and Frohman.[14] It was announced with great fanfare by *Moving Picture World*, in a publicity-focused version of the truth:

> Uncommon interest attaches itself to the production of this drama, partly because of the world wide popularity which Wilde's masterpiece has enjoyed on the stage through many years, and partly because of the insistent refusal of the executors of the Wilde estate for a long time to permit a picturization.[15]

Readers might infer that the Estate's artistic scruples had delayed 'picturization'. Not so: it was that old dispute about rights.

Regardless, *Lady Windermere* was finally going to Hollywood and she wasn't the only one. The migration of journalists, fiction writers, artists, actors, playwrights, directors, and impresarios to capitalize on the Hollywood boom is well documented. In 1920 the population of Los Angeles was 576,000; by 1930 it had more than doubled to 1,230,000.[16] Attracted by the promise of glamour and fame, this flood of hopefuls helped transform Los Angeles into 'the Holy Grail of American ambition'.[17] The attraction of Hollywood was clear. In a case that could stand for innumerable others, when Van Vechten's novel *The Tattooed Countess* (1924) was adapted for the screen as *A Woman of the World* (1925), starring Pola Negri, it bore scant relation to his novel and he disliked it.[18] His objections were assuaged when a cheque for $7,500—the largest he had ever received—arrived from Famous Players-Lasky for the rights.[19]

Among the new arrivals was Lubitsch. Originally an actor, by his twenties he was an established film-maker in his native Germany. Despite an unsuccessful first foray to Hollywood a year earlier, in 1922 a contract from Mary Pickford lured him back across the Atlantic, this time for good. Falling out with Pickford—though *Rosita* (1923), their sole joint venture, was well received—Lubitsch was snapped up by Warner Brothers on a dream deal: three years, six pictures, and total control from determination of the cast and crew to the final edit.

While *Lady Windermere* was probably a default choice for adaptation, being the Wilde play Warner Brothers was able to acquire, it was singularly apt for Lubitsch and for the time. It would definitively answer questions hitherto far from settled: Could the American screen be Wildean? Did it want to be Wildean? And if so, how? At the time, it was far from clear that even Wilde could be Wildean on-screen. For the comedic Wilde had, as yet, hardly been seen in movies and not in adaptations of his comedies. With the notable exception of Roscoe Arbuckle's 1918 star turn as a slapstick Salome, in America as in Europe, silent film had lingered on Wilde's tragic heroes. Meanwhile the British film adaptations of *Lady Windermere* and *A Woman of No Importance* emphasized the melodrama that remained in Wilde's original plays, to the point where little if any comedy remained.

The role of Lubitsch as director signalled that Warner Brothers had something different in mind for their *Lady Windermere*. In a happy confluence, his ambitions as a director in mid-1920s Hollywood enabled Wilde and American cinema to resolve another problem they shared: how to be at once naughty and nice. There had always been tensions between the public's love of Wilde and propriety. His mainstream success in twentieth-century America had been made possible by an image makeover which put the trials and their subject firmly off-stage. Shadowy suggestiveness brought a frisson of sexual impropriety, but this had to stay in the background. The *léger* tone and light sampling of fin-de-siècle motifs in new decadent writing assisted the cause by steering away from overt references to 'the love that dare not speak its name'. But this rehabilitation of Wilde's reputation was intrinsically fragile. His queer side perennially threatened to break out and indeed kept doing so: in the Maud Allan trials, Frank Harris's *Oscar Wilde, His Life and Confessions* (1916), Nazimova's *Salome*, and those forged Wilde letters by 'Dorian Hope', which used sexual slang and innuendo and discussed male prostitutes.[20]

At a time when the movie industry was implementing new regulations, Wilde thus posed both a threat and an opportunity. The threat was that he and his works offered *sin* rather than *naughtiness*, and if it were sin there would be trouble. The Motion Picture Producers and Distributors of America (MPPDA), established in 1922 under Will H. Hays, heralded an era of industry self-regulation in an atmosphere of suppressed panic about the morality of the movies.[21] The point of self-regulation was to avoid a worse fate: mandatory government censorship. With a stated intention 'to keep the screen clean and wholesome',[22] the MPPDA provided thirteen assurances; for instance that 'the producers of motion pictures refrain from [. . .] [t]hematically making prominent an illicit love affair which tends to make virtue odious and vice attractive'.[23] A specific agreement, known as 'the Formula', governed cinema adaptations of plays and novels: it would be necessary 'to exercise every care that only books or plays which are of the right type are used for screen presentation'.[24] The very suggestion of Wilde might contravene any one of the rather nebulous regulations set out by the MPPDA.

The opportunity was Lubitsch. Having made his name in Germany with sex comedies, in Hollywood he ambitiously set about creating a sophisticated visual language of erotic play that evoked things unshowable onscreen. *Lady Windermere* was filmed at a time when 'sophisticated comedies' were beginning to find ways to depict situations and morals 'on the edge of what censors or more conservative viewers would tolerate'.[25] Of course, Wilde was a past master on this front. *Lady Windermere* had been conceived in 1892 amid a parallel culture of moral tentativeness and illicit desire and, like Lubitsch, Wilde had to work with and around censorship. Liberally borrowing characters and plot conceits from conventional nineteenth-century fallen-woman melodramas, he reworked these into a subtle but devastating subversion, in a semblance of light-hearted fun and frivolity. That helped *Lady Windermere* get the Lord Chamberlain's approval, where *Salome* failed months later.[26]

When Lubitsch set out to produce a film that was—as he himself put it— 'Wilde-ish . . . in spirit', he wanted to capture the subtle, light wit of Wilde's epigrams with their ability to put sex into the air.[27] Wilde's style and attitude to morality suggested a way to do just that—one that might expand the language of the sophisticated comedy. The big problem was words, or lack thereof. Lubitsch's seemingly impossible challenge was how to translate Wilde's witty words into silent moving pictures.

Hollywood Boom

Wilde's style and Hollywood were already coming together when Lubitsch arrived on the West Coast. Some of the new decadents were starting to head out there. Van Vechten was one of them. Having begun his career as a novelist with *Peter Whiffle* (1922), a sensual Bildungsroman deeply indebted to *À rebours* and *Dorian Gray*, his next novel brought its tale of hedonistic experimentation to a climax in the setting of—where else?[28] Staying at the Ambassador Hotel on Wilshire Boulevard in January 1927, he decided to write a Hollywood novel.[29] *Spider Boy* (1928) is the story of gauche playwright Ambrose Deacon, who takes a train West from New York and mistakenly ends up in Hollywood where he careens through a series of misunderstandings and mishaps. Like Harold Lloyd's comic on-screen characters, Ambrose is an Everyman who would go unnoticed in the crowd if only things would stop happening to him.[30] Despite—or because of—his increasingly desperate attempts to leave Hollywood, protesting that he has no interest in making movies, he is courted by top movie executives and pursued by larger-than-life silent screen star Imperia Starling, who imprisons him in her opulent Beverly Hills home so that Ambrose has to mount several escape attempts. The more he desperately tries *not* to sign a contract with a top Hollywood studio, the more the studio bosses think he is playing hard to get and offer him ever-larger sums. In the end, he gives up, submitting to both the executives, who rewrite 'his' script so extensively that it no longer bears any relation to his own work, and to the film star, whom he reluctantly marries.

The plot of 'going Hollywood' had become familiar in 1920s film comedies. Van Vechten's madcap novel captures the kinetic energy and farcical mishaps of successful films like Mack Sennett's *Small Town Idol* (1921).[31] At the same time it exemplifies the new decadence, illustrating what some had suspected for years: Hollywood was the new Mecca of decadence, the only place where such sumptuous collections of luxury goods and displays of excess could truly exist for their own sake in the 1920s. Describing Starling's vast Beverly Hills residence and the movie studio in an accumulation of rich, sensual details, Van Vechten creates a catalogue of objects in a style characteristic of fin-de-siècle decadent novels to evoke immersive, almost overwhelming, sensuality.[32] At its centre are the film stars, who have themselves become works of art: living to drink and to simply *be*—and be photographed by the fan magazines—while being paid vast sums. The decadent dream incarnate.

By 1927 Van Vechten's own Hollywood sojourn was part of an established trend. Nazimova had set up home in Beverly Hills in 1918. Two erstwhile Salomes, Mimi Aguglia and Evelyn Preer, and an onstage Dorian Gray, Edwards Davis, also went West, where a string of smaller parts awaited them.[33] For others, movie fame meant that Wilde faded into the background of their pre-Hollywood careers. We've already mentioned D. W. Griffith's turn in *Salome* onstage in New York before he became a film director. Others include Bela Lugosi—the eponymous *Dracula* (1931)—who starred as Lord Henry in the first Hungarian film adaptation, entitled *The Royal Life*. Ernest Thesiger had trodden the boards many a time in *Lady Windermere* and twice in *Earnest* before finding fame as the ultimate camp villain in the B-movie classics, *The Old Dark House* (1932) and *Bride of Frankenstein* (1935).[34]

This background in Wildeanism and new decadence, which hopefuls brought with them out West, is forgotten in most accounts of how Hollywood became Hollywood.[35] Perhaps it doesn't suit the story the conventional wisdom wants to tell. Or maybe it's because so many who found success there seemed to be born again in the process, their old life no longer relevant. Take Ben Hecht, the ultimate Hollywood migrant. In 1928 Herman J. Mankiewicz sent an oft-quoted cable urging Hecht to join him in Hollywood: 'Millions are to be grabbed out here and your only competition is idiots. Don't let this get around.'[36] Hecht went straight away. His wild double success at doctoring others' scripts, while writing original ones at lightning speed, made him Hollywood's most prolific screenwriter. His triumph swept away all that went before in accounts of his life, including his own memoirs.[37] Yet when Hecht got Mankiewicz's wire, he was a successful journalist and fiction writer on the literary scenes of Chicago and New York. His short stories and essays, which appeared frequently in *The Little Review*, like his novels published by Boni and Liveright in New York, were studded with the motifs of the Anglo-European fin de siècle: adding a touch of class and creating a frisson of transgression in these tales of would-be decadents in modern-day Chicago.

Hecht was not precious about artistic originality or fidelity to his sources. His pragmatism was a stronger impulse than his decadence ever was. So he sampled the ennui, opulent tastes, and witty epigrams of the decadent anti-hero in order to give his stories a fashionable edge.[38] Sometimes his neo-decadents found themselves in a naturalist dilemma novel; elsewhere they were at the centre of a whodunit.[39] Either way, they were like Van Vechten's movie stars: decadents recast in the midst of a modern metropolis moving to the rhythms of a fast-paced plot.

Elsewhere too decadents were outliving the fin de siècle or being born again. In a series of comic mysteries—a dozen novels (1926–39) and fifteen films (1929–47), hugely popular in their day—S. S. Van Dine created what Raymond Chandler unkindly called 'the most asinine character in detective fiction'.[40] Philo Vance is a flippant Manhattan flâneur and art collector, with an English accent acquired at Oxford, who solves crimes in his spare time. The District Attorney even advises him not to wear a green carnation: a reference to Wilde's appearance at the premiere of *Lady Windermere*, when the same bloom symbolized homosexual desire.[41] Or again, the transatlantic bestseller *The Green Hat* (1924) by Michael Arlen alludes to Walter Pater's famous description of the *Mona Lisa* to evoke its main figure, Iris March, while Dorian Gray's misdemeanours are echoed in the downfall of golden boy Napier.[42] Set in Mayfair's Shepherd Market, Arlen's nostalgic eye knows well that Half Moon Street is home to Algernon in *Earnest*, while in real life Robbie Ross spent his last years at number 40. It lingers longingly on what it refers to as this 'street of ghostly dandies'.[43]

Like Hecht, Van Dine and Arlen went to Hollywood. They may not have fully realized it at the time, but their decadence-inflected novels already looked towards the movies. For these novels jettisoned the forms of fin-de-siècle fiction, understanding that the kind of meandering odyssey of sensations and feelings catalogued in exhaustive detail back then, was a dead end. At the level of sentence, the overwrought, wearyingly overabundant evocations and constructions of nineteenth-century decadence could hardly appeal as mass-market fiction.[44] And anyway bestsellers are not made by a self-involved man having sensual experiences alone in heavily draped rooms. Those novels were too elitist in their frames of reference, too languid to sustain a cracking plot, even if they wanted to, which they didn't. When Wilde incorporated the suspense of sensation fiction, the horror of the gothic novel, and the cross-examination and chase sequences of the emerging detective genre into *Dorian Gray*, he was anticipating this turn. Only by creating a compelling narrative would the public take notice. Such became the essence of the new decadent novel: 'magenta, warmer, léger', to recall Van Vechten's description of decadence à la 1922, in comparison to its fin-de-siècle precursor. An amorphous magpie genre, new decadence fused decadent character traits and motifs with mystery-driven plots; defined at the level of narrative by naturalism, or the emerging vernacular of hard-boiled mass-market fiction.[45]

Scenario writers were in demand and there were even lucrative competitions to find new talent. One such, run by the *Chicago Daily News* and the Goldwyn Film Company in September 1921, offered a first prize of $30,000—equivalent to over $400,000 today.[46] *The Photodramatist*, a newly founded industry magazine, carried numerous advertisements for writers, editors, and more, as well as articles explaining how to make it as a scenario writer in Hollywood, which was, declared one such, 'the intellectual center of western America. For photodramatists [...] the end of an uphill trail, a vantage point from which to assail the mountain peaks of art'.[47] Hecht's *Daily News* colleague Charles MacArthur, with whom he would write films including *The Front Page* (1931), headed to Hollywood from Chicago. So did the multitalented Wallace Smith, another who started out as a reporter. Moving from words to pictures, Smith's explicit Beardsleyesque illustration for Hecht's novel *Fantazius Mallare* (1923) got himself, Hecht, and their publisher prosecuted for sending 'lewd, lascivious, and obscene' literature through the US postal service—but more of that later.[48] In Hollywood Smith switched back to words again with a successful third career as a screenwriter, cut short by his premature death from a heart attack in 1937. His twenty-six film credits included *Bulldog Drummond* (1929) and *Friends and Lovers* (1931).

Some of these writers had, like Hecht, moonlighted in the film studios of New York and Chicago before heading to California. Others tried their luck with no prior experience in moving pictures. Samuel Hoffenstein was one of the latter. Like Nazimova, Hoffenstein was a Russian immigrant weaned on Wilde and decadence. In 1916 while working as a journalist on the *New York Evening Sun*, his poetry collection *Life Sings a Song* appeared. It used the tropes and verse styles of the 1890s—death or ennui defining every poem—with a strong sense of its own belatedness.[49] A relative latecomer to Hollywood, he found immediate success with an Oscar nomination for the screenplay adaptation of *Dr Jekyll and Mr Hyde* (1931), starring Fredric March. A second screenwriting nomination followed for *Laura* (1944). Writers like Hoffenstein were paid expeditiously for their work, beneficiaries of Hollywood's desire to boost its cultural capital, or at least to keep up with consumer demand for more movies. F. Scott Fitzgerald—yet another Hollywood hopeful whose early novels were rooted in decadence[50]—later fictionalized the culture of these newly arrived writers in *The Last Tycoon* (1940): 'There was lassitude in plenty—California was filling up with weary desperados. And there were tense young men and women who lived back East in spirit while they carried on a losing battle with the climate.'[51]

America's Wilde resonated with the growing number of immigrant filmmakers from Europe too. Alfred Hitchcock learnt about post-Wildean dandy style from going to the theatre with his mother in London. He read *Dorian Gray* 'several times' as an adolescent, and one of his favourite sayings in later life was from *The Ballad of Reading Gaol*: 'Each man kills the thing he loves.' Of course, the emotions and practicalities of killing a loved one would be the subject of his biggest screen successes.[52] We know from Chapter 3 that Wilde was a star in Moscow; it was a similar story elsewhere, with *Salome* proving especially popular in France, Italy, and Germany.[53] While *Salome* was Wilde's best-known work on the Continent, others and his own star persona were also familiar. In 1902 Max Reinhardt had produced an unlikely double bill of *Salome* and *Bunbury* (*Earnest* retitled) at the Kleines Theater in Berlin, which helped to kick off Germany's Wilde craze.[54] There were over 200 translations of Wilde's works into German between 1900 and 1934.[55] In 1921 alone, five of his plays were performed on the Berlin stage.[56] It was out of this theatrical culture that Samuel (later Billy) Wilder came to Hollywood, via Paris, from Berlin. Likewise, Lubitsch came up through the Berlin theatre and was in Max Reinhardt's ensemble between 1911 and 1918.[57] These weren't Wildeans as such, but they were products of a time and place in which Wilde was a shared point of reference—a rich resource on which to draw for plot and style.

Wilde, Beardsley, and the new decadence were simply part of the imaginative fabric of Hollywood. In 1927 *Picture-Play Magazine* noted that Hollywood starlets read the works of Anglo-American decadence and would regularly 'prattle to you of Ronald Firbank and Van Vechten—these being, apparently, the flappers' favorites'.[58] Firbank himself was 'very elated' when he was approached for the film rights to his novel *Caprice* shortly before his death.[59] The silent movie star Louise Brooks described her celebrated on-screen style in the early 1920s as 'decadent black-and-white Aubrey Beardsley makeup cover[ing] a sprinkling of Kansas freckles'.[60] Earlier, in 1918 Eugene O'Brien, then a matinee idol, told *Motion Picture Magazine* that Wilde was his favourite writer.[61] Meanwhile, the magazine *Shadowland* (1919–23) juxtaposed full-page picture spreads on the latest movies with essays that showed an easy familiarity with European and American decadence. One regular contributor was Frank Harris, recent author of the sensational *Oscar Wilde, His Life and Confessions*. In the magazine, he and others wrote profiles on fin-de-siècle decadents.[62]

There were no battle lines between West Coast moviemakers and East Coast literati. Hollywood was the pleasure dome the literary set loved to hate. At the Cocoanut Grove, night spot of the stars at the Ambassador Hotel, Ralph Barton caricatured H. L. Mencken, Theodore Dreiser, Joseph Hergesheimer, Paul Morand, and George Jean Nathan, surrounded by Erich von Stroheim, Reinhardt, Lubitsch, and many stars including Greta Garbo, John Gilbert, John Barrymore, and Ronald Colman.[63] Such intermingling between Hollywood and the literati of decadence extended well beyond Los Angeles, even across the Atlantic. At Paul Robeson's opening night party for *Show Boat* in London on 26 November 1928, Van Vechten, Vyvyan Holland, Evelyn Waugh, M. P. Shiel, and Rebecca West rubbed shoulders with Noël Coward, Ivor Novello, Fred and Adele Astaire, Tallulah Bankhead, and Cecil Beaton.[64] A marvellous party indeed. In another possible world, had Wilde's life not ended in that Paris hotel room in 1900, he would surely have been there too, now an elder statesman, his transgressions forgiven in the jazz age, at least in liberal circles, exchanging bons mots with Van Vechten.

Even the thought of Wilde's son, Vyvyan chatting to Fred Astaire over cocktails in St John's Wood is tantalizing because it seems so unexpected. In those days though more people moved with ease between the entertainment and literary worlds. Coward, another of Robeson's guests, is a prime example. Steeped in Wilde's work and friends himself with Wilde's own friends, he began his career writing Wildean pastiches.[65] Coward's carefully cultivated lifelong persona of impenetrable camp charm, with extravagant fashion choices just beyond the limits of good taste, were based on the half-fantasy that he was, as he put it, 'a weedy sensualist in the last stages of physical and moral degeneration'.[66] From London, Coward migrated to New York, and from there to Hollywood in the early 1930s. Throughout, his circle encompassed fin-de-siècle decadents, society types, and the new show-business elite. In 1926 he visited Wilde's old friend André Gide in Paris, before partying with Lady Diana Cooper and Cole Porter—who wrote about the tedium of endless pleasure with the wit of Wilde himself—in Venice.[67] For Coward, Porter, and Hecht alike, Wilde and the decadent movement signalled rebellion and 'art for its own sake'. This was the spirit they took West, and which helped shape Hollywood.

Decadent Style in Hollywood

That Hollywood was the ultimate fantasy pleasure town made it an attractive proposition for new decadents and wannabes alike. It could have been a location in a Firbank novel: a new exotic paradise, created even as the cosmopolitan centres of fin-de-siècle Europe had been jolted out of gaiety into grim seriousness by the First World War. London, Paris, Naples, and Florence were now overlaid with the memory of conflict, while New York for all its sophistication reeked of finance and toil. Los Angeles by contrast was a town made for creating art, with seemingly endless budgets and (in the beginning) no moral stricture; where pleasure was the main imperative after work. In his sensational memoir-cum-gossip-book *Hollywood Babylon* (1965), Kenneth Anger lovingly records the excesses of the silent-era stars: the Roman plunge pool in Pola Negri's living room; Marion Davies's 100-room mansion, with its all-gold salon and marble bridge-spanned swimming pool; Gloria Swanson's leopard-upholstered Lancia and her $6,000 a year budget for perfume; or the Garden of Alla with its tropical gardens and all-female pool parties, which feature in Van Vechten's research notes for *Spider Boy*.[68]

Anger may exaggerate some of Hollywood's opulence, but its existence is not in question, and this extended to the new purpose-built movie theatres. The first film venues had been flea pits: dens of perversion, rich with the 'promise of a saturnalia in suspense', but sorely lacking in glitz or scale.[69]

As movie-going became part of nightlife, new theatres were constructed like magnificent palaces, modelled on exclusive hotels and the homes of the wealthiest.[70] These immersive spaces of luxury allowed ordinary people to see themselves, framed in gilt mirrors, amidst tapestries, crystal chandeliers, rugs, red velvet, domes, and pillars.[71] The Paramount Theatre on the Upper West Side, which opened in 1926, had ten themed rooms to evoke old-world glamour, from the Venetian Room to the Chinoiserie and Peacock Alley.[72] Such adornments and indulgences 'signaled a release from everyday inhibitions, tapping the quest for post-Victorian freedom'.[73] They were emblematic of a country conscious of its wealth and ready to enjoy its leisure time.

Despite the elective affinities of Hollywood's off-screen excesses and its depiction of epic indulgence in movies by DeMille and von Stroheim with the decadent dream of unbridled pleasure, this scale and excess owes very little to Wilde specifically. The direct influence of Wilde on-screen in the early 1920s was trickier. In truth, Hollywood studios didn't at first know quite what to do with his works or those of the new decadence. Not that they weren't interested. As David Weir has written, the influential critic James Huneker's 'prolific endorsements of decadent authors in the press put them at odds with Puritanism and Main Street respectability and contributed to the fashion for silent screen scenarios derived from *fin-de-siècle* literature'.[74] In addition to the buzz around bringing Wilde's plays to the screen, there were adaptations of several other decadent novels.[75] But this raised an issue. What would—or could—such films look like, in style and content, given increased anxiety over the national image of Hollywood and its movies?

That atmosphere of moral caution goes a long way to explain the lack of studio support for Nazimova's *Salome*. In the era of the MPPDA it became increasingly necessary to balance the fashionable naughtiness of new decadence with the propriety necessary to receive studio backing and nationwide distribution. The problem was how to do this. While new decadent novels had effectively repackaged themes and motifs from Wilde and decadence in a fresh and fast-paced form, it was not clear how the visual language of cinema could encompass either their witty satire of prevailing ethical norms or their sensuality. Adaptations of new decadent fiction tended to dispense with these qualities altogether. Van Dine's Philo Vance novels, as adapted in a series of films from 1929 starring William Powell, became straightforward crime dramas with a well-dressed leading man. When *The Green Hat* was filmed as *A Woman of Affairs*, starring Garbo, obscuring its source novel was a prerequisite of its passing the MPPDA.[76] The movie is still edgy; its director, Clarence Brown, devised new editing techniques and visual symbolism to imply the novel's depictions of homosexuality, syphilis, and drug abuse.[77] But no trace remains of the nostalgia in Arlen's prose, which positioned Iris March and her lovers as the last in a line of decadents. Or again, in the adaptation of Hecht's *The Florentine Dagger* (1935), the novel's decadent motifs are variously revised, ironized, or dismissed. Thus where the novel describes the main protagonist's 'grey and scarlet mask of ennui', the film comments that he looks like 'something of a Dracula type'.[78] The wider processes at work here are subtle and complex. This was not just about dumbing down or getting past the censors. Times had changed, and new forms were emerging. This parallels, perhaps, the way T. S. Eliot and Ezra Pound struck through words and phrases in Eliot's original draft of *The Waste Land* (1922) which rooted it in decadence.[79] Both cases show a culture moving on, erasing its workings to create a form that appears entirely new.

One possibility then, was that, as the Wildeans reached the West Coast, Wilde's influence would fade from view. Eventually it did, but not before reshaping American movies—once film-makers found a way to fully realize the cachet of Wilde's style on the big screen. As of the early 1920s, it might seem that Wilde has gone as far as he will go in the movies: a few adaptations, based on his current popularity and the movies' focus on adaptation in the early years of feature films. His charismatic anti-heroes, Dorian and Salome, helped expand the range of the cinematic hero; both translated well to the plot-driven movies of the feature-length silents. What was lost, however, at that point, was any meaningful sense of Wildean style. The symbolism of *Salome* had featured in Nazimova's film, but it was already out of time: overly portentous in the mass entertainment world of American movies. Wilde's epigrammatic style was different, or at least it had the potential to be. No adaptation had come close to realizing his wit on-screen, but then no movies featured actual speech until 1927. Written on title cards, Wilde's sparkling words became leaden.

There were ways not to do it. The 1916 British screen adaptation of *Lady Windermere* is a case in point. A new Beardsley-style poster was designed for the US release in 1919, capitalizing on the artist's stateside revival. Alas, the film was not as sophisticated as the poster implied. As Wilde wrote it, *Lady Windermere* was on a cusp between nineteenth-century melodramas and Henrik Ibsen's moral problem plays. It opens with Lady Windermere planning her birthday party, only to be shocked when her husband implores her to invite the notorious Mrs Erlynne. That night, fearing that her husband is having an affair with Mrs Erlynne and not suspecting for a moment that Mrs E is in fact her long-lost mother, Lady Windermere flees to Lord Darlington's house to take up his offer of an affair. Mrs Erlynne pursues her, determined not to let her imperil her marriage and lose everything, as she herself had done. When Darlington and Lord Windermere return unexpectedly, Mrs Erlynne saves her daughter's reputation by pretending that it is she who has gone to Darlington's house; thereby sacrificing her own chance of social rehabilitation, while Lady Windermere is able to slip out unseen.

Though faithful to Wilde's plot, this *Lady Windermere* adaptation is a long way from the spirit of his play, and further still from those Beardsleyesque posters. Capitalizing on 'naïve' public taste for sentimental dramas with a strong homiletic message, it doubles down on the play's moral melodrama from the very first intertitle:[80]

> There is the same world for all of us, and good and evil, sin and innocence, go through it hand in hand. To shut one's eyes to half of life that one may live securely is as though one blinded oneself that one might walk with more safety in a land of pit and precipice.[81]

In Wilde's play these are Lady Windermere's words to her husband in Act 4. Moving them to the beginning has the effect of foregrounding the play's most uncontroversial moral message. The film that follows reconceives Wilde's comedy as a melodrama, often spelt out in his own words—but with much judicious editing—on the intertitle cards.

In 1919, when this *Lady Windermere* had its US release, Wilde's play was second only to *Earnest* in popularity with repertory and am-dram groups, and the film was not unsuccessful at the box office. Most critics ignored it, but *The Film Daily* mourned its departures from Wilde's play and savaged the result for being 'as entertaining as a telephone directory'.[82] To be fair, this was a casualty of the challenges of translating Wilde's fun to the silent screen in a context of moral pressure. Shorn of the energy of Wilde's epigrammatic wit, the plot lends itself to a straightforward morality tale, and so that's what it became. One of Wilde's greatest assets, his stylistic naughtiness, went AWOL. Perhaps the adaptors fought shy of this. Alternatively, the challenge of bringing verbal wit to life in pictures alone may have defeated them.

Ernst Lubitsch's *Lady Windermere*

Aesthetic infidelities notwithstanding, we owe a debt to this bowdlerized British version. In practical and legal terms, without it Lubitsch's adaptation might never have been made. Piecing together the puzzle, it seems Warner Brothers bypassed the Wilde Estate by purchasing the copyright granted to the Ideal Film Company in London, and then struck a separate deal with Daniel Frohman. Hollywood was now free to film *Lady Windermere*.

But how? Lubitsch's brilliance was to steer skilfully past Scylla and Charybdis: eschewing both the overwrought overabundance of decadence on-screen, as conjured up by earlier epics, and the melodramatic pull of *Lady Windermere*'s plot. Instead, he found a way to channel the *léger* tone that the new decadence liked best about Wilde, but which had not hitherto translated successfully to the screen. Style and naughtiness would be key. The effect was far-reaching. After Lubitsch, Wilde's influence in Hollywood would be felt not only or even mainly in direct adaptations of his work. It was bigger than that: filtered into an elegant fresh cocktail—new decadence mixed with the jazz age and flapper feminism—which the broader culture lapped up.

In Berlin Lubitsch had developed rapidly from a star and director of slapstick farces to a pioneer of new cinematic techniques.[83] Moving to the United States in 1923, he evolved further into one of the leading pioneers of *sophisticated comedy*: steering away from farce and slapstick, as well as the overwrought sensations of sentimental melodrama. Out went moralizing and emotional showdowns; in came restraint and understatement.[84] *Lady Windermere* marked a critical moment in this evolution, at a point in Lubitsch's career when he had things to learn from Wilde. He had seen how effective understated satire could be in Charlie Chaplin's critically acclaimed *A Woman of Paris* (1923).[85] That film had been pivotal in the development of sophistication as a style: 'it definitively altered the way such comedies were made'.[86] In his next film Lubitsch went beyond Chaplin. *The Marriage Circle* (1924), with its innovative use of close-ups, continuity editing techniques, and facially oriented acting, announced a new auteur—or at least an incipient one.[87] This was the beginning of sophisticated comedy, with its stylistic restraint and abdication of moral judgement.

In *Lady Windermere* Lubitsch goes another step further, stylistically and morally. The acting is more subtle, the direction more experimental. On the film's release in December 1925 he published an article in the *New York Herald*, explaining that this adaptation rested on his ambition to create a *purely visual* language for the silent screen—refracted through 'Wilde-ish... spirit'.[88] He defends the complete absence of Wilde's own epigrammatic wit from the film's title cards: 'Motion picture audiences might well ask why, with such splendid material to work on, did I eliminate the most famous lines of Wilde's play when I might have welded them into the pictures as subtitles?'[89] His answer is clear, and worth quoting at length, both for its thoughtful brilliance and its summary of the precise ways in which Wilde, via Lubitsch, would profoundly influence and shape Hollywood style:

> The searching hand of a director burrows under words—hundreds of them—words garnished this way and that to clothe their purpose in different guises, to clutch the purpose that motivates a play or a novel. The discriminating director discards the useless verbiage and garners the thought, the idea, the intangible breathing thing that feeds the printed page, and he prepares to tell the same tale again, this time with living persons on the screen. Realizing [. . .] the poor, vitiated photoplay that would result if the literal letters of his epigram[s] were used, I tried to stalk and bag the game hiding under his words and translate that [. . .] into a moving picture.[90]

Does it work? Though none of Wilde's epigrams appeared as title cards on-screen, Lubitsch knew how much these words mattered. He 'insisted that the actors speak dialogue written in [Wilde's] script, so that the emotion and expression would come naturally from the scene's content'.[91] Lubitsch also knew what effect he wanted: 'Let me say from the first I sought that underlying thought that gave birth to each of these terse gems and tried to show in action and motion the very identical reaction'.[92] He creates a visual language to express the absurdity of conventional morality—as the play's epigrammatic wit does—while making barely a ripple on the surface of propriety.

When Ronald Colman saunters into Scene 1 as Lord Darlington, we can well imagine him commenting to Lady Windermere (May McAvoy), as he does in Act 1 of Wilde's play, that 'It is absurd to divide people into good and bad. People are either charming or tedious'.[93] Here, though, the images do the talking. Never has the term 'picturization' been more apt. Darlington takes Lady Windermere's outstretched hand in a close-up (Fig. 4.1 (a)) and he goes to kiss it, but she withdraws (Fig. 4.1 (b)); so he instead ducks down to kiss the same hand, in its new more compromising position against her breast (Fig. 4.1 (c)). Or in the next scene, as Lady Windermere embraces her husband (Bert Lytell), he attempts to reach behind himself for an envelope on his desk addressed to the notorious Mrs Erlynne (Irene Rich) before she sees it. The shot cuts to a close-up of his hand creeping towards it, before she pulls his arm back into their embrace. Windermere tries again . . . his hand stretches across the desk, cannot quite reach the envelope, but another

(a)   (b)

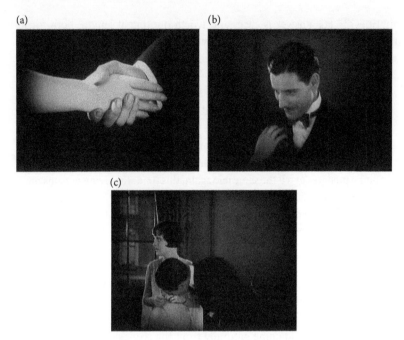

(c)

Fig. 4.1 In *Lady Windermere's Fan* (1925)
(a) Lord Darlington (Colman) takes Lady Windermere's (McAvoy's) hand
(b) She withdraws her hand as he goes to kiss it
(c) She turns away but he kisses her hand, now resting on her breast

hand—Darlington's—sweeps it into his. The camera cuts to a confused and sombre Windermere, followed by Darlington, turned away, his face showing the effort of appearing casual as he adjusts his bow tie.

Lubitsch's *Lady Windermere* teems with such brief, seemingly inconsequential moments. If not producing 'the very identical reaction' to Wilde's words, as Lubitsch hoped, they visibly share his subversive view: minor transgressions from society's rigid moral codes are to be judged according to their charm, not their morality. Moreover, they do so using analogous techniques to those of Wilde. As Amanda Anderson has written, the Wildean epigram works by the way that it 'enacts an ironic detachment—it pulls back and comments upon a topic, a prior response, a set of conditions... reversing the terms, refusing niceties, using the traditional form of moral observation to thwart moral piety'.[94] This is precisely what Darlington's kiss and deft handling of the letter do: depicting niceties refused and an ironic detachment from the morals implied beneath manners. With such moments, Lubitsch realizes that Wildean decadence is at least as much about the playful clandestine defection from normative ethics as it ever was about epic scenes of debauchery. In fact such scenes of debauchery are few and far between in Wilde's work or Lubitsch's. These are both artists interested in what goes on behind closed doors and beneath impeccable manners, engaging their audience in imagining what that might be, understanding the imagining is more tantalizing than anything that could be shown.

Wilde helped Lubitsch to realize the power of satirical understatement on-screen. As such, the 1925 *Lady Windermere* adaptation is a major advance, not only on the 1916 British version, but also in comparison to contemporary slapstick comedies and Lubitsch's earlier films. We see this satirical understatement above all in the way Lubitsch dramatizes the spectacle of *looking*. If Wilde's play was about talking, Lubitsch is all about looking. It is a further twist on the facial acting that Lubitsch had been developing since *Madame DuBarry* (1919), and which achieved a new art of repressed expression in *The Marriage Circle*.[95] For in *Lady Windermere*, the second glance, the unseen observation, an exchange of looks, and in particular the side-eye, all convey the ephemeral essence of passion and dissent from propriety. In his star turn as Darlington, Colman conveys ironic distance as he pointedly directs his eyes away from his co-stars, off-camera, at moments when untruths maintain the appearance of respectability. It happens after Windermere conceals the incriminating letter; when Darlington watches Windermere dismiss his own car to take an anonymous taxi; and, later, when Lady Windermere tells him that her husband has never met Mrs Erlynne. As he is held in a static medium close-up, his face remains impassive and his hooded eyes move off-camera to look into the middle distance, acknowledging a secret which the audience shares about the passions and truths behind the manners that uphold this society. Physical action is minimized, mirroring the stasis of Wilde's drawing-room conversations, and as the eyes dance they look behind the manners depicted on-screen as well as the Production Code to which the film must adhere.

And yet in replacing talking with looking, Lubitsch is again taking a cue from Wilde, whose stage directions make significant references to staring, glaring, glancing, and watching.[96] In Lubitsch's hands this is often comic, as in Darlington's satirical performance of looking away. The appearance of the Duchess of Berwick (Carrie Daumery), Lady Plymdale (Billie Bennett), and Mrs Cowper-Cowper (Helen Dunbar) makes the effect more ostentatious. In Wilde's play, when Mrs Erlynne first appears, Lady Plymdale

'glares with indignation at Dumby' for his attention to her and then comments, 'I really must have a good stare at her. [Goes to door of ball room
and looks in]'.[97] In Lubitsch's adaptation, Mrs Erlynne first appears at the
horse races and *having a good stare at her* becomes a moment to satirize
society's moral opprobrium and nosiness. A close-up shows the Duchess
of Berwick, Lady Plymdale, and Mrs Cowper-Cowper sitting in the stand.
They are not interested in the horses. In turn they put their binoculars to
their eyes and the camera cuts to Mrs Erlynne, shown in a masked point-
of-view shot (Fig. 4.2). Later, at the birthday party, the same trio, sitting in
a row, avert their eyes from Lord Windermere when he spies Mrs Erlynne.
But, as he goes to greet her, a medium close-up of their awkward meeting
cuts first to show the ladies in a static close-up watching intently and then to
the wall above them. In turn each rises into the frame to peer at the assumed
couple, before disappearing back down into their seat. If Wilde suggests the
significance of looking to Lubitsch, then the latter uses the movie camera
to realize its witty potential. His close-ups and continuity editing create a

Fig. 4.2 The Duchess of Berwick (Daumery), Lady Plymdale (Bennett), and
Mrs Cowper-Cowper (Dunbar) watch the notorious Mrs Erlynne through
binoculars in *Lady Windermere's Fan*

new mode of dry visual humour—one that would not be possible onstage. Lubitsch directs our eyes and, as he does so, he makes looking epigrammatic with a juxtaposition of images both amusing and unexpected. These eyes underscore the visual motif of concealment running through Wilde's play, with the climax of the play/film of Lady Windermere's concealment in a curtain.

It is with the movie camera that Lubitsch's adaptation becomes more Wilde-ish than Wilde's play. For it is Darlington, no less, behind this movie camera. Darlington's is the spirit and perspective channelled by Lubitsch and his photographer, Charles Van Enger. Darlington's satirical eye and agnosticism on any question of morality define the camera's perspective from *Lady Windermere*'s opening moments; inviting the viewer to share his values and seek the charm, rather than the moral import, in life. In consequence, the screenplay rebalances Wilde's script. The melodramatic scenes in the original are minimized or cut out entirely. New scenes spring to life out of Wilde's stage directions to exploit the kineticism of cinema and expand a sense of Wilde-ish playfulness, as in the performative peering of the dowagers at the racecourse. In the most insightful essay on Lubitsch and Wilde, Charles Musser writes that 'To be faithful to the spirit of Wilde on the level of treatment may mean being transgressive and irreverent towards the play itself'.[98] Or as Cole Porter put it: 'I'm always true to you, darlin', in my fashion | Yes, I'm always true to you, darlin', in my way.' Porter's 1948 lyric adapted Ernest Dowson's decadent poem, 'Non Sum Qualis Eram Bonae sub Regno Cynarae' (1894).[99] Although Musser is quite right, he elides the fact that in 1925 Lubitsch decisively shaped what exactly 'the spirit of Wilde' would mean henceforth. The way in which Lubitsch adapted Wilde helped to create *which* Wilde we know today. Lubitsch chooses to be faithful in his fashion to Wilde the wit; not Wilde the melodramatist, nor the tragedian. Those Wildes on which his fame was propelled across Europe and in America's Salomania are gone. They didn't suit the public's taste anymore.

Lubitsch's Wilde-ish spirit expands the screenplay in dimensions Wilde could not have imagined, but would surely have applauded. In a new scene, for example, Lord Augustus (Edward Martindel) follows Mrs Erlynne to make her acquaintance. The following sequence takes up the suggestion of Wilde's stage direction at the end of Act 2 in which Mrs Erlynne exits and Lord Augustus 'follows her in a bewildered manner'.[100] Lubitsch uses a static camera to show Mrs Erlynne walking, left to right, across the screen. On the wall above her there is a huge sign and finger pointing to the exit (Fig. 4.3 (a)). As she exits screen left, there is a moment of empty screen before Lord

Augustus appears walking briskly behind her across the screen. The scene cuts and the camera now tracks Mrs Erlynne walking on the left side of the screen, while Augustus catches her up. As he advances, the screen is masked, right to left, until it covers them both, just as he removes his hat in greeting (Fig. 4.3 (b)). The camera is at play here, showing us that in Lubitsch's hands, love is a flirtation, no more.[101] It is not Wilde's *Lady Windermere*, but it feels like it should be. Love is treated with the utmost seriousness by Wilde, and even by his Darlington. He's sentimental that way, a sincere Victorian. But love reconceived through Wilde-ish spirit is a game: it is Augustus pursuing Mrs Erlynne or Darlington kissing a place he should not. As Wilde-ish spirit diffuses through the film, it begins to feel as though this is the only Wilde there ever was.

If Lubitsch is more Wilde-ish than Wilde was, Wilde also makes Lubitsch more Lubitschean than he had yet been in 1925. Wilde's style was integral to eliciting a new kind of Lubitsch comedy, based around the grammar of understatement and implied transgression. Like Wilde, Lubitsch understood how censorship offered opportunities for witty innuendo and he emerges in *Lady Windermere* as a master of visual wit, as if to show Wilde that 'witty words are not the only form of witty language'.[102] Though the first reviews were decidedly mixed,[103] *Lady Windermere* is a landmark in the development of his style, foreshadowing the famous Lubitsch Touch: 'the effect created *between* images—by what is not shown, by ellipses'.[104]

At the same time, *Lady Windermere* helped define a new archetype on-screen too, one which would also become essential to Hollywood comedy:

(a)   (b)

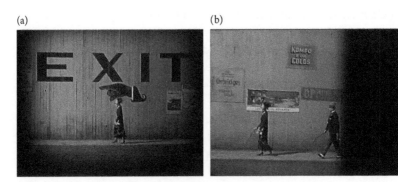

Fig. 4.3 In *Lady Windermere's Fan* (1925)
(a) Mrs Erlynne (Rich) walks from the races
(b) As Lord Augustus (Martindel) catches up with Mrs Erlynne (Rich), the screen is masked from the right-hand side

the witty woman of the world. Mrs Erlynne—errant mother and sensual adventuress—is one of Wilde's greatest heroines. Defying the conventions of Victorian melodrama from which Wilde's play begins, she is a dynamic and unapologetic older woman who enjoys and uses her sex appeal. When she comments to Augustus, 'I can fancy a person dancing through life with you and finding it charming', the audience knows that dancing through life is exactly what she intends to do.[105] Not for her the waltz but the polka and tango. Her dancing is fun, passionate, and sensual. Neither the 'angel in the house' nor a tragic fallen woman, she dances to affirm that her course through life will be guided by pleasure and charm, not by moral obligations. As she herself tells Windermere in Wilde's play, 'if a woman really repents, she has to go to a bad dressmaker, otherwise no one believes in her. And nothing in the world would induce me to do that'.[106] Lubitsch and Irene Rich in the role of Mrs Erlynne take up this spirit: we see it in the knowing ironic smiles and looks which replace her verbal wit, as well as her defiant strides across the screen as Augustus struggles to catch up.

Such female defiance was not new to film adaptations of Wilde. It had quite literally been seen before, in Nazimova's *Salome*. Beyond Wilde's authorship, these two share a specific cinematographic link: they were both shot by Van Enger.[107] In the racecourse scene, when Mrs Erlynne is pictured through a masked camera in profile, as if watched through binoculars, she wears a peacock-feather skullcap, eyes down, her lips slightly parted with the pleasure of being an object of desire. She holds the pose and we watch her just as the dowagers do (Fig. 4.4). Mrs Erlynne's pose is very similar to that of Salome's as she imagines herself in possession of Herod's white peacocks, filmed by Van Enger three years earlier. There, as Salome, Nazimova is pictured in profile tipping her peacock-feathered head to the stars, her eyes closed and mouth open with the pleasure of using her beauty to get things (Fig. 4.5). This line between Mrs Erlynne and Salome shows that the defiant Wildean heroine wasn't dead, even after the fallout from Nazimova's film. But to make it in Hollywood, she would have to go about her pleasure-seeking in a different way: armed with cutting remarks instead of a sword. She refuses tragedy. And this is what makes Mrs Erlynne a new kind of cinematic character, a new kind of naughty woman. She is defined by ironic distance from the moral values of a society whose rules she never truly accepts. Like Darlington, she acquiesces to its rituals while wryly defecting from the morals that had seemed enshrined in them. She rises above society with a smile or a remark: a precedent for the fast-talking dame of 1930s screwball comedies, 'who existed apart or beyond the more stolid

Fig. 4.4 Mrs Erlynne (Rich) in the race stand as the dowagers watch on

conventions of movie womanhood' because of the way in which they fused together the good girl, bad girl, sexual desirability, and intelligence.[108]

Lubitsch's visual wit prepares the ground for the plot's broader revision of what it means to be—to quote the original title and final subtitle of Wilde's play—'A Good Woman'. The pious Lady Windermere has gone to Darling-ton's house with the intention of having an affair with him. When Lord Darlington comes back to the house with Lord Windermere and others, her reputation and marriage is saved by Mrs Erlynne, who hides her till the arrivals can be distracted and she can exit. She is the 'Good Woman'. Lubitsch knew as well as Wilde that society depends on deception. There are three undisclosed secrets left at the end of Wilde's play—that Lady Winder-mere went to Darlington's rooms; that Mrs Erlynne is her mother; and that Mrs Erlynne was not at Darlington's home to see Lord Augustus.[109] These also remain undisclosed at the end of Lubitsch's film. His *Lady Windermere* did not give audiences the fallen women they expected to see or an ending in which 'the good ended happily, and the bad unhappily'.[110]

Wilde had performed a dramatic volte-face with the conventions of the melodrama on the stage. Now his play helped to define a way to do this on-screen too, in an analogous context of Puritanical strictures. The *Lady*

Fig. 4.5 Salome (Nazimova) in the dream sequence of *Salome*

Windermere adaptation was just the start, and indeed only of one the elements. But it is essential to Lubitsch's evolution into one of the progenitors of screwball comedy.

The *Lady Windermere* That Never Was

In 1929 the new decadent scene in American literary life was all but over. Looking back at the decade, H. L. Mencken claimed that only James Huneker had remained a true decadent. 'The rest went this way and that way—into popularity, into preciosity, into futility and banality,' he commented; 'Some even fetched up in the movies!'[111] In July of the previous year he had wired Van Vechten full of theatrical concern for their mutual friend, novelist Joseph Hergesheimer. 'Joe has gone to Santa Monica to visit Lasky,' he wrote; 'I suspect the worst. He is writing fillums again.'[112] The 'fillums' were a bit of fun, in Mencken's eyes. They couldn't be taken seriously, even when his friend was going to meet Jesse L. Lasky: the head of Famous Player-Lasky, soon to become Paramount Pictures.

Mencken was too stuffy to see that popularity and the movies were exactly where decadence was heading. Only it wouldn't be Huneker or Van Vechten, or any of the established decadent writers from New York's literary scene, who would make it big there. Cinematic innovators were the ones who would realize Wilde's full potential on the screen. Lubitsch comes closest to showing us what a Wildean cinema would look like, precisely because his adaptation of *Lady Windermere* does not merely adapt Wilde's first play. Rather, it asks: if Wilde were a film-maker, thinking in the language not of words but of images, what would his films look like? This is the moment when Wilde's adaptations cross over into a style that would become integral to the formation of American cinema. Although Lubitsch was the first film-maker to take Wilde seriously as a stylist, he was not to be the last. Repurposing the works, figures, and styles of Wilde or decadence for the big screen would be most effective in ways that would expand the artistic scope of cinema for a mass market, as we'll see.

Sadly, even as aesthetics leapt forward, their advance was blocked by renewed wrangling over rights. The copyright sparring between Frohman and the Wilde Estate recommenced in 1934, when Warner Brothers sought the talking-film rights for a new sound adaptation of *Lady Windermere*. What began as a welcome enquiry to the Estate, about using Wilde's spoken words in addition to the silent film rights they already owned, quickly soured into a four-way transatlantic disagreement.[113] Some accord had been reached with Frohman earlier, but now that was in tatters and it all ended acrimoniously in 1936. There was to be no film.[114] The what-ifs are tantalizing. Had Warner Brothers remade *Lady Windermere* in the mid-1930s, would it have anticipated that studio's screwball comedies like *The Awful Truth* (1937) or melodramas focused on strong thwarted women, like *Now, Voyager* (1942) and *Mildred Pierce* (1945)? Watching Lubitsch's *Lady Windermere*, it is difficult not to linger on what other things might have been.

What would he have done with *The Importance of Being Earnest*? Or a talkie adaptation of *An Ideal Husband*?

In the event, there would not be another US-made cinema adaptation of Wilde's social comedies until *The Fan* (1949), directed by Otto Preminger. Framing the story of *Lady Windermere's Fan* in post-war Britain, this begins with a now elderly Mrs Erlynne at an auction house trying to claim the fan, then going to Lord Darlington's house only to find it has been requisitioned to distribute food parcels. Like British adaptations of *An Ideal Husband* (1947) and *The Importance of Being Earnest* (1952), *The Fan* was camp and earnest but oddly sexless—despite a script co-written by Dorothy Parker. The fact is that these adaptations are not where the energy of Wilde's afterlife is at all. By the time they were made, his influence had long evolved and broadened into something else: Wilde-ish spirit sans Wilde. Nor was there just one way for film-makers to be Wilde-ish. If for Lubitsch this meant an ironic and subtle take on the tension between manners and morals, others would mine Wilde very differently, finding violence and even horror.

5

The Gangster as Aesthete

Schmucks, heels, and dirty double-crossing rats. By the early 1930s these were the radicals of the American big screen: stars of the new crime movies. The figure of the gangster exploded into cinemas for the first time in *Underworld* (1927) in a high-speed getaway car, amid a riot of bullets, and it would be fair to say that any connection with Dorian Gray, Salome, or Mrs Erlynne is far from obvious. Earlier and direct adaptations of Wilde's works are easy to spot. Even Roscoe Arbuckle's Salome skit gave clear pointers to his influences. With the so-called 'new decadence', Wilde and decadence began to take on a life of their own, and as they did so they also helped to create a new American icon—the gangster. But how?

The first clue is in the title sequence, where we see that *Underworld* is written by Ben Hecht. It was his first Hollywood scenario and at the inaugural Academy Awards it won him the Oscar for Best Original Story. Not that he went to the awards ceremony. Though he quickly became a top screenwriter and five further Oscar nominations would follow, Hollywood's self-congratulatory parties never appealed to Hecht. He was at home not in Los Angeles but downtown in Chicago and New York. Rewind a few years and he was a crime reporter and aspiring writer of decadent fiction, living above his means in Chicago. *Underworld* was his first attempt at marrying aestheticism with his reporter's knowledge of organized crime on-screen. It would not be the last. To be a true decadent you have to be the heir to a fortune or a successful criminal. Hecht—born to immigrant Jews from Minsk—was neither; but back in Chicago, full of restless energy, he had dreams. That his reading in British, French, and American decadence still 'haunted' him decades later did not especially mark him out, at a time when, as we know, these works had a bohemian cache.[1] He came of age in the 1910s as a young crime reporter (just 17 when he started), first for the *Chicago Daily Journal*. Later, at the *Chicago Daily News*, he was one of many drawn to the languorous poses and sensual imperatives of the fin de siècle.[2] Not only *Dorian Gray* but also *The Hill of Dreams* by Arthur Machen (1907), *Mademoiselle du Maupin* by Théophile Gautier (1835), *Spiritual Adventures* by Arthur Symons (1905), and Joris-Karl Huysmans's *À rebours* and *En route*

Wilde in the Dream Factory. Kate Hext, Oxford University Press. © Kate Hext (2024).
DOI: 10.1093/9780191987335.003.0005

(1895), all appear on his list of 'Fifty Books That Are Books'.[3] He fashioned himself after Charles Baudelaire (Fig. 5.1) and when his great friend, Margaret Anderson, editor of *The Little Review*, remarked that he reminded her of a decadent poet, so keen was he to fulfil the role that he also became well versed in Ernest Dowson, Paul Verlaine, and Stéphane Mallarmé.[4]

In a piquant case of art seeking to improve on life, the selfish thrill-seekers of decadent novels made Hecht dissatisfied with the real-life hoodlums he reported on. In contrast to fiction, he complained that the modern American criminal was 'an artificial and uninteresting disappointment'.[5] Things would be different in his own short stories and films. An inveterate reuser of good material, Hecht's bad guys were romantics filched from the decadent movement: Dorian Grays kicking back in smoke-filled speakeasies on the South Side; Des Esseinteses holed up in a beautifully appointed apartment under siege from the FBI; or wise guys quoting Algernon Charles Swinburne over dinner at Delmonico's. Aesthetes as much as criminals, they live for fine, intense sensual experiences, be it in their ostentatious sartorial choices or exhaustive self-indulgences.

Fig. 5.1 Portrait photograph of Ben Hecht (1918)

The essential duality of aestheticism and criminality takes us back to *Dorian Gray* and *Raffles*. It is all but missing from the history of the cinematic bad guy, or, if noticed, it causes puzzlement. In his magisterial study of films noirs, James Naremore ponders why the gangsters in *Underworld* are peculiarly 'aestheticized', vehemently endorsing Andrew Sarris's view that 'its gangster protagonists [. . .] have about as much connection to waking reality or to the hard-boiled tradition as the motorcyclists in Cocteau's *Orphée*.[6] *Underworld*'s gangsters are indeed aestheticized but this is not so peculiar. Their aestheticism wasn't unprecedented or isolated. Nor was realism Hecht's aim. He developed the gangster aesthetes in *Underworld* out of his reading of fin-de-siècle decadence and his own new decadent short fiction. On-screen, post-*Underworld*, the aestheticism of the Hechtian gangster utterly defines the plots of *Little Caesar* (1931) and *Scarface* (1932); it also featured, for example, in *The Roaring Twenties* (1939 as the genre evolved. By 1943, when the decadent-poet-turned-screenwriter Samuel Hoffenstein adapted Wilde's short story 'Lord Arthur Savile's Crime', it was entirely fitting that Lord Arthur be played by Edward G. Robinson—typecast as the ultimate turnip-headed gangster ever since he took the title role in *Little Caesar*. There was no one better to embody the duality of a man capable of both delicate artistic appreciation and cold-blooded murder.

Hecht's gangsters embody a different side of Wilde's naturalization as an American citizen to that we've seen so far. We've begun by looking at how his influence took shape as camp, flamboyant, audacious: embodied by Alla Nazimova's Salome, Lubitsch's Lord Darlington and Mrs Erlynne, and—looking ahead to later chapters—we'll see how it re-emerged in screwball comedies and Vincente Minnelli's musicals, where pleasure for its own sake pirouettes into glorious Technicolor to the music of George Gershwin. Gangster films show how the influence of Wilde and decadence took a different but no less vital turn, as it underpinned the alpha-male gangster's nihilistic individualism. Unaccustomed as we are to thinking about Wilde and gangsters together, it makes sense. As we saw with *Raffles*, aestheticism—or art and pleasure for its own sake—is a rejection of industrious work ethics in place of which the individual lives on his own terms. It affirms intense ephemeral pleasures indulged against the backdrop of inevitable death. It desires rare and exotic goods that confirm the exquisite tastes of their consumer. It is a life lived fast for thrills regardless of the cost to others. In short, it has much in common with the mythology of the gangster. It was Hecht's genius to exploit this affinity.

The gangster started to become the epitome of modern criminality at the same time as Salomania and the Beardsley craze were fading away. It was a phenomenon born of Prohibition laws, which saw organized criminal gangs spread across America's major cities, fuelled by bootlegging profits and into a national crime wave. This was the epoch in which 'Big Jim' Colosimo, Al Capone, and John Dillinger put Chicago at the centre of organized crime. The press portrayed them as seductive anathemas to the values of society in their nihilistic pursuit of pleasure, beautiful possessions, and sexual fulfilment, slinking about the city at night. Seen through the lens of urban America in the 1920s, decadence offered a literary correlative to a general association between organized crime and extravagant style. Jonathan Munby draws the real-life gangster as 'someone who had thrown off the straitjacket of bourgeois moral rectitude', inhabiting in its stead a 'world of fulfilled desires contrasted strongly with the "official" doctrine of deferred gratification and hard work'.[7] In the public imagination the gangster's willingness, and even pleasure, in committing violent criminal acts went along with excessive but stylish consumerism. Newspapers peddled this as glamour porn: listing, alongside his crimes, the finest details of his tailored suits and tuxedos, spats, rare jewellery, cigarette cases and lighters, as well as the furniture in his home, from antiques and art deco furniture to Persian rugs and priceless works of art.[8] This was an immersive fetishization that mirrored the 'cataloguing' descriptions of sensual objects in decadent and new decadent novels.

When we try to trace the aesthetic gangsters of *Underworld* and those catalogued descriptions of sensual objects back through the tried and tested routes of cultural history, the trail quickly goes cold. The official prehistory of on-screen gangsters starts with D. W. Griffith's one-reel film, *The Musketeers of Pig Alley* (1912), which was the first film to depict groups of criminals on the streets of New York. Shot on location and containing several of the ingredients that were to become integral to the gangster genre, it nevertheless epitomizes a middle-class social reform agenda in its depiction of what it called 'New York's Other Side'.[9] There is street crime and an arresting shoot-out finale, but not an aesthete in sight. The screen gangster's famous literary antecedents are no more illuminating. The first hard-boiled crime stories, published in *The Black Mask* magazine in December 1922, were 'The False Burton Combs' by Carroll John Daly and 'The Road Home' by Dashiell Hammett. These were tales of organized crime, secret identities, hot pursuits, shadowy escapes, and shoot-outs with no space for exegeses

on beauty and pleasure. Their prose was spare, muscular, fragmented, vernacular; the very antithesis of the jewelled styles of decadent writing. This
December 1922 issue altered the direction of *The Black Mask*, setting a trend
for hard-boiled style as well as subject matter. Even so, half-hidden connections between latter-day decadence and American popular culture can
be found in the most unlikely places. *The Black Mask* was founded by H.
L. Mencken and George Jane Nathan in 1920 with the express aim that it
would fund their decadence-infused literary journal, *The Smart Set*.[10] When
in those heady days, groundbreaking modernist writing appeared against 'a
background chorus of decadent voices' in that journal and others, it also
sat alongside pulp fiction. The staff of *The Smart Set* and *The Black Mask*
shared the same editorial partnership and occupied the same building, 25
West 45th Street in Manhattan.[11] Such circumstantial evidence cannot prove
a case, but it makes a larger point that has dropped out of cultural history:
Oscar Wilde lurks in the backstory of many a hard-boiled wise guy.

If the aesthetic gangster is partly obscured by what we think we know
about the origins of the gangster in fiction, it is equally concealed by the way
we tend to see Wilde today. The fact that theft, burglary, and murder were
integral to the pursuit of decadent pleasures was discussed in Chapter 2 and
it is essential here. Before Hecht, the aesthetic criminal had already evolved
through Dorian Gray's backstreet dealings with 'thieves and coiners' to E. F.
Hornung's amateur cracksmith Raffles, with his conception of burglary as
an art for its own sake, and the Raffles-inspired cat-burglar figure of Dorian
in Thanhouser's two-reeler.[12] Hecht and the gangster mythology he helped
create go further again. In the now-familiar moves of Wilde criticism it is
often forgotten that, as Neil Sammells writes, 'Wilde's world is one of violent potential, a potential that is distanced, ironized, refracted through the
stylistics of wit'.[13] Hecht knew that and so did Hoffenstein. In the atmosphere
created by burgeoning mob activity, this 'violent potential' was a powerful
element of Wilde's stories and plays. It is not a trivial fact that from the ninth
floor of the Fine Arts Building in Chicago, *The Little Review*'s editors looked
out across the South Side—controlled by 'Big Jim'.[14] The magazine's material
situation thus affected what its editors saw in the decadent styles and ideas
that intermingled with fledgling modernism on their pages.

The editorial direction of the little magazines refashioned Wilde as a
hard man in direct ways. In the 1910s, as Friedrich Nietzsche's vision of
the Übermensch was making waves in American letters, bringing together
thinkers of various backgrounds, his ideas and Wilde's coalesced and fused
between the covers of *The Little Review* and *The Smart Set*.[15] Viewed in a

long shot, Wilde was not so different from Nietzsche. Both, H. L. Mencken declared, were exemplars of how not to be like other people: twin foes in the fight against the 'depressing Puritan philosophy' of their present.[16] Mencken claimed not to like Wilde very much but what he admired was his egotistical chutzpah, which, when positioned next to Nietzsche, became his dominant characteristic.[17] In an editorial essay setting out *The Little Review*'s central principles Margaret Anderson proceeds similarly, taking just a paragraph to move from explicit emulation of Wilde's 'new Beauty' and 'new Hellenism' to her own imperative to 'rebel . . . to soar and flash and flame, to be swamped at intervals and scramble to new heights, to be young and fearless and reckless and imaginative'.[18] The editorial is followed by an epigram from Wilde's *De Profundis*: 'The supreme vice is shallowness. Whatever is realized is right.'[19] This is Wilde read through Nietzsche, with Wilde framed as a Yes-saying rebel. While dynamic combativeness is not unfamiliar in Wilde's essays and dialogues, it has much more in common with Nietzsche as conceived by George Burman Foster in the pages of the same magazine, in the feature articles he published there every month for two years (1914–15).[20] Close up, there are far more differences than similarities, and Nietzsche himself would have abhorred the association with Wilde given his own repudiation of 'art for art's sake'.[21] Regardless, in Chicago and New York, Nietzsche's status changed the frame through which Wilde was seen, making him less queer, less flamboyant, and more aggressively rebellious.

Mencken's own sub-Wildean epigrams, first published in *The Smart Set* around the same time, illustrate what this version of Wilde would look like:

The modern husband is afraid to be polite to his wife in public. People will always think that he owes her money.[22]

The only silly thing about a man's effort to keep his wife and her sweetheart apart is his belief that they don't realize the existence of each other.[23]

A gentleman is one who never strikes a woman without provocation.[24]

The first kiss is always stolen by the man. And the last one is always begged for by the woman.[25]

Tucked between the poetry, stories, and articles in *The Smart Set*, these epigrams might evade scrutiny. They shouldn't though because some are quite shocking, with the humour founded on relentless misogyny, shading

into casual violence. Throughout, this is rooted in the style and irreverence that Mencken admired in Wilde, with occasional direct references to
him.[26] Make no mistake, the misogyny has its roots in Wilde too. As Elaine
Showalter avers, Lord Henry's bons mots in *Dorian Gray* are contemptuous
of women:[27]

> American girls are as clever at concealing their parents, as English women
> are at concealing their past.[28]

> My dear boy, no woman is a genius [. . .] Women represent the triumph of
> matter over mind, just as men represent the triumph of mind over morals.[29]

> Women [. . .] inspire us with the desire to do masterpieces, and always
> prevent us from carrying them out.[30]

In Mencken's epigrams the misogyny is magnified and decontextual-
ized, producing a very different overall effect. While, in *Dorian Gray*,
Henry's witticisms help to legitimize desire between men, Mencken positions his speaker as a straight, potentially violent male whose witty
rejection of normative ethics underlines his independence. Here *straight-
ness* is crucial. Mencken's aggressive assertion of straight masculinity in
these epigrams diminishes Wilde's queerness, stressing rather his credentials as a rebel against social conformity. This twist in Wilde's posthumous influence may not sit comfortably with the twenty-first-century
Oscar, camp icon and social progressive. While each fresh cohort of
critics fashions Wilde anew, they should not forget those predecessors
who saw him, no less legitimately, through the different lenses of their
own era.

How Wilde was conceived by *The Little Review* and *The Smart Set* is not,
in the end, all that significant beyond literary curiosity. *The Little Review*'s
circulation was between 700 and 2,000;[31] *The Smart Set* reached around
20,000 in its Mencken–Nathan years.[32] It is their influence beyond literary circles that matters when we consider how Wildeanism seeped into
American culture, and this is where Hecht comes in. Hecht called himself
Mencken's 'disciple'; Mencken was his 'hero', his 'alma mater'.[33] Mencken
published Hecht's stories in *The Smart Set* from 1915, often alongside his
own misogynistic epigrams. Hecht's genius, first in his fiction and then
on-screen, was to fuse American new decadence with Mencken's Nietzsche-
inflected Wilde and Prohibition-era Chicago, to create a new archetype: the
gangster as aesthete, first in his fiction then on-screen.

Ben Hecht's Chicago Fiction

In a Chicago where gangsters and the literati lived cheek by jowl, Hecht moved with particular vigour across their worlds. He spent his days and a good part of his nights as a crime reporter and the time in-between writing fiction and opinion pieces for *The Smart Set* and *The Little Review*. He knew the gangsters on the South Side as friends. When Big Jim was shot 'by parties unknown' inside one of Hecht's favourite haunts, Colosimo's, in the power struggle that ultimately resulted in Al Capone becoming the boss of the Chicago Outfit, Hecht helped to pay for the funeral.[34] It seems unlikely that anyone else discussed their writing with both the decadent writer Arthur Machen and Al Capone; Hecht did, though history does not relate how the conversations went.[35]

Latter-day decadents and modern American criminals are the two types Hecht knew best from his reading and working life. They jostled and merged in his imagination so that, from 1915, he was writing prolifically about aesthetes who were criminals and criminals who were aesthetes, laying the foundations for his aesthetic gangsters on-screen. These were energized into life by his alpha-male individualism and his militant view that 'art for art's sake' was not a retrograde notion. In a fiery dialogue with Anderson he raged that 'The perfumes of Araby are short-lived in a slop jar [. . .] Remember, too, that this is America, 1915, and not Greece, B.C. 400'.[36] His fiction was set in modern Chicago, portrayed, in his words, with the 'dynamo beltings of modernity' and complete with electric signs, five-and-dime stores, skyscrapers, movie theatres, and streetcars.[37]

For Hecht, 'America, 1915' meant not only modernity but also a new focus on the backstreets and dives, the streetcars and tenement buildings. He sought to capture the fact that 'art for art's sake' was not the preserve of a wealthy elite. Like those regional bohemians discussed in Chapter 1, the imperatives of art and pleasure were aspirational for Hecht's fictional heroes, lifting them out of the workaday world. Whereas authors like Van Vechten and Huneker came from wealth and assumed a position of cultural and economic privilege in their writing, Hecht was acutely aware of being an outsider in their uptown milieu. He disdained 'a more refined taste in haberdashery and bon mots, and a yen for imitating Oxford graduates'.[38] In 'The Simple Art of Murder' (1944), Raymond Chandler would write that Dashiell Hammett 'took murder out of the Venetian vase and dropped it into the alley'.[39] Hecht performs the same act of transportation with aestheticism. This begins with his short stories, dozens of them, in which the denizens of his half-imagined downtown come to life as working-class Wildeans and a new breed of streetwise criminals, liberally sprinkled with the kind of Nietzschean chutzpah Mencken loved. There is the convict hiding out watching the beautiful snow fall as the police close in; the impoverished widow who embezzles her husband's insurance to stage the most lavish funeral her neighbourhood had ever seen; the reporter intoxicated with cocktails in a downtown jazz club. What connects them is that they are all sensualists. Rainstorms, heavy fog, dancing in a nightclub, a day trip out of town: such are the settings for their stolen moments away from work and everyday worries, where Hecht's flâneur-narrator records ordinary people immersed in unreflective pleasure for its own sake.[40]

On occasion—and only on occasion—there are direct references to Wilde and fin-de-siècle decadence. In 'Queen Bess' Feast', two young men are invited to a party at the house of Bess, a notorious sex worker. Reviled by the police, Bess lives by selling alcohol and a good time, blowing her profits on more and various pleasures.[41] Sex work was rife in Chicago, where it predated bootlegged liquor as the centre of organized crime.[42] Not that such issues of legality are Hecht's focus here: his theme is Bess's pursuit of pleasure. Presenting the young men with a set of Oscar Wilde's works, she invites them to what they imagine and hope will be a 'Black Mass', like the one at the climax of Huysmans's decadent novel par excellence, *Là-bas* (*The Damned*, 1891).[43] These references to fin-de-siècle decadence function like those in *The Green Hat* and the *Van Dine* mysteries, teasingly conjuring up seductive worlds of self-indulgence. In Hecht's imaginative geography, consumerism plays a similar role. In another story, 'The Sybarite' uses her husband's life insurance to pay for the most lavish funeral her neighbourhood has ever seen. She doesn't care that she is left penniless afterwards because she is sustained by the 'thrilled' feelings and 'gentle ecstasy' that this splash has produced. Similarly, in 'Michigan Avenue', Chicago's main retail street is 'consecrated to the unrealities so precious to us', with its shoppers pursuing their 'unreal life [. . .] of secret grandeurs'. Or again, in 'The Little Fop', the title figure fastidiously aspires 'to a fashion illustration in one of the magazines' but without the money or taste to fulfil that role.[44]

For the most part, allusions to the decadent movement are tucked within Hecht's characterizations of criminal aesthetes in the downtown. In 'Where the "Blues" Sound', the scene is a speakeasy where people dance in a wild trance to the music of the blues:

This is the immemorial bacchanal lurching through the kaleidoscope of the
centuries. Pan with a bootlegger's grin and a checked suit. Dionysus with
a saxophone to his lips. And the dance of Paphos called now the shimmie
[sic].[45]

The 'stylistics of wit' that were Wilde's stock-in-trade are gone here, replaced
by spare descriptions, fragmented sentences, and vernacular dialogue. New
decadents like Arlen and Huneker had also refused Wildean style, but they
turned instead to naturalism. For all that Hecht tried naturalism elsewhere,
here his style is that of a hard-boiled reporter. Like the stories in *The Black
Mask*'s heyday, his narrator has the low, husky half-whisper of Humphrey
Bogart, disillusioned, detached, but immersed too in the underworld of
which it speaks. The allusions to illicit pleasures are still firmly rooted in
the decadent movement. Bacchus (or Dionysus) had appeared as a symbol
of sensual reawakening in Walter Pater's 'A Study of Dionysus' (1876) and
'Denys L'Auxerrois' (1887), and later in Arthur Machen's *Hill of Dreams*.
In this Chicago bar, Dionysian frenzy is reborn as the shimmy, with its
syncopated rhythms and astringent chords, together with overtly sexual-
ized wiggles, which vanquished the decorum of formal dancing. In these
moments of heightened consciousness the wall between legality and illegal-
ity thins to the point of transparency. Right and wrong are all but irrelevant
in this world where pleasure is the measure of all things. Yet we are gently
reminded by the presence of the bootlegger, romanticized here as a latter-
day Pan, that alcohol was a criminal matter in Chicago before National
Prohibition started. The bootlegging industry was already taking shape
there, as organized crime branched out from prostitution to liquor.[46] Hecht's
bootlegger, like the Dionysian saxophonist, is very much an aesthete—a
purveyor, like Hecht, of pleasure for its own sake—with his criminality a
necessary component.

In Hecht's Baudelairean vision of Chicago, artists, thrill-seekers, and
lovers of beautiful things are located right next to sex workers, bootleggers, murderers, and thieves. They are all wanderers around the backstreets
and bars, where they pursue excitement at any cost. Shrugging off the ethical responsibilities assumed by social realism and pulp fiction in the same
period, Hecht sees Chicago through the eyes of an aesthete. He is interested
not in social reform (as Griffith was) or redefining the terms of ethics (unlike
Wilde or Ernst Lubitsch) but only in the opportunities of pleasure for its
own sake in the reduced circumstances of the city he knows, whose teem-
ing anonymous streets conceal many a deviant and criminal act. Watching

people on the rainy streets at night, Hecht's narrator considers how they 'lie, quibble, cheat, steal, fourflush and kill, each and all inspired by the solacing monomania that every one of their words and gestures is a credible variant of perfection.'[47] The potential for danger is part of the allure. In 'Fog Patterns' the flâneur-narrator entertains thoughts of what would happen 'If a terrible murder were created in a marvellous fog...'[48] The allusion to Charles Baudelaire's 'The Painter of Modern Life' (1863) is obvious. The really striking thing is that Hecht's narrator almost wants there to be a murder for the thrill it would produce.[49]

The 1919 Volstead Act and National Prohibition thereafter precipitated a new interest in the thrill-seeker who lives outside the law. In Chicago, alcohol was banned in two-thirds of its precincts prior to National Prohibition, and Hecht reflects this by emphasizing the criminality of his aesthetes rather than the aestheticism of his criminals. His 1917 story 'The Devil Slayer' gives a new emphasis to the setting of the speakeasy: here, illicit pleasures carry a risk and come at a cost.[50] Hidden in a basement on a South Side backstreet, the Yellow Tavern is secretly protected from the law by police captains and politicians who know its owner Tony Mallato. When a crusading priest persuades the narrator to take him there to see for himself its 'plague' of drunkenness and debauchery, the narrator plans to corrupt the priest with alcohol and beautiful women.[51] The plan begins well. After rounds of whiskey and wine with Mallato, and a dance with a sex worker, a spell is cast: Around us rose melodies of joy, the cacophony of mirth and wit and lusty souls. Before our eyes man and woman revelled in the true basement bacchanaelia [sic].[52]

This is the 1920s beginning to roar into being and, with it, the jazz age that would later be fixed in the literary imagination by the novels of F. Scott Fitzgerald, one of Hecht's Hollywood drinking buddies. As in 'Where the "Blues" Sound', the scene is identified specifically as bacchanalian, looking back to the fin de siècle and the classical decadence. The bar's name, too, is no accident, evoking the luxuriant 'disease' of decadence via The Yellow Book, as well as the yellow-backed novel that corrupted Dorian Gray and the racy French nineteenth-century yellow-backed novels on which both were based.

However, 'The Devil Slayer' has a twist. The priest is bluffing our bootlegger friends: he uses his inside information to lead a police raid on the bar. In the story's closing paragraphs the indulgent pleasures of the speakeasy at night are replaced by the language of moral authority as the narrator reads a newspaper report on the raid. There, in black and white, the Yellow Tavern is reviled by the Associated Deacons and Deaconesses Moral Improvement League as a 'haunt of wickedness' with 'sights which beggar description', nonetheless described in all their indecency, depravity, and debauchery.[53] As the conflict between pleasure and authority—or organized crime and the law—takes centre stage here, 'The Devil Slayer' quite suddenly becomes a very different kind of story to 'Where the "Blues" Sound'. While the story's moral is dispensed with lashings of irony, it marks a watershed in both Hecht's writing and the afterlife of decadence. It realizes the dramatic tension and irony of society's self-appointed moral guardians that Hecht would bring with him to Hollywood.

The pleasures Hecht idealized gave way to a focus on the criminal figures he knew best from Chicago, though not exactly as he knew them. His disappointment with the real-life criminals he encountered as a reporter was assuaged by aestheticism, which added depth and intrigue to his fictional characters.[54] In 'The Bomb Thrower', for example, the eponymous figure stands on the street, his back against a skyscraper, expecting at any moment to be apprehended for a bomb attack he has committed. We don't know much about his crimes or their motivations, and that doesn't matter anymore. Suddenly conscious of his mortality, the fugitive has become an aesthete, who 'could think only with his eyes', and for whom the only things that matter are immediate sensations.[55] As he waits for his inevitable arrest or death, the sights and sounds of the city are intensified into vivid colours, shapes, and patterns. His impressions are cinematic, appearing like 'the play of shadows' and evoked by Hecht's narrator as a montage of images.[56] These images become more abstract with every passing moment: 'Curves of people, blur and drip of people' turn into 'changing hieroglyphs of dots' and 'combinations of yellow, blue and lavender hats'.[57] Transfigured into colours, shapes, and patterns, this is a world where political or religious ideologies have become immaterial—giving the fugitive a fresh sense of his freedom and power. There are no direct references to Wilde or bacchanalian frenzy here, or to any of the fin-de-siècle works Hecht knew so well. The visible scaffolding of these influences has been left behind and Hecht, like his bomb thrower, has internalized the principles of the aesthete. He *is* an aesthete. The abstract images of the city street reflect Walter Pater's idealization of painting as 'a space of colour', while his impressions gain piquancy from being set against 'the valley of the shadow of death', like those impressions of Baudelaire's flâneur.[58]

'The Bomb Thrower' repackages the ideas of aestheticism into mass-market fiction. In other short stories, such as 'Manhunt' and 'The Yellow

Goat', Hecht returns to its dramatic conceit: a crime committed, a police hunt, and the heightened sensations of the criminal at large in the city. The cinematic visuals and dramatic potential here were likely as obvious to Hecht as they are to us. So it was to the movies he went and where we now follow him.

Underworld, *Little Caesar*, and *Scarface*

When the writer Jules Barbey D'Aurevilly read Huysmans's *À rebours* he famously commented that 'After such a book, it only remains for the author to choose between the muzzle of a pistol or the foot of a cross'.[59] What he meant, of course, is that if the decadence of *À rebours* is to be taken seriously then there is no alternative to self-annihilation or religious conversion. It would be simply impossible to continue with such a godless, brutally self-indulgent life, hurtling through intense sensations without purpose. Something would have to give.

The screen gangsters of the 1920s and 1930s share this hedonistic nihilism with the decadent. Their motivations are plucked from Hecht's stories: bacchanalian revelries, the pleasures of illicit alcohol partaken in speakeasies, being pursued through the city streets—all set against the certain knowledge that it could all end at any moment. The muzzle of a pistol (or to be more exact, a revolver) is almost invariably their fate. With Hecht's eye for the market he surely realized that the tensions between organized crime and the authorities had potential on the Hollywood screen. His *Underworld* far outshone the smattering of earlier films about street crime. It is a criminal Bildungsroman that introduced some of the defining features of the gangster genre: high-stakes heists, a glamorous moll, increasing tensions between buddies in the nihilistic pursuit of power and wealth. In all this, Hecht drew on his earlier fiction's imperatives of consumption and pleasure, portraying the gangster lifestyle as positively alluring. Or at least he began to. Like his short fiction, his screen treatments were impressionistic; they focused on sensations rather than the plot, which was worked out along the way with director Josef von Sternberg.[60] Hecht emphasized sensations with his characteristic desire to—as he put it—'skip the heroes and heroines, and to write a movie containing only villains and bawds'.[61] This focus would be definitive. At its core *Underworld* and the gangster films it inspired dramatize the tension between the individualist's unbridled pleasure and the law. They depict the idealized criminal living against the clock, with his exquisite connoisseurship set in shocking contrast to his violent acts.

As *Motion Picture News* notes, *Underworld* was 'corking stuff!' and it became one of the biggest-grossing films of 1927 as well as one of the last silent pictures.[62] It begins with Rolls Royce Wensel (Clive Brook) witnessing the bank heist described in this chapter's opening paragraph. The perpetrator, Bull Weed (George Bancroft), buys his allegiance and pressures him into joining the criminal gang. What develops is a ménage à trois in which the increasingly close friendship between Rolls Royce and Bull is paralleled in the relationship between Rolls Royce and Bull's girlfriend, Feathers McCoy (Evelyn Brent). When Bull is convicted of murder, it seems that only Rolls Royce and Feathers can save him. But will they?

Remember that this is the film Naremore singles out as being peculiarly aesthetic. It is certainly poles apart from the documentary realism of *The Musketeers of Pig Alley* or the still-shockingly realistic *The Public Enemy* starring James Cagney (1931). Yet against the backdrop of Hecht's fiction-writing career *Underworld* seems not so much peculiar as inevitable, revivifying the downtown aestheticism and bootleggers he had already created on the page for the demands of the screen. Thrilling set-pieces place criminality at the centre of the action, erasing any line between right and wrong, and making excitement and sensual experience all that matter.

After the bank heist, these sensual moments reach a climax with the Bootleggers' Ball and end with a siege showdown that reworks the end of 'The Bomb Thrower', with Bull on the run, waiting for the police to arrive. The extended Bootleggers' Ball sequence is at the structural centre of the film, where it operates like the speakeasy scene in 'The Devil Slayer'. Framed by the drama of criminals versus police, it immerses the viewer in the illicit pleasures of covert Prohibition-era partying. In one of his first US films, director von Sternberg works with Hecht's emphasis on thrills in the scenario to bring their seductive sensuality to life. The ball begins with crowds of tuxedoed partygoers, foxtrotting amongst the streamers and necking cocktail after cocktail at the bar. Each shot fades into the next, creating an impression of excess that recalls the epic scenes directed by DeMille or von Stroheim earlier in the decade. This, the intertitles declare, is 'a devil's carnival'. Is it despite this or because of it that the scene is so enticing? Probably the latter. As the night reaches a climax the shots become shorter and more fragmented. An image of one partygoer in a distorting mirror (Fig. 5.2) is followed by a montage of laughing, swaying faces in ever-shorter takes until it cuts suddenly to the aftermath of slumped, exhausted bodies

Fig. 5.2 A man sees himself in a distorted mirror near the end of the Bootleggers' Ball sequence in *Underworld* (1927)

surrounded by the debris of champagne and streamers. Bacchanalian? Of course it is. This is another case of 'the true basement bacchanaelia [*sic*]', as Hecht called it in 'The Devil Slayer'. It epitomizes how *Underworld* embeds its audience with its criminal anti-heroes, sweeping us up into their heightened consciousness. We not only identify with them; we want to be there with them.

The Bootleggers' Ball sequence is only the most overt and extended depiction of sensual pleasure in *Underworld*. There are many more. Von Sternberg's cinematography emphasizes that these pleasures are at once the rationale for the crimes Bull and Rolls Royce commit and their counterpoint. On Feathers's first appearance, the camera cuts away from her to follow a single stray vane, in close-up, floating and spiralling from her ostrich feather boa down the stairs, into the hand of a man on the floor below. Von Sternberg's camera is characteristically 'languid and caressing' as it captures the vane, moving almost imperceptibly in the air, spiralling and suggesting the gentle, ephemeral touch of luxury, just beyond reach.[63] In another seductive close-up, Feathers's face is backlit, in profile, gently caressed by the vanes in her feather boa as she looks up with unrequited desire at Rolls

Royce. Illicit sensations are central both to the scenario and the aestheti-cism of von Sternberg's direction, and they provide the modus operandi for *Underworld*'s gangsters. Not power, not violence. Sensual experiences, all-encompassing in the film, are made possible by a life of crime and offer a seductive reason for such a career choice.

Underworld is critical in the history of the gangster movie because it makes sensations the motivation for organized crime, adding a compelling new psychological dimension and depth to the otherwise simple power-crazed figures of earlier movies. Its connection between sensual pleasures and organized crime takes the 'violent potential' always present in Wilde's writing and realizes it with relentless immediacy. Since the early days of multi-reel feature films, Dorian and Salome had each been reimagined as sensational criminals with their misdemeanours magnified on-screen for a culture and a medium that thrived on exciting stories. Separately, Lubitsch's *Lady Windermere* had shown how Wilde's style could take on a life of its own, beyond his words and scenes. Now, as *Underworld* took Hecht's aes-thetic criminals into the cinemas, their violence threw sensual pleasure into a new relief, as the seductive counterpoint to thrilling gangland crime.

Off-screen, soaring crime rates and the Wall Street Crash helped cement the popularity of this new genre. The window between the advent of 'talkies' in 1927 and imposition of the Hays Code in 1934 gave the gangster a disturb-ing, compelling voice. Edward G. Robinson's last words in *Little Caesar*—'Is this the end of Rico?'—became a national catchphrase, while the charismatic pugnacity of Cagney in *Public Enemy* and Paul Muni in *Scarface* made them into stars. At once the worst nightmare of law-abiding people and folk heroes who could sock it to the system on guts and nerve, their legends thrived on the immediacy and scale of cinematic images. Over sixty gangster movies were made in Hollywood between 1930 and 1935, but it was *Little Caesar* and *Scarface* in particular—two of the most famous and influential—that took up the concerns of *Underworld* to ingrain them in American culture. Each is notionally based on a novel squarely in the tradition of *The Black Mask*'s hard-boiled writing. The crucial difference is that in the movie adap-tations their central figures are motivated by something not present in the source novels at all: aestheticism.

In *Little Caesar*, Rico's love of opulent things and sensual pleasures is an ingenious way to develop his character (Fig. 5.3). He is not a meathead or a butcher but an aspiring connoisseur of the beautiful. Director Mervyn Le Roy uses the camera to fetishize luxury items with lingering extreme close-ups of a tiepin, a diamond ring, a diamond-encrusted pocket watch, for

Fig. 5.3 Little Rico (Robinson) hits the big time in one of his new outfits in *Little Caesar* (1931)

example, to show Rico's obsession with high-status consumer goods and their motivating role in his life of crime. This fetishization charts Rico's ascent to the top of organized crime. It reaches its apotheosis in his apartment, which is opulent, furnished with antiques, large paintings, and deco chairs, its polished surfaces festooned with cocktails and cigars. The catalogued descriptions that made glamour porn out of real-life gangsters in the newspapers are brought to luxuriant life here on the screen. When Rico's showdown with his former best-friend Joe (Douglas Fairbanks Jr.) is played out on this set, the homoerotic tension between them is intensified by the apartment's ambience, and it sets off the chain of events that will end in Rico's death.

Hecht himself developed the figure of the gangster aesthete in his story for *Scarface* (1932), directed by Howard Hawks and Richard Rosson. The plot is notionally based on Armitage Trail's 1929 novel of the same name, inspired, in turn, by Capone (nicknamed 'Scarface'). However, again, aestheticism is a significant addition to the screenplay. The movie's plot follows Tony Camonte (Muni) as he rises through the ranks of the Chicago mob. While his decisive violence enables him to accumulate power and wealth,

this ultimately causes all-out gang warfare as he stops at nothing to control the city's liquor trade. Hecht's scenario removes references to Camonte's
military service, which in the novel had underpinned his ambitions for
gangland expansion. The result is a focus very different from the original source—or indeed Brian De Palma's 1983 remake, starring Al Pacino.
Hecht's screen story fashions Camonte around the accumulation of luxury
goods, something Trail mentions only once in passing. From the Havana
cigar and velvet robe that Camonte first covets as a newbie assassin visiting
his boss, to the brocade robe, diamond-encrusted tiepin, carved four-poster
bed, and dozens of handmade shirts he goes on to buy with the profits of
bootlegging, the film's scenario is studded with exotic, exclusive objects. It
is virtually an inventory of products, all purchased by Camonte to show off
his top-drawer cultural capital.

Camonte's tastes are not fashionable. When Poppy (Karen Morley) visits his new apartment, she finds it stuffed with objets d'art he has bought
at auction, and a butler completes the effect. Her response is unenthusias-
tic. 'Kind of gaudy isn't it?' she ventures. Camonte doesn't care. Historian
of the American gangster, David Ruth, notes that *Scarface* positions the
pursuit of sensuous pleasure as the source of true fulfilment in the underworld.[64] We know that this was an ethos close to its screenwriter's heart.
Camonte is a pastiche of Des Esseintes in Huysmans's *À rebours*, one of
Hecht's favourite books and, like Des Esseintes, he curates his apartment
both to embody his personality and consolidate it. Their homes are sensory
pleasure domes set in contrast to the turbulent world outside, punctuating
the plot with visions of luxuriant space, as when Camonte wanders around
his precious objects and furniture in his patterned silk robe. Pleasuring no
one except himself, he seeks sensation after sensation, object after object, in
wilful disregard of bourgeois morality or taste. As such, *Scarface* conjures
up not only *À rebours* but also *Dorian Gray*. Camonte's initial awe at sensual experiences and exclusive purchases develops into a realization that he
can exert power over people, as he seeks out increasingly intense thrills to
the point of exhaustion and self-annihilation. The movie's final climax is
a graphic gangster version of Dorian's and Des Esseintes's self-destruction.
Camonte's final night has the same hypersensitivity and mania that define
those fin-de-siècle decadents. Each is at once protected and imprisoned by
the home he has fashioned, high on the pleasures they can create within,
but also, ultimately, driven mad in the egotistical reverie of overindulgence.[65] Even under police siege inside (Fig. 5.4), Camonte believes he
can triumph as he fires from his window at the police below. When tear

Fig. 5.4 Tony Camonte (Muni) under siege in his house beautiful in *Scarface* (1932)

gas fills the rooms, he has no choice but to flee—and is shot dead on the steps.

Scarface and *Little Caesar* are no more Wildean than *Underworld*. It would be difficult to discern the roots of their peculiar aestheticism had Hecht not left a trail of clues. Yet just as the ghosts of fin-de-siècle decadence haunt Eliot's *Waste Land*, these films wouldn't be what they are without Wilde and the decadent movement. The imperative of collecting sensations and ostentatious goods provides the psychological conceit and dramatic impetus for the gangster, creating the seductive 'villains and bawds' Hecht envisaged.

Lord Arthur Savile's (Gangland) Crime

On 22 July 1934, John Dillinger was leaving a screening of *Manhattan Melodrama* (1934), starring Clark Gable, at the Biograph Theatre, near Chicago's Lincoln Park. On the run since escaping from prison six months earlier, this notorious leader of the Dillinger Gang was going to see a gangster movie. The FBI swooped and fired as Dillinger attempted to pull a gun, and after a chase he was shot dead. This event illustrated what many feared: that real-life

THE GANGSTER AS AESTHETE   133

gangsters loved and were inspired by the bad guys on-screen. Dillinger even looked a little like Gable, who made a life of crime seem like a far better fate than the law and order which ultimately triumphs in the final reel of the film.

A year later, the newly stringent MPPDA announced a moratorium on gangster movies.[66] Fears that movies were damaging to Christian morality and calls that they should be subject to censorship date back to before the landmark *Mutual Film Corporation* v. *Industrial Commission of Ohio* ruling and Griffith's spirited pamphlet against censorship in 1915. These calls first peaked in 1922 with the foundation of the MPPDA for self-regulation. Anxieties were piqued by gangster movies and talking pictures. In 1929 the Catholic Church had drawn up the Motion Picture Production Code, which proposed core principles for the moral content of movies. In theory these were adopted soon after. However, in practice, the new code was frequently ignored until 1934 when a new head, Joseph Breen, started enforcing it.[67] When the gangster genre was revived in the late 1930s, it was filtered through a moralistic social consciousness which had never wholly gone away. That wasn't Hecht's idea of gangster movies at all. Though he played the game, working as an uncredited script doctor on *Angels with Dirty Faces* (1938) and *Kiss of Death* (1947) among others, he had no truck with their moralizing denouements. Instead, he threaded his aesthetic rebels into movies that went under the radar of the code. Thus in the crime comedy *Crime Without Passion* (1934), Claude Rains's homme fatal recites the opening lines of Swinburne's sadomasochistic poem 'Dolores' (1866) to his girl-friend. Or again, Hecht's adaptation (with Charles MacArthur) of Emily Brontë's *Wuthering Heights* (1939) reimagines Heathcliffe through the lens of decline, sensualism, and perversity that Pater and Swinburne also detected in the novel.[68] Maybe it takes a decadent to see just how decadent *Wuthering Heights* is. Ever prolific, Hecht's energies went elsewhere, though, and we'll return to him in Chapter 6 to see his integral role in screwball comedy.

Meanwhile a different writer brought the gangster's aestheticism vividly back to life and he takes us back to Wilde. *Flesh and Fantasy* (1943) is a curious anthology film featuring separate short stories loosely connected by their supernatural premises. The second of these is an adaptation of 'Lord Arthur Savile's Crime', with a screenplay by erstwhile decadent poet Samuel Hoffenstein. Its plot is fairly faithful to Wilde's comic short story in which a palm reader tells the horrified Lord Arthur that he is fated to be a murderer, and we follow his farcical attempts to commit the deed before he gets married. In Hoffenstein's screenplay, Wilde is reread through the Hollywood gangster. 'Little Rico' himself, Edward G. Robinson, takes the lead role, now

Americanized and rechristened as Marshall Tyler in a performance that brings that gangster aestheticism full circle. 'Lord Arthur Savile's Crime' was always violent. It contains perhaps the most vivid examples of Wilde's 'violent potential'. This is a world where a charming dinner guest may be armed with a dagger, poisoned bonbons can be purchased over the counter, and an international network of criminals can provide an explosive clock, with no questions asked.[69] Robinson's magnetic, volatile screen presence embodies the underlying tension of such homicidal possibilities in Wilde's story. The first scene opens in a lamplit drawing room, where he is in evening dress partaking of drinks over genial conversation. Could we believe the charming and impeccably dressed Tyler capable of cold-blooded murder? But of course. Cinema audiences had seen it all before in his most famous gangster movies: Robinson the elegant dandy, turning on a dime into Robinson the merciless killer.

The script is not only faithful to Wilde's story, it also suggests Hoffenstein's close attention to it. To be sure, Lord Arthur is renamed, most of the dialogue is new and the location modern, while the ending is altered in deference to the code. Still, when Podgers hands Tyler/Arthur his business card, the address shown in close-up is the very same as Wilde wrote: '103a West Moon Street, London'.[70] When Tyler buys poison for the attempted murder of his aunt, his fabricated reason for needing the poison is a mastiff with 'incipient rabies': the exact reason given by Arthur in Wilde's story.[71] Then, as Podgers reads Tyler's palm in the new scene, an apparent non sequitur frames the all-important verdict on Tyler's fate:

TYLER: I'm here to listen to the future, Mr Podgers, not the past.
PODGERS: But they're the same, the future and past, Mr Tyler. For isn't the future forever passing into the past? Even the next little moment—look! ... Now it's the past.

This sentiment is not in Wilde's story. The source here is Hoffenstein's own decadence-inspired poetry, which was preoccupied with transience. Ultimately it looks back to Pater's anxious turn to 'your moments as they pass', entertaining the possibility, alongside Pater, that experience comes down to 'a single moment, gone while we try to apprehend it, of which it may ever be more truly said that it has ceased to be than that it is'.[72]

The adaptation's departures from Wilde's story show a keen awareness of its cinematic potential within the evolving genre of the gangster film-noir thriller. In Wilde's original, Podgers's revelation that Arthur will commit a murder is not stated directly. Chapter 1 ends with Podgers taking out a small magnifying glass to read his palm and chapter 2 begins as Arthur flees the house, 'with face blanched by terror, and eyes wild with grief'.[73] The revelation itself could not be lost from the screen adaptation in this way. The art of suggestion that was Wilde's gift to Lubitsch did not extend so far. Instead, Podgers (Thomas Mitchell) makes the shocking declaration— 'Murder. You're going to kill someone'—set against the sound of a steam train approaching at increasing speed and emitting a loud, long, high-pitched toot. The auditory metaphor of an approaching train was becoming famil-iar in Hollywood thrillers—the toot or whistle corresponding to violence, unnerving the audience with a suggestion of fearful screaming.[74] Later, Tyler is on his way home when—as Podgers has also foretold—his car is caught in crossfire as police chase criminals through the deserted street and a bullet hits the windscreen. Needless to say, Wilde wrote no such scene, but it is entirely congruent and injects a cinematic climax that affiliates his story to the gangster films and the emerging noirs.

Elsewhere this cinematic reworking of Wilde is apparent in the way Tyler wrestles with his own conscience about becoming a murderer. The original story has Arthur wandering the streets, contemplating his gruesome fate and taunted by the inanimate objects he passes:

Murder! The very night seemed to know it, and the desolate wind to howl it in his ear. The dark corners of the streets were full of it. It grinned at him from the roofs of the houses.[75]

As he passes a Marylebone church, 'dark arabesques of waving shadows' interrupt the still scene. Walking towards Portland Place, 'he feared that he was being followed'. The word 'Murder' on a hoarding resonates as he thinks of how one day a reward poster may bear his own name.[76] The doppelgänger had long been a feature of the movies. As noted earlier, Hoffenstein also wrote the screenplay for *Dr Jekyll and Mr Hyde* (1931) while, as the star of *The Whole Town's Talking* (1935), Robinson played both a mild-mannered clerk and the dangerous fugitive for whom he is mistaken.[77] In *Flesh and Fantasy*, as Tyler tries to come to terms with his fate, an invisible split screen creates an alter ego (also played by Robinson) to taunt him in a montage of unsettling vertiginous shots. His spectral face appears in the shop window of a deserted night-time street, in a mirror, in the glass of his spectacles, and reflected in a polished table (Fig. 5.5), all the time inciting him to murder.[78]

Fig. 5.5 Tyler Marshall/Lord Arthur Savile (Robinson) taunted by his alter ego in a polished table in *Flesh and Fantasy* (1943)

With this, Wilde was again being reinvented, showing that his imagination lent itself to the concerns and aesthetics of cinema. It was hardly the kind of feature film Robert Ross or Vyvyan Holland had envisaged. Back in 1917, as Ross and Martin Holman tried to engineer Wilde's posthumous US film career from London, 'Lord Arthur Savile's Crime' had been their best hope for a successful adaptation, though in the end it was only produced as a minor film in Hungary.[79] During 1932–3 Holland discussed worldwide film rights for 'Lord Arthur' at length, via Norman Croom Johnson, with the British-based writer and director St John Legh Clowes but the deal fell through.[80] What Hoffenstein did was arguably the best possible adaptation of the story at just the right time. Between the eras of the gangster movie and film noir, *Flesh and Fantasy* exploited the chilling duality of the Wildean hero, realizing the cinematic imagination of what Wilde wrote before cinema ever existed.

* * *

What kind of figure did Wilde cut in Hollywood by the early 1930s? It seems that the craze for all things Wildean was ending. The threat—or promise— posed by Nazimova's avant-garde *Salome* was long since over. The so-called 'new-decadence' was no more. Writers like Van Vechten, S. S. Van Dine, and Michael Arlen, who recycled motifs and elements of decadent style in the 1920s, had moved on in various ways, having subsumed Wilde—in part— into middlebrow novels. In short, in the places we might usually expect to see it, the influence of Wilde and decadence more broadly was becoming fainter. If we look literally and directly for Wilde in 1930s' Hollywood, he is hardly to be found.

Gangster pictures took his influence and that of decadence in a new direction. The gangster drew on the tacitly embedded associations of 'art for art's sake', giving him some of the complexity that Hecht wanted to infuse into the American criminal. But this also turned the decadent into something strikingly modern and different: it drew out Wilde's aggressive egotism and all but uncoupled it from homoeroticism, to help create an all-American bad guy, rooted in a different reading of Wilde that, post-queer theory, we have forgotten. Still, the immersive overabundance of sensations for their own sake reaches their horrific zenith in the violence of the Hechtian gangster, feeding off the playful, nonchalant, casual, and often-submerged violence and thrill-seeking of the decadent.

After Hecht the lines of influence between decadence and American crime movies become more blurry. It would be excessive to claim the Hollywood crime-film genre for decadence per se. But once you notice, and with Hecht as the crucial midwife, the crime thriller and the gangster film often evoke the decadent tradition—not least in the subtle ways they gesture beyond the moral restrictions of mainstream films to suggest subversive aesthetic and sexual values at odds with the Production Code.

Lest anyone still find this a stretch, I call Niles from *Frasier* as a witness. In 2012 the Williamstown Theatre Festival staged a version of *The Importance of Being Earnest* which transplanted the play from 1890s' London to Prohibition-era New York. David Hyde Pierce, who conceived and directed this production, explained to *Playbill* how it came about:

What I've discovered [. . .] is that the way Oscar Wilde and his characters use language is weirdly similar to the way Damon Runyon's characters use language. The characters from Guys and Dolls have a similar kind of heightened use of words—a very hyper-articulate way of speaking.

He started to read through *Earnest*

'using that dialect'—a very urban New York way of speaking—'just for fun, and the more I did it, the further I got into the play, the more I started to hear the underlying structure and brilliance, which I had frankly sort of forgotten, because I take it for granted.[']81

Hyde Pierce goes on to explain how this specific framing serves to defamiliarize and refresh the play:

'By making these characters essentially members of an organized crime family, the relationships become very powerful. When people are concealing their identities, when they have buried secrets, when money's an issue, when family connection's an issue, all of that takes on a clearer and stronger tone when you're dealing with gangsters.'

Yes, 'you're dealing with gangsters' when you're dealing with Wilde.

6

A Wildean Universe

From Epigrams to Screwball Talk

There is an insistent buzz at the door. David (played by Cary Grant, on the brink of becoming a matinee idol) opens it absent-mindedly. He stands 6′ 1″ tall, tanned, muscular—and he is dressed only in a negligee trimmed with feathers.

Anarchy ensues. 'Who are you?' demands the old lady at the door (May Robson). 'Well, who *are* you? . . . Why are you wearing *these* clothes?' After a barrage of questions, David, bewildered and frustrated, cracks. 'Because I just went gay all of a sudden!' he declares, leaping into the air and flourishing his arms in the indignant lady's face (Fig. 6.1). He doesn't yet know that she owns the house he is in.

This moment from the ultimate screwball comedy, *Bringing Up Baby* (1938), is outrageous, camp, 'Wilde-ish', and Wildean in very different ways to the gangster movie. It plays with the innuendo around the term 'gay', which, like 'camp', was beginning to emerge into mainstream usage as a euphemism for homosexuality at the time.[1] As David turns away from the door, suddenly crestfallen, he mumbles apologetically, 'I'm just sitting in the middle of 42nd Street waiting for a bus'. For sophisticated cinema audiences it was this line ad-libbed by Grant that made the force of his 'gay' really resonate. Its cultural context is forgotten today, but in the 1930s 42nd Street was the primary cruising strip for male and cross-dressed sex workers, as well as a major bus station. Police officers often heard 'waiting for a bus' as an excuse for suspicious loitering.[2]

This gender-bending is not the main thing, though, linking *Bringing Up Baby* to Oscar Wilde—or at least not directly. David's camp outburst marks a climax in the farcical confusions that have led him, a serious and respected palaeontologist, to the point of insanity chasing around the countryside, in clothes and a house that are not his own, after the pet leopard of an heiress (Katharine Hepburn) he has been trying to avoid. With this in mind, the deeper link between Wilde and *Bringing Up Baby* is that this cult movie epitomizes Maria DiBattista's observation: screwball comedies can only exist in

Wilde in the Dream Factory. Kate Hext, Oxford University Press. © Kate Hext (2024).
DOI: 10.1093/9780191987335.003.0006

Fig. 6.1 David (Grant) answers the door to a shocked Aunt Elizabeth (Robson) in *Bringing Up Baby* (1938)

a 'Wildean Universe'.[3] Like Wilde's society comedies, the world of screwball comedy is one that turns on witty one-liners, opening ever-wider circles of farce with misinterpretations and mistaken identities, while satirizing alpha-masculinity in spacious, stylish rooms.

That Wilde is one of the originators of screwball comedy is a commonplace amongst film critics. His influence mingles with that of George Bernard Shaw, Harley Granville-Barker, and, later, Clifford Odets, alongside Arthur Schnitzler, Noël Coward, and others.[4] The idea that screwball comedy is 'Wildean' conveys a general sense that there's something queer about screwball characters and situations, somehow descended from Oscar. Looking at the genre in the context of Wilde's popularity in the United States, the contours of his influence on it become clearer. The widespread popularity of Wilde's social comedies—especially *The Importance of Being Earnest*—in 1920s' US repertory and university theatre productions comes first. We then saw how Ernst Lubitsch set his mind to translating Wilde's epigrammatic wit into a 'Wilde-ish . . . spirit' in his adaptation of *Lady Windermere*.

Even so, the turn to comedy in the movies is moot. With the notable exception of Roscoe Arbuckle's star turn as a slapstick Salome and Lubitsch's *Lady Windermere*, silent film in America, as in Europe, had lingered more on Wilde's tragic heroes. The adaptations of *Salome* and *Dorian Gray*, like the 1916 *Lady Windermere*, played up Wilde's melodrama. In a sense, the gangster too was an evolution of this serious Wilde. There is a fundamental dichotomy between Salome and Dorian, who ultimately suffer for their queer desires, and Algernon Moncrieff, whose 'Bunburying' uses humour to make reality conform to itself in *Earnest*.[5] In the latter case, it is not the queer individual who must pay for their failure to fulfil society's ideal of normative sexual behaviour; now it is reality itself that is remade as queer. In Hollywood this begins with Mrs Erlynne's refusal to succumb to what society expects of her and the way in which Lubitsch translates the Wildean epigram into the visual language of cinema. Just as surely as Salome's tragedy has its Hollywood legacy in melodramas like *Sunset Boulevard*, the queer humour inaugurated by *Earnest* lives on in screwball comedies like *Bringing Up Baby*.

Screwball comedy emerged in Hollywood soon after talking pictures and as increasingly strict censorship regulations were redefining the film industry. As noted in Chapter 5, the timing was no coincidence. After *The Jazz Singer*, an explosion of talking pictures was one of the factors that made a stricter code of conduct for the film industry seem essential to the country's self-appointed moral guardians.[6] Despite the studio moguls' stated imperative of moral education, the 'talkies' threatened to reflect the graphic language and lewd jokes common on the New York stage.[7] When, in 1934, the Motion Picture Production Code, or Hays Code, was enforced under Joseph Breen, Hollywood was quick to respond: first by seeming to fall into line and, second, by parodying the rules. Most famously, Clark Gable and Claudette Colbert erected 'The Wall of Jericho' between their beds in *It Happened One Night* (1934) to poke fun at the blunt Puritanism of the code. In *The Scoundrel* (1935) Noël Coward sums up the view of many Hollywood screenwriters when his character quips, 'I refuse to make money improving people's morals. It's a vulgar way to swindle the public. Selling them the things they least need: virtue and dullness.' In practice, film-makers had no choice but to peddle virtue, or at least to appear to. Obscenity received only one sentence in the code: 'obscenity in word, gesture, reference, song, joke, or by suggestion (even when likely to be understood only by part of the audience) is forbidden.'[8] It was a definition conveniently broad enough to cover a multitude of sins, including violence and blasphemy. Naturally though, the censors were most interested in sex. The problem for film-makers in dealing with dialogue and more stringent regulations was how to get around their different demands, and to do so in such a way that the getting-around would become part of the entertainment.

This is where Wilde comes in, and not for the first time. In 1915, *Dorian Gray*'s homoeroticism was a suggestive touch and in 1925 Lubitsch captured that 'Wilde-ish spirit' in his direction. Now, in the 1930s, Wilde was one of the figures who helped Hollywood comedy find its voice. It was a voice—quite literally—descended from the epigrammatic dialogue of Wilde's society comedies in the form of screwball wit to whisper and laugh behind the censors' backs. This verbal comedy of evasion, suggestiveness, and—crucially—play was piqued by slapstick and farce, creating a world in which conventional rules of morality and decorum are turned upside down. Such epigrammatic wit, especially between the sexes, conjured up another world of naughty possibilities hidden in plain sight.[9] As screwball comedy evolved, this world expanded into that 'Wildean universe' DiBattista recognizes. Isn't that what Wilde himself had done to evade and ironize Victorian Puritanism? Like the strategies employed by his *Dorian Gray* to attempt to avoid the censure of Mrs Grundy, movies in the era of the Production Code encrypted subjects that were taboo, and did so in order to create a new pleasure; the pleasure of imagining the unsayable.[10]

It was an avowed Wildean who started all this: Ben Hecht, again. Having moved to Hollywood and helped to establish the big screen gangsters, he distanced himself from that burgeoning genre. He wrote the screenplay for *The Scoundrel*, including that Wildean quip on virtue and dullness quoted above, by which time he'd written or co-written over half a dozen comedies. With studio heads desperately seeking writers who could produce screenplays 'on the edge of what censors and more conservative viewers would tolerate', Hecht would become the ultimate screenwriter and widely credited as one of the defining forces of the screwball comedy.[11]

The Importance of Being Epigrammatic

America's easy familiarity with Wilde's social comedies and the rise of new decadence had provided fertile ground for Hecht to develop his epigrammatic wit. His first novel *Erik Dorn* (1921) is the Bildungsroman of a charismatic dandy called Erik, who chafes in modern America but comes to realize that it is not possible to live for pleasure alone. Erik's epigrammatic speech establishes him as a Wildean figure at the outset: 'There are two kinds of newspapermen,' he jokes in the novel's opening pages; 'those who try to write poetry and those who try to drink themselves to death. Fortunately for the world, only one of them succeeds.'[12] Like Lord Henry in *Dorian Gray*, Erik is a walking compendium of this kind of epigram, ironizing the bourgeois values of the life he leads: 'A conscience is an immediate annoyance, whereas ideals are charming procrastinations';[13] 'Observing married couples is a post-graduate course in pessimism.'[14] Erik's epigrams are metonyms for the detached, playful, transgressive dandy that he aspires to be. For the Wildean epigram encapsulates a rebellion against conventional morality, or at least it kicks verbally over the traces, believing that rebellion might be possible. It puts the speaker in a position of ironic detachment from society and does so always with a devil-may-care smile.[15] As Erik's epigrams reject society's values, they open the possibility of pleasure for its own sake unbridled by responsibility.

So far, so Wildean. Still, there is a crucial difference between Erik and Lord Henry, who he'd like to be. Whereas Henry goes on living life for pleasure beyond the end of *Dorian Gray*, Erik is brought to book for his hedonism. When he travels to Germany as a reporter in the chaos of the First World War, he must face suffering and life-and-death responsibility for the first time. Reading the last letter of a close friend, put to death after the end of the war, he is gripped by grief. Realizing how selfish his life has been, he utters, ' "I have no phrases, dear friend. Let my tears be an epigram." '[16] It is a sombre farewell to the Wildean epigram and the idea that it is possible to play fast and loose with ethics and responsibility anymore. *Erik Dorn* turns into, and turns out to be, a morality tale after all.

The epigram was not dead though, as Hecht well knew. Unlike almost any other decadent writer, bar Wilde himself, he was a pragmatist. He'd been an excellent journalist and a good fiction writer but above all he built his early fame by flouting the law in the service of self-publicity. His second novel *Fantazius Mallare* parodied *À rebours* by Huysmans (as his screenplay for *Scarface* would later) with the express purpose of courting controversy. In this aim it succeeded admirably. When Hecht feared he had not included enough shocking material, he added a seven-page preface to the novel 'Dedicated to my Enemies' and his illustrator, Wallace Smith, drew a prefatory image of a man masturbating against a tree.[17] In an echo of the *Ulysses* trials of Hecht's close friends Margaret Anderson and Jane Heap, they were duly charged, alongside the publisher Pascal Covici, with distributing 'lewd, lascivious, and obscene' literature through the US postal service. A Hecht

Defense League was founded. Clearly enjoying the whole episode enormously, he had cards printed with his own bon mot: 'There are no obscene words. There are only obscene readers.'[18] This of course references Wilde's own epigrammatic defence of *Dorian Gray* in his Preface to the novel's second edition:

> *There is no such thing as a moral or immoral book.*
> *Books are well written, or badly written. That is all.* [...]
> *It is the spectator, and not life, that art really mirrors.*

Just as Wilde had simplified Walter Pater's aesthetic principles into epigrammatic form to defend *Dorian Gray* from its moral critics, so Hecht took Wilde's Preface and boiled it down further to one core message that literature has no moral responsibility. In Hecht's imagination he was Wilde: Mark Two, and *Fantazius Mallare* was his *Dorian Gray*. He would be a martyr for his art—at least if it would make him wealthy and successful. His sequel, *The Kingdom of Evil: A Continuation of the Journal of Fantazius Mallare* (1924), took self-indulgence to such an extreme that it became grotesque. Much later, the make-up artist for *Citizen Kane* (1941), Maurice Seiderman, saw parallels between the novel's central character and the character of Charles Foster Kane that he was creating for Orson Welles. So much so, that he engaged someone to read extracts from the novel to Welles in the make-up room.[19]

Although Hecht would turn out to be unique, his kind of witty dialogue was not rare in the 1920s. With silent movies booming in the 1920s, it was one of the ways in which live theatre could assert its superiority to 'the flickers'. The continued popularity of Wilde's society comedies was such that when NBC ran its first programme of coast-to-coast radio adaptations in 1929, its first production was *Earnest*.[20] This was an apt choice, for conversation was Wilde's great gift. He'd found writing action difficult and sought refuge in long scenes of dialogue, making his scripts perfect for radio performance.[21] Nevertheless NBC's choice is another turn in Wilde's posthumous American reputation. Just a decade or so earlier, his words were omitted from silent adaptations of his own works. The ostentatious alignment of the name 'Oscar Wilde' with irreverent and suggestive wit may have been too blatant for the fledgling movie industry. Or maybe it was because—with the notable exception of Lubitsch—it seemed cinema could not do justice to Wilde before synchronous sound.

The NBC adaptation could be assured of an audience familiar with *Earnest*. It had always been the most popular of Wilde's plays in America, performed far more than any other. It concerns Jack and Algernon, who are anything but earnest. They casually blend fiction into their lives in order to pursue pleasure with impunity. Jack pretends to visit his imaginary brother Ernest in order to get away from his home in the country and romance Gwendolen in town, while Algernon avoids responsibilities that bore him in town by pretending to visit his imaginary friend Bunbury in the country. When Algernon decides to visit Jack at home, though, and meets Jack's young ward Cecily in the guise of 'Ernest', a chain of misunderstanding is unleashed in which the identity of 'Ernest' and the question of who is engaged to whom has farcical consequences.

This plot was soon legendary. However, it was not the plot that people responded to first when they saw *Earnest*; it was the dialogue. Early in the new century US notices and reviews of *Earnest* had often focused on Wilde's 'sparkling' or 'witty' dialogue.[22] As Algernon and Jack open the play, their dandyism is writ large by their epigrammatic wit:

'The amount of women in London who flirt with their own husbands is perfectly scandalous. It looks so bad. It is simply washing one's clean linen in public.'[23]

'I hate people who are not serious about meals. It is so shallow of them.'[24]

'Relations are simply a tedious pack of people, who haven't got the remotest knowledge of how to live, nor the smallest instinct about when to die.'[25]

Epigrammatic dialogue like this pulls away from its original context and transcends it to become an independent quotable entity.[26] At the same time it is the counterpart of the play's absurd plot, relentlessly ironizing Victorian moral values at the level of the sentence. The epigrams quoted above and many others create a parallel universe—a Wildean Universe no less—in which illicit sex is better than marriage, nice food is more impor- tant than telling the truth, no one likes their family, and bearing the name 'Ernest' is more important than doing good deeds.[27] It is, in short, the very antithesis of what Joseph Breen and the Motion Picture Production Code stood for.

Notwithstanding the cultural contexts of minstrelsy discussed in Chapter 1 and still pertinent in the 1910s and 1920s, and Wilde's continued high profile, when we think about the plot of *Earnest* in relation to America's vision of itself in the 1920s, its success is still surprising. For this, Wilde's last completed play, is his most amoral, surreal, and—crucially—camp society comedy. Its verbal wit creates an atmosphere of utter irreverence in which sincerity, marriage, and masculinity are mercilessly parodied. Its values, such as they are, are utterly at odds with the pervasive myth that American men in this period defined themselves by self-made, industrious work, sports, and monikers of robust heteronormativity.[28] *Earnest's* popularity does, however, correlate strongly with America's largely-forgotten early-twentieth-century gay cultures, and the 'vogue for effeminacy' that they helped to create in the 1920s and early 1930s.[29] The cultural historian George Chauncey has shown that these cultures were very familiar in New York.[30] Bohemian circles comprised a mixture of gay and straight groups, and drag balls attracted large numbers of curious spectators, while the image of the 'fairy' grew familiar in the city's culture and 'pansy acts' became a feature of the uptown club scene.[31] In New York's various fledgling gay circles, the identity of the 'queer' in particular resonated with the contemporary popularity of Wilde's plays. The self-styled queer tended to be middle class, fashioned with an effeminate sartorial style and exaggerated good manners. His persona aspired to the sophistication of the English gentry, at the same time as he took to 'burlesquing gender conventions with a sharp and often sardonic camp wit'.[32] In short, the New York queer had much in common with Lord Henry, Darlington, Algernon, and Jack.

As the image of the queer dovetailed with *Earnest*, it highlighted the sexually subversive dimensions of Wilde's play as never before. Since they first appeared on the stage across the English-speaking world, Wilde's plays had succeeded in front of largely conservative audiences—and indeed they continue to do so today. Still their subversive edge was never lost. As Alan Sinfield has commented, they 'flirt, at least, with the danger that prevailing values might not be satisfactory, or might not prevail. In the face of such a production, some audience members will retreat into conformity, while others will entertain more radical possibilities'.[33] For those radical audience members and others who entertained the possibility of breaching the bounds of 'normal' values, Jack and Algernon are an inspiration and ones whose potential is made flesh by the real-life 'queers' of New York. Jack and Algernon are so unapologetically naughty, so outrageous, and at the centre of the mischief-making with which their characters ironize Victorian values is their queerness. They are not homosexual but, as Sinfield argues, their attitudes and behaviour put into play the idea that they very well might be.[34] The best example is the most famous: Algernon's fictional friend 'Bunbury', whose frequent illnesses enable him to shirk unwanted engagements. Making dear Bunbury into a verb for Algernon's secret jaunts to the country ('Bunburying'), the name becomes, as Derek Jarman said in another context, 'confession as innuendo'.[35] Its alliteration and rhythm relish its own naughtiness as it celebrates the pleasures of a double life.[36]

As Wilde knew better than anyone, once the values that your audience thought it could take for granted are suspended and replaced with a nod and a wink, anything is possible. When Cecily ventures that novels with happy endings are depressing, her governess Miss Prism declares that in her novel, 'The good ended happily, and the bad unhappily. That is what Fiction means'.[37] The Wildean Universe would not be like that. Transplanted into 1920s America the ironizing of Puritanical morals in Wilde's plays was in sympathy with the spirit of the jazz age, giving him a new lease of life. To these jazz age Americans, Wilde wasn't some remote Victorian; he was their contemporary, to be embraced and reinvented by a culture more suited to him than his own. In 1923 an ecstatic reviewer in Indianapolis lauded a new production of *An Ideal Husband* as 'a Tiffany diamond, a nearly priceless gem'.[38] The metaphor is telling: it denotes something that is sparkling, chic, and modern. But of course Wilde always intended to be modern, setting all his social comedies conspicuously in the Present.[39] In 1920s America, epigrammatic dialogue was his primary marker of distinction and modernity. Most often, this modernity was underscored by the production design. The plays were performed in contemporary dress, sometimes strikingly à la mode. The 1922 Dakota Playmakers' production of *Earnest* caused quite a stir, being costumed in the latest fashions. The ladies' extravagant gowns were imported from Paris, with several costume changes to show off, for example, Gwendolen's sea-green crêpe gown trimmed with 400 pearls and her 'gown of rainbow coloured satin'.[40] Heady fare for Grand Forks, North Dakota, showing once again how Wilde's sparkle appealed not only to literary elites and urban sophisticates.

Even as Wilde's plays showed themselves to be modern, offstage the Wildean epigram was taking on a life of its own. Other fledgling epigrammatists understood whence their style came, as one of the greatest, Dorothy Parker, acknowledged in 1927:

> If, with the literate, I am
> Impelled to try an epigram,
> I never seek to take the credit;
> We all assume that Oscar said it.[41]

While far from Parker's best lines—in a career that included writing the Hollywood screenplay for *The Fan*, the 1949 adaption of *Lady Winder-mere*—they capture the culture's easy familiarity with the Wildean epigram. Tallulah Bankhead, who starred in the London stage adaptation of Michael Arlen's *The Green Hat*, provides some of the most memorable examples. 'It's the good girls who keep diaries,' she said; 'the bad girls never have time.'[42] She commented on several occasions, as a boast or a promise: 'I'm as pure as the driven slush.'[43] Of course, Bankhead's bons mots mirror Wilde's epigrams insofar as they centre on a reversal of conventional wisdom regarding 'good' and 'purity'. Morality is not jettisoned, but playfully inverted.[44] As in *Earnest*, nothing overtly sexual is said. There is, though, a clear hint of another world; call it a subculture, or a Wildean Universe, in which normative values do not apply. Bankhead's unwritten diary entries allude to Gwendolen's line in *Earnest*: 'I never travel without my diary. One should always have something sensational to read in the train.'[45] Whatever is going on between those sheets, it is clearly more entertaining than anything that should be read by respectable people.

Bankhead reinvigorated the epigram as the centrepiece of the one-person show otherwise known as her life. Her remarks were energized by the ambiguous distinction between her private life and public persona. High-profile cocaine use and bisexuality—she was, she reportedly said, 'ambi-sextrous'![46]—gave her epigrams an edgy plausibility. The Motion Picture Production Code Committee's 'Doom Book' comprised a list of 150 actors and actresses considered 'unsuitable for the public' and when it was presented to the studios, Bankhead was at the top under the heading: 'Verbal Moral Turpitude'.[47] Little wonder that she was not able to make a career in Hollywood, though she spent time in Los Angeles and became a perennial part of Alla Nazimova's 'Sewing Circle'.[48]

It was nothing new to use epigrams to defect from the values society held dear. Bankhead's genius lay in publicly brandishing them to signal that she was a strong, independent, and sexually liberated woman. Less clear is whether her witty one-liners were a part of a trend. There is some evidence from Bankhead's friends and associates in the overlapping circles of the international lesbian literati that it might have been. Dolly Wilde, for instance, cultivated the connection with her uncle Oscar with humour that 'charmed and amused whole rooms-full of sophisticates in the salons and clubs'.[49] In Nazimova's Sewing Circle, wit was deployed as an ostentatious badge of otherness.[50] More specific evidence goes little further than a fragment here and there, but they indicate a link in the feminist evolution in

Wildean wit, from the unapologetically funny independence of Wilde's own witty women to the screwball heroine. In Wilde's second social comedy, *A Woman of No Importance* (1893), when Lord Illingworth asks Mrs Allonby, 'What do you call . . . a bad woman?', she replies, 'Oh! the sort of woman a man never gets tired of'.[51] In *Lady Windermere's Fan*, Mrs Erlynne refuses to play out the tragic fallen-woman trope of Victorian fiction.[52] 'Repentance is quite out of date,' she tells Lord Windermere; 'And besides, if a woman really repents, she has to go to a bad dressmaker, otherwise no one believes her. And nothing in the world would induce me to do that.'[53] Bankhead, habitually glamourous in silk gowns, furs, and pearls, would surely concur.

Looking further afield to Paris there are also stylistic parallels with Bankhead's sometime-friend, the expatriate playwright, poet, and novelist Natalie Clifford Barney. Openly lesbian and polyamorous throughout her long life, writing in both French and English, for sixty years she had an influential salon on the Left Bank. Barney was one of those American disciples who met Wilde during his 1882 tour, as a child on Long Island.[54] His influence is clear in her own several volumes of epigrams:

'*Elle m'a initié au plaisir,—je ne lui ai jamais par-donné*'
['She introduced me to pleasure—I have never forgiven her.'][55]

'*La gloire: être connu de ceux qu'on ne voudrait pas connaître*'
['Fame: to be known by those whom one doesn't want to know'][56]

'*Il vaut mieux être un amant qu'aimer un amant*'
['It is better to be a lover than to love a lover'][57]

'*Marié: n'être ni seul ni ensemble*'
['Married: to be neither alone nor together'][58]

Harnessing the Wildean epigram to assert her independence and intelligence, Barney was also innovative in the way she uttered them. As Joan Schenkar perceptively notes, in Barney's epigrams there is an absence of

the encompassingly Parnassian quality of Oscar's [. . .] often to their advantage. They are far less like proclamations from Oscar's Imaginary Academy of Fine Ideas and far more like crystalline splinters from Natalie's Golden Bowl of Life.[59]

Indeed, these 'crystalline splinters' reject the studied quality of Wilde's witticisms and those of Bankhead. They are defined by a new naturalism, produced with the effect of spontaneity.

It is Noël Coward who best articulates this naturalization of the epigram. By 1925, when he had his first comedy hit in New York with *Hay Fever*, the epigrammatic wit he borrowed copiously from Wilde in his early plays had evolved into a new pared-down style; as he himself put it, 'more natural and less elaborate'.[60] Coward felt this suited the times better. As he explained in regard to his *Easy Virtue* (1924): 'My object in writing it [was] primarily to adapt a story, intrinsically Pinero in theme and structure, to present-day behaviour; to compare the *déclassée* woman of to-day with the more flamboyant *demi-mondaine* of the nineties'.[61] The fin de siècle was still an avowed inspiration but Coward had developed a new philosophy. 'Wit ought to be a glorious treat like caviar', he wrote; 'never spread it about like marmalade'.[62] Together with the sense of spontaneity, this rarity would become the keynote of the Wildean epigram in 1920s and 1930s America.

Mae West's Verbal Seductions

It was not Coward or Bankhead but another strong independent woman who would first take the epigram to Hollywood. Mae West first developed epigrammatic dialogue for the gay characters in her Broadway plays *Sex* (1926), *The Drag* (1927), and *The Pleasure Man* (1928).[63] These were among the 'sex plays' popular with Broadway audiences in the mid-to-late 1920s, and they introduced the modish terms 'queer', 'camp', and 'gay' into stage dialogue, borrowing from Manhattan's gay and drag subculture.[64] The epigrammatic witticisms West wrote for the stage were not Wildean exactly. As Lilian Schlissel notes, they turned rather on New York slang, which 'came out of the speakeasies, and the jokes she used were familiar routines of burlesque'.[65] Queer and sexy with it, West's plays swapped the show of restraint and innuendo of Wildean epigrams for spectacle and shock. What connected Wilde to West's plays was not textual influence but circumstance. *The Pleasure Man* followed an acclaimed stage adaptation of *Dorian Gray* at the Biltmore Theatre, in midtown Manhattan.[66] Opening on Broadway on 1 October 1928, it was raided by police during its second performance; the entire cast of fifty-four was arrested for indecency.[67] Newspapers photographed them in full drag flouncing, hands on hips, towards the waiting police cars and smiling at the cameras (Fig. 6.2).

Fig. 6.2 Cast members of Mae West's show, *The Pleasure Man*, are arrested (4 October 1928)

The juxtaposition of *Dorian Gray* and *The Pleasure Man* is coincidental as far as we know. It is though telling. In 1920s' New York, gay culture was very visible. If this was a closet, its doors were wide open and everyone could hear the party inside. West very publicly reminded straight audiences, who mostly knew little of drag shows or the clandestine delights of 42nd Street, that epigrammatic dialogue was queer and the outrageous way she did so made it seem queerer than ever. Her plays helped make the epigrammatic dialogue of Wilde's stage characters, with their commitment to pleasure and dismissal of normative morality, all the more legible as a code for sexual deviance on the New York stage. West was not alone in such signalling. The tradition of the post-Wildean comedy is seen in Allen Norton's *The Convolvulus* (1914), Coward's play *The Vortex* (1927), and *The Green Bay Tree* (1933), a Broadway hit for the now-forgotten Mordaunt Shairp. Each begins with unmistakable allusions to the concerns and epigrammatic dialogue of Wilde's society comedies. With this they establish sexual deviance and irony at the centre of the play—only to wrong-foot the audience by using it not, as Wilde did, to challenge normative values, but as the root of their human tragedies.[68]

West used the Wildean epigram for her own ends too, but those ends were quite different. She followed Erlynne, Bankhead and Barney in using wit as a tool to assert her sexual independence and confidence. When West was signed to Paramount Pictures in 1932, she faced the challenge of adapting her stage success for the movies. Her references to the homosexual demi-monde might inflame the authorities in New York but she mostly got away with it. She wouldn't get away with it in Hollywood given the new levels of vigilance over the screen. Although the Production Code had not yet come into full effect, overt depictions of gay characters and love affairs were taboo, as was the kind of graphic language featured in West's stage scripts. Perhaps she consciously looked to Wilde as a blueprint for how witty talk could hide subversive sexuality. She certainly 'cherished and idealized the 1890s', setting several of her films in that era.[69] She may also have been channelling the fashionable and flirtatious epigrams in vogue thanks to Bankhead, Barney, and others. At all events, Wildean wit was perfectly suited to what she sought to achieve on-screen: a naughty frisson in place of the graphic language of her stage productions.

The plots of West's films hardly matter. Suffice it to say that they are varia-tions on a theme. Always in the starring role herself, West upstages men who desire her, negotiates close encounters with criminals, performs songs and burlesques, and even appears in a lion-taming act in *I'm No Angel* (1933), before she ultimately triumphs by outsmarting everyone and falling in love. All this is just a vehicle for her standout wit and sex appeal. Most of her wise-cracks have the illusion of spontaneity—that naturalism again—delivered as a riposte over a sequined shoulder while she stalks off in an implausi-bly tight dress, with a man or men in hot pursuit.[70] Many of her brief quips are modelled on the stage dialogue of *The Pleasure Man*, a transference that made perfect sense to West, as she saw both women and gay men as groups oppressed by straight men.[71] At climactic moments, though, she'll produce an epigram that is classically Wildean in its wit. In her most commercially successful film, *I'm No Angel*, she tells Jack (Cary Grant), 'When I'm good I'm very good, but when I'm bad I'm better'. And later, 'Well, it's not the men in your life that counts, it's the life in your men'. Her epigrams sub-vert straight power relations in a new crystalline form absent from her stage plays. In doing so, they connect the Wildean epigram to female sexual provo-cation and assertiveness on the big screen for the first time, empowered against men who speak in dull prose. Sometimes Oscar is all but quoted:

'I generally avoid temptation unless I can't resist it', she declares in *My Little Chickadee* (1940). The sentiment is from Lord Darlington, who tells Lady Windermere, 'I can resist everything except temptation'.[72] As in Wilde's epigrams, the power (and fun) comes from the way that West treats Victorian morality—still very much integral to the epigram—as a subject for derision. Here, in a shift from her stage successes, epigrams empower sexually knowledgeable women. In so doing, West gives us Wildean wordplay brought down from the heights of third-person address in a more radical way than Bankhead had, filtered through West's drawl and pout, as she stands just a little too close to her male foil. West knew better than anyone that there is an electricity as an epigram is uttered. It's nothing less than a moment charged with possibility in which normative values are suspended, in which it seems possible to move the moral boundaries or simply draw new ones. West's charismatic screen presence brings Wildean wordplay and wit to sizzling visual life. She is the epigram re-embodied in wonderfully new ways.

High art it wasn't. As Neal Gabler notes, Paramount's movies 'didn't ennoble the audience; they whisked them away to a world of sheen and sex where people spoke in innuendo, acted with abandon, and doubted the rewards of virtue'.[73] Paramount was also home to Lubitsch from 1928, and there he made the definitive comedies *One Hour with You* and *Trouble in Paradise* (both 1932). It was a good home for West, with her combination of subversive wit and platinum-blonde glamour. As knowing off-screen as on, West understood well that box-office success required a tricky tightrope-walk and balance between satisfying the cinema-going public's appetite for titillation and entertainment, and evading the censors.[74] How she brought this off was in part a throwback. Recalling that, in the 1910s, Wilde's *Dorian Gray* had been performed on the vaudeville circuit, West revivifies the connection between variety performance, bawdy innuendo, and witty epigrams.

Indubitably a sex symbol, at least as troubling for the censors was the way that West's epigrammatic dialogue positioned her as suggestive and deviant.[75] In trying to make sense of her, contemporaries reached for the central figures of the decadent movement. Her friend Cecil Beaton commented in appreciation of her signature style that 'Aubrey Beardsley might have drawn the canary-white tendrils weaving over the hourglass figure as a landlocked mermaid'.[76] Others took this heady mix of excess, glamour, and perversion as an affront, or even as a symbol for the final throes of decadent capitalism. In 1934, at the height of West's fame, the Marxist critic Robert Forsythe portrayed her as 'a complete treatise on decay'; specifically locating her in a tradition of sexual perversion which began with Oscar Wilde and spelt doom for the bourgeoisie. He called her performances

the direct result of a sybaritic life which finally results in profound boredom for lack of any further possible stimulation or titillation. It is invariably associated with those twin elements of perversion, sadism and masochism, and generally reveals itself among the thinned-out representatives of a dying class.[77]

How wrong he was. As another great female hustler of the Broadway stage—Rose in Stephen Sondheim's *Gypsy*—would declare thirty years later, 'Finished? We're just beginning and there's no stopping us this time . . .'

The Front Page to *The Scoundrel*

When Mae West arrived in Hollywood, Ben Hecht was there working on his own scripts. Thanks to Bankhead, West, Hecht, and others—including Wilde himself, through revivals of his plays—Wildean wit already had a cultural status and profile as something sophisticated and modern, teetering on the brink of dangerous transgression.

Hecht picked the right time to pitch up in Hollywood. Ever the opportunist, he was quick to resurrect the epigrammatic wit that his first novel purported to kill off. That was then. Now, he knew—and knew that he knew—how to write Wildean wit better than anyone. His extraordinary skills would make him 'the most influential writer in the history of the American movies, creating a new and exciting language for the screen.'[78] The flair for dialogue that he'd first shown in *Erik Dorn* would mean he was to be a sought-after scriptwriter as the talkies became the only game in town, when movies needed words to match their dazzling images. Hecht's many screenplays, like West's, come via the Coward school of wit: used sparingly, like caviar. As for West, the fact that epigrams could hide a multitude of sexual sins while creating a frisson of suggestion was a bonus—one that would become increasingly useful as the Production Code came into effect.

Hecht's epigrams created a new archetype for cinema: the charismatic, morally reprehensible male anti-hero, first seen in *The Front Page* (1931), co-written with his former *Chicago Daily News* colleague, Charles MacArthur. Based on their 1928 play of the same name, it takes a typical day in the newsroom of a busy paper as its focus. Wit and rapid-fire dialogue define its irreverent, ironic tone. Take, for instance, the moment when Roy Bensinger (Edward Everett Horton), a crime reporter, comments: 'That jail is reeking with germs [. . .] It's amazing to me that those prisoners can live long enough to get hung.' At one level this is a trivial example. Bensinger is not a central character and his comment is peripheral to the plot's main concerns. Neither is the epigram weaponized, as in Wilde's work, to subvert truth or sexual morality. Yet this remark is more than just a cheap laugh. By suggesting that an unpleasant odour is more serious than impending execution, it ironizes death row in aesthetic terms. Its humour turns on taking trivial things seriously and vice versa, the art of destabilizing established values that Wilde created. And it isn't only what Bensinger says, it's how he says it. The camp hauteur of Horton's screen persona as he tosses off the bon mot takes for granted the association between witty epigrams and the queer outsider, established by Wilde and celebrated by Manhattan's gay cabarets and drag acts.[79] Sophisticated audiences may have noted the gentle nod to those predecessors. Most audiences would not, but the line would be amusing anyway.

As Hecht developed his screen dialogue, its humour often turned on the relationship between epigrammatic wit and queerness. His screenplay for *Design for Living* (1933)—directed by none other than Lubitsch—famously retained none of the words from Coward's original stage comedy of the same name. It is the story of a ménage à trois, comprising two best friends (Fredric March and Gary Cooper) who fall in love with Gilda (Miriam Hopkins), much to the disgust of her own best friend, Max (Horton again). The scenario alone signals how Coward and Hecht liked to subvert monogamous, heterosexual relationships. But there's more going on too. When the love triangle ends in acrimony, Gilda marries Max and they retire to their bridal suite:

MAX: Do you love me?
GILDA: Oh Max. People should never ask that question on their wedding night. It's either too late or too early.

The naughty quip puts Gilda in the same position as Mae West: a woman whose sexual playfulness overturns gendered expectations of male authority. Her Wildean tone is at once louche and self-assured, with an air of unassailable authority. At the same time, Hecht's script is having fun with Horton's camp persona, using innuendo to raise questions about where his own sexual interests really lie. Even this brief example shows that an epigram embedded in a screenplay is never only an epigram because its seductions radiate through the viewer's perceptions of a scenario and the characters. It is not *straight* in either sense of the word. Rather, its humour slyly queers the Christian moral values that the Production Code explicitly upheld on-screen.

Above all, *Design for Living* and *The Front Page* showed that language itself could become the motivating energy, even the theme, of a production.[80] That hadn't really been done since Wilde's plays, but on-screen it was even better thanks to the art of the close-up. Close-ups showed audiences the immediacy of repartee in a way that can be lost in a theatre space. As a technique it is perfect for Wilde's wit. Screenplays are still chronically undervalued in film studies and critics have missed the way in which Hecht's words energized sound comedy into screwball. But in the fusion of witty talk, physical comedy, and farce that is the essence of screwball at its zenith in the late 1930s, and which is focal in discussions of the genre, talk in fact came first, setting the pace and tone of the very different kind of comedy.

By the mid-1930s Hecht was experimenting with how he could harness epigrammatic wit into a new form of fast-paced dialogue. His screenplay for *The Scoundrel* is a prime example. It is the story of Tony Mallare (played by Noël Coward), a publisher who lives for pleasure alone. In a reversal of Frank Capra's later *It's a Wonderful Life* (1946), he dies and returns as a ghost only to discover that he cannot find a single person to mourn his death. He is given one month to find someone to cry for him or he will never rest in peace. Hecht—in control of the script for which he and MacArthur won the Oscar for Best Story—brings the language of his anti-hero closer to the decadent than ever before on film. As if to declare his intentions his hero's name, Tony Mallare, reuses the surname from his banned novel *Fantazius Mallare*. It's an in-joke of the kind in which Hecht specialized. True to his name, Mallare's epigrammatic language marks him out as an immoral dandy at the outset. 'If only women were as charming during a love affair as they are after it's over, how much longer one's mad devotion would last', he quips in the opening scene. At one level this is a male echo of Mrs Allonby's line in *A Woman of No Importance*: 'Men always want to be a woman's first love. That is their clumsy vanity. Women have a more subtle instinct about things. What we like is to be a man's last romance.'[81] The big difference is pace. Epigrammatic dialogue in Wilde's plays had been coloured by luxuriant ennui and occasional melodrama. In *The Scoundrel* ennui has been swept aside; the melodramatic set pieces are gone too. Now it is the restless and nervous energy of anxiety that defines epigrammatic wit. Coward's delivery is infused with the rapid speed and physical movement of the busy, modern city and specifically that of the newsroom. Spat out, in the office, as he clutches a phone, this is machine-gun dialogue of the kind that also featured in Hecht's gangster films. There are parallels between this kind of anxious-paced scene and the neurotic energy of decadent prose, with its overwrought syntaxes.[82] Here, though, the epigram has well and truly crossed the Atlantic and become a naturalized US citizen.

In 'The Critic as Artist', Gilbert waxes lyrical on his desire for a literature that moves with 'words that are winged with light'. He explains his view that modern literature has focused on visual effects at the expense of its melody and metre and envisages 'the true rhythmical life of words and the fine freedom and richness of effect that such rhythmical life produces'.[83] Wilde's drawing-room dialogues have their rhythm, but it's a rhythm of languid imagination not real life. Hecht achieves Gilbert's dream. His dialogue is 'winged with light', free and moving with the rhythm of the city. As Mallare begins another epigram, we can see *The Scoundrel* as a transitional film between Wilde's society plays and screwball banter: 'I call anyone who's clever enough to see through me a friend and . . .' There he is interrupted mid-sentence by a lawyer who chips in, '. . . Anyone who doesn't a sweetheart'. Here the measured streams of epigrammatic wit in Wilde's plays are reworked into fast adversarial repartee. Talking over each other, finishing each other's sentences; these would be two of the defining characteristics of screwball comedy dialogue. This scene is also an example of how the form of talking pictures helped to realize the epigram's potential to be thoroughly modern. Without the actors needing to project to the back row or necessary pauses for audience laughter and applause after a witticism, cinema could reflect the dynamism of the dialogue with close-ups and the camera's shot-reverse shot.

Hecht's epigrams are on the surface brief innocuous interjections: caviar to add savour and flavour to a scene. They are, though, more than just that. His anti-heroes repurpose audacious epigrams to define a new kind of male lead on-screen, one quite different from the cracker-barrel comedian of slapstick comedy. Taking his cue from West and Bankhead, these are no longer abstract assertions of truth but personalized and naturalized. Mallare is a modern-day dandy, in the form of a middle-class womanizer, queered by his wit and Coward's persona. The new anti-hero thus created is a charming cad. Morally reprehensible, he can bring off adultery, theft, fraud, and even murder with a smile and an ironic put-down. He is a social deviant, bundling together queerness with other modes of sexual transgression into a general sense of naughtiness that seduces the audience into forgiving him.

Just how radical this was is another question. Sensational as Hecht's epigrammatic anti-heroes are, they ultimately transgress rather than topple moral order. In the first place, Hecht's anti-heroes come into being in the dramatic moment when they reject normative ethics with a witty line. Their epigrams needle at the Production Code and the Christian ethics that it symbolized, but they do not offer a constructive thesis to put in its place. Wilde reached again and again for a way to move beyond the ethical limitations of epigrammatic wit.[84] Hollywood perhaps realized that it didn't really care to try too hard. Its wit kicks over the traces, and that's enough. In *The Scoundrel*, as in *Design for Living* and *The Front Page*, Hecht and MacArthur situate epigrammatic wit within a narrative arc that restores moral order— or at least some semblance of it—by the final reel. It's a similar story in West's films: her wisecracks ironize conventional morality and yet her lead female characters are in fact very moral. A classic tart with a heart, with a strong commitment to justice, kindness to those in need, and monogamy—with the right man. Her morals and Hecht's hardly aligned with the code's staid idea of how good and evil be depicted on-screen but this moral order was never seriously under threat.

Twentieth Century, *Bringing Up Baby*, and *The Awful Truth*

Now we come back to Cary Grant's negligee. By the time *Bringing Up Baby* was filmed in 1938 any direct influence from Wilde had become difficult to trace. A new form had evolved with no clear link to 1890s' decadence beyond a series of elective affinities. The epigrams are very few, replaced by faster-moving quips. And yet this repartee, together with comic cross-dressing and mistaken identities, crystalizes screwball comedy as a Wildean Universe. It began with the epigrams but in a fully Wildean Universe the playfulness and social subversion encapsulated in a well-deployed epigram come to define the whole film. The essence of the screwball is that key moral terms—'dignity', 'duty', 'truth', 'sacredness', 'sincerity'—are called into question, their values radically revised or cast asunder with irony.[85] Like Lubitsch's *Lady Windermere* this is not just about a funny line of dialogue or even a handsome man answering the door in a woman's negligee. Rather, it's a whole attitude to morality which irreversibly destabilizes the values that the Production Code sought to uphold, and does so with such fun. This radical destabilization is what is quintessentially Wildean, toppling gender norms, truth, and sexual ethics alike. It truly is, as DiBattista writes—borrowing Wilde's epigraph to *Earnest*—'trivial comedy for serious people'.[86]

Twentieth Century (1934), again written by Hecht and MacArthur, is the first film to show us what would happen if the naughty irony contained within the moment of the epigram were to saturate an entire movie. That moment of subversive possibility, ordinarily contained and constrained within the epigram as a discrete amusement, runs riot across its scenes. It is a whole movie set within a Wildean Universe. Hitherto, typical plots featured one person who defects from society's values. Fun is had, but eventually our hero is reined in (however imperfectly) before the closing credits. Here, by contrast, the lead character's ironic dismissal of agreed norms spans out into a wholesale revision of those values, with no 'back to normal' at the end.

Twentieth Century is a madcap retelling of George du Maurier's novel *Trilby* (1894). John Barrymore, who had starred in Warner Brothers' *Svengali* three years earlier and of course the 1920 *Dr Jekyll and Mr Hyde* adaptation discussed in Chapter 2, is Oscar Jaffe: a Svengali-like figure who crafts Lily's (Carole Lombard's) career, only to lose her when she becomes famous. DiBattista perceptively notes that 'Lily might have been imagined by Oscar Wilde, had Wilde wanted to represent how Americans, famed for the unaffected "naturalness" of their social manners and verbal style, might take up the pleasures of affectation'.[87] Lily and Oscar are Wildean without ever uttering an epigram, because their relationship is suffused with irony and amusing untruths; they each adopt multiple identities and in every moment blur the line between sincere emotion and stylish affectation.

In a further development of the genre, melodrama and sentiment are vetoed. These qualities were essential to Wilde's first three social comedies. It was part of their Victorian heritage. Silent comedy was not averse to either, and we saw earlier how film-makers played up the melodrama in adaptations of *Dorian Gray*, *Salome*, and *Lady Windermere*. In the talkies, though, both began to look dated and, like the Jewish comedies to which they were also indebted, screwball parodied them. As Jaffe, Barrymore, one of the greatest actors of stage and screen, appears prematurely aged by drink and drugs into a vision of decadence, with his beautiful ruined profile, to ham up the melodrama and sentiment of the parts that brought him fame.

At the moment when Jaffe congratulates Lily on her triumphant stage debut, he effuses, his voice dripping in emotion, 'The beauty and glamour that were mine for a little while during those rehearsals when you thought I was so cruel now belong to the world forever and ever more . . . Would you let me kiss you goodbye?' Becoming tearful as he kisses her, she suddenly clings to him, imploring in sympathy, 'Oscar don't leave me, I'm nothing without you'. She does not see what we do: his expression changes to impassive calculation, and the camera cuts to his foot as it discreetly closes the door behind them. He has got what he wanted. This is heterosexual love made into an absurd farce: a parody exposing the performative basis of the boy-meets-girl plots celebrated in any number of box-office smashes, including Barrymore's own. Sincerity has no currency here. Like the world conjured up by *Earnest*, ironic masks are all that exist. The true feelings of these characters are unknown. Perhaps there are no true feelings. In such a context, one shared by Lubitsch, death and love exist only at an ironic distance, where they do not signify any more than a bad review or an unflattering dress. Later, when Jaffe is abandoned by Lily, he becomes manic and paints over her name on the play posters; his colleagues watch with their arms folded, commenting only 'What's Rembrandt up to?' His threats of self-harm are dismissed by them: 'He wouldn't kill himself, it'd please too many people.' The lines are not Wildean but the attitude is. Hecht had been cultivating it since 1915 and a culture familiar with *Earnest* had no problem getting the message. It would be hard to watch those hackneyed emotional tropes unironically ever again.

The negligee scene comes at the climax of David's humiliations in *Bringing Up Baby*. This scene understands the irony and insincerities of Barrymore's performance in *Twentieth Century*, for both films were directed by Howard Hawks. As their lives become entangled in increasingly anarchic ways, David's attempts to get away from Susan are thwarted by the energy of her playful deceptions. Her actions draw him and everyone around her into absurd situations, confusions, and assorted indignities that far outstrip those in the short story on which it was based.[88] *Bringing Up Baby* was a box-office flop on its first release, and according to its director Howard Hawks its anarchism was to blame. Years later in an interview with Peter Bogdanovich, he said:

> I think the picture had a great fault and I learned an awful lot from that. There were no normal people in it. Everyone you met was a screwball and since that time I have learned my lesson and I don't intend ever again to make everybody crazy. If the gardener had been normal, if the sheriff had been just a perplexed man from the country—but as it was they were all way off center. It was a mistake I realized after I'd made it and I haven't made it since.[89]

Hawks may not be sincere; *Twentieth Century* has 'no normal people in it' either. This quibble aside, the 'fault' of *Bringing Up Baby* exemplifies a culture that had been suffused with the Wildean. Through those am-dram productions and cheap editions, with the persona of the queer and the high-profile epigrammatic wit of Bankhead and others, Wilde's comedy had become widely identified with sophistication, fun, and salacious naughtiness. Like *Earnest*, *Bringing Up Baby* has no moral centre. The film jettisons a moral order, even a revised one. At the beginning, the film's universe is centred on patriarchy and serious study. We are left instead, at the end, with matriarchy, chaos, and fun. More importantly, David realizes that he loves Susan for her enormous capacity for deception and her relentless humiliation of him—even as she accidentally destroys the brontosaurus skeleton which it was his life's work to complete. The film ends with them sitting on the scaffolding above a heap of its bones. The world of play ushered into being is never brought to heel.

Bringing Up Baby shows that the Wildean Universe would be cinematic in ways that Wilde could not have dreamt of. Not only the negligee, but Baby the Leopard, the loon mating calls, and the hilarious imprisonment of the lead characters revivify the connection between decadence and slapstick first made by Carl Van Vechten's novel *Spider Boy*. The pratfalls, chases, and comedy animals remind us that decadence shares in the dream of slapstick comedy: its anarchism, rebellion, and insouciance in the rejection of conventional behaviour. Moreover, slapstick imbues such a rejection with unbridled fun—and it's fun that is the keynote. Grant was the perfect star to bring such free play to life. He'd learnt stilt-walking, pratfalls, and gymnastics in music hall and vaudeville, giving him a singular facility with slapstick among Hollywood's leading men.[90] His persona married slapstick to the possibility of sexual anarchy. His mid-Atlantic accent, exaggerated good manners and wit conjured up something of the 'queer' persona that had emerged in 1920s New York even before he put on that feather-trimmed negligee, while persistent gossip about his relationship with Randolph Scott added to the uncertain effect.[91]

When film critics have termed screwball comedy 'Wildean', that's because no other term fully captures its atmosphere. We find this Wildeanism or Wilde-ish spirit in George Cukor's classic society comedies—*The Women* (1939), say—which place Wildean techniques of impersonation, punning, connotative play, and farce to indicate the absurd conventions of heterosexual courtship in which romance is performative, while teasingly suggesting a lesbian relationship between two of the central figures.[92] Of course there were other influences on screwball, but none do what Wilde does with morality. It is only in a Wildean Universe that *The Awful Truth* can celebrate deception as the centre of a heterosexual relationship. Married couple Jerry (Grant, again) and Lucy (Irene Dunne) separate when each is caught out in a lie and they suspect each other of adultery. Truth has limited currency here. 'There's nothing less logical than the truth', Lucy declares at the outset, recalling Algernon's comment that 'The truth is rarely plain and never simple.'[93] It's an idea that radiates through the movie as it does through *Earnest*, implicating Wildean disagreements over the nature of truth and frequent funny lies, while reminding us of the deceptions that provide a happy ending in *Lady Windermere*. This is a film without a moral compass. No figure represents morality. When such qualities as duty, dignity, and responsibility appear—which they frequently do—they are made to look ludicrous. It is never revealed to the characters or the audience whether Lucy and Jerry were really having affairs with other people, and within the logic of the film it doesn't matter: when they reconcile for the film's happy ending, it is on the basis that they have fun together regardless of—or even because of—their indiscretions. So *The Awful Truth* reminds us that screwball comedy is not romantic comedy. It is too cynical, too ironic about that possibility of monogamous, heteronormative happiness. Produced during the worst years of the Depression, screwballs like *The Awful Truth* offered escapism from such dull norms, offering a possibility to remake the world according to one's own values, in what for most viewers was a fantasy world of drawing rooms and grand pianos, walk-in wardrobes and black-tie dinners.

* * *

Meanwhile, Wilde's plays were beginning to receive a more hostile reception in Manhattan. A major revival of *Earnest* at the Vanderbilt Theatre, New York, in 1939 was roundly criticized for being too dated. 'You cannot help admiring the brilliance of some of the results,' a review from the *New York Post* noted, before continuing with an increasingly familiar refrain; 'Yet you soon get heartily sick of the trick. You find yourself resenting the emptiness of the writing. You begin to feel as if you had lived on a diet of truffles for a month.'[94] For every New York critic who found Wilde fresh and funny, there was another who found his plays dated, stagey, slow, and sentimental. A review of *Lady Windermere* onstage sums up the general tone: '1932 people indulging in eighteen-ninety sentiments and sentimentality are neither believable nor worth paying to listen to.'[95] At first glance these responses to Wilde look a little ironic given his role in screwball dialogue. Really, they are all too understandable. Wilde's wit does sound ponderous alongside the agile exchanges emerging on-screen. In a decade where comedy was almost invariably set in a glitzy version of contemporary America, there were no new US screen adaptations of Wilde's society plays, despite their recent and widespread popularity and the opportunities of synchronic sound. As we know, there were other reasons for this: the ongoing dispute between Daniel Frohman and the Wilde Estate that scuppered Warner Brothers' *Lady Windermere*. But perhaps it's just as well there were not more adaptations. The epigram was moving on beyond its master, leaving his plays looking old-fashioned by comparison.

7

The Aesthete as Monster

On 10 October 1938, Leslie and Sewell Stokes' acclaimed play *Oscar Wilde* transferred from London to Broadway with Robert Morley in the title role. The Stokes' representation of Wilde's sexuality was shocking. Their play's depiction of his life after prison would help mythologize him for decades after as a tragic genius with a fatal flaw, whose last years were miserable and drunken. Like *Salome* in 1892, *Oscar Wilde* was not granted a licence for public performance by the Lord Chamberlain's Office in London. Instead, it was first performed in the United Kingdom at the Gate Theatre Studio, a private theatre club in Soho.[1] On Broadway, it was a critical and commercial success, bringing Wilde himself back to the forefront of public consciousness, even as his social comedies were fading from popularity.

The New York notices attracted the attention of a young would-be actor called Laird Cregar, living in his car in Los Angeles. Cregar is all but forgotten today; his career was all too brief. But on 22 April 1940, due to his persistence, *Oscar Wilde* opened at the legendary El Capitan Theatre on Hollywood Boulevard, to an audience largely comprising movie people. It was produced on a shoestring budget put together by Cregar and screenwriter Charles O'Neil. Cregar himself took the dream role of Wilde.[2] The plot centred on the trials, using texts from the court transcripts to draw Wilde as a brilliant man, fatally flawed by compulsive indiscretions and hubris. Audiences watched Wilde flirt with much younger men in private at the height of his fame before he defended 'the love that dare not speak its name' from the witness box.[3] Cregar's imposing stage presence as a tall, 300-pound, reportedly bisexual man, was held in tension with his at-times emotional performance to embody Wilde as he had not been seen before.

Today his star turn would likely look melodramatic and excessively sentimental.[4] However, as the curtain went down on opening night, the audience's reception was rapturous:

> It was as if the audience at the El Capitan had witnessed an unholy miracle. Oscar Wilde's ghost had risen from his angel-with-phallus-decorated grave in Paris, taking possession of a 26-year-old L.A. vagrant and happily

Wilde in the Dream Factory. Kate Hext, Oxford University Press. © Kate Hext (2024).
DOI: 10.1093/9780191987335.003.0007

serving as the 'bludgeon' he'd needed to strike Hollywood right between the eyes. The opening night audience stood and cheered, a thunderous reception reported as 'unbelievable' and 'extravagant.'[5]

The notices were laudatory. Among them, a headline in the *Los Angeles Daily News* ran, 'LAIRD CREGAR, A NEW STAR, EMERGES IN OSCAR WILDE.'[6] The *Los Angeles Examiner* rhapsodized, 'Laird Cregar gives one of the best performances I have seen on the coast. He IS Oscar Wilde.'[7] John Barrymore, who met Wilde and had been cast as Dorian Gray, was among those who attended in the opening weeks.[8] Soon, *Screenland* reported, 'all of Hollywood was talking about the astounding man who was bringing Oscar Wilde to life nightly at El Capitan Theatre. It was considered downright illiterate not to have seen the play at least once. Everybody at 20th Century-Fox saw it several times.'[9]

The way *Oscar Wilde* brought its eponymous figure's transgressions back into the foreground was not to everyone's taste. Having seen it, Spencer Tracy told Ed Sullivan that he 'felt sort of unclean, because to a normal person the topic is almost obscene.'[10] He illustrates a background hum of critical opprobrium about Wilde that was growing a little louder in the 1940s. Delight in Wilde's naughtiness had made up for much in the 1910s and 1920s, when he felt practically like a contemporary misfit. While such delight waned, the opprobrium remained. In New York, books on Wilde were published in greater numbers, from the first account of the tour, *Oscar Wilde Discovers America [1882]* by Lloyd Lewis and Henry Justin Smith (1936) and Frances Winwar's study *Oscar Wilde and the Yellow' Nineties* (1940), to Edouard Roditi's moralistic *Oscar Wilde* (1947). However, *The Atlantic* condemned Winwar's study for focusing on a subject 'such has no serious person would wish to examine, still less recall, still less to dwell upon [. . .] the courses of squalid delinquency almost subhuman.'[11]

Vocal hostility to Wilde does not obscure the fact that the Stokes' play begins the next chapter of his afterlife in Anglo-American culture. It was the basis for one of two 1960 films on Wilde's life, beginning a slow turning point that would see him transcend his published writings as a countercultural icon and superstar. That's looking ahead, though. For our purposes, *Oscar Wilde* marks a different turning point in Wilde's influence. It is one in which sexual transgression comes together with the epigrammatic dandy in a new kind of monster and homme fatal. In this turn, the moralistic currents of the era matter because they shape a darker Wilde than that seen on-screen before.

Cregar's stage performance made him famous overnight but, when he was signed by Twentieth Century Fox, having got their attention at El Capitan, his association with Wilde became a liability. He was directed away from the kind of leading-man roles he really wanted. Like Roscoe Arbuckle and Charles Laughton before him but worse, his size—noted in reviews as making him resemble Wilde—was refigured as an unmanly and sinister threat. He was typecast as a corrupted detective and stalker in *I Wake Up Scream-ing* (1941); a sexually twisted murderer in the title role of *The Lodger* (1944) (Fig. 7.1); and a murderous pianist in *Hangover Square* (1945). These are Cregar's most famous films and in all of them he stars as men leading double lives: outwardly respectable and talented in the daytime, at night they creep through the backstreets committing terrible acts. So Cregar made his name onstage as one brilliant man leading a double life; now on-screen he played others: clandestine criminals with a hint, or more than a hint, of sexual per-version. Unsurprisingly, his association with Wilde persisted and, before his untimely death in December 1944, he was in the frame to star as Lord Henry in Albert Lewin's adaptation of *The Picture of Dorian Gray* (1945).[12]

In the broader cultural context of late 1930s and 1940s America, Cregar's typecasting as a violent, sinister criminal was all too predictable. Amid a 'homosexual panic' and defensive assertions about the manliness of men of the 1930s and 1940s, disguised depictions of gay men were everywhere.[13] Very few, if any, were triumphant like the title figure of *Oscar Wilde*. Its

Fig. 7.1 Laird Cregar, starring as the eponymous Lodger, creeps in the East End backstreets (1944)

revivification of connections between Wilde, criminality, and sex between men was timely and dangerous. Maybe that's why Spencer Tracy felt so sullied. Was Cregar's Wilde too affirmative and sympathetic in a culture than contained more Tracys than Nazimovas? From the former point of view, Wilde's triumph onstage was an aberration: a witty and defiant gay man hitting back against the system, even though this system ultimately breaks him like a butterfly on the wheel. Strictly speaking, gay characters could not appear on-screen due to the Production Code, but Vito Rosso shows how 'they continued to emerge in this period as subtextual phantoms representing the very fear of homosexuality'.[14] In other words, they were—to borrow from *The Atlantic* review above—'almost subhuman': monstrous queers, appearing in B-movie horrors and films noirs, whose very being served to underline the danger of desire between men. We have traced the influence of decadence on the movies from 'fantastic crime', as Pater called it, to Dorian Gray and Raffles, and through to the high-octane gangsters of the early 1930s. Their crimes could be fatal and serious. Only now, though, did the decadent's criminality mutate into a very real threat to America.

Oscar Wilde, Queer Monster

In the 1930s, B-movie horrors showed the disturbing underside of the cosmopolitan and sexually liberal values of the screwball comedy. Before he ever took to the stage, it was in these films that Cregar's typecasting became almost inevitable. For, in the enveloping doom that is the stock-in-trade of the horror film, the very same qualities that caused laughter in the screwball star were integral to the violent threat of the monstrous queer: verbal wit, a camp manner, dapper dress sense, cavalier attitude to truth, and ultimate absurdity. The urban sophisticates of *Bringing Up Baby* and *The Awful Truth* played with witty repartee, double lives, and dandified sexual ambiguity for laughs. Repackaged in a gothic set with a score by Franz Waxman, though, such characteristics became sinister. Or, encapsulated in an image, Cary Grant in a negligee is one person's idea of a joke but another's idea of an aberration. Is that why, when Grant was cast against type as a witty but deceptive and potentially homicidal husband in *Suspicion* (1941), it was not as shocking as it should have been? That Grant, too, screwball's most charismatic star, could have within him the potential to do truly terrible things was all too believable. While screwball comedy remained a popular genre into the early 1940s, the shadow of horror loomed. In *Arsenic and Old*

Lace (1944) a newly married man—Grant again—discovers that his elderly aunts are serial murderers and ends up unwittingly involved in covering up murder.

Wilde and *Dorian Gray* are part of the origin myth for Hollywood's queer monsters.[15] Harry M. Benshoff puts that Wilde's novel created 'the quintessential imagery of the monster queer—that of a sexually active and attractive young man who possesses some terrible secret which must perforce be locked away in a hidden closet'.[16] He goes on to suggest that the end of Wilde's life in exile and decline established the image of 'the pathetic and slightly sinister homosexual dandy'.[17] How far we can take this argument? Benshoff doesn't trace the evolution from Wilde to Hollywood and, by the 1930s, the influence is diffused and mixed up with other queer monsters from the fin de siècle. A potential genealogy is evidenced in my preceding pages, as they work through the homoeroticism of Dorian's cross-dressed kiss with Sybil in Thanhouser's adaptation (1915) and the camp fashioning of Dorian in the German *Das Bildnis des Dorian Gray* (1917); the addition of a Lord Henry figure with Wilde's dialogue in the adaptation of *Dr Jekyll and Mr Hyde* (1920); Bela Lugosi's early role as Lord Henry in the Hungarian adaptation of *Dorian Gray* (1917) before he emigrated to the United States and made the role of Dracula his own in 1931. When 'art for art's sake' comes to underpin the screen gangster's criminal motivations and epigrams evolve into screwball comedy, the horrific possibilities are in kept in abeyance, but they never go away.

The rise of the horror flic brings this potential back with full force. Here, disaggregated aspects of Wilde's popular persona and characters are brought together in a mythology of the monster, punctuated by direct references to Wilde and Beardsley. In the pre-Production Code talkie, *The Old Dark House* (1932), directed by James Whale, Ernest Thesiger's homicidal character, Horace Femm, brings together the era's dominant ideas of gay men: a dandified appearance, effeminate behaviour, witty dialogue, and European accent.[18] The plot is little more complex than the title. A group of Americans get stranded at an old dark house in Europe, where they are at the mercy of its oddly hospitable inhabitants, Femm and his sister. Femm was such a hit that Thesiger appeared as the very similar Septimus Pretorius in *Bride of Frankenstein* (1935). His monster queers are far from the young and nubile Dorian Gray. They are   illustrating Benshoff's point—elderly and emasculated, in Victorian costume, like period relics. Thesiger had learnt from the master. Chapter 4 noted that in his early career he starred in several productions of *Lady Windermere's Fan* and *The Importance of Being Earnest.*

These included playing Algernon in a West End production described by Robert Ross as 'the best performance of that play that he had ever seen'.[19] In *Lady Windermere*, he made the role of Charles Dumby his own, taking it on several times between 1911 and 1930, including in one version he also produced.[20] Thesiger's association with the afterglow of decadence also included performing the role of Master of Ceremonies on the opening night of the Cave of the Golden Calf, the Mayfair nightclub where 'the cult of Wilde could continue to worship' with murals based on Russian ballet, ragtime music, and recitations of Wilde's stories, among its various broadly decadent charms.[21] The characters of Femm and Pretorius are no less than the flip side of Thesiger's onstage dandies. Their effeminate attention to sartorial correctness and 'manners over morals!' now becomes menacing.[22]

The link between Wilde and monstrous desire is explicit in *Mad Love* (1935). When the homicidal Dr Gogol (Peter Lorre) imprisons the object of his obsessive love, Yvonne (Frances Drake), voices in his head repeat: 'Each man kills the thing he loves.' For Dr Gogol, this lamentation from Wilde's *Ballad of Reading Gaol* becomes a recommendation. At this horrific climax, his eyes fix on her, suddenly possessed by a plan, and he advances reciting the *Ballad* aloud. Never mind that his obsession is with a woman; homosexuality was rolled in with other forms of perversity in Hollywood, as in broader 1930s' American culture.[23] The effect is to reify Wilde's role as an originator—*the* originator—of sexual deviancy, with his murderous threat to the innocent coded in epigrams. For audiences familiar with the epigrammatic dandy and Wilde's society comedies it makes sense and may have been part of a larger sensationalization of the phrase in popular culture. After all, 'The Trials of Oscar Wilde' had featured on the first cover story of pulp magazine *Courtroom Stories* in 1931.[24] Dr Gogol, Femm, and *Courtroom Stories* marked a repositioning of Wilde as a cartoonish grotesque that could be dismissed because he was more funny than scary, now safely sequestered in the remote past, in Europe.

Dr Gogol is also a reminder. In the Preface I mentioned that *The Greatest Show on Earth* features Buttons the clown, played by James Stewart, on the run after the murder of his wife, which he protests was a mercy killing. Close to capture, as he stands outside the big top, he utters: 'Each man kills the thing he loves.' We will never know whether this is a deliberate intertextual reference to Dr Gogol as well as Wilde. It could have been because the script doctor brought in to improve this, Cecil B. DeMille's last, film was none other than Hollywood's most prolific screenwriter and new-decadent novelist Ben Hecht. These allusions would certainly make the film—often cited as the worst winner of the Best Picture Oscar—more interesting, with the line's conflicting resonances in Wilde's original poem and Hollywood horror, inviting the viewer who gets both references to question Buttons's self-serving account of why he killed his wife.

Elsewhere, broader decadent aesthetics influenced B-movie horrors. *The Black Cat* (1934), loosely based on Edgar Allan Poe's short story of the same name, borrows Aubrey Beardsley's style to underline the monstrous sexuality of its villain. A young couple travelling in Europe become stranded at the mountaintop house of a mad scientist (Boris Karloff) with the former friend (Bela Lugosi) he has not seen since the war, and who wants vengeance for the mysterious disappearance of his wife. As these old foes are brought back together, the former friend is increasingly affected by the presence of his host's strange black cat, which comes to signify an evil presence in the house. According to the director and co-writer Edgar Ulmer, the artistic inspiration for *The Black Cat* was not really Poe's short story but Beardsley's 1894 illustrations for it (Fig. 7.2).[25] Remember, during the 'Vogue of Beardsley' his style influenced a number of high-profile illustrators.[26] While *Vanity Fair*'s Ralph Barton had translated Beardsley's minimal witty lines into caricature, Ulmer takes Beardsley's grotesque contortions of curve and proportion and turns them into horror. Ulmer creates two-tone tableaux like Beardsley's woodcuts, dramatizing large black shapes next to expanses of white space, divided by clean, minimalist lines. The solid black cat appears repeatedly in sharp menacing silhouette against a white wall. Such stark images reinforce Ulmer's intention that, in his words, the Karloff and Lugosi characters should appear 'as aberrant as possible. A stable of misfits, members of the decadent aristocracy of the countryside'.[27]

Wilde's ghost-like presence in American culture again metamorphoses into a creative force. It does so in a very different way to what we saw in comedy: screwball unleashed the decadent's epigrams and transformed them into the quintessential American voice of moral insouciance. Horror had wit, but it was a genre that dealt in moral absolutes. In its dichotomy between good and evil, it was clear which side Wilde, decadence, and everything associated with them was on. And what was that *everything*? Sex of course. Sex alone was bad enough but the queer monster's Wildean characteristics suggested perversion and its association with violent danger. Coming at the end of this decade-long association between horror, decadence, and the queer, it's hardly surprising that Cregar's stage role as Wilde—*the* fatally flawed, sexually deviant man who originated monster queer myth on-screen—saw him typecast as a murderous villain.

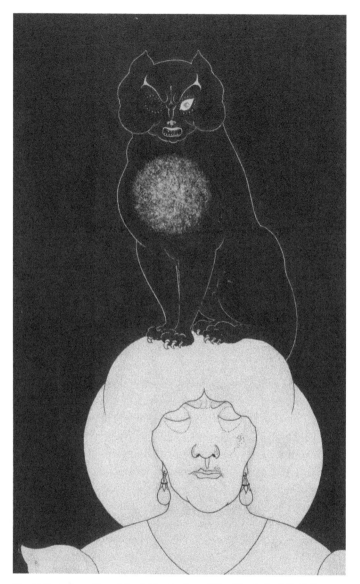

Fig. 7.2 Aubrey Beardsley's illustration, 'The Black Cat' (1894)

Decades later, James Whale's decadent heritage as director of *The Old Dark House* and *Bride of Frankenstein* became central to the fantasy biopic *Gods and Monsters* (1998).[28] The film's plot is premised on a master–disciple relationship between the elderly Whale (Ian McKellen) and his young, working-class gardener (Brendan Fraser). Borrowing the dynamic between Basil Hallward and Dorian for this central relationship and using motifs from Wilde's novel, intermingled with the image of Frankenstein, *Gods and Monsters* dramatizes the question of whether the gardener would ultimately harm the friend who loves him, but with a very different ending. The monster is redeemed.

Laura, The Big Sleep, and *A Double Life*

With the rise of film noir in the 1940s, the moral landscape becomes more muddled than B-movie horror allowed. As James Naremore writes, the noir audience watches on, disorientated because they can no longer fully distinguish between good and evil.[29] In this genre—a hybrid of crime thrillers, horrors, and gothic romances, filtered through the visual aesthetics of German expressionism—the queer monster evolves into the homme fatal. He has returned from the exotically European settings of the horror flick, and is indeed more menacing in a lounge suit, sipping cocktails in Manhattan. Like the B-movie monster he is physically vulnerable and sexually suspect, fatally prone to hubris. In common with the femme fatale, too, he has a mysterious allure and erotic fatality, which masks his secret threat.[30]

Just such a figure is at the centre of *Laura* (1944). Based on the novel by Vera Caspary, the movie focuses on the murder of eponymous socialite and career woman Laura (Gene Tierney). As Detective Mark McPherson (Dana Andrews) investigates her relationship with Svengali-figure Waldo Lydecker (Clifton Webb), the mystery of her murder becomes indistinguishable from the mystery of her identity and McPherson's growing obsession with her. Its primary screenwriter was Samuel Hoffenstein, one-time decadent poet and screen adaptor of 'Lord Arthur Savile's Crime' in *Flesh and Fantasy*. In *Laura*, he turns once again to Wilde: having been brought in to overhaul the first draft of the script, his main contribution was to recreate the character of Waldo around Clifton Webb.[31] He turned Waldo from Caspary's more marginal would-be hero and romantic fantasist into an older effeminate aesthete, whose amorality ultimately leads him to murder without compunction. Waldo's bons mots, which do not appear in Caspary's novel, put him in contrast with the straight-talking police detective hero. 'You seem to be completely disregarding something more important than your career,' he quips to Laura: 'my lunch.' Elsewhere, 'In my case self-absorption is completely justified. I have never discovered any other subject quite so worthy of my attention', and again, 'I'm not kind, I'm vicious. It's the secret of my charm'. In another departure from the novel, Waldo first appears in a Romanesque marble bath next to a leopard-skin chair and proceeds to dress in dandyish attire, complete with a cane and buttonhole.[32]

Waldo's epigrammatic wit and taste for decadent living is our giveaway that he is the villain. He is leading a double life as a murderer as well as a man of culture. Like Thesiger, Webb had form as a dandy leading a double life. In 1939 he starred as John Worthing in the badly reviewed *Ernest* on Broadway, noted in Chapter 6.[33] Jack is, of course, 'Jack' when he is in the country and 'Ernest' in town.[34] For, as he explains to Algernon, 'a high moral tone can hardly be said to conduce very much to either one's health or happiness'.[35] Jack's voice resonates through Webb's insouciant delivery of Waldo's epigrams, while his prioritization of lunch over Laura's career reminds us of the way that Jack snaffles cucumber sandwiches and bread and butter, when Algernon tries to discuss the serious matter of Gwendolen.[36] The difference is that Waldo is a real louse. He is the kind of man Jack might become thirty years on, still with a taste for only the very best, but with his patter grown hackneyed and his moral subjectivism having taken him far into the kind of debauchery that is little more than an amusing possibility in Wilde's play.

Realizing that he will never possess Laura, Waldo murders a woman he has mistaken for her and later attempts to discredit Detective McPherson. Then, in another departure from Caspary's novel, he creeps into Laura's apartment in a second murder attempt. Here, at the film's climax, decadent poetry makes a dramatic appearance. She is listening to Waldo on the radio, in a pre-record, reading Ernest Dowson's poem, 'Vitae Summa Brevis Spem Nos Vetat Incohare Longam' (1896). He is shown in an extreme low-angle shot loading a rifle as it begins:

> They are not long, the weeping and the laughter,
> Love and desire and hate:
> I think they have no portion in us after
> We pass the gate.

The shadow of death that was always integral to decadent sensibility is here a literary corollary to noir murder. He intends to kill them both—but he doesn't of course. Laura overpowers him in her bedroom and McPherson arrives just in time to save her, while another cop shoots Waldo dead and the movie ends.

The Big Sleep (1946) incorporates Wilde and decadence into its male protagonist in more morally complicated ways. Based on Raymond Chandler's 1939 novel, with a screenplay by William Faulkner, its Philip Marlowe (Humphrey Bogart) is at the centre of a confused moral landscape.[37] The ill and elderly General Sternwood (Charles Waldron) sets off the film's chain of murder, seduction, and partial revelation when Marlowe comes to his house to discuss a private investigation.[38] 'You are looking, sir, at a very dull survival of a very gaudy life', Sternwood tells private eye Marlowe, from his wheelchair. The scene is set in Sternwood's orchid-filled hothouse as per Faulkner's stage directions:

[Shot] 7. GREENHOUSE CHOKED WITH ORCHID PLANTS

Marlowe, following Norris between the crowding tendrils and branches. The place is oven-hot, damp with sweat, green with gloom. Marlowe is already reacting to it, is already mopping his face with his handkerchief.

[Shot] 8. MED. CLOSE SHOT—GENERAL STERNWOOD

In a wheelchair in the center of the greenhouse, in a cleared space about which the plants crowd and hover.[39]

These personifying descriptions intensify the claustrophobic hothouse flowers in Chandler's original scene.[40] The perfume of orchids, Sternwood comments, 'has the rotten sweetness of corruption' and he embodies this himself. Orchids encode overindulgence and sexual perversion, unspeakable in the Production Code era. They emasculate him, linking him and the wild behaviour of his daughters with an excessive and lascivious past. How exactly? The decadent movement brought orchids and exoticism together with carnal perversity and death through their overwhelming scent.[41] Lord Henry comments that the orchid is 'a marvellous spotted thing, as effective as the seven deadly sins', before Dorian's near collapse in a hothouse, a metaphor for his self-destructive pursuit of exotic aesthetics and erotic experiences.[42] Chandler and Faulkner know what they are doing with Sternwood's orchids. Faulkner cut his teeth at University of Mississippi doing Beardsley-style illustrations and in his novel *Absalom, Absalom!* (1937), when Bon's ultimately devastating heritage becomes apparent, he is described as 'an elegant and indolent esoteric hothouse bloom'.[43]

Chandler was familiar with Wilde's epigrams and life story too.[44] In the novel's hothouse scene used by Faulkner Marlowe's alpha masculinity is set in contrast with Sternwood's effeminacy by an allusion to Wilde himself:

STERNWOOD: You didn't like working for Mr. Wilde?
MARLOWE: I was fired for insubordination. I seem to rate pretty high on that.[45]

This mention of 'Wilde' is a little in-joke of the kind Chandler likes to make. Of course Marlowe would not like working for Mr Wilde and his statement to this effect distances him from the suggestion of homosexuality imbued in the name.[46] It's another example of how the scaffolding of decadence is dismantled to create modernism. For Faulkner transferred Chandler's knowing lines to his (equally knowing) draft script but they were later cut by Jules Furthman, who refocused its dialogue on the sexual energy between Bogart and Lauren Bacall (playing Vivian Sternwood).[47] In the final cut, the sharp-suited, hard-boiled Marlowe is still the antithesis of the famous Wilde and the overwhelming sensuality of the hothouse. His 'Mr Wilde' is not mentioned but, pacing back and forth, sweating and uncomfortable, talking with Sternwood, Marlowe reveals he doesn't like orchids. 'I hate them', he states, with odd decisiveness for a man who doesn't look like he'd give much thought to ornamental flowers.

Marlowe cannot be contained within the perfumed, effeminate atmosphere of the hothouse just as he could never be happy working for Mr Wilde. He is, though, Wildean in a different and covert way. His dialogue features paradoxes, bons mots, one-liners, and wisecracks structured like Wilde's epigrams, as a binary that undermines conventional moral sentiment. It was during the Wilde trials that 'the epigram becomes the tool par excellence of an oppositional masculinity'.[48] For Marlowe, as for Wilde, epigrammatic speech signifies charisma, intellectual superiority, and—crucially—an opposition to socially acceptable forms of masculinity, like the white-collar worker or the husband.[49] Only, the straight, hard-boiled private eye takes Wildean wit from homosexual characters and makes it into a defining feature of heterosexual manliness.[50] He reinscribes epigrammatic wit as a quality of urban modernity and heterosexual seduction, framed with a 'concrete efficacy' that makes speech his most effective weapon.[51] Max Beerbohm said that Wilde used 'style like a silver dagger'.[52] Marlowe calls attention to the fact that Wilde's verbal wounds are inflicted more like silver bullets. His epigrammatic wit is discharged with accuracy and without need of force, while the assailant retains a cool distance.

This dialogue is accompanied by Marlowe's flâneur-like mastery of LA night-time streets. On these streets, the plot spans out from the hothouse and, with crime after crime, reveals 'a wider corruption that is too deep to be eradicated, infamously ending with an unsolved murder'.[53] David Thompson suggests somewhat uncertainly that 'The Big Sleep abandons story and genre as easily as one of its girls stepping out of her clothes . . . There's a prospect of decadence in that, I think'.[54] There is certainly a prospect of decadence in The Big Sleep and one that is at least as vital as its relationship with literary modernism. Noir and modernism developed in tandem, both underpinned by a critique of Enlightenment rationalism, industrial technology, and social democracy.[55] However, the restless pleasure-seeking and ennui of decadence are also integral to The Big Sleep and films noirs more broadly. In the middle of the plot's spiralling complexities, the repartee between Marlowe and Vivian arrests the conventional forward-driven narrative of the crime thriller. This instead becomes a film about smart talk, in which verbal play for its own sake is reproduced in the erotic desires that it brings into being. The temporal logic of the plot is decadent, defined by its denial of futurity, driven by the pleasure of repartee and inexorable death.[56] Resolution of the plot or the crime at its centre becomes secondary, even forgotten.

In a different sense too, decadence was becoming unbounded. The definition of 'decadence' in literature and the arts was always vexed. Now it was losing its identity in other traditions and new currents. The figure of the decadent was integral to the menace and charm of the male leads in The Big Sleep and Laura, but Wilde has no immediately obvious connection with either. They signal that, in the end, the only way to be true to Wilde is to take him in vain, making his style and dandies the genesis of new forms. Anyway, Wilde's plots and misfits had modern aspects but by the 1940s their Victorian foundations creaked too. To recapture their modernity, adaptations would have to be bold and experimental. The conventions of Hollywood adaptation in the 1940s were not up to the task, or even interested in it. Instead, Wilde's stories were put into period costumes as measured against, and in service of, an uncertain present following US entry to the Second World War.

Hollywood was at the forefront in making a case for this distant-seeming conflict. Between 1942 and 1945, it produced sixty-eight films set in Allied countries, with the trend peaking in 1943, the year in which Mrs Miniver won the Oscar for Best Picture.[57] These films portrayed Great Britain as sympathetic and quaint. Adaptations of Wilde's works followed suit. The

Canterville Ghost (1944) took the direction of heritage cinema that would define it for a couple of decades. Based on his 1887 short story of the same name, the movie fully exploits Wilde's comic contrast between the historic Canterville Chase, in England, and its new American inhabitants, as Sir Simon (Charles Laughton), a ghost who has haunted the house for hundreds of years, makes mischief. *The Canterville Ghost* was perfect wartime entertainment, bringing together American and British stars in a warm story that showed off British history. It has an affected plummy voice-over and comic set pieces with Sir Simon, not to mention Margaret O'Brien's star turn as the young girl who befriends the ghost, now with the addition of American GIs stationed at the castle. It couldn't fail to be a commercial success, albeit of quite a different kind to those Wilde adaptations of the 1910s and 1920s. For its success was not fuelled by Wilde's name but by the star power of its actors, whose names appeared above the title with a photo of them together on the exhibition poster. Wilde is relegated to small text near the bottom.[58] Likewise, *The Fan*, mentioned in Chapter 4 mummifies *Lady Windermere* as a prestige drama, within a framing narrative of Second World War London. This is the city after the Blitz: the fan is being auctioned and Lord and Lady Windermere, we're told, were killed in the first air raids. When Mrs Erlynne (Madeleine Carroll) goes to Lord Darlington's (George Sanders's) house and finds it being used for the war effort, looking around in wonder, she reimagines how it looked in 1892. Now Darlington is, one of the workers tells her, 'practically a museum piece!' Mrs Erlynne is aghast. 'A museum piece?' She gasps, 'My dears, Lord Darlington was once the most dangerous man in London.' It is not only Darlington who is a museum piece; the adaptation treats Wilde's play in this way too.

American culture was changing, and if we look to *The Canterville Ghost* and *The Fan* instead of *The Big Sleep* and *Laura*, it appears that the excitement and threat posed by Wilde had been absorbed and neutralized. Even *Salome* was now safe. In *DuBarry was a Lady* (1943), an ambitious and ultimately unsuccessful musical starring Gene Kelly, Salome takes the guest spot in a standout number written by Roger Edens and E. Y. Harburg and performed by Virginia O'Brien, accompanied by Tommy Dorsey and his Orchestra:

> With seven veils
> She wowed the males
> And made the hall of fame,
> And this modern swinging stuff and thing

All dates back to this dame.
Salome was the grandma of them all,
She had the stuff that makes your motor stall.

Here, in mad comical lyrics, Salome's Dance of the Seven Veils is conceived as the origin of swing, reframed as bourgeois, with her striptease and
necrophilia euphemized away. The immediacy and raw sexiness of Irving
Berlin's 1909 lyrics for 'Sadie Salome Go Home' and its place in the music
hall are a distant memory.

This was a vision of the future. Wilde's position in culture was to go on
shifting in this direction for a while yet. Meanwhile, though, it was a suave
English dandy, Ronald Colman, who would bring the real embodied threat
of sexual transgression à la Wilde back full circle to meet Wilde's social
comedies. Twenty-two years after his career-defining role as Lord Darlington in Lubitsch's *Lady Windermere*, Colman won the Oscar for Best Actor
in George Cukor's noir thriller *A Double Life* (1947).[59] Anthony John (Colman) is a successful stage actor and loving husband, who is secretly unable to
distinguish between his roles and his own life. As he becomes immersed in
rehearsals for *Othello*, he embarks on a double life, acting on his necrophiliac
fantasies of murdering women. As it turns out, then, Darlington was still 'the
most dangerous man in London'. The double life had been a defining interest of American cinema since the silent era: this common theme brought
Dorian Gray together with *Dr Jekyll and Mr Hyde* in 1920. And it is another
great tale of a double life—that at the centre of *Earnest*—that frames John's
descent into madness. A large poster for a fictional production of *Earnest*,
starring John, hangs in his agent's office as they discuss whether he will take
the ill-fated role of *Othello*. Wilde's play becomes a leitmotif for the secret life
that he begins, one that subverts all the fun of *Earnest*'s 'Bunburying' into
a sexually perverted fantasy of being one person at home and quite another
elsewhere.

Dorian Gray Turned Noir

When Dorian appeared on the American screen for the first time in
thirty years in *The Picture of Dorian Gray* (1945), he would have been at
home in the company of Waldo Lydeker or General Sternwood in his party
days. He would, given the chance, hang out in alleyways with Anthony John.
In short, he was an *homme fatal* shaped by the emerging conventions of

film noir. Rereading Wilde's novel through this MGM's big-budget adaptation, and in the context of the 1915 Thanhouser version, we realize, though, that Dorian always was a film-noir homme fatal really, and *Dorian Gray* was always a crime thriller.

The screenwriter, director, and producer of this *Dorian Gray*, Albert Lewin, was no ordinary Hollywood film-maker. Even at a time when the movie industry comprised people from very diverse professional backgrounds, university professors were few. Lewin had studied English literature at New York University, Harvard, and Columbia, before teaching literature at the University of Missouri. Then he moved to Hollywood.[60] His *Dorian Gray* was solidly rooted in the source novel, using substantial sections of Wilde's dialogue, as might be expected from a literature professor. There were changes that seem to straighten Wilde's novel into the mould of a prestige realist melodrama.[61] Gladys (Donna Reed) becomes a major character and Dorian's love interest, while David (Peter Lawford), her would-be suitor, puts heterosexual desire at the centre of the plot. It was also shot in black and white, which was commonly associated with realism, in contrast with the camp 'fantasy and spectacle' of 1940s Technicolor.[62] One of the early screenplay drafts even retitled it *The Picture*, distancing it from Wilde's novel.[63]

The title was, though, changed back and, when we look closely, Lewin's *Dorian Gray* is not straight at all. Echoing reviews of Nazimova's *Salome*, a reviewer of *Dorian Gray* noted that 'pseudo-intellectuals' would notice 'the insinuations [. . .] and hidden wonders in Oscar Wilde', while others in the audience would be bored by the talking.[64] The figure of Dorian provides the first clue as to just how queer those 'insinuations' are and we'll come back to those. First, it's worth noting that, had Lewin had his way, Dorian would have been much queerer even than he appears. Lewin recalled how, years later. It began with an urgent and secretive phone call from the film's art director Cedric Gibbons, as the film prepared for pre-production:

Gibby was the only close friend of Greta Garbo around the studio, and he had been deputed to tell me that Garbo wanted to play Dorian. Indeed, it was the only role she would come back to the screen for. Of course, I moved heaven and earth to set it up. But everyone had a fit: the censorship problem, formidable anyway, would have become insurmountable with a woman.[65]

Had it been possible for Garbo to play Dorian, she would have followed female actor Varvara Yanova, who starred as a cross-dressed Dorian in the 1915 Russian adaptation of *Dorian Gray*. Closer to home, Garbo's ambition recalls the determination of her friend, Nazimova, with *Salome*. There had long been rumours about Garbo's sexuality, rumours that her roles did nothing to assuage. She didn't care. In the pre-Production Code film *Queen Christina* (1933) she played the title role as the rebel monarch, refusing to marry and performing a cross-dressed kiss with her maid. When she pitched to be the next Dorian, Garbo had not made a film since 1941, resisting all attempts to lure her back to the screen, so she must have really wanted that role. Russo reports that the full truth was even more deliciously shocking than Lewin's account: Garbo wanted to play Dorian opposite Marilyn Monroe as Sybil Vane.[66] It could never have happened. The strict Production Code would have ruled out the casting, and before the script got to that stage, the patriarchal head of MGM, Louis B. Mayer, would have scuppered it.[67]

It is striking that Lewin's response to Garbo was so enthusiastic. Exactly why, we cannot know. Could he see the artistic or commercial value of the casting? Did he see Dorian as queer? It might have been all three reasons or none. Still, his attitude is quite a contrast with the story of Samuel Goldwyn's decision to produce a movie based on Radclyffe Hall's *The Well of Loneliness* (1928). When told that the novel is about a lesbian, he retorted, 'So what? We'll make her an American.' As Russo notes, the story may be apocryphal and the film was never made. But the facts don't matter; the point is that it captures the spirit of a truth. Americanism and its cinema were presented as an anathema to lesbian and gay identity in the 1930s and 1940s, and so the latter could be 'laundered off the screen' in a fantasy of all-American heterosexual romance or made into something monstrous.[68]

Lewin did neither. His Dorian was to be sexually subversive, with or without Garbo. Hurd Hatfield was cast in the role. With discretion essential, Lewin signalled his defection from Hollywood's moral codes with subtlety, while fitting into the popular genres of its time. The carefully composed mise-en-scène is the first suggestion of its queer intents. For it transfers the catalogued descriptions of luxuriant objects featured in Wilde's novel to the screen. The screenplay's description of Basil's studio is typical:

> The studio opens upon an enclosed garden, visible through the huge window across which long tussore-silk curtains are stretched. Under the trees in the garden is a profusion of verdure. Long grass, lilac, rose, flowering

thorn, daisies, and laburnum. In a corner of the studio is a divan of Persian saddle-bags, in another corner a piano.[69]

Lewin's attention to detail here befits an English professor, incorporating objects that appear on Wilde's opening pages.[70] The accumulation of exotic and sensual objects fetishizes the mise-en-scène. On-screen, as the camera lingers in deep focus it operates like the novel's accumulation of descriptions to arrest the forward movement of the narrative. 'I got involved in making the picture exquisite,' Lewin remembered later; 'I went to town on every set-up.'[71] At the end of the first draft script, in a note apparently to himself, he even typed: '(It was with this quotation that the picture began. Now the design is complete.)'[72] It is indeed a highly wrought work of art.

Then there is Dorian's Picture itself, which arrests the narrative in a different, shocking way: irrepressibly and riotously over-the-top from its first alteration and through each of its six appearances in 'glorious Technicolor' that interrupts the black-and-white camera used for the rest of the movie. Artist Ivan Le Lorraine Albright expands the minimalist descriptions in Wilde's novel, which are repeated in Lewin's stage directions.[73] Its visual interruption indicates a more fundamental tension in the surface show of realism. When Dorian appears on the Technicolor canvas as a luridly multicoloured, disfigured monster he may evoke some of the emotions essential to the horror genre—shock, revulsion, fear—but the main effect of the grotesque image on the canvas is camp and comedic.

In *Laura* and *The Big Sleep*, the villain's effeminacy ultimately serves to reify the alpha-male leading man. *Dorian Gray* is different, with its title character at the centre of his own queer noir. His face becomes another of the objets d'art to fill Lewin's screen, appearing framed by archways, door frames, and mirrors.[74] There is something darker here too, in the way that Hatfield's Dorian brings together androgyny and clandestine danger. His blank illegible expressions, aquiline bone structure, and brooding looks led contemporary reviewers to liken him to a young Katharine Hepburn, Dracula, and even Dr Caligari.[75] He lures Sybil, Basil, and Alan to their deaths, and wrecks the life of Adrian and countless others. When Adrian appears in Bluegate Fields, in an enlarged role, he even recites several lines of Wilde's *Ballad of Reading Gaol*, implicating homoerotic desire in Dorian's misdemeanours.[76]

With homme fatal Dorian at its centre, *Dorian Gray* may begin as a prestige realist melodrama, but it soon becomes a crime thriller. The notorious Bluegate Fields in East London's Docklands is like a noir city, its streets unnavigable, disconnected, and in a state of architectural collapse, pictured in darkness and mist.[77] In the context of emerging noir thrillers, Lewin was pragmatic to bring this feature of Wilde's novel to the fore. Earlier we saw how Wilde's visual suggestions had been a source of cinematic inspiration, noting, for example, how the lighting descriptions in *Dorian Gray* are incorporated into the design for *Dr Jekyll and Mr Hyde* in 1920 and how Wilde's focus on eyes and seeing are made focal by editing techniques in Nazimova's *Salome* and Lubitsch's *Lady Windermere*. Lewin also works from Wilde's descriptions which, to his 1940s' view, anticipate the noir city and its chiaroscuro lighting.[78]

On the night of Basil's (Lowell Gilmore's) murder, the noir shadows reach beyond the Docklands to take over West London and the movie itself. Lewin's rescripting between 1943 and 1945 moves the fateful meeting between Basil and Dorian from the last third of the plot to the middle. Taking its cue again from Wilde, who writes that '[t]he lamp-light struggled out through the fog' that night, Lewin's scene begins with low lighting diffused through fog as Basil calls out Dorian's name.[79] Having passed Basil already, Dorian pauses and looks down, steeling himself, as a deep-focus shot holds them together in the frame. The shot asks what their relationship is now and what will happen next. In effect, the movie turns into a thriller and never looks back. High-contrast chiaroscuro lighting defines its visual aesthetics, intensifying the psychological drama and suspense, and positioning the scene within the emerging noir genre. Lewin's scripts transcribe Wilde's lighting directly into its stage directions. So, as Dorian takes Basil up to the attic to see the Picture, Wilde writes, 'The lamp cast fantastic shadows on the wall and staircase'.[80] This description appears word for word in Lewin's stage directions and the 'fantastic shadows' are realized on-screen by director of photography Harry Stradling.[81] As Dorian and Basil enter the house, an establishing shot decentres them so that the spindles of the staircase are cast as elongated bar-like shadows across the wall in the centre of the frame (Fig. 7.3). This chiaroscuro lighting, shot at sharp vertiginous angles, was to become one of the most characteristic visual effects in noir.[82] Stradling had created a very similar effect in *Suspicion*: at the film's tense climax, Johnnie (Cary Grant) carries a glass of milk—famously containing a light bulb to create an unnatural glow—up the stairs to his new wife (Fig. 7.4). Low lighting casts the distorted shadows of the staircase spindles, like bars, over him and against the wall. As he walks up those stairs towards the camera, the audience does not know whether he is poisoning her with the milk. What we do know is that the charming Johnnie is in considerable debt; he has been

Fig. 7.3 Basil (Gilmore) and Dorian (Hatfield) arrive at Dorian's house on the night of the murder in *The Picture of Dorian Gray* (1945)

Fig. 7.4 Johnnie (Grant) ascends the stairs with the milk for his sick wife, lit by a light bulb, in *Suspicion* (1941)

Fig. 7.5 Close up of Dorian as he stabs Basil, with the lamp revolving, casting shadows across the attic

sorely disappointed by his wife's dowry; he is a compulsive liar. Stradling's lighting design as Dorian and Basil enter Dorian's house effectively poses a parallel question to that as Johnnie ascends the staircase: we know that he is an irresponsible dandy, a petty criminal, even, but would he resort to murdering the person who loves him most; the only person who could offer him redemption? We all know how it ends for Basil.

Literary critics tend to term Wilde's lighting 'gothic', contextualizing its style in the literary history that influenced it. Noir film-makers show another way to understand it, not by what it developed out of but what it developed into. It is the beginning of a new tradition in artificial light effects rather than merely an end of gothic ones. Those 'fantastic shadows' expand their dramatic potential into a noir design that defines Basil's murder scene. Stabbed by Dorian, Basil slumps forward in his chair, knocking the gas lamp above the table. As the lamp revolves on its cord it casts light around the low-lit, shadowy room, illuminating first the picture, and silhouetting Dorian as he stabs Basil again and again and again. It continues to swing while the camera cuts to a close-up of Dorian's impassive face, alternately casting it into light and shade (Fig. 7.5). There is no revolving lamp in Lewin's stage directions so it is likely that Stradling conceived the idea. It certainly creates 'fantastic shadows'. Although chiaroscuro lighting was becoming common to noir, influenced by German expressionism, this fast, revolving movement is innovative. Noir thrillers paint in light and shade, with the noir protagonist fearing the threat in the shadows and bringing these into the light of revelation. Here, though, it is light that threatens to expose Dorian: the revolving lamp is a visual metaphor for Dorian's exposure and powerlessness in the face of a situation that has moved beyond his control, used again when he inadvertently kills himself.

With Basil dead, what could come next in a noir *Dorian Gray* but a criminal investigation? Seeming once again to follow Wilde, Lewin builds on the interrogatory dialogue Wilde wrote for Basil and foregrounds this dimension of Henry's (George Sanders's) dialogue in the scene at Lady Narborough's house following Basil's disappearance. Henry speaks Wilde's line: ' "By the way, Dorian, you ran off very early last night. You left before eleven. What did you do afterwards: Did you go straight home? [. . .] Did you go to the club?" '[83] In the novel, Henry responds irreverently to Dorian's attempt to fabricate an alibi: ' "My dear fellow, as if I cared." '[84] The subject is then dropped. By contrast, in the adaptation, Henry continues the interrogation with new dialogue written by Lewin: 'There are two hours unaccounted for Dorian. I suspect they bear investigation. Or perhaps they will not.' Mystery is integral to Wilde's novel. With this, Lewin begins a timely expansion of Wilde's own preoccupation with mystery and its resolution in the story. After Basil's murder, the word 'curiosity' is the most frequently used word in the novel. It appears throughout Lewin's stage directions too, shaping the actors' performances around often-futile truth-seeking. For example, 'Dorian Gray, filled with curiosity about places and people remote from his own experience, wandered the half-world of London';[85] Sybil has 'a curious look';[86] 'curious stories' are said to be current about Dorian;[87] 'Dorian examines the portrait curiously';[88] Henry even asks questions '(Curiously)';[89] James Vane arrives at Selby and 'looks curiously about the station'.[90]

Such curiosity reminds us that *Dorian Gray* was conceived at a dinner party on 30 August 1889, held at the Langham Hotel in London. The host? Publisher of *Lippincott's Monthly Magazine*, J. M. Stoddart. The guests? Arthur Conan Doyle, Oscar Wilde, and Irish MP Henry Gill. Stoddart wanted Conan Doyle and Wilde to each contribute a novella to his magazine.[91] Over dinner they discussed literature and Doyle offered Stoddart his second Sherlock Holmes story, 'The Sign of Four'. He described murders therein and Wilde recounted how his own Dorian was to kill

Basil.[92] Later Wilde also agreed to write for *Lippincott's* and probably delivered his manuscript, a couple of months after the publication of Doyle's story, in late March or early April 1890.[93] There is only a brief account of the evening, no more than I've written, but Basil's cross-examination makes me wonder whether they talked of detection that night. Almost certainly, Wilde was conscious of writing as the detective novel was coming into being. In his novel, on the night of his death, Basil presents Dorian with a barrage of questions.[94] Like Holmes's interrogations, Basil's presentation of circumstantial evidence and questions to the suspect are plain, succinct, and assertive in style.[95] Later, Henry and the Duchess at Selby Royal also use interrogation as repartee as she quizzes him on subjects including beauty, love, and faith.[96]

Lewin capitalizes on the detective element in *Dorian Gray*. In his script, following Basil's death, Lord Henry's epigrammatic dialogue shifts into a different mode of rapid-fire mastery of his scenes, in which he cross-examines Dorian and others. Developing the Holmes-style interrogation and Wildean curiosity into the film's driving force is a logical move for the 1940s' market. It was noticed by contemporary critics. 'DORIAN GRAY IS ARTISTIC HORROR "KITTY O'DAY": A WHODUNNIT FUN DISH', the *Hollywood Reporter* gushed in its headline, referencing another recent detective drama.[97] As the sleuth, Henry revivifies the connection between Wildean wit and the hard-boiled wisecracking of the private dick. He has all the wit and irreverence of Philip Marlowe in period dress, something emphasized by the casting of Sanders, who had starred as private eye Gay Falcon in the eponymous RKO Pictures B-movie series (1941–2), and as the detective to Cregar's monster in both *Hangover Square* and *The Lodger*. In new scenes, Dorian and Gladys even visit Scotland Yard to discuss Basil's disappearance, while David acts like a private eye, trailing Dorian and bribing his servants to get into the attic. As the film enters its final quarter, it becomes a race to the climax, with the law closing in, and even a chase after Dorian—led inevitably by Henry—ending in vain with his unintentional suicide as he destroys the Picture.

When Henry and company arrive in the attic to find a disfigured Dorian dead on the floor and his Picture once more intact, there is no resolution. Throughout the movie, the moments when Dorian's resplendent Technicolor Picture appear on-screen defy all aesthetic logic. As they do so, they also reject the logic of realism and the detective's drive to make sense of all the evidence. And so, while David and Gladys are ultimately reconciled in a heterosexual love match and—in a twist that surely pleased the Production Code arbiters and fooled no one—Dorian and Henry beg forgiveness from

God, the ending is unsettled. The movie closes, like *The Big Sleep*, with an unsolved murder and a chain of events that will never be unravelled, despite the relentless detective work that has driven the plot forward. In the final shot, *Rubaiyat of Omar Khayyam* (1859) is propped up against a sphinx, in the foreground, as David and Gladys hurry out of the house.

After *Dorian*

The sets for Lewin's Bluegate Fields were seen on-screen again soon after *Dorian Gray*. Preparing to shoot *Ziegfeld Follies* on the MGM backlot, Vincente Minnelli decided to use the sets for Bluegate Fields for his 13-minute 'Limehouse Blues' ballet sequence. This brings us back to this book's Preface which began with the *Follies*.[98]

Like 'This Heart of Mine', 'Limehouse Blues' features Fred Astaire and Lucille Bremer, and it too tells a love story in miniature, based around the 1922 standard of the same name. This time it is an unrequited love, performed as a 'dramatic pantomime'. It opens on *Dorian Gray*'s Dockland sets, and the camera follows an immigrant worker (Astaire) as he moves through its bustling streets, past dock workers, pearly kings and queens, and drinkers in pubs. As he goes, Astaire is charting the ghost scenes of Dorian's debauchery. However, he is a romantic, captivated by a mysterious elegant woman (Bremer), who stops to admire a fan in a shop window. The ballet takes shape when he is caught up in a burglary and, as he lies dying, he imagines owning the fan and dancing with the woman.

Hollywood's queer monsters and hommes fatals had no such romantic aspirations. As Lewin and Stradling make Dorian their contemporary with the aesthetics of noir, they ask us to reconsider how the movies of others with an avowed interest in the horrific potential of decadence—say, Whale, Hecht, Hoffenstein, Faulkner, Cukor—incorporate its figures, language, and styles into their films to create queer monsters. Had the dandy not always been a little too well groomed? Had their witty words not always served to hide true feelings in a way as suspicious as it is alluring? Did we not always wonder at the dark side of the deceptions we found so amusing?

Wilde's associations with horror, double lives, and queer monsters continued to resonate though the ostensible connections become less and less immediate as Wilde's scandal and popularity faded. The title of *The Man in Half Moon Street* (1945) is a nod to the street in which Algernon lives in *Earnest*, and it reminds us that Michael Arlen made the same reference in

The Green Hat.[99] Written by Barré Lyndon, in the same year he wrote *Hang-over Square*, *The Man in Half Moon Street* filters *Dorian Gray* through the spectre of the ageing monster queer with a scientific twist: Julian Karell (Nils Asther) is a man whose appearance has not altered for decades despite the passing years or any of the terrible things he has done, thanks to a potion created by his mentor (Reinhold Schünzel) to stop ageing. As he prepares to marry, though, he fears that his secret will be found out. He is running out of the medicine, his body is ageing rapidly, and suspicions are aroused by an old painting that looks like him. As he moves to do whatever is neces-sary to stay young and keep his secret, his behaviour becomes increasingly erratic and destructive. He kidnaps a young man to experiment on, but time is running out.

Fifteen years after Lewin's *Dorian Gray*, another admirer of Wilde's novel, Alfred Hitchcock, directly borrowed Stradling's lighting effects—those 'fan-tastic shadows' inspired by Wilde's description—for the terrifying climax of *Psycho* (1960). Lila (Vera Miles) has got into Norman's (Anthony Perkins's) house. As he pursues her, she flees to the basement and discovers his mother sitting with her back to the door. It is as she turns the mother around that the truth is revealed: she is in fact a shrunken corpse.[100] Lila screams, knocks the light bulb above Mrs Bates, and it casts light and shade across the room as Norman runs in wearing his mother's clothes with a knife in his hand to murder Lila, as he had her sister (Janet Leigh). The cult sexploitation film *The Secret Life of Dorian Gray* (1970) also took up Stradling's lighting design to dramatize Basil's (Richard Todd's) murder. Director Massimo Dal-lamano even emphasizes its effect by replotting his murder at the beginning of the film, and having the first half of the story unfold as Dorian's (Helmut Berger's) flashback while he sits by the fire watching Basil's overcoat burn.

Oscar Wilde, Hollywood Rebel

Conclusion

'To be premature is to be perfect', Wilde wrote in 'Phrases and Philosophies for the Use of the Young'.[1] He believed in his more robust periods that he was premature too, writing in a century that he had already outgrown. Perhaps at times we could almost imagine Wilde in a trilby and trench coat as he takes a Lucky Strike from his lips and grinds it into the sidewalk—a wise guy, a chancer, chauffeur-driven through the iron gates to the dream factory in the mornings and stalking the downtown streets of Los Angeles at night. If we could conceive of such a Wilde, one who could outlive almost all his decadent contemporaries, would he write dark thrillers, like *Underworld* and *The Man in Half Moon Street*, or screwball comedies, like *Twentieth Century* and *The Awful Truth*?

Wilde was, of course, more Victorian than he ever wished to believe, or indeed, sometimes, than his critics wish to admit. He would be at least as likely to haunt the Café Royal drinking hock and seltzers with Arthur Symons, talking over old times, as to be on the West Coast sipping martinis. His sense that there might be, at least for his works, a more propitious future was not, though, wrong. When he set his social comedies in The Present, he was willing them always—whenever and wherever they were—to be contemporary and relevant. His combination of suggestive wit, malleable plots and characters, bound up with his personal notoriety, mellowed into naughtiness by the passage of time, ensured that they, like *Salome* and *Dorian Gray*, were just that—at least up to a point.

Lord Darlington, Mrs Erlynne, Jack Worthington, Salome, and Dorian resonated through early twentieth-century popular culture because they were already in that *present*. Their radical individualism, with its pursuit of pleasure and ability to shrug off normative values with a witty remark, was a spirited if subtle protest against Puritanism and how it defined the American movie industry. As Wildean characters evolved via Raffles and Salomania, the Salomes of Bara and Nazimova, and the innuendo of that 'Lubitsch Touch', there was alchemy too. Successive acts of adaptation and

Wilde in the Dream Factory. Kate Hext, Oxford University Press. © Kate Hext (2024).
DOI: 10.1093/9780191987335.003.0008

adoption Americanized Wilde, creating the conditions in which he became 'Wilde-ish' and Wildean, filtering into the culture and becoming, eventually, untraceable among the numerable other influences that made the American movies the movies. In the selective popular memory of the twelve decades since his death, Wilde has become ever more Wilde-ish.[2] On his 1882 tour, he'd aspired to the condition of entertainer and over the following decades his style helped to define entertainment.

The screen adaptations of his plays and fiction were then just the beginning. A different kind of beginning. Robbie Ross's hope was that adaptations might rehabilitate Wilde's reputation, as his own work as editor and executor had. In reality, it was the market and the Estate's dispute with Frohman, as well as changing popular tastes, that were to define Wilde on-screen. His legacy never lost its dangerous edge and, in the moments when it threatened to take over, he and his works seemed to be the very antithesis of the family entertainments they have, against all odds, become. Gangsters, horror monsters, and noir villains were Wilde's progeny too—a further stage in how his characters and the broader ideas and styles of the decadent movement diffused into popular culture. This was not Ross's Wilde. Neither is it the Wilde often written. Still, it is a crucial reconception of Wilde that helped to make him the pop culture figure he is today.

Material conditions define how far we can understand this history. We may never know for sure whether Lois Weber really adapted *Dorian Gray* in 1913. Unless there is a stunning archival discovery, like that of Roscoe Arbuckle's *The Cook*, we will never see Theda Bara's 1918 *Salome* movie or the 1921 British adaptation of *A Woman of No Importance*. What we do know is that when Wilde goes to the movies, he's an entertainer, a sensation; a sophisticated wit, uncoupled from Wilde the critic or the writer of *De Profundis*. The excitement of Wilde's homicidal anti-heroes, the straight sexiness of *Salome* onstage, and the assertive and 'fallen' woman who is an unapologetic wit: these were good box office. Salome and Mrs Erlynne are the wicked great-aunties of the devil-may-care witty women in screwball comedy. Lord Darlington and Jack help to make a casual and comic relationship with the truth into one of the charismatic qualities of the screwball hero. This naughty and illicit Wilde appeals to the exhilaration of outraging the system and the terms of the American Dream with a hedonistic counter-aspiration in which sensuality and desire are all that matter. It is the alternative dream of a culture open to the free play of truth, ethics, and sexual politics. One in which anything goes.

Through the lens of American cinema, Wilde looks different too. Hollywood's interest in his works—from what its studios adapted to the concerns they elaborated on and those they ditched—help us see Wilde's modernity. The scopophiliac gaze in *Salome*, the autonomous movement of Dorian's Picture, and its electrical lighting effects were filmic before there was film, so of course film-makers seized on these aspects while academics have tended to overlook them. Wilde's epigrams were reworked into quips that helped to show how screen dialogue could move, and as they did, they showed how dialogue can become the anarchic energy for a Wildean Universe on-screen.

Hollywood highlights the frisson of possibility as well as the danger of Wilde's sexuality before he was made over into a gay icon, while it also reminds us, on the big screen, of the sheer joy of quietly and elegantly defecting from what society expects us to do. Its hedonism and dreaming created a culture that soon subsumed Wilde completely amongst innumerable other influences. However, as it did so, it created the conditions in which Wilde would come back to be recognized as a very modern superstar. Without Hollywood, Wilde would not have become Wildean, and, without Wilde, Hollywood would not be quite the same Hollywood either.

Notes

Preface

1. Nicholas Frankel, *Oscar Wilde: The Unrepentant Years* (Cambridge, MA: Harvard University Press, 2017), 6–7.
2. Frankel, *Oscar Wilde*, 235–6.
3. Frankel, *Oscar Wilde*, 277–81, 10–11.
4. Oscar Wilde, *The Complete Letters of Oscar Wilde*, ed. Merlin Holland and Rupert Hart- Davis (London: Fourth Estate, 2000), 972.
5. Oscar Wilde, *The Picture of Dorian Gray* (Oxford: Oxford University Press, 1998), 206.
6. Frankel, *Oscar Wilde*, 149; Wilde, *Complete Letters*, 964.
7. Simon Pure, 'The Londoner', *The Bookman* (September 1919): 41.
8. Oscar Wilde, *The Ballad of Reading Goal*, in *The Annotated Prison Writings of Oscar Wilde*, ed. Nicholas Frankel (Cambridge, MA: Harvard University Press, 2018), 323.
9. 'Art for art's sake' was coined as 'art pour l'art' by Théophile Gautier in his Preface to *Mademoiselle du Maupin* (1835), 29. When it appeared in Algernon Charles Swinburne's *William Blake: A Critical Essay* (1868), 91, the questions begged by the phrase were in common currency in London's literary circles. Walter Pater included it at the climax of his anonymous review essay, 'Poems by William Morris' (1868). Here he contemplates what makes life worth living if it is, as he assumes, but 'a brief interval'. He settles, scandalously at the time, on 'passion' as his answer: 'Only, be sure it is passion, that it does yield you this fruit of a quickened, multiplied consciousness. Of this wisdom, the poetic passion, the desire of beauty, the love of art for art's sake, has most; for art comes to you professing frankly to give nothing but the highest quality to your moments as they pass, and simply for those moments' sake' (312). This essay was infamously edited and republished under Pater's name as the Conclusion to *Studies in the History of the Renaissance* (1873).

Chapter 1

1. John Cooper, 'The Lecture Tour of North America: A Flagship Project', last modified 2022, last accessed 17 January 2023, https://www.oscarwilde

inamerica.org/lectures-1882/lecture-intro.html; Michèle Mendelssohn, *Making Oscar Wilde* (Oxford: Oxford University Press, 2018), 80.

2. Wilde met Walt Whitman with their mutual friend Joseph M. Stoddart at his home in Camden, NJ, on 18 January and again 10 May 1882. Roy Morris Jr. discusses the meeting *in Declaring His Genius: Oscar Wilde in North America* (Cambridge, MA: Harvard University Press, 2013), 55–9, 166–7. Wilde's meeting with Henry James is the subject of Mendelssohn's *Henry James, Oscar Wilde, and Aesthetic Culture* (Edinburgh: Edinburgh University Press, 2007). Their first encounter was at the home of Judge Edward G. Loring in Washington DC on 22 January 1882: *Henry James, Oscar Wilde*, 27–9.

3. His first book of collection, *Poems* (1881), was published in Boston during the tour. His play, *Vera; or, The Nihilists* (1882), was first produced in New York in 1883, when it closed after a week. See Matthew Sturgis, *Oscar Wilde: A Life* (London: Head of Zeus, 2018), 295.

4. Wilde's lecture 'The Practical Application of the Principles of Aesthetic Theory to Exterior and Interior House Decoration, with Observations upon Dress and Personal Ornaments' was first delivered on 11 May 1882. It was first published by Robert Ross. See Wilde, 'House Decoration', in *Essays and Lectures*, ed. Robert Ross (London: Methuen & Co, 1908), 165.

5. Oscar Wilde, 'The English Renaissance of Art', in *Essays and Lectures*, ed. Ross, 142.

6. Oscar Wilde, 'Oscar Wilde in Omaha', *Omaha Weekly Herald* (24 March 1882), in *Oscar Wilde in America: The Interviews*, ed. Matthew Hofer and Gary Scharnhorst (Champaign: University of Illinois Press, 2010), 100.

7. See Mendelssohn, *Making Oscar Wilde*, 287 n. 9.

8. Mendelssohn makes the point that Wilde was not in fact the prototype for Bunthorne in *Patience*. However, it was a mutually beneficial fantasy for publicity purposes: *Making Oscar Wilde*, 58–60.

9. Mendelssohn, *Making Oscar Wilde*, 151–2.

10. Mendelssohn, *Making Oscar Wilde*, 150–65.

11. Sturgis, *Oscar: A Life*, 292–6.

12. The phrase originally appeared in 'The Two Loves', a sonnet by Alfred Douglas, which was the subject of Gill's line of questioning to Wilde. See Oscar Wilde, quoted in Sturgis, *Oscar Wilde: A Life*, 570.

13. Anon., 'Queensberry Held', *The Evening World* [Night Edition] (9 March 1895): 1. Chronicling America: Historic American Newspapers, shorturl.at/beiP3 See also, as example, the first report on Queensberry's arrest: Anon., 'Wilde Strikes Back', *The Evening World* [Night Edition] (2 March 1895): 6. Chronicling America: Historic American Newspapers, shorturl.at/wzNV7; Anon., 'The News This Morning', *New-York Tribune* (3 March 1895): 1. Chronicling America: Historic American Newspapers. shorturl.at/mqD26

14. Anon., 'Oscar Wilde Jailed', *The Evening World* [Night Edition] (6 April 1895): 1. Chronicling America: Historic American Newspapers. shorturl.at/goPT0

15. The accusation was originally reported as 'To Oscar Wilde, posing as a som-domite [*sic*]' meaning sodomite, and this was the form of words heard in court. Matthew Sturgis suggests that it read, 'For Oscar Wilde ponce and Somdomite [*sic*].' Sturgis, *Oscar Wilde: A Life*, 540.

16. Anon., 'Oscar Wilde Jailed', 1.

17. Anon., 'Wilde's Career Ended', *The Sun* (6 April 1895): 1. Chronicling America: Historic American Newspapers. shorturl.at/KMO04

18. Anon., 'Wilde Agt. Queensberry', *New-York Tribune* (4 April 1895): 12. Chron-icling America: Historic American Newspapers. shorturl.at/flsxz

19. Anon., 'Wilde Denies All', *The Evening World* (30 April 1895): 7. Chronicling America: Historic American Newspapers. shorturl.at/hkpx0

20. Anon., 'Wilde Defends Himself', *Evening Star*, Washington DC (30 April 1895), 1. Chronicling America: Historic American Newspapers. shorturl.at/blpDK. Over the following days this report was syndicated to regional newspapers including *Los Angeles Herald* (1 May 1895): 3; Chronicling America: Historic American Newspapers. shorturl.at/jCI69; *The Superior Times* (4 May 1895): 1. shorturl.at/fTUX0

21. Oscar Wilde, 'Phrases and Philosophies for the Use of the Young', in *Complete Works of Oscar Wilde* (London: Book Club Associates, 1976), 1205.

22. David Weir, *Decadent Culture in the United States: Art and Literature against the American Grain, 1890–1926* (Albany, NY: State University of New York Press, 2007), 18–19.

23. For information on the New York productions, see Robert Tanitch, *Oscar Wilde on Stage and Screen* (London: Methuen, 1999), 101–2, 199–200, 226–7, 260. The Articles of Agreement with Marbury and producer Charles Frohman are housed in the Papers of Robert Ross and Vyvyan Holland relating to the Literary Estate of Oscar Wilde, Bodleian Library, Oxford, MS 7018/1 Folder 7.

24. James Crump, *F. Holland Day: Suffering the Ideal* (Santa Fe, NM: Twin Palms Publishers, 1995), 16. Only one—very warm—letter survives from their corre-spondence: Wilde to Holland Day, 11 August 1890, in *The Complete Letters of Oscar Wilde*, 445–6.

25. These included Walter Pater's 1887 short story 'Duke Carl of Rosenmold', republished as *Duke Carl of Rosenmold: An Imaginary Portrait* (Boston: Copeland & Day, 1897) and Ralph Adams Cram's 1893 novel, *The Decadent: Being the Gospel of Inaction* (Boston: Copeland & Day, 1894).

26. Crump, *F. Holland Day*, 4.

27. See Emily S. Rosenberg's *Spreading the American Dream: American Economic and Cultural Expansion, 1890–1945* (New York: Hill and Wang, 2011), 7 ff.,

which locates the Columbian Exposition of 1893 in Chicago as a crucial point in the formation of the American Dream concept.

28. Frederick Jackson Turner's 'The Significance of the Frontier in American History' (1893) argued that American democracy and the distinct American character had been formed on the Frontier. In the 1890s his thesis 'attained the status of revealed truth': H. W. Brands, *The Reckless Decade: America in the 1890s* (Chicago: University of Chicago Press, 2002), 2. Brands's *Reckless Decade* is the most focused discussion of the currents and tensions that defined the 1890s in America.

29. Shirley Everton Johnson, *The Cult of the Purple Rose* (Boston: Richard G. Badger, 1902), 104.

30. Johnson, *Cult*, 108.

31. Paul K. Saint-Amour, *The Copywrights: Intellectual Property and the Literary Imagination* (Ithaca, NY: Cornell University Press, 2003), 120; Gregory Mackie, *Beautiful Untrue Things: Forging Oscar Wilde's Extraordinary Afterlife* (Toronto: Toronto University Press, 2019), 124.

32. Howard Dietz, *Dancing in the Dark: An Autobiography* (New York: Bantam Books, 1976), 14, 37.

33. David Weir, *Decadence and the Making of Modernism* (Amherst: University of Massachusetts Press, 1995), 189.

34. Margaret C. Anderson, 'A Real Magazine', *The Little Review* 3, no. 5 (August 1916): 1. Modernist Journals Project.

35. Paul Vanderham, *James Joyce and Censorship: The Trials of Ulysses* (London: Macmillan, 1998), 37–54.

36. Arthur Symons, 'Bertha', *The Little Review* 4, no. 11 (March 1918): 51–3; Hecht, 'Nocturne', *The Little Review* 5, no. 1 (May 1918): 45–52; Hecht, 'Lust', *The Little Review* 5, no. 2 (June 1918): 14–20. Modernist Journals Project.

37. Kirstin MacLeod, 'Making It New, Old School: Carl Van Vechten and Decadent Modernism', *Symbiosis* 16 (2012): 209. David Weir notes, for example. how Ralph Adams Cram's short fiction drew Poe and Wildean decadence together: see *Decadent Culture in the United States*, 71.

38. Douglas Mao, 'The Naughtiness of the Avant-Garde: Donald Evans, Claire Marie, and *Tender Buttons*', in *Decadence in the Age of Modernism*, ed. Kate Hext and Alex Murray (Baltimore: Johns Hopkins University Press, 2019), 197–228.

39. I say showman-in-training because Wilde's early lectures were not wholly successful from the point of view of performance. In *Making Oscar Wilde*, 74–8, Mendelssohn traces how Wilde developed his style after these early challenges.

40. Joanna Levin, *Bohemia in America, 1858–1920* (Stanford, CA: Stanford University Press, 2010), 257–70.

41. For a larger discussion of *The New Bohemian*, the wide influence of which is belied by its brief existence, see Levin, *Bohemia in America, 1858–1920*, 267–8.

42. [Anon.,] 'April Magazines', *Evening Journal* (20 April 1917): 13. Chronicling America: Historic American Newspapers. shorturl.at/ky259

43. Emanuel Haldeman-Julius, quoted in Melanie Ann Brown, 'Five-Cent Culture at the "University in Print": Radical Ideology and the Marketplace in E. Haldeman-Julius's Little Blue Books, 1919–1929', PhD diss., University of Minnesota, 2006, 37.

44. Quoted in 'Forcing a Writer', *New York Sun* (18 May 1919): 5. Chronicling America: Historic American Newspapers. shorturl.at/bIUW8

45. Walter Pater, *Studies in the History of the Renaissance* (Oxford: Oxford University Press, 1998), 152.

46. Wilde, quoted in W. B. Yeats, *The Collected Works of W. B. Yeats*, Volume III: *Autobiographies*, ed. Douglas Archibald and William O'Donnell (New York: Scribner, 1999), 124.

47. Jonathan Freedman, *Professions of Taste: Henry James, British Aestheticism, and Commodity Culture* (Stanford, CA: Stanford University Press, 1990), 113–14.

48. Freedman, *Professions of Taste*, 113.

49. Louis Marcorelles, quoted in James Naremore, *The Films of Vincente Minnelli* (Cambridge: Cambridge University Press, 1993), 4; *The Films of Vincente Minnelli*, 8.

50. Vincente Minnelli, *I Remember It Well* (New York: Doubleday, 1974), 39.

51. Minnelli, *I Remember It Well*, 49–51.

52. Emanuel Levy, *Vincente Minnelli: Hollywood's Dark Dreamer* (New York: St Martin's Press, 2009), 21.

53. Minnelli, *I Remember It Well*, 50.

54. Vincente Minnelli, *Casanova's Memoirs*, ed. Joseph Monet (London: W. H. Allen, 1953).

55. Levy, *Vincente Minnelli*, 70–1.

56. Weir, *Decadence and the Making of Modernism*, 189.

57. Ben Hecht, *Erik Dorn* (New York: G. P. Putnam's Sons, 1921), 21–2.

58. Ben Hecht, *Child of the Century: The Autobiography of Ben Hecht* (New York: Signet Books, 1954), 237.

59. Ben Proctor, *William Randolph Hearst: The Later Years, 1911–1951* (New York: Oxford University Press, 2007), 5–6; Frank M. Robinson and Lawrence Davidson, *Pulp Culture: The Art of Fiction Magazines* (Portland, OR: Collectors Press, 1998), 13–14.

60. 'Advertisement: "The Importance of Being Earnest"', *Keowee Courier* (25 February 1914): 1. Chronicling America: Historical American Newspapers. shorturl.at/beksT

61. Burton Rascoe, 'The Bible of the Nineties', *New-York Tribune* (8 October 1922): 7. Chronicling America: Historical American Newspapers. shorturl.at/ctP37. For an example of one of the profiles of Wilde that appeared in the press, see John D. Williams, 'Oscar Wilde Nineteen Years After', *New York Sun* (3

November 1918): 5. Chronicling America: Historical American Newspapers. shorturl.at/dikqs

62. Richard Le Gallienne, 'The Coming Back of Oscar Wilde', *Munsey's Magazine* 66, no. 2 (March 1919): 262.

63. David Weir discusses how *The Chap-Book* fashioned itself as an American *Yellow Book*: see Weir, *Decadence Culture in the United States*, 101–12.

64. Timothy K. Conley, 'Beardsley and Faulkner', *Journal of Modern Literature* 5, no. 3 (September 1976): 342–3.

65. Gregory Mackie, 'Aubrey Beardsley, H. S. Nichols, and the Decadent Archive', *Volupté: Interdisciplinary Journal of Decadence Studies* 3, no. 1 (2020): 49–74. DOI: 10.25602/GOLD.v.v3i1.1403.g1517

66. In 1914 Barton turned from the romanticized style of Charles Dana Gibson that characterized his earliest cartoons, to Aubrey Beardsley. This change was precipitated by his move from Kansas City to New York, where he soon shared the popular enthusiasm for European fin-de-siècle culture. At first, Beardsley's stylistic influence was highlighted by his choice of subjects. His drawings of Salome's Dance of the Seven Veils and La Toilette recalled Beardsley's illustrations for Wilde's *Salome* in both style and subject, whilst others incorporated decadent-Beardsleyesque motifs, such as the peacock feather, now worn in the headdress of a cocktail-sipping flapper. For a fuller account, see Bruce Kellner, *The Last Dandy: Ralph Barton, American Artist, 1891–1931* (Columbia: University of Missouri Press, 1991), 39.

67. Sturgis, *Oscar Wilde: A Life*, 434–6.

68. The first major production of *Salome* opened at the Astor Theatre in New York on 28 January 1906. For extracts from contemporary reviews, see Tanitch, *Oscar Wilde on Stage and Screen*, 143. The American premiere was on 12 November 1905, when *Salome* was produced by the Progressive Stage Society at the Berkeley Lyceum, New York, on a triple bill with *The Revolt* by Auguste Villiers de L'Isle Adam and *On the Road* by Clara Kuge. Jerry Morris's archive blog entry features photographs of dozens of documents, advertisements, and other ephemera related to the society, including several related to their *Salome* production. See Morris, 'Julius Hopp and the Progressive Stage Society 1904–1906', My Sentimental Library, 30 March 2020, last accessed 17 January 2023, https://blog.mysentimentallibrary.com/2020/03/.

69. H.H.K., 'The "Salome" of Wilde and Strauss', *New-York Daily Tribune* (23 January 1907): 7. Chronicling America: Historical American Newspapers. shorturl.at/rsxL4

70. Heirich Conried, 'Opera Wars, 1903–1908: Parsifal, Salome, and the Manhattan Opera Company', in *Grand Opera: The Story of the Met*, ed. Charles Affron and Mirella Jona Affron (Oakland: University of California Press, 2014), 61–5.

71. 'Sadie Salome Come Home', quoted in Charles A. Kennedy, 'When Cairo Met Main Street: Little Egypt, Salome Dancers, and the World's Fairs of 1893 and

1904', in *Music and Culture in America, 1861–1918*, ed. Michael Saffle (New York: Garland, 1998), 288–9. For the lyrics in full see: Irving Berlin, 'Sadie Salome, Go Home!' 1909. Sadie Salome.com, last accessed 17 January 2023. http://sadiesalome.com/about.html?KeepThis=true.

72. Megan Girdwood, *Modernism and the Choreographic Imagination: Salome's Dance after 1890* (Edinburgh: Edinburgh University Press, 2021), 60, 35. https://doi.org.uoelibrary.idm.oclc.org/10.1515/9781474481649

73. Petra Dierkes-Thrun, *Salome's Modernity: Oscar Wilde and the Aesthetics of Transgression* (Ann Arbor: University of Michigan Press, 2011), 92–4.

74. Girdwood, *Modernism and the Choreographic Imagination*, 58.

75. [Anon.,] 'Life and Ginger at the Garrick', *Wilmington Evening Journal* (12 October 1909): 2. Chronicling America: Historical American Newspapers. shorturl.at/hACPQ

76. For a typical example of Davis's billing with his *Dorian Gray* show, below 'The Famous "Diving Venus"', see the advertisement for the Orpheum Theatre in *Goodwin's Weekly* (10 September 1910): 10. Chronicling America: Historical American Newspapers. shorturl.at/hFO67

77. Carl Van Vechten, *In the Garret* (New York: Knopf, 1920), 292.

78. Quoted in Addell Austin Anderson, 'The Ethiopian Art Theatre', *Theatre Survey* 33 (November 1992): 136.

79. Anderson, 'The Ethiopian Art Theatre', 135–6.

80. Unfortunately, very little information is available on this production. See the anonymous review: 'Negro Art Group', *Variety* 96 (24 July 1929): 68. Lantern: Media History Digital Library. shorturl.at/grvRX

81. Mendelssohn, *Making Oscar Wilde*, 91–3.

82. Stefano Evangelista, 'Introduction: Oscar Wilde—European by Sympathy', in *The Reception of Oscar Wilde in Europe*, ed. Evangelista (London: Continuum, 2010), 7–8.

83. Robert L. Caserio, 'Queer Modernism', in *The Oxford Handbook of Modernisms*, ed. Peter Brooker et al. (Oxford: Oxford University Press, 2010), 200.

84. Van Vechten, *In the Garret*, 292–3.

85. Dierkes-Thrun, *Salome's Modernity*, 93–4.

86. Quoted in Tanitch, *Oscar Wilde on Stage and Screen*, 203.

87. Daniel Brown, 'Wilde and Wilder', *PMLA* 119, no. 5 (October 2004): 1226.- Jstor. https://www.jstor.org/stable/25486118

88. Brown, 'Wilde and Wilder', 1226.

89. Brown, 'Wilde and Wilder', 1229 n. 2.

90. Ronald H. Wainscott, *The Emergence of Modern American Theater, 1914–1929* (New Haven: Yale University Press, 1997), 7–10.

91. Allen Norton, *The Convolvulus* (New York: Claire Marie Press, 1914).

92. When *The Turning Point* premiered in New Haven the plagiarism was identified immediately. See e.g. [Anon.,] 'The Turning Point Produced', *Evening Star* (1 March 1910): 15. Chronicling America: Historical American Newspapers. shorturl.at/lqUZ6

93. For information on the Broadway Production of *Oh, Earnest!*, see Tanitch, *Oscar Wilde on Stage and Screen*, 269. It is also possible to trace the origins of this production via the contemporary newspaper reports. Originally titled *Tangles* and produced by P. T. Rossiter, it opened out of town before transferring to the Royal Theatre, on W 45th Street, under its new title. The book and lyrics were by Francis DeWitt, with music by Robert Hood Bowers: [Anon.,] 'Broadway Briefs', *The Daily Worker* (2 April 1927): 8. Chronicling America: Historical American Newspapers. shorturl.at/luNS5.

94. The Library of Congress's *Chronicling America* National Digital Newspaper Program has made over 1.5 million newspaper pages across 600 national historic titles available to search online: https://www.loc.gov/ndnp/. Using their search facility I've counted each separate production mentioned or reviewed in the newspapers: some are touring productions, first performed in New York or ending there, and most are regional productions. This figure is, however, only a ballpark figure given that many more local newspapers have not been digitized.

95. The New York opening is noted in Tanitch, *Oscar Wilde on Stage and Screen*, 105–6. Representative reviews of the tour include the following: Julia Chandler Manz, 'The New Year Will Find Fun and Frolic in Local Playhouses', *The Washington Herald* (27 December 1914): 5; Chronicling America: Historical American Newspapers. shorturl.at/aBRTW; [Anon.,], 'Margaret Anglin here this week will present Oscar Wilde's Brilliant Comedy, "Lady Windermere's Fan" at Jefferson', *The Birmingham Age-Herald* (7 February 1915): 1; Chronicling America: Historical American Newspapers. shorturl.at/ixzL6; 'America's foremost actress, Margaret Anglin' [Advertisement], *Evening Journal* (9 March 1915): 9; Chronicling America: Historical American Newspapers. shorturl.at/nBIW4.

96. There are numerous reviews and advertisements in local papers, showing the scale of Wilde's popularity for university productions. To take just two examples, University of Nevada Theta Epsilon Society performed Earnest at Carson City Opera House in aid of their athletics fund. See *The Importance of Being Earnest* [advertisement], *The Carson City Daily Appeal* (8 February 1909): 4; Chronicling America: Historical American Newspapers. shorturl.at/koPRU; University Players from the University of Missouri toured the state with public performances of *Earnest* in 1917: *The Importance of Being Earnest* [advertisement], *The Daily Missourian* (29 April 1917): 6. Chronicling America: Historical American Newspapers. shorturl.at/ayCGL

97. See e.g. [Anon.,] 'What to See this Week at Local Theatres', *Los Angeles Herald* (22 November 1908): 3. Chronicling America: Historical American Newspapers. shorturl.at/bFRSZ

98. Newspaper archives provide numerous cases, most of which are entirely lost except for a line or small notice in the local newspaper. For some examples of slightly more substantial accounts of small amateur productions, see the following. There was a production of *Lady Windermere* in aid of the library fund for the University of Washington's extension programme: [Anon.,] [Untitled,] *Washington Standard* (28 May 1915): 8; Chronicling America: Historical American Newspapers. shorturl.at/eRW05; a benefit performance of *Earnest*, for Providence Hospital in Oakland, CA: [Anon.,] 'Ideals, Not Cash, Inspire This', *The San Francisco Call* (2 December 1906): 44. Chronicling America: Historical American Newspapers. shorturl.at/iuIP2.

99. [Anon.,] 'Society', *Sunday Star* (8 January 1911): 1. Chronicling America: Historical American Newspapers. shorturl.at/ey369

100. 'The Importance of Being Earnest' [Advertisement], *The Mt Sterling Advocate* (17 April 1917): 5. Chronicling America: Historical American Newspapers. shorturl.at/lVW46

101. [Anon.,] 'Town Drama Club Opens Second Season', *Daily Star-Mirror* (8 October 1920): 4. Chronicling America: Historical American Newspapers. shorturl.at/bSZ39

102. [Anon.,] 'A Fool There Was', *El Paso Herald* (24 July 1913): 4. Chronicling America: Historical American Newspapers. shorturl.at/vCE36

103. A number of high-profile contemporary reviews hailed Wilde as a new departure for the British stage. For example, following the premiere of *Lady Windermere*, William Archer, a key figure in bringing Ibsen's plays to the London, wrote that *Lady Windermere* 'is on the highest plane of modern English drama, and furthermore, it stands alone on that plane [...] Wilde has no rival among his fellow-workers for the stage.' [Signed Review of Arthur Pinero's *The Second Mrs Tanqueray*,] 3 June 1893, in *Oscar Wilde: The Critical Heritage*, ed. Karl Beckson (London: Routledge, 1974), 169. Henrik Ibsen's *Pillars of Society* (1877) was first performed in England in 1880 and it had little impact. The first full London production of *A Doll's House* (1879) was not until 1889, followed by a private production of *Ghosts* (1891). In the period c.1891–3 the 'Ibsen Campaign' marked the slow beginning of 'Ibsenism' in the English theatrical world, though the large majority of critics were hostile to Ibsen's work in the 1890s: see Katherine E. Kelly, 'Pandemic and Performance: Ibsen and the Outbreak of Modernism', *South Central Review* 25, no. 1, special issue: *Staging Modernism* (Spring 2008): 12–35.

104. Gregory Mackie, 'The Function of Decorum at the Present Time: Manners, Moral Language, and Modernity in "an Oscar Wilde Play"', *Modern Drama*

52, no. 2 (Summer 2009): 149, 157–8. Project Muse. https://doi.org/10.1353/mdr.0.0099

105. Mendelssohn, *Making Oscar Wilde*, 231–2.

106. Mendelssohn, *Making Oscar Wilde*, 231–7.

107. Freedman, *Professions of Taste*, 114.

108. Wainscott, *Modern American Theater*, 3.

109. See e.g. 'Book Club Meets' [Notice], *The Daily Times* [5 o'clock edition] (17 November 1921): 5. Chronicling America: Historical American Newspapers. shorturl.at/tKNO2

110. Henry James to Mrs Hugh Bell, 23 February 1892, in *Letters*, Volume III: *1883–1895*, ed. Leon Edel (London: Macmillan, 1981), 372.

111. Until 1912, the Motion Picture Patents Company limited the length of films to 20 minutes.

112. Charlie Keil and Ben Singer, 'Introduction: Movies and the 1910s', in *American Cinema of the 1910s: Themes and Variations*, ed. Keil and Singer (New Brunswick, NJ: Rutgers University Press, 2009), 19.

113. Ross became the literary executor of Wilde's estate on 14 August 1906 following his fallout with Alfred Douglas over the publication of *De Profundis* (1905): see Laura Lee, *Oscar's Ghost: The Battle for Oscar Wilde's Legacy* (Stroud, Gloucester: Amberley Publishing, 2017), 183.

114. There's no evidence in his meticulous letters that he knew about Wilde's twentieth-century reception in the US. The Wilde estate retained the US performance rights for *Salome*. Charles Frohman was the original US rights holder for *Lady Windermere* (1892), *A Woman of No Importance* (1893), *An Ideal Husband* (1895), and *Earnest* (1895), and he produced the premieres of these plays in New York. The wider problem, and one that endured long after Ross's death when Vyvyan Holland took control of the estate, was that Wilde's copyrights were disorganized. In his final years, in grave financial difficulty, Wilde had sold the rights to some of his works to several different people. For an account of this confusion, see Paul K. Saint-Amour, *The Copywrights: Intellectual Property and the Literary Imagination* (Ithaca, NY: Cornell University Press, 2003), 91–114.

115. Letter from Robert Ross to Martin Holman, 4 March 1915, in Papers of Robert Ross and Vyvyan Holland, MS 7018/1 Folder 2.

116. In his role as executor and his role as editor of the *Collected Works of Oscar Wilde* (1908), Ross's aims were to bring the Estate out of bankruptcy and to rehabilitate Wilde's image. As an editor, 'The first order of business was to demonstrate to the public at large that there was nothing dangerous or corrupting in his writing [. . .] His guiding principle was not to show readers the most authentic Wilde, but the best version of Wilde' (Lee, *Oscar's Ghost*, 180). There is evidence everywhere of the same approach in Ross's handling

of the estate. For a full discussion of this, see Mackie, *Beautiful Untrue Things*, 34–6.

117. The letters pertaining to Wilde's potential in American cinema only detail hopes and ideas between Ross and Holman. See Papers of Robert Ross and Vyvyan Holland, MS7018/1 Folders 2 and 8.

118. Letter from Holman to Ross, 9 August 1917, in Papers of Robert Ross and Vyvyan Holland, MS 7019/1 Folder 8; underlined in original.

119. Letter from Holman to Ross, 12 February 1917, in Papers of Robert Ross and Vyvyan Holland, MS 7018/1 Folder 8.

120. The only evidence that the Wilde Estate would be involved in an American film adaptation of Wilde's work is correspondence regarding a Mr Campbell. Holman writes to Ross that he was 'asking for a list of everything of Wilde's for the U.S.A., a big filming company wants some Wilde material, and I hope to get off the "Vera" [*sic*]. If I can get the play taken I can probably manage for them all the world rights of "The Canterville Ghost": with money spent on it the latter should make a really beautiful film': letter from Holman to Ross, 2 October 1917, in Papers of Robert Ross and Vyvyan Holland, MS7018/1 Folder 8.

121. Following Charles Frohman's death on the *Lusitania* in 1915, his brother Daniel took control of the copyrights. Ross and Holman suspected Marbury and Daniel Frohman of not informing them fully about the American accounts and complained of Frohman's 'very unbusinesslike methods': letter from Holman to Ross, 8 February 1917, in Papers of Robert Ross and Vyvyan Holland, MS 7018/1 Folder 8. The Famous Players Film Company became Famous-Players Lasky in 1916 and ultimately took the now-familiar name of Paramount Pictures in 1936. For a full account of the studio's early evolution, see Neal Gabler, *An Empire of Their Own: How the Jews Invented Hollywood* (London: Doubleday, 1988), 21–46; for Daniel Frohman's involvement in the Famous Players Film Company, see esp. 29–33.

122. Letter from Holman to Ross, 19 April 1917, in Papers of Robert Ross and Vyvyan Holland, MS7018/1 Folder 8.

123. See e.g. the dispute with Frohman over rights for *An Ideal Husband*: letters from Holman to Ross, 21 March and 19 April 1917, in Papers of Robert Ross and Vyvyan Holland, MS 7018/1 Folder 8.

124. For example, he produced *The Prisoner of Zenda* on stage in New York (1897) and it was adapted to the screen by his Famous Players Film Company in 1913; he produced *A Lady of Quality* on stage in 1897 and then on film for Famous Players Film Company in 1913.

125. Records are incomplete but there were British film adaptations of *Lady Windermere* (1916) and *A Woman of No Importance* (1921; lost). The former is discussed in Chapter 4.

126. Letter from Holman to Ross, 8 February 1917, in Papers of Robert Ross and Vyvyan Holland, MS7018/1 Folder 8.

127. Rob King, '1914: Movies and Cultural Hierarchy', in *American Cinema of the 1910s*, ed. Keil and Singer, 117–18.

128. King, '1914: Movies and Cultural Hierarchy', 118–19.

129. There is little trace of this film. However, brief accounts can be found in the following: [Anon.,] 'Film Fancies', *The New York Clipper* (15 November 1913): 9; Lantern: Media History Digital Library, shorturl.at/iJ257; [Anon.,] 'A Florentine Tragedy', *Motography* 10, no. 1 (December 1913): 32. Lantern: Media History Digital Library. shorturl.at/fxGJQ

130. 'A Florentine Tragedy', *Motion Picture News* 13, no. 2 (October 1913–January 1914): 39.

131. *Variety* 29, no. 5 (January 1913): 28. The Orpheum had hosted a much-publicized and popular play-adaptation of *Dorian Gray* a few years earlier, but reviews for the very different *Florentine Tragedy* were mixed. See press notices, e.g. *Motography* (19 April 1913): 32. Lantern: Media History Digital Library. shorturl.at/mUVZ4. See also Edward Davis's impassioned defence of Oscar Wilde, published in the week before his production: Davis, 'The Rehabilitation of Oscar Wilde', *Los Angeles Herald* (21 August 1910): 4. Chronicling America: Historical American Newspapers. shorturl.at/nRT89

132. [Advertisement], *The Moving Picture World* 16, no. 1 (April–June 1913): 213, 297, 400. Lantern: Media History Digital Library. shorturl.at/bglLP

133. David Pierce, *The Survival of American Silent Feature Films: 1912–1929* (Washington DC: Library of Congress and Council on Library and Information Resources, 2013), 21. https://www.loc.gov/programs/static/national-film-preservation-board/documents/pub158.final_version_sept_2013.pdf Accessed 19 January 2023.

134. The 1913 *Dorian Grey* [*sic*] adaptation by the New York Film Company is cited very briefly by multiple books and websites of secondary criticism. It is said to have been written for the screen by the pioneering film-maker Lois Weber, who is also rumoured to have starred as Sybil, and directed by Phillips Smalley. However, there is no primary evidence for its having reached production. Moreover, Lois Weber's involvement does not add up. In 1913 she and Smalley were producing one or two one-reel films per week for their own Rex Film Company based in Los Angeles, and since 1912 a subsidiary of the Universal Film Manufacturing Company. I am grateful to Shelley Stamp, Weber's biographer, for responding to my question about the possibility of this production.

Chapter 2

1. David Wark Griffith, 'The Rise and Fall of Free Speech in America', *The Griffith Project*, Volume 11: *Selected Writings of D. W. Griffith: Indexes and Corrections to Volumes 1–10*, ed. Paolo Cherchi Usai (London: BFI, 2007), 151.

2. Griffith, 'The Rise and Fall of Free Speech in America', 145–7.

3. Ben Singer calls Griffith 'an immoral moralist' in his essay 'Griffith's Moral Profile', in *A Companion to D. W. Griffith*, ed. Charlie Keil (London: Wiley, 2017), 34. The racism of Griffith's film *Birth of a Nation* (1915) made it singularly controversial on its release but it broke box-office records.

4. Larry May, *Screening Out the Past: The Birth of Mass Culture and the Motion Picture Industry* (Chicago: University of Chicago Press, 1983), 60–81.

5. May, *Screening Out the Past*, 100.

6. May, *Screening Out the Past*, 100.

7. May, *Screening Out the Past*, 98.

8. Russell Merritt, 'Rescued from a Perilous Nest: D. W. Griffith's Escape from Theatre into Film', *Cinema Journal* 21, no. 1 (Autumn 1981): 7, 27. Jstor. https://www.jstor.org/stable/1225002

9. *Hollywood: A Celebration of the American Silent Film*, dir. Kevin Brownlow and David Gill, Episode 2, 'In the Beginning' (Thames Television, London, 1980).

10. Shushma Malik, 'The Criminal Emperors of Ancient Rome and Wilde', in *Oscar Wilde and Classical Antiquity*, ed. Kathleen Riley, Alastair J. L. Blanchard, and Iarla Manny (Oxford: Oxford University Press, 2018), 308.

11. Charles Baudelaire, 'The Painter of Modern Life', in Baudelaire, *The Painter of Modern Life and Other Essays*, trans. and ed. Jonathan Mayne (London: Phaidon, 2006), 7. The close relationship between the flâneur and the criminal is taken up by Walter Benjamin in *Charles Baudelaire: A Lyric Poet in the Era of High Capital*, trans. Harry Zohn (London: Verso, 1997), 41. For more on this connection, see Tom MacDonough's 'The Crimes of the Flâneur', *October* 102 (Autumn 2002): 101–22.

12. Malik, 'The Criminal Emperors', 308–9.

13. James Naremore, *More Than Night: Film Noir in Its Contexts* (Berkeley and Los Angeles: University of California Press, 1998), 70–1; see T. S. Eliot, 'The Lesson of Baudelaire', *Tyro: A Review of the Arts of Painting, Sculpture, and Design* 1 (Spring 1921): 4.

14. Arthur Symons, *Wanderings* (London: J. M. Dent and Sons Ltd, 1931), 77.

15. Dominic Janes, *Oscar Wilde Prefigured: Queer Fashioning and British Caricature, 1750–1900* (Chicago: University of Chicago Press, 2016), 163–4.

16. Janes, *Oscar Wilde Prefigured*, 162–3.

17. Walter Pater, *Miscellaneous Studies* (London: Macmillan, 1928), 30.

18. Pater, *Miscellaneous Studies*, 26.

19. Pater, *Miscellaneous Studies*, 30.

20. Pater, *Renaissance*, 86.

21. Christopher S. Nassar, 'Oscar Wilde's "Lord Arthur Savile's Crime" and *The Picture of Dorian Gray*: Point Counterpoint', *ANQ: A Quarterly Journal of Short Articles, Notes and Reviews* 27, no. 3 (2014): 137–43.

22. Wilde, *Dorian Gray*, 207.

23. Wilde, *Dorian Gray*, 141. For a more extensive discussion of how ancient Rome influences Dorian's attitude to crime, see Malik, 'The Criminal Emperors', 314–16.

24. Wilde, *Dorian Gray*, 123–43.

25. Wilde, *Dorian Gray*, 138 ff.

26. 'Walter Pater, 'A Novel by Mr. Oscar Wilde', *The Bookman* (November 1891): 59–60.

27. Simon Joyce, 'Sexual Politics and the Aesthetics of Crime: Oscar Wilde in the Nineties', *ELH* 69, no. 2 (Summer 2022): 502–3. Jstor. https://www.jstor.org/stable/30032029

28. D. Michael Jones, 'E. W. Hornung's Raffles and the Aesthetic Movement: The Rhetoric of Romance Masculinity', *English Literature in Transition, 1880–1920* 59, no. 1 (2016): 45. Project Muse. muse.jhu.edu/article/603457.

29. Lee O'Brien, 'Wilde Words: The Aesthetics of Crime and the Play of Genre in E. W. Hornung's Raffles Stories', *English Studies* 96, no. 6 (2015): 660. Ingenta Connect. https://doi.org/10.1080/0013838X.2015.1045731 For a discussion of examples, see O'Brien, 'Wilde Words', 660–3.

30. Jones, 'E. W. Hornung's Raffles and the Aesthetic Movement', 44–5.

31. E. W. Hornung, *Raffles: The Amateur Cracksman* (London: Penguin, 2003), 25–6.

32. Jones, 'E. W. Hornung's Raffles and the Aesthetic Movement', 45.

33. For two typical examples of this intimate plotting together, see 'The Ides of March' and 'Gentlemen and Players', in Hornung, *Raffles: The Amateur Cracksman*, 6, 50.

34. Letter from Wilde to the Editor of the *Scots Observer*, 9 July 1891, in *Complete Letters of Oscar Wilde*, 439.

35. Charles Musser, *Before the Nickelodeon: Edwin S. Porter and the Edison Manufacturing Company* (Berkeley and Los Angeles: University of California Press, 1991), 406.

36. Musser, *Before the Nickelodeon*, 406.

37. Federico Pagello, 'A. J. Raffles and Arsène Lupin in Literature, Theatre, and Film: On the Transnational Adaptations of Popular Fiction (1905–1930)', *Adaptation* 6, no. 3 (March 2013): 276. Oxford Academic. https://doi.org/10.1093/adaptation/apt002

38. As discussed in Chapter 1 n. 134, there is no primary evidence that a film of *Dorian Gray* was produced in 1913 despite its being cited in passing by numerous secondary critics.

39. 'The Picture of Dorian Gray' [advertisement], *Motion Picture News* 12, no. 3 (July–October 1915): 18. shorturl.at/klE19 Lantern: Media History Digital Library.

40. Harry M. Benshoff, *Monsters in the Closet: Homosexuality and the Horror Film* (Manchester: Manchester University, 1997), 21.

41. Benshoff, *Monsters in the Closet*, 21.

42. See Anthony Slide, *Silent Topics: Essays on Undocumented Areas of Silent Film* (London: Scarecrow Press, 2004). As Slide notes, most silent films from the 1910s have been lost (*Silent Topics*, 41–6). See also Richard Barrios, *Screened Out: Playing Gay in Hollywood from Edison to Stonewall* (London: Routledge, 2003), 15–22.

43. Lee Grieveson, *Policing Cinema: Movies and Censorship in Early-Twentieth-Century America* (Berkeley and Los Angeles: University of California Press, 2004), 198–201.

44. Edwin Thanhouser, quoted in Martin Danahay, 'Richard Mansfield, *Jekyll and Hyde* and the History of Special Effects', *Nineteenth Century Theatre and Film* 39, no. 2 (Winter 2012): 65. Taylor & Francis Online. https://doi.org/10.7227/NCTF.39.2.4

45. Wilde, *Dorian Gray*, 179.

46. Judith Buchanan, '*The Picture of Dorian Gray* (1915)', video commentary, last accessed 19 January 2023, https://vimeo.com/ondemand/thanhouserloc.

47. Joseph F. Spillane, 'The Road to the Harrison Narcotics Act: Drugs and Their Control, 1875–1918', in *Federal Drug Control: The Evolution of Policy and Practice*, ed. Jonathon Erlen and Joseph F. Spillane (New York: Pharmaceutical Products Press, 2004), 8–9.

48. Quoted in Spillane, 'The Road to the Harrison Narcotics Act', 8–9.

49. Eve Kosofsky Sedgwick, *Epistemologies of the Closet* (Berkeley and Los Angeles: University of California Press, 2008), 171–2.

50. Sedgwick, *Epistemologies of the Closet*, 172.

51. Jeff Nunokawa, 'The Importance of Being Bored: The Dividends of Ennui in *The Picture of Dorian Gray*', *Studies in the Novel* 28, no. 3, special issue: *Queerer than Fiction* (Fall 1996): 357.

52. Nunokawa, 'The Importance of Being Bored', 357–8.

53. Paul Foster, 'Kingdom of Shadows: Fin-de-Siècle Gothic and Early Cinema', in *Monstrous Media/Spectral Subjects: Imaging Gothic Fictions from the Nineteenth Century to the Present*, ed. Fred Botting and Catherine Spooner (Manchester: Manchester University Press, 2015), 30.

54. Kate Hext, 'Victorians in the Closet: Oscar Wilde's Monstrous Hollywood Legacy', *Victorian Literature and Culture* 49, no. 4, special issue: *The Scales of Decadence* (Autumn 2021): 716–19. https://doi.org/10.1017/S1060150320000303 Cambridge Core.

55. Wilde, *Dorian Gray*, 87.

56. Wilde, *Dorian Gray*, 215–16.

57. Wilde, *Dorian Gray*, 125.

58. Danahay, 'Richard Mansfield, *Jekyll and Hyde* and the History of Special Effects', 67.

59. James Kotsilibas-Davis, *Good Times, Great Times: The Odyssey of Maurice Barrymore* (New York: Doubleday, 1977), 327–8, 354–6.

60. Kotsilibas-Davis, *Good Times, Great Times*, 221.
61. [Unsigned,] 'Filming Oscar Wilde Story', *Variety* (May 1919): 66. Lantern: Media History Digital Library. shorturl.at/bdvBR
62. The movie broke box-office records when it opened at the Rivoli in March 1920: see [Unsigned,] 'Super-Special Now Available', *Motion Picture News* 21, no. 18 (3 April 1920): 3. Lantern: Media History Digital Library. shorturl.at/IKNU3
63. Wilde, *Dorian Gray*, 18.
64. This adaptation of *Salome* is discussed in Chapter 3.
65. Sturgis, *Oscar Wilde: A Life*, 398.
66. Wilde, *Dorian Gray*, 127–8.
67. Dierkes-Thrun, *Salome's Modernity*, 94.
68. [Unsigned,] 'Maud Allan', *Variety* 11 (June 1908): 4. Lantern: Media History Digital Library. shorturl.at/DGIRU
69. Charlie Keil, '1913: Movies and the Beginning of a New Era', in *American Cinema of the 1910s: Themes and Variations*, ed. Charlie Keil and Ben Singer (New Brunswick, NJ: Rutgers University Press, 2009), 95–6.
70. As Dierkes-Thrun explains, 'the word clitoris [was] a code for lesbianism and degeneracy'. See *Salome's Modernity*, 112.
71. Philip Hoare, *Wilde's Last Stand: Scandal and Conspiracy during the Great War* (London: Duckworth Overlook, 1997), 90.
72. Hoare, *Wilde's Last Stand*, 91.
73. For a full account of the allegations and their context, see Hoare, *Wilde's Last Stand*, 88–94.
74. Dierkes-Thrun, *Salome's Modernity*, 84, 120.
75. Hoare, *Wilde's Last Stand*, 137–72.
76. F. Cunliffe-Owen, 'Pemberton-Billing and the "Black Book"', *New York Sun* (7 July 1918): 12. Chronicling America: Historic American Newspapers. shorturl.at/iqxW5
77. Justine Brown, *Hollywood Utopia* (Vancouver: New Star Books 2002), 29.
78. *Hollywood: A Celebration of the American Silent Film*, ed. Brownlow and Gill, Episode 2, 'In the Beginning'.
79. Dierkes-Thrun, *Salome's Modernity*, 141–2.
80. Ellen Crowell, 'The Ugly Things of Salome', in *Decadence in the Age of Modernism*, ed. Kate Hext and Alex Murray (Baltimore: Johns Hopkins University Press, 2019), 51.
81. Theda Bara, 'The Curse on the Moving Picture Actress', *The Forum* (July 1919): 83–93, at 92. The Unz Review. shorturl.at/cfIT3
82. Nigel Waymouth, interview with Kate Hext, 15 August 2015, London.
83. Dierkes-Thrun, *Salome's Modernity*, 84.

84. Shelley Stamp, 'Women and the Silent Screen', in *The Wiley-Blackwell History of American Film*, Volume I: *Origins to 1928*, ed. Cynthia Lucia, Roy Grundmann, and Art Simon (London: Wiley-Blackwell, 2012), 2–3. onlinelibrary.wiley.com

85. The screen scenario was written by the prolific and acclaimed Léonce Perrett, with Wilde's play credited as its basis.

86. [Anon.,] 'A Modern Salome', *Motion Picture Magazine* (February–July 1920): 436. Lantern: Media History Digital Library. shorturl.at/fsvTU

87. Sam Stoloff, 'Normalizing Stars: Roscoe "Fatty" Arbuckle and Hollywood Consolidation', in *American Silent Film: Discovering Marginalized Voices*, ed. Gregg Bachman and Thomas J. Slater (Carbondale, IL: Southern Illinois University Press, 2002), 161.

88. For a comprehensive discussion of the history of the prop head of John the Baptist onstage, see Crowell, 'The Ugly Things of Salome', 47–70.

89. This argument is the subject of Ellis Hanson's 'Salome, Simile, *Symboliste*', in *Decadent Poetics: Literature and Form at the British Fin de Siècle*, ed. Jason David Hall and Alex Murray (Basingstoke: Palgrave, 2013), 141–62.

90. Cleopatra and Salome were already paired in the cultural imagination. Sarah Bernhardt had played Cleopatra in the 1880s and 1890s before being in line to star as Salome in the first aborted production, whilst the Ballets Russes added the Dance of the Seven Veils to their 1909 production of *Cleopatra*, starring Ida Rubinstein, who had taken the lead role in their production of Salome the previous year.

91. Gregg Merritt, *Room 1219: The Life of Fatty Arbuckle, the Mysterious Death of Virginia Rappe, and the Scandal that Changed Hollywood* (Chicago: Chicago Review Press, 2016), 1–13, 41–6, 203–4.

92. [Unsigned,] *Teleny, or The Reverse of the Medal* (n.p.: Gay Erotica Classic, 2013), 108–10.

93. Hilary A. Hallett explores the imagery used by the press to contrast Arbuckle with Rappe and define the public mood in the wake of the incident in *Go West, Young Women! The Rise of Early Hollywood* (Berkeley and Los Angeles: University of California Press, 2013), 183–9.

94. *Hollywood: A Celebration of the American Silent Film*, dir. Brownlow and Gill, Episode 3, 'Single Beds and Double Standards'.

95. Kenneth Anger, *Hollywood Babylon* (New York: Dell Publishing, 1975), 44.

Chapter 3

1. At the time of its release, the film was officially titled *Douglas Fairbanks in Robin Hood*, an indication of Fairbanks's star power.

2. Patricia White, 'Nazimova's Veils: *Salome* at the Intersection of Film Histories', in *A Feminist Reader in Early Cinema*, ed. Jennifer M. Bean and Diane Negra (Durham, NC: Duke University Press, 2002), 61.

3. Sturgis traces Marbury's work as Wilde's American agent in *Oscar: A Life*, 451, 493, 503, 660. Gavin Lambert discusses how Nazimova and Marbury might have come to know each other in New York in *c.*1905, and Marbury's likely role in introducing her to Charles Frohman, in Lambert, *Nazimova: A Biography* (Lexington: University Press of Kentucky, 2021), 153–5.

4. 'Nazimova in Oscar Wilde's "Salome" ' [advertisement], *Motion Picture News* (January–February 1923): 756. Lantern: Media History Digital Library. shorturl.at/hnsMY

5. Nazimova, quoted in Malcolm H. Oettinger, 'The Complete Artiste', *Picture-Play Magazine* (March–August 1923): 57. Lantern: Media History Digital Library. shorturl.at/dBHI6

6. Nazimova, quoted in Oettinger, 'The Complete Artiste', 57.

7. Note that English editions and adaptations of Wilde's play almost invariably spelt the title without the acute accent on its last letter, but Nazimov'as title is written '*Salomé*' as in Wilde's French language edition. Many reviews of Nazimova's adaptation rendered the title in the former way. I have Anglicized Nazimova's title for consistency.

8. Kenneth Anger reports the rumour that the cast were all gay. See Anger, *Hollywood Babylon*, 163.

9. Jonathan Freedman, *The Jewish Decadence: Jews and the Aesthetics of Modernity* (Chicago: University of Chicago Press, 2021), 85.

10. James W. Dean, 'Nazimova's "Salome," A Film with a Mental Kick in It', *Albuquerque Sunday Herald* (18 June 1922): 3. Chronicling America: Historic American Newspapers. shorturl.at/eiqvy

11. This information is featured in the advertisement cited in n. 4: 'Nazimova in Oscar Wilde's "Salome" ', 756.

12. Dean, 'Nazimova's "Salome" ', 3; [Anon.] 'Censors Believe Movies Reason for Boys' Crime', *The Indianapolis Times* (26 August 1922): 6. Chronicling America: Historic American Newspapers. https://shorturl.at/adhN4

13. 649 West Adams Boulevard. Theda Bara sold the house to Roscoe 'Fatty' Arbuckle in 1919, who filled it with rare antiques and partied even harder than Bara.

14. Bara, 'The Curse on the Moving Picture Actress', 86.

15. Charles Keil, 'The Movies: The Transitional Era', in *American Literature in Transition, 1910–1920*, ed. Mark Van Wienan (Cambridge: Cambridge University Press, 2018), 319.

16. There were 'her-own' movie companies headed by stars including Helen Gardner, Florence Turner, Clara Kimball Young, and Lois Weber—writer and star of the fabled 1913 *Dorian Gray*.

17. Nazimova, quoted in Oettinger, 'The Complete Artiste', 57.

18. Lucy Fischer, *Cinema by Design: Art Nouveau, Modernism, and Film History* (New York: Columbia University Press, 2017), 72–3.

19. S. L. M. Barlow, 'The Movies—An Arraignment', *The Forum* (January 1922): 40. The Unz Review. https://www.unz.com/print/Forum-1922jan-00037

20. Harlow Robinson, *Russians in Hollywood, Hollywood's Russians: Biography of an Image* (Boston: Northeastern University Press, 2007), 17.

21. Artistically very diverse films in this category include Josef von Sternberg's directorial debut, *The Salvation Hunters* (1925), Paul Fejos's *The Last Moment* (1928), Charles Vidor's *The Bridge* (1929), Charles Klein's and Leon Shamroy's *The Tell-Tale Heart* (1928), and Boris Deutsch's *Lullaby* (1929).

22. See David E. James, 'Hollywood Extras: One Tradition of "Avant-Garde" Film in Los Angeles', in *Unseen Cinema: Early American Avant-Garde Film, 1893–1941*, ed. Bruce Charles Posner (New York: Black Thistle Press/Anthology Film Archives, 2001), 45–6.

23. 'Nazimova with Metro', *Moving Picture World* (28 July 1917): 582. Lantern: Media History Digital Library. shorturl.at/bhITX

24. A number of critics refer to Nazimova's house as 'The Garden of Allah', however the 'h' was added in the late 1920s when she no longer owned it. See Alla Nazimova's poem 'Not that it Matters' (1926), included in the appendix of Lambert's *Nazimova*, 399.

25. Eva recited Wilde's short stories on her stage tours and identified with 'the tragedy, the public scandal, the humiliation' of his life as she tried to come to terms with her own sexuality. See Robert A. Schanke, *Shattered Applause: The Lives of Eva Le Gallienne* (Carbondale: Southern Illinois University Press, 2010), 47.

26. Axel Madsen, *The Sewing Circle: Hollywood's Greatest Secret; Female Stars Who Loved Other Women* (London: Robson Books, 1998), 2–3.

27. Dolly Wilde, quoted in Joan Schenkar, *Truly Wilde: The Unsettling Story of Dolly Wilde, Oscar's Unusual Niece* (Cambridge: Da Capo Press, 2000), 31. There is some disagreement about when they met. Joan Schenkar writes that it may have been in 1926 (*Truly Wilde*, 145–7). Gavin Lambert's *Nazimova*, 282–3, suggests a slightly different account in which Nazimova and Dolly meet in 1925.

28. Liz Brown, *Twilight Man: Love and Ruin in the Shadows of the Clark Empire* (London: Penguin 2021), 117.

29. Brown, *Twilight Man*, 138.

30. Brown, *Twilight Man*, 122–5. Clark postponed a plan to publish them privately due to concerns over litigation from Douglas but they eventually appeared in an edition of 250 in 1924: see *Twilight Man*, 127, 141.

31. Brown, *Twilight Man*, 123.

32. Letter from Carl Van Vechten to Fania Marinoff, 22 June 1922, in Carl Van Vechten Papers, 1833–1965, New York Public Library, Series 3, b. 36, Letters from Carl Van Vechten to Fania Marinoff.

33. Mercedes de Acosta, 'Memory', in *Moods* (New York: Moffat, Yard & Company, 1919), 3.

34. De Acosta, 'Disgust', in *Moods*, 10.

35. Vincent Sherry, *Modernism and the Reinvention of Decadence* (Cambridge: Cambridge University Press, 2014), 70–81.

36. Brown, *Hollywood Utopia*, 41.

37. Herbert Howe, 'A Misunderstood Woman', *Photoplay* (January–June 1922): 25. Lantern: Media History Digital Library. shorturl.at/dhxUW

38. Brown, *Hollywood Utopia*, 64.

39. Diana McLellan, *The Girls: Sappho Goes to Hollywood* (London: Robson Books, 2001), 33; White, 'Nazimova's Veils', 64.

40. Anger, *Hollywood Babylon*, 44.

41. Anon. [Ed Roberts], *The Sins of Hollywood: An Exposé of Movie Vice!* (Los Angeles: Hollywood Publishing Co., 1922), 74.

42. Carl Van Vechten, *Spider Boy: A Scenario for a Moving Picture* (New York: Alfred A. Knopf, 1928), 60.

43. Sheldon Hall and Steve Neale, *Epics, Spectacles, and Blockbusters* (Detroit: Wayne State University Press, 2010), 38.

44. A couple of years earlier, she attempted to obtain the rights to Pierre Louÿs's *La Femme et la Pantin* (*The Woman and the Puppet*, 1898). The problem with rights was most likely because an adaptation was already under contract with Goldwyn Pictures. It was released as *The Woman and the Puppet* (1920), starring Geraldine Farrar and is thought to be lost. Later adaptations included *The Devil is a Woman* (1935), starring Dietrich and directed by Josef von Sternberg.

45. June Mathis and Alla Nazimova, 'Aphrodite', undated [1920], 13-f.91, 1, in Margaret Herrick Library, Los Angeles.

46. Pierre Louÿs, *Aphrodite*, trans. Lewis Galantière (New York: Modern Library, 1933), xiv.

47. Lambert, *Nazimova*, 232.

48. Mathis and Nazimova, 'Aphrodite', 1.

49. Mathis and Nazimova, 'Aphrodite', 17, 36, 17.

50. Mathis and Nazimova, 'Aphrodite', 44.

51. Mathis and Nazimova, 'Aphrodite', 45.

52. Mathis and Nazimova, 'Aphrodite', 47.

53. Lambert, *Nazimova*, 237.

54. Lambert, *Nazimova*, 251, 260–1.

55. David Weir, 'Alla Nazimova's *Salomé*: Shot-by-Shot', *Volupté: Interdisciplinary Journal of Decadence Studies* 2, no. 2 (Winter 2019): 181. DOI: 10.25602/GOLD.v.v2i2.1348.g1467

56. Melanie C. Hawthorne, ' "Comment Peut-on Être Homosexuel?": Multinational (In)Corporation and the Frenchness of *Salomé*', in *Perennial Decay: On the Aesthetics and Politics of Decadence*, ed. Liz Constable, Dennis Denisoff, and Matthew Potolsky (Philadelphia: University of Pennsylvania Press, 1999), 170.

57. Oscar Wilde, *Salome*, in Wilde, *The Importance of Being Earnest and Other Plays* (Oxford: Oxford University Press, 1998), 91, line 1050. In the original text, the word 'Mystery' was not capitalized.

58. Oscar Wilde, *The Ballad of Reading Gaol*, in *The Annotated Prison Writings of Oscar Wilde*, ed. Nicholas Frankel (Cambridge, MA: Harvard University Press, 2018), 323.

59. Wilde, *Salome*, 74, lines 373–5.

60. Kenneth Anger, 'Diva of Decadence: Salomé (1922)', in *Unseen Cinema: Early American Avant-Garde Film, 1893–1941*, ed. Bruce Charles Posner (New York: Black Thistle Press/Anthology Film Archives, 2001), 96.

61. Quoted in Helen Sheehy, *Eva Le Gallienne: A Biography* (New York: Alfred A. Knopf, 1996), 86.

62. This is one of the main theses of Richard Abel's study, *Americanizing the Movies and 'Movie-Mad' Audiences, 1910–1914* (Berkeley and Los Angeles: University of California Press, 2006).

63. Betsy F. Moeller-Sally, 'Oscar Wilde and the Culture of Russian Modernism', *SEEJ* 34, no. 4 (1990): 460. Jstor. https://doi.org/10.2307/308194

64. Stefano Evangelista, 'Introduction', 2-6; Rainer Kohlmayer and Lucia Kramer, '*Bunbury* in Germany: Alive and Kicking', in *The Reception of Oscar Wilde in Europe*, ed. Evangelista (London: Continuum, 2010), 189.

65. Evgenii Bershtein, ' "Next to Christ": Oscar Wilde in Russian Modernism', in *The Reception of Oscar Wilde in Europe*, ed. Evangelista, 294–9.

66. Anna Kovalova, ' "The Picture of Dorian Gray" Painted by Meyerhold', *Studies in Russian and Soviet Cinema* 13, no. 1 (January 2019): 66. Taylor & Francis Online. doi.org/10.1080/17503132.2019.1556429 I am grateful to Jon Stone for pointing out that the most prominent Russian director of the 1910s, Evgenii Bauer, made some complex films including a 1915 adaptation of *Bruges-la-morte*, titled *Daydreams*.

67. Kovalova, ' "The Picture of Dorian Gray" Painted by Meyerhold', 71.

68. Kovalova, ' "The Picture of Dorian Gray" Painted by Meyerhold', 70–1; Vsevolod Meyerhold, *The Picture of Dorian Gray* (1915), ed. and trans. Anna Kovalova and Ekaterina Ivanenko, *Studies in Russian and Soviet Cinema* 13, no. 1 (January 2019): 93 ff. Taylor & Francis Online. doi.org/10.1080/17503132.2019.1557407

69. Bershtein, ' "Next to Christ" ', 293.

70. Annabel Rutherford, 'The Triumph of the Veiled Dance: The Influence of Oscar Wilde and Aubrey Beardsley on Serge Diaghilev's Creation of the Ballets Russes', *Dance Research: The Journal of the Society for Dance Research* 27, no. 1 (Summer 2009): 93–107. Jstor. https://www.jstor.org/stable/40264008

71. Jonathan Stone, 'The Journal as Archive: *Vesy* and the Russian Reader's Encounter with Decadence', *Volupté* 3, no. 1 (Summer 2020): 75–91, at 77. DOI: 10.25602/GOLD.v.v3i1.1404.g1518

72. See Léon Bakst, 'Tailpiece for Salome', *Mir iskusska* 5, no. 5 (1901): 287; border design for 'List of Pictures', *Mir iskusska* 7, no. 2 (1902): 109.
73. I am grateful to Sasha Dovzhyk for this information. See Sergei Makovskii, 'Ob illiustratsiiakh Birdsleia', in *Salomeia* by Oskar Uail´d, trans. Konstantin Bal´mont and Ekaterina Andreeva (St Petersburg: Panteon, 1908), 125–31.
74. Sasha Dovzhyk, 'Aubrey Beardsley in the Russian "World of Art"', *British Art Studies* 18 (November 2020): 33–6. https://doi.org/10.17658/issn.2058-5462/issue-18/sdovzhyk
75. Wilde, *Salome*, 65, line 7. The image of Salome's feet as white doves is evoked again by Herod shortly before the Dance of the Seven Veils: *Salome*, 84, line 799.
76. For an example amongst the *Salome* drawings, see Aubrey Beardsley, 'Enter Herodias', in 'Aubrey Beardsley illustrations for *Salome* by Oscar Wilde', accessed 26 January 2023, British Library Online, https://www.bl.uk/collection-items/aubrey-beardsley-illustrations-for-salome-by-oscar-wilde.
77. Olga Matich, *Erotic Utopia: The Decadent Imagination in Russia's Fin de Siècle* (Madison: University of Wisconsin Press, 2005), 142–54.
78. Nicoletta Misler, 'Seven Steps, Seven Veils: Salomé in Russia', *Experiment* 17 (2011): 155. Research Gate. DOI:10.1163/221173011X611888.
79. Fischer, *Cinema by Design*, 80.
80. Dierkes-Thrun, *Salome's Modernity*, 134–5.
81. [Anon.,] 'Too Much and Too Little on the Russian Stage', *The Literary Digest* (30 May 1914): 1317.
82. George Jean Nathan, 'The Popular Play', *The Smart Set* (June 1918): 136. Modernist Journals Project.
83. Elliot Robert Barkan, *Immigrants in American History: Arrival, Adaptation, and Integration* (Santa Barbara, CA: ABC Clio, 2013), 594.
84. George Martin Day, *The Russians in Hollywood: A Study in Culture Conflict* (Los Angeles: University of Southern California Press, 1934), 2.
85. Robinson, *Russians in Hollywood, Hollywood's Russians*, 16.
86. Olga Matich discusses the myth or partial myth of the Russian aristocrat in Hollywood, noting at the outset that 'The stereotype of the Russian aristocrat in Paris turned cab driver is rivalled in Hollywood by the figure of the aristocrat or tsarist general as movie extra reliving his past on the silver screen' (Matich, 'The White Emigration Goes Hollywood', *Russian Review* 64, no. 2 (April 2005): 187–380, at 187, https://doi.org/10.1111/j.1467-9434.2005.00357.x). This myth was emblematized by the plot of *The Last Command*. As Matich argues, though, it is highly likely that many Russian immigrants in Hollywood romanticized or entirely fabricated their backgrounds.
87. Robinson, *Russians in Hollywood, Hollywood's Russians*, 15.
88. Lambert, *Nazimova*, 248–9.
89. James, 'Hollywood Extras', 44–52.

90. James, 'Hollywood Extras', 44–52.

91. Quoted in Conley, 'Beardsley and Faulkner', 342–3.

92. Pam Cook, 'Picturing Natacha Rambova: Design and Celebrity Performance in the 1920s', *Screening the Past* 40 (September 2015), http://www.screeningthepast.com/2015/08/picturing-natacha-rambova-design-and-celebrity-performance-in-the-1920s/.

93. Dean, 'Nazimova's "Salome"', 3.

94. Cook, 'Picturing Natacha Rambova'.

95. Dierkes-Thrun, *Salome's Modernity*, 141. Rambova was involved professionally, romantically, and indeed scandalously with Kosloff between 1916 and 1917: see Michael Morris, *Madam Valentino: The Many Lives of Natacha Rambova* (New York: Abbeville Press, 1991), 44–52.

96. Oscar Wilde, *Lady Windermere's Fan*, in *The Importance of Being Earnest and Other Plays* (Oxford: Oxford University Press, 1998), 44, lines 332–4.

97. Narraboth is listed as the Young Syrian is Wilde's play-text.

98. See Pamela Robertson, *Guilty Pleasures: Feminist Camp from Mae West to Madonna* (Durham, NC: Duke University Press, 1996), 12. Robertson begins this history of female camp with Mae West.

99. Weir, 'Alla Nazimova's *Salomé*: Shot-by-Shot', 188.

100. Dierkes-Thrun, *Salome's Modernity*, 134–5. Dierkes-Thrun also discusses the parallels between Wilde's Salome and Ibsen's heroines in detail: *Salome's Modernity*, 133–7. Caserio argues that Wilde and Ibsen are both queer in the sense that the portrayal of queer identity is central to their works as a personal liberation from bourgeois morality and the binary sexual identity of heterosexual/homosexual; see 'Queer Modernism', 201–3.

101. Wilde, *Salome*, 74, lines 372.

102. Lois Cucullu, 'Wilde and Wilder Salomés: Modernizing the Nubile Princess from Sarah Bernhardt to Norma Desmond', *Modernism/modernity* 18, no. 3 (September 2011): 499–503. Project Muse. https://doi.org/10.1353/mod.2011.0057

103. Wilde, *Salome*, 65, lines 20–1.

104. Wilde, *Salome*, 70–1, lines 194, 205–6, 268, 270.

105. Wilde, *Salome*, 85, line 831.

106. Wilde, *Salome*, 65, lines 9–10.

107. Weir, 'Alla Nazimova's *Salomé*', 204.

108. Eliot L. Gilbert, ' "Tumult of Images": Wilde, Beardsley, and "Salome"', *Victorian Studies* 26, no. 2 (Winter 1983): 143–5. Jstor. https://www.jstor.org/stable/3827003

109. Lambert, *Nazimova*, 288–90, 299–302.

110. McLellan, *The Girls*, 47–52.

111. See Catherine Maxwell, 'Carnal Flowers, Charnel Flowers: Perfume in the Decadent Literary Imagination', in *Decadence and the Senses*, ed. Jane Desmarais and Alice Condé (Oxford: Legenda, 2017), 32–50.

112. There have been three major productions of *Sunset Boulevard*. In this discussion I am referring to the first production in Los Angeles (1993) which transferred to Broadway (1993-4) and the London revival (2016). These runs shared many of personnel, including the star, Glenn Close, as Norma Desmond, and Costume Designer Anthony Powell.
113. *Sunset Boulevard* (2016), English National Opera, London Colosseum, 1 April–7 May 2016. Choreographer Stephen Mear, Costumes by Tracy Christensen and Anthony Powell, Director Lonny Price.

Chapter 4

1. Wilde, quoted in Richard Ellmann, *Oscar Wilde* (London: Vintage, 1988), 340.
2. Mackie, *Beautiful Untrue Things*, 96.
3. Mackie, *Beautiful Untrue Things*, 96–7.
4. Mackie, *Beautiful Untrue Things*, 71, 108.
5. Holland, quoted in Mackie, *Beautiful Untrue Things*, 89.
6. MacLeod, 'Making It New, Old School', 201–11.
7. Carl Van Vechten, 'Ronald Firbank', in Van Vechten, *Excavations: A Book of Advocacies* (New York: Alfred A. Knopf, 1926), 172.
8. I have written at length about the relationship between Van Vechten and Firbank elsewhere. See Kate Hext, 'Rethinking the Origins of Camp: The Queer Correspondence of Carl Van Vechten and Ronald Firbank', *Modernism/modernity* 27, no. 1 (January 2020): 165–83. Project Muse. https://doi.org/10.1353/mod.2020.0007
9. Edmund Wilson, *The Shores of Light: A Literary Chronicle of the Twenties and Thirties* (New York: Farrar, Straus and Young, 1952), 72.
10. Letter from Vyvyan Holland to Norman Croom-Johnson, 7 October 1931, in Papers of Robert Ross and Vyvyan Holland, Bodleian Library, Oxford, MS 7018/2 Folder 1. In 1967 the programme notes accompanying a screening of Nazimova's *Salome* stated that Holland's new translation of *Salome* had provided the basis for Nazimova's title cards. There doesn't appear to be evidence that Holland had any direct involvement with the production.
11. For examples of the US release notices, see '*Lady Windermere's Fan*' [advertisement], *Moving Picture World* (7 June 1919): 1422; Lantern: Media History Digital Library. shorturl.at/cFPQT 'Princess Theatre' [advertisement], *The Brattleboro Daily Reformer* (21 September 1922): 4. Chronicling America: Historic American Newspapers. shorturl.at/gltQ4
12. The correspondence from this period is not included in the archived papers collected in the Papers of Robert Ross and Vyvyan Holland in the Bodleian Library. However, a letter dated 18 October 1934 from John W. Rumsey, President of the American Play Company, summarizes the discussions he held with the Estate in 1923 while introducing an enquiry regarding the worldwide

talking-film rights to *Lady Windermere's Fan*. See letter from John W. Rumsey to Parker Garrett Associates, 18 October 1934, in Papers of Robert Ross and Vyvyan Holland, MS 7018/4.

13. For the details and origins of this disagreement, see discussion in Chapter 1.

14. Warner Brothers reached a deal with Frohman and the producers of the British adaptation, the Ideal Company, which owned the rights to produce a silent adaptation of *Lady Windermere* in the UK. [Unsigned,] 'Star and Director Guests of the Warners in New York', *Moving Picture World* (24 October 1925): 634. Lantern: Media History Digital Library. shorturl.at/dgAX3; See also Charles Musser, 'The Hidden and Unspeakable: On Theatrical Culture, Oscar Wilde, and Ernst Lubitsch's *Lady Windermere's Fan*', *Film Studies* 4, no. 1 (Summer 2004): 19. DOI: https://doi.org/10.7227/FS.4.2

15. [Unsigned,] 'New Lubitsch and Chaplin Get Underway at Warners', *Moving Picture World* (3 October 1925): 416. Lantern: Media History Digital Library. shorturl.at/swBLT

16. Saverio Giovacchini. *Hollywood Modernism: Film and Politics in the Age of the New Deal* (Philadelphia: Temple University Press, 2011), 14.

17. Leo Braudy, *The Hollywood Sign: Fantasy and Reality of an American Icon* (New Haven: Yale University Press, 2011), 43.

18. Carl Van Vechten, 'Hollywood Parties', *Vanity Fair* (June 1927): 86.

19. Carl Van Vechten, Daybook, 3 October 1925, in Carl Van Vechten Papers, 1833–1965, New York Public Library, Day Books 1901–1930 [Incomplete], ZL-434 Reel 1.

20. Mackie, *Beautiful Untrue Things*, 70–1.

21. Jennifer Fronc, *Monitoring the Movies: The Fight Over Censorship in Early Twentieth-Century America* (Austin: University of Texas Press, 2017), 128–35.

22. [Unsigned,] 'Producers Take Drastic Step to Assure', *Moving Picture World* (19 March 1921): 240; Lantern: Media History Digital Library. shorturl.at/apHQ1; [Unsigned,] '100 Per Cent. Clean Screen Productions', *Moving Picture World* (19 March 1921): 241. Lantern: Media History Digital Library. shorturl.at/agqK9

23. [Unsigned,] 'Producers Take Drastic Step to Assure', 240.

24. Lee F. Hanmer et al., 'Resolution Passed by Association of Motion Picture Producers, Inc., (California)', 25 July 1924, 1, Zepfanman.com, last accessed 21 January 2023, https://www.dropbox.com/s/66ftwacjheu3h2y/1924-06-19-formula-0162.pdf?dl=0.

25. Lea Jacobs, *The Decline of Sentiment: American Film in the 1920s* (Berkeley and Los Angeles: University of California Press, 2008), 2.

26. Sos Eltis, *Revisiting Wilde: Society and Subversion in the Plays of Oscar Wilde* (Oxford: Oxford University Press, 1996), 59–62. On *Salome* and the Lord Chamberlain, see Ellmann, *Oscar Wilde*, 372–4.

27. Ernst Lubitsch, 'Lubitsch Talks of Epigrams on Screen', *The New York Herald, New York Tribune* (27 December 1925): 3.
28. For a fuller discussion of *The Blind Bow-Boy*, see Kate Hext, 'Making Decadence New: Carl Van Vechten's Cinematic Fiction', in *Decadence: A Literary History*, ed. Alex Murray (Cambridge: Cambridge University Press, 2020), 362–3.
29. Edward White, *The Tastemaker: Carl Van Vechten and the Birth of Modern America* (New York: Farrar, Straus and Giroux, 2014), 231.
30. See Alex Clayton's discussion of Harold Lloyd's comic persona in *The Body in Hollywood Slapstick* (Jefferson, NC: McFarland, 2007), 84.
31. For other examples, see *Merton of the Movies* (1924); *The Extra Girl* (1923); *In Hollywood with Potash and Perlmutter* (1924).
32. 'The party entered a huge hall, hung with tapestries and Spanish shawls and oriental rugs, punctuated with Iberian chests, Moroccan ottomans, Flemish cabinets, Empire commodes, and Italian refectory tables. Everywhere flowers bloomed, spikes and clusters of them, in huge blue porcelain and terra-cotta jars. The procession of footmen mounted the grand staircase with the luggage.' Van Vechten, *Spider Boy*, 55.
33. Evelyn Preer was a pioneering African American actress on both stage and screen. Working with African American film-maker Oscar Micheaux, she made over ten films. In Hollywood, she took smaller parts in, for instance, *The Blonde Venus* (1932). Mimi Aguglia had consistent parts in Hollywood movies into the 1950s. These ranged from an uncredited role in *The Last Man on Earth* (1924) to Guadalupe in *The Outlaw* (1943); Edwards Davis had a large number of character roles, including *Kildare of Storm* (1918) and *The Sea Hawk* (1924).
34. Thesiger corresponded with Vyvyan Holland directly and negotiated for the rights fee to be waived. We do not have the letter between Thesiger and Holland, but Holland relays this fact to Norman Croom-Johnson: see letter from Holland to Croom-Johnson, 29 April 1931, in Papers of Robert Ross and Vyvyan Holland, MS7018/2. Despite the wrangling over American rights to Wilde's plays, there was no dispute that Holland personally owned the UK stage rights to *Earnest* and *Lady Windermere* outright.
35. Weir, *Decadence and the Making of Modernism*, 189.
36. Mankiewicz, quoted in Julien Gorbach, *The Notorious Ben Hecht: Iconoclastic Writer and Militant Zionist* (West Lafayette, IN: Purdue University Press, 2019), 92.
37. Adina Hoffman's biography, *Ben Hecht: Fighting Words, Moving Pictures* (New Haven: Yale University Press, 2019), begins to address this blind spot with attention to Hecht's first literary career in Chicago and New York.
38. Ben Hecht, *The Florentine Dagger* (London: George Harrap & Co Ltd, 1924), 11, 106–7.

39. Hecht's naturalistic novels include *Erik Dorn* (1921) and *Gargoyles* (1922). His whodunnit, *The Florentine Dagger* (1923), reworks the same kind of decadent character.

40. Raymond Chandler, *The Simple Art of Murder* (London: Vintage, 1988), 10.

41. See S. S. Van Dine, *The Benson Murder Case* (New York: Felony & Mayhem, 2018), 7–8, 11, 14. On the green carnation, see Sturgis, *Oscar Wilde: A Life*, 442–3.

42. For the allusion to the *Mona Lisa*, see Michael Arlen, *The Green Hat* (London: The Boydell Press, 1984), 186. The evocation of Dorian is most marked when the naïve narrator sees Napier 'in a curious moment [...] down a villainous alley near the East India Docks when through a lighted window I was astonished to see Napier's white, thin, fine face and those dark fevered eyes. He was talking earnestly to an old man and a very pretty young girl who was crying [...] He was a strange, secret, saintly youth, a favourite of gods or men': *The Green Hat*, 130–1. Dorian goes to the East India Docks for opium and sex workers: see Wilde, *Dorian Gray*, 180–2.

43. Arlen, *The Green Hat*, 98.

44. Arthur Symons, 'The Decadent Movement in Literature', *Harper's Monthly Magazine* (November 1893): 866–7.

45. Brooks E. Hefner, *The Word on the Streets: The American Language of Vernacular Modernism* (Charlottesville: University of Virginia Press, 2017), 140.

46. [Unsigned,] 'The $30,000 Scenario Contest: National in Scope', *The Photodramatist* 3, no. 4 (September 1921): 6. Lantern: Media History Digital Library. shorturl.at/EUX12; [Unsigned,] 'Film Producers are Calling: "Author—AUTHOR!"', *The Photodramatist* 3, no. 11 (April 1922): 35. Lantern: Media History Digital Library. shorturl.at/euwY4

47. Ted Le Berthon, 'This Side of Nirvana', *The Photodramatist* 3, no. 4 (September 1921): 15–16. Lantern: Media History Digital Library. shorturl.at/jnpU8

48. William MacAdams, *Ben Hecht: The Man Behind the Legend* (New York: Charles Scribner's Sons, 1990), 70–1.

49. See e.g. 'Crêpe on the Door', 'Romance', and 'Dead', in Samuel Hoffenstein, *Life Sings a Song* (New York: Wilmarth Publishing Company, 1916), 18, 35–6, 39–42. This element in Hoffenstein's work is discussed by Benjamin De Casseres in his 1916 Preface to the collection.

50. In his first semi-autobiographical novel, *This Side of Paradise* (1920), Amory Blaine's education pivots on his discovery of *The Picture of Dorian Gray* and 'the misty side streets of literature' it leads him to: Joris-Karl Huysmans, Walter Pater, Théophile Gautier. See F. Scott Fitzgerald, *This Side of Paradise* (London: Penguin, 2000), 47–8, 98.

51. F. Scott Fitzgerald, *The Last Tycoon* (London: Penguin, 2001), 97.

52. For a full discussion of Hitchcock's interest in Wildean decadence, including its influence on his early films, see Kate Hext, 'Decadence on the Silent

Screen: Stannard, Coward, Hitchcock, and Wilde', *Volupté* 2, no. 2, special issue: *Decadence and Cinema* (Winter 2019): 21–45. DOI: 10.25602/GOLD.v.v2i2.1339.g1460

53. Evangelista, 'Introduction', 7–8.
54. Kohlmayer and Krämer, '*Bunbury* in Germany', 190–2. It was after seeing this production that Marcel Rémy composed the music for Maud Allan's 'The Vision of Salome', discussed in Chapter 1: see Girdwood, *Modernism and the Choreographic Imagination*, 59.
55. Kohlmayer and Kramer put the figure at over 225 in '*Bunbury* in Germany', 192. Robert Vilain puts the figure at 'over 250' in 'Tragedy and the Apostle of Beauty: The Early Literary Reception of Oscar Wilde in Germany and Austria', in *The Reception of Oscar Wilde in Europe*, ed. Stefano Evangelista (London: Bloomsbury Academic, 2010), 173.
56. Musser, 'The Hidden and Unspeakable', 17–18.
57. Kristin Thompson, *Herr Lubitsch Goes to Hollywood: German and American Film after World War I* (Amsterdam: Amsterdam University Press, 2005), 19.
58. Carroll Graham, 'The Stroller', *Picture-Play Magazine* 27 (September 1927–February 1928): 52. Lantern: Media History Digital Library. shorturl.at/bjkq9
59. Osbert Sitwell, in Ifan Kyrle Fletcher, *Ronald Firbank: A Memoir* (London: Duckworth, 1930), 140.
60. Louise Brooks, *Lulu in Hollywood: Expanded Edition* (Minneapolis: University of Minneapolis Press, 2000), 20.
61. Hazel Simpson Naylor, 'He has an English Accent, but his Last Name's O'Brien', *Motion Picture Magazine* (November 1918): 58–60, 120. Lantern: Media History Digital Library. shorturl.at/cBNUW
62. See Frank Harris, 'Arthur Symons', *Shadowland* 5, no. 2 (January 1922): 47, 66, 74; Lantern: Media History Digital Library. shorturl.at/osvX4; Frank Harris, 'George Moore', *Shadowland* 4, no. 6 (April 1921): 37, 68; Llewelyn Powys, 'The Wayward Poet of England', *Shadowland* 7 no. 4 (December 1922): 3, 76; Benjamin De Casseres, 'Baudelaire: Ironic Dante', *Shadowland* 7, no. 5 (July 1921): 45, 72.
63. Ralph Barton, 'A Tuesday Night at the Cocoanut Grove', *Vanity Fair* (June 1927): 62–3.
64. Van Vechten writes an account of this occasion, concluding, 'Everybody gay. An amazing party. Home at 3': Van Vechten, Day Book, 26 November 1928, in Carl Van Vechten Papers, 1833–1965, Box 112.
65. For a discussion of Coward's ambivalent relationship with Wilde's legacy, see Hext, 'Decadence on the Silent Screen', 25–7.
66. Coward, quoted in Lahr, *Coward the Playwright* (Berkeley and Los Angeles: University of California Press, 2002), 19.

67. Philip Hoare, *Noël Coward: A Biography* (London: Sinclair-Stevenson, 1995), 162.

68. Anger, *Hollywood Babylon*, 101–9, 163. The Garden of Alla appears in Van Vechten's handwritten notes for *Spider Boy*, in Carl Van Vechten Papers, 1833–1965, Box 113.

69. Ben Hecht, *1001 Afternoons in Chicago* (Chicago: Covici-McGee, 1922), 127. In this and other descriptions of movie theatres in his fiction, Hecht is indebted to Arthur Symons's *London Nights* (1897) and *Silhouettes* (1896).

70. May, *Screening Out the Past*, 150–66.

71. May, *Screening Out the Past*, 156; Brown, *Hollywood Utopia*, 49.

72. Brown, *Hollywood Utopia*, 49.

73. May, *Screening Out the Past*, 156.

74. Weir, *Decadent Culture in the United States*, 193.

75. See e.g. *Wild Oranges*, a novel by Joseph Hergesheimer (1918), adapted as a film of the same name by King Vidor in 1924; Edgar Saltus's novel, *The Palister Case* (1919), adapted with the same title (1920); and *Daughters of the Rich*, also a novel by Saltus (1909), adapted with the same title (1923).

76. Carmen Guiralt, 'Self-Censorship in Hollywood During the Silent Era: *A Woman of Affairs* (1928) by Clarence Brown', *Film History* 28, no. 2 (2016): 84–7. Jstor. https://doi.org/10.2979/filmhistory.28.2.04

77. Guiralt, 'Self-Censorship in Hollywood', 89 ff.

78. Hecht, *The Florentine Dagger*, 11.

79. T. S. Eliot, *The Waste Land: A Facsimile and Transcript*, ed. Valerie Eliot (London: Faber & Faber, 2011). See discussion in Sherry, *Modernism and the Reinvention of Decadence*, 264–79.

80. Jacobs, *The Decline of Sentiment*, 82.

81. I have quoted the lines used on the intertitle card in the adaptation. These correspond to Wilde, *Lady Windermere*, 58, lines 397–401.

82. [Unsigned,] 'Screen Version of Wilde Drama a Flivver', *The Film Daily* (8 June 1919): 21. Lantern: Media History Digital Library. shorturl.at/aivTY

83. Richard W. McCormick, 'Transnational Jewish Comedy: Sex and Politics in the Films of Ernst Lubitsch—From Berlin to Hollywood', in *Three-Way Street: Jews, Germans, and the Transnational*, ed. Jay Howard Geller and Leslie Morris (Ann Arbor: University of Michigan Press, 2016), 170.

84. In *The Decline of Sentiment*, 79, 91–9, Jacobs uses *A Woman of Paris* as a model to outline the features of sophisticated comedy.

85. Scott Eyman, *Ernst Lubitsch: Laughter in Paradise* (New York: Simon and Schuster, 1993), 104–6.

86. Jacobs, *The Decline of Sentiment*, 91.

87. Kristin Thompson, 'Lubitsch, Acting and Silent Romantic Comedy', *Film History* 13, no. 4, special issue: *Before Screwball* (2001): 400–1. Jstor. https://www.jstor.org/stable/3815457

88. Lubitsch, 'Lubitsch Talks of Epigrams on Screen', 3.
89. Lubitsch, 'Lubitsch Talks of Epigrams on Screen', 3.
90. Lubitsch, 'Lubitsch Talks of Epigrams on Screen', 3.
91. Eyman, *Ernst Lubitsch*, 113.
92. Lubitsch, 'Lubitsch Talks of Epigrams on Screen', 3.
93. Wilde, *Lady Windermere*, 10, lines 117–19.
94. Amanda Anderson, *The Powers of Distance: Cosmopolitanism and the Cultivation of Detachment* (Princeton: Princeton University Press, 2001), 158.
95. Thompson, 'Lubitsch, Acting and Silent Romantic Comedy', 400.
96. For example, see Wilde, *Lady Windermere*, 27, line 223; 27, line 245; 32, line 413; 33, line 459. As noted in Chapter 3, *Salome* also features frequent references to looking.
97. Wilde, *Lady Windermere*, 27, lines 232–3.
98. Musser, 'The Hidden and Unspeakable', 16.
99. 'Always True to You in My Fashion' was written for the stage musical *Kiss Me Kate* (1948) and it appeared in the MGM film adaptation in 1953. Dowson's original poem features the repeated refrain, 'I have been faithful to thee, Cynara! in my fashion'. In 1913 Holbrook Jackson, the first chronicler of decadence, singled out 'Cynarae' as the most complete expression of the decadent attitude. See his *The Eighteen Nineties: A Review of Art and Ideas at the Close of the Nineteenth Century* (London: Grant Richards, 1922), 65. Dowson's poems also provided inspiration for the titles of the novels *Gone with the Wind* by Margaret Mitchell (1936) and the teleplay *The Days of Wine and Roses* by J. P. Miller (1958), adapted as feature films in 1939 and 1962 respectively.
100. Wilde, *Lady Windermere*, 35, line 514.
101. See e.g. Darlington's declaration of love for Lady Windermere: Wilde, *Lady Windermere*, 28–9, lines 285–310.
102. Linda Costanzo Cahir, 'A Shared Impulse: The Significance of Language in Ernst Lubitsch's "Lady Windermere's Fan"', *Literature/Film Quarterly* 19, no. 1 (1991): 8. ProQuest. https://shorturl.at/nCIQ6
103. Eyman, *Ernst Lubitsch*, 115.
104. McCormick, 'Transnational Jewish Comedy', 182.
105. Wilde, *Lady Windermere*, 26, lines 210–11.
106. Wilde, *Lady Windermere*, 54, lines 256–8.
107. Thompson, *Herr Lubitsch Goes to Hollywood*, 28.
108. Maria DiBattista, *Fast-Talking Dames* (New Haven: Princeton University Press, 2001), 180.
109. Ellmann, *Oscar Wilde*, 364.
110. Oscar Wilde, *The Importance of Being Earnest*, in *The Importance of Being Earnest and Other Plays* (Oxford: Oxford University Press, 1998), 273, lines 52–3.

111. H. L. Mencken, 'Introduction', in *Essays by James Huneker* (New York: Scribner's, 1929), x.

112. Letter from H. L. Mencken to Van Vechten, 28 July 1928, in Carl Van Vechten Papers, 1833–1965, Box 23, folder 8.

113. Telegram from Western Union Cablegram from American Play Company to Parker Garrett & Co, 18 October 1934, in Papers of Robert Ross and Vyvyan Holland, MS 7018/4.

114. An agreement to divide copyright proceeds for the disputed plays between the Estate and Frohman is outlined in a letter from Norman Croom-Johnson to Vyvyan Holland. It suggested that the Estate would take a two-thirds share and Frohman would take the remaining one-third. See letter from Croom-Johnson to Holland, 19 October 1934, in Papers of Robert Ross and Vyvyan Holland, MS 7018/4. It is not clear whether any adaptation rights were sold according to this agreement, but there is mention that the worldwide film rights for *The Importance of Being Earnest* were sold in 1932 in a letter to Frohman's London agent: see letter from Croom-Johnson to Gertrude Butler, 25 October 1934, in Papers of Robert Ross and Vyvyan Holland, MS 7018/4. The correspondence related to Warner's proposed adaptation is collected in the same box: MS 7018/4. Read in sequence, it tells a compelling story of delays. The existing agreement is undermined when Frohman and the American Play Company declare that he should have a higher 50 per-cent stake; this causes an impasse that ends with the issuing of contracts by Warner Brothers, only to have the contract rejected by Frohman.

Chapter 5

1. Ben Hecht, *Gaily, Gaily* (London: Elek Books, 1963), 187.

2. MacAdams, *Ben Hecht*, 68.

3. Ben Hecht, 'Fifty Books That Are Books', last accessed 26 January 2022, https://ilxor.com/ILX/ThreadSelectedControllerServlet?boardid=55&threadid=97564.

4. MacAdams, *Ben Hecht*, 35, 67–8.

5. Ben Hecht, 'The Sermon from the Depths', *The Little Review* 2, no. 3 (May 1915): 40. Modernist Journals Project.

6. Naremore, *More Than Night*, 55.

7. Jonathan Munby, *Public Enemies, Public Heroes: Screening the Gangster from Little Caesar to Touch of Evil* (Chicago: University of Chicago Press, 1999), 24–5.

8. David E. Ruth, *Inventing the Public Enemy: The Gangster in American Culture, 1918–1934* (London: University of Chicago Press, 1996), 1, 63, 66–7.

9. Munby, *Public Enemies, Public Heroes*, 21–4.

10. Gabrielle Dean, 'Cover Story: *The Smart Set*'s Clever Packaging, 1908–1923', *Journal of Modern Periodical Studies* 4, no. 1 (2013): 15. Project Muse. muse.jhu.edu/article/524287

11. Weir, *Decadence and the Making of Modernism*, 177.

12. Wilde, *Dorian Gray*, 138; Hornung, *Raffles*, 26. For a full discussion of how the decadent criminal evolved through these works, see Chapter 2.

13. Neil Sammells, 'Pulp Fictions: Oscar Wilde and Quentin Tarantino', *Irish Studies Review* 3, no. 11 (Summer 1995): 43. Taylor & Francis Online. doi.org/10.1080/09670889508455492.

14. In this period the South Side included Michigan Avenue.

15. Jennifer Ratner-Rosenhagen, *American Nietzsche: A History of an Icon and His Ideas* (Chicago: University of Chicago Press, 2012), 21–36.

16. H. L. Mencken, 'Portrait of a Tragic Comedian', *The Smart Set* 50, no. 1 (September 1916): 281. Modernist Journals Project. The great intellectual historian of Nietzsche's reception in Great Britain, Patrick Bridgwater, argues that 'Nietzsche found such ready acceptance in advanced intellectual circles at the turn of the century' because 'some of his areas of concern were, or sounded, familiar to English readers from writers such as Pater and Wilde': Bridgwater, *Anglo-German Interactions in the Literature of the 1890s* (Oxford: Legenda, 1999), 240–1. Could it be the same story in America? Quite possibly. Huneker knew Wilde's work well, having met him on his 1882 tour, by the time he first read Nietzsche.

17. Mencken, 'Portrait of a Tragic Comedian', 284.

18. Margaret C. Anderson, 'Our First Year', *The Little Review* 1, no. 11 (February 1915): 2–3. Modernist Journals Project.

19. Oscar Wilde, *De Profundis*, in *The Annotated Prison Writings of Oscar Wilde*, ed. Nicholas Frankel (Cambridge, MA: Harvard University Press, 2018), 281. Wilde's original text uses an 's' in 'realises'. It's difficult to see why Anderson used this quotation since its sense is somewhat lost when taken out of the context of Wilde's address to Alfred Douglas about his need to face up to his behaviour.

20. In *The Little Review* between 1914 and 1915, Jennifer Ratner-Rosenhagen (*American Nietzsche*, 104) argues that George Burman introduced Nietzsche as ' "the Prophet of a New Culture" whose life and thought heralded an exalted image of modern man'. For a discussion of Burman's articles in *The Little Review*, see Ratner-Rosenhagen, *American Nietzsche*, 104–6.

21. Friedrich Nietzsche, *Twilight of the Idols*, trans. Richard Polt (Cambridge, MA: Hackett, 1997), 64–5.

22. [Anon.,] *The Smart Set* 53, no. 1 (September 1917): 118. Modernist Journals Project.

23. [Anon.,] *The Smart Set* 53, no. 1 (September 1917): 122. Modernist Journals Project.

24. H. L. Mencken, *A Little Book in C Major* (New York: John Lane, 1916), 61. This collection brings together many of Mencken's epigrams from *The Smart Set*.

25. [Anon.,] *The Smart Set* 47 no. 3 (November 1915): 202. Modernist Journals Project.

26. Mencken, *C Major*, 23.

27. Elaine Showalter, *Sexual Anarchy: Gender and Culture at the Fin de Siècle* (London: Virago, 1992), 176–7.

28. Wilde, *Dorian Gray*, 33.

29. Wilde, *Dorian Gray*, 46.

30. Wilde, *Dorian Gray*, 77.

31. Alan Golding, 'The Little Review (1915–1929)', in *The Oxford Critical and Cultural History of Modernist Magazines*, Volume II: *North America 1894–1960*, ed. Peter Brooker and Andrew Thacker (Oxford: Oxford University Press, 2012), 70.

32. Sharon Hamilton, 'American Manners: *The Smart Set* (1900–1929); *American Parade* (1929)', in *The Oxford Critical and Cultural History of Modernist Magazines*, Volume II: *North America 1894–1960*, ed. Brooker and Thacker, 234.

33. Hecht, *A Child of the Century*, 168.

34. Hecht, *Gaily, Gaily*, 86–8.

35. We do know that Machen was not impressed by his young acolyte. He wrote later, 'I am afraid Ben Hecht is a thoroughly worthless fellow. But I dare say he will make money': letter from Arthur Machen to Montgomery Evans, 25 September 1923, in *Arthur Machen and Montgomery Evans: Letters of a Literary Friendship, 1923–1947*, ed. Sue Strong Hassler and Donald M. Hassler (Kent, OH: Kent State University, 1994), 22.

36. Ben Hecht, 'The Reader Critic', *The Little Review* 2, no. 9 (December 1915): 42. Modernist Journal Project.

37. Hecht, *1001 Afternoons in Chicago* (Chicago: Covici-McGee, 1922), 153.

38. Hecht, *Gaily, Gaily*, 34.

39. Chandler, *The Simple Art of Murder*, 15.

40. To trace the examples listed here, see Hecht, 'Ripples', 265–8; 'Fog Patterns', 27–30; 'Jazz Band Impressions', 223–5; 'Nirvana', 127–30; and 'The Snob', 72–5, all collected in Hecht, *1001 Afternoons in Chicago* (page refs. are to this collection).

41. Hecht, 'Queen Bess' Feast', in Hecht, *1001 Afternoons in Chicago*, 185–8.

42. Marc Mappen, *Prohibition Gangsters: The Rise and Fall of a Bad Generation* (New Brunswick, NJ: Rutgers University Press, 2013), 10–11.

43. Hecht, *1001 Afternoon in Chicago*, 186.

44. Hecht, 'The Sybarite', 61, 62; 'Michigan Avenue', 54, 53; and 'The Little Fop', 85, all collected in Hecht, *1001 Afternoons in Chicago* (page refs. are to this collection).

45. Hecht, 'Where the "Blues" Sound', in Hecht, *1001 Afternoons in Chicago*, 119.
46. Mappen, *Prohibition Gangsters*, 10–12.
47. Hecht, 'Confessions', in Hecht, *1001 Afternoons in Chicago*, 185.
48. Hecht, 'Fog Patterns', 29.
49. Chapter 2 discusses Baudelaire's place in the evolution of the decadent criminal.
50. Ben Hecht, 'The Devil Slayer', *The Smart Set* 53, no. 1 (September 1917): 128. Modernist Journals Project.
51. Hecht, 'The Devil Slayer', 128.
52. Hecht, 'The Devil Slayer', 126.
53. Hecht, 'The Devil Slayer', 128.
54. Ben Hecht, 'The Bomb Thrower', *The Little Review* 7, no. 3 (September 1920): 18–23. Modernist Journals Project.
55. Hecht, 'The Bomb Thrower', 21.
56. Hecht, 'The Bomb Thrower', 18.
57. Hecht, 'The Bomb Thrower', 18, 19, 19.
58. Pater, *Renaissance*, 89; Baudelaire, 'The Painter of Modern Life', 7. The piquancy of sensual pleasure in Pater's *Renaissance* is intensified by his consciousness, famously expressed in the Conclusion, that 'we are all under sentence of death but with a sort of indefinite reprieve [...] we have an interval, and then our place knows us no more' (153).
59. Jules Barbey D'Aurevilly originally made this remark at the close of his 1884 review of *À rebours* in *The Constitutional*. Huysmans quoted it in his 1903 Preface to the novel: Joris-Karl Huysmans, 'Preface Written Twenty Years After the Novel', trans. Patrick McGuiness, in Huysmans, *Against Nature*, trans. Robert Baldick (London: Penguin, 2003), 308.
60. John Baxter, *Von Sternberg* (Lexington: University of Kentucky Press, 2010), 67–9.
61. Hecht, quoted in Baxter, *Von Sternberg*, 67.
62. [Anon.,] 'Pictures and People', *Motion Picture News*, 9 September 1927 (July–September 1927): 763. Lantern: Media History Digital Library. shorturl.at/qDI37
63. Gabler, *An Empire of Their Own*, 204.
64. Ruth, *Inventing the Public Enemy*, 115.
65. For discussion of Des Esseintes's relationship with his house, see Jessica Gosling, ' "Things Worldly and Things Spiritual": Huysmans's *À rebours* and the House at Fontenay', in *Decadence and the Senses*, ed. Jane Desmarais and Alice Condé (Oxford: Legenda, 2017), 69.
66. Munby, *Public Enemies, Public Heroes*, 19–20.
67. Donald Crafton, *The Talkies: America's Transition to Sound, 1926–1931*, Volume IV of *History of the American Cinema*, ed. Charles Harpole (Berkeley and Los Angeles: University of California Press, 1999), 475–6. See also Nora

Gilbert, *Better Left Unsaid: Victorian Novels, Hays Code Films, and the Benefits of Censorship* (Stanford, CA: Stanford University Press, 2013), 6–8.

68. See Walter Pater, *Appreciations with an Essay on Style* (Evanston, IL: Northwestern University Press, 1987), 242; Arthur Symons, 'A Prelude to Life', in *The Memoirs of Arthur Symons: Life and Art in the 1890s*, ed. Karl Beckson (London: Pennsylvania State University Press, 1977), 17.

69. Sammells, 'Pulp Fictions', 43; Wilde, 'Lord Arthur Savile's Crime', in Wilde, *The Complete Short Stories* (Oxford: Oxford University Press, 2010), 3–32, at 5, 17–18, 24–5.

70. Wilde, 'Lord Arthur Savile's Crime', 11.

71. Wilde, 'Lord Arthur Savile's Crime', 17.

72. In Hoffenstein, *Life Sings a Song*, see esp. 'The Prescience of Immortality' (37–8), 'Oh! Quiet Night' (75), and 'To a Cabaret Singer' (80–3); Pater, *Renaissance*, 153.

73. Wilde, 'Lord Arthur Savile's Crime', 11.

74. For contemporary examples, see *The 39 Steps* (1939), *Spellbound* (1941), and *Gaslight* (1944), all of which juxtapose the sound of a train whistle with the protagonist's mortal fear to heighten tension. For a discussion of the metaphorical significance of trains in films noirs, see Nicholas Christopher, *Somewhere in the Night: Film Noir and the American City* (New York: Free Press, 1997), 96.

75. Wilde, 'Lord Arthur Savile's Crime', 12.

76. Wilde, 'Lord Arthur Savile's Crime', 12–13.

77. Hext, 'Victorians in the Closet', 722–3.

78. The following year, Robinson's off-screen friend Gene Kelly devised the 'Alter-Ego Dance' for *Cover Girl* (1944). Kelly's dance with his alter ego in a deserted street suggests a parallel with, or even an influence from, Tyler's alter ego.

79. There is reference to a proposed French film adaptation of 'Lord Arthur Savile's Crime' in a letter from Holman to Ross, 8 February 1917, in Papers of Robert Ross and Vyvyan Holland, Bodleian Library, Oxford, MS7018/1 Folder 8.

80. For the correspondence concerning the proposed sale of the worldwide film rights for 'Lord Arthur Savile's Crime' in 1933–4, see Papers of Robert Ross and Vyvyan Holland, MS7018/3 Folder 1. Letters spanning over a year show the estate's considerable interest in selling the film rights: negotiations advanced as far as a draft contract and price (£1,000), both included in the papers. When this deal fell through by early 1934, the Estate, led by Vyvyan Holland, investigated alternative buyers for the film rights to 'Lord Arthur Savile's Crime' (which they priced at £2,000) alongside 'The Canterville Ghost' (£2,000), 'The Sphinx Without a Secret' (£500), and *The Ballad of Reading Gaol* (£500): see letters from N. Croom-Johnson to Vyvyan Holland, 17 and 18 January 1934, in Papers of Robert Ross and Vyvyan Holland, MS7018/3 Folder 1.

81. Hyde Pierce, quoted in Mervyn Rothstein, 'David Hyde Pierce Reimagines *The Importance of Being Earnest*, With a "Mob" Twist', *Playbill* (25 June 2012), last accessed 17 January 2023, https://www.playbill.com/article/david-hyde-pierce-reimagines-the-importance-of-being-earnest-with-a-mob-twist-com-195055.

Chapter 6

1. Ronald R. Butters, 'Cary Grant and the Emergence of Gay Homosexual', *Dictionaries: Journal of the Dictionary Society of North America* 19 (1998): 188–9.
2. George Chauncey, *Gay New York: Gender, Urban Culture, and the Makings of the Gay Male World, 1890–1940* (New York: Basic Books, 1995), 18 n.
3. DiBattista, *Fast-Talking Dames*, 105.
4. Peter Swaab, *Bringing Up Baby* (London: BFI, 2010), 8–9.
5. Caserio, 'Queer Modernism', 200.
6. For a useful discussion of this and other contributing factors involved, see Crafton, *The Talkies*, 472–4.
7. Crafton, *The Talkies*, 472.
8. 'MPPDA Code', quoted in Crafton, *The Talkies*, 475.
9. Screwball comedy broadly falls into two categories: the comedy of the sexes, which I'm focusing on here, and class comedies, such as *It Happened One Night*, *My Man Godfrey* (1936), and *The Lady Eve* (1941). Both categories feature wisecracking but do not tend to feature epigrams.
10. Gilbert, *Better Left Unsaid*, 2, 46. On *The Picture of Dorian Gray*, as discussed in Chapter 1, Wilde argued in a letter to the *Scots Observer* that 'what Dorian Gray's sins are no one knows'. Wilde uses allusions and implications to evoke Dorian's homosexual encounters throughout the novel and these are discussed in Chapter 2. Nicholas Frankel discusses the ways in which the novel's 1890 text was edited in his 'Textual Introduction', in *The Uncensored Picture of Dorian Gray*, ed. Frankel (Cambridge, MA: Belknap Press, 2011), 35–53.
11. Jacobs, *The Decline of Sentiment*, 2.
12. Ben Hecht, *Erik Dorn* (New York: G. P. Putnam's Sons, 1921), 20.
13. Hecht, *Erik Dorn*, 28.
14. Hecht, *Erik Dorn*, 31.
15. For a full discussion of Wilde's epigrams, see Anderson, *The Powers of Distance*, 147–73.
16. Hecht, *Erik Dorn*, 367.
17. As David Weir notes, the former reportedly influenced Allen Ginsberg's poem *Howl* (1956). See Weir's *Decadence and the Making of Modernism*, 180.
18. MacAdams, *Ben Hecht*, 70–1. Like a true Wildean, Hecht reused this epigram in his novel, *Humpty Dumpty* (New York: Boni & Liveright, 1924), 299.

19. Weir, *Decadence* and *the Making of Modernism*, 191.
20. [Advertisement,] 'National Broadcasting Co., Inc', *Radio Doings* (5 July 1930): 16. Lantern: Media History Digital Library. shorturl.at/bwIPZ.
21. Jerusha McCormack, 'Wilde's Dublin, Dublin's Wilde', in *Oscar Wilde in Context*, ed. Kerry Powell and Peter Raby (Cambridge: Cambridge University Press, 2013), 19.
22. For examples, see [Anon.,] 'Theatres', *The Seattle Star* (25 July 1901): 2; [Anon.,] 'Theatre', *New York Daily Tribune* (4 December 1910): 6; [Anon.,] 'The Belasco Theater—Opening of Arden Company in Wilde Play', *The Washington Herald* (12 May 1907): 4. Chronicling America: Historical American Newspapers.
23. Oscar Wilde, *The Importance of Being Earnest*, in *The Importance of Being Earnest and Other Plays* (Oxford: Oxford University Press, 2008), 259, lines 242–4.
24. Wilde, *Earnest*, 260, lines 278–9.
25. Wilde, *Earnest*, 268, lines 592–5.
26. Anderson discusses the 'transferability' of the epigram: *The Powers of Distance*, 148.
27. Mackie, 'The Function of Decorum at the Present Time', 147–9.
28. Michael Kimmel, *Manhood in America: A Cultural History* (Oxford: Oxford University Press, 2011), 120 ff.
29. Chauncey, *Gay New York*, 318; see also Chauncey's broader discussion of the visibility of the gay scene in New York, at 1–23.
30. Chauncey suggests that there is good reason to believe that the New York scene is reflected in other cities and towns across the US but further research would be necessary to confirm the fact: see *Gay New York*, 12.
31. Chauncey, *Gay New York*, 67–103.
32. Chauncey, *Gay New York*, 105–6.
33. Alan Sinfield, *The Wilde Century: Effeminacy, Oscar Wilde and the Queer Moment* (London: Cassell, 1994), 75.
34. Sinfield, *The Wilde Century*, 70–3.
35. Jarman, quoted in Hoare, *Noël Coward*, 129.
36. Wilde, *Earnest*, 257–9, lines 177–257.
37. Wilde, *Earnest*, 273, lines 52–3.
38. Walter D. Hickman, 'Ton of Acting Bestowed on Wilde; Palos and Palet, Art Landry Are Hits', *The Indianapolis Times* (5 June 1923): 3. Chronicling America: Historical American Newspapers. shorturl.at/hpU05
39. At the beginning of each of the social comedies, Wilde specifies that the time is 'The Present'; Mackie, 'The Function of Decorum at the Present Time', 149.
40. [Anon.,] 'Society', *Grand Forks Herald* (20 February 1922): 10. Chronicling America: Historical American Newspapers. shorturl.at/hyP69

41. Dorothy Parker, 'On Oscar Wilde', *Life* (2 June 1927), 13.
42. Bankhead, quoted in Ronald Blythe, *The Pleasures of Diaries: Four Centuries of Private Writing* (London: Pantheon, 1989), 3.
43. Bankhead reproduces the bon mot in her autobiography, *Tallulah: My Autobiography* (Jackson: University of Mississippi Press, 2004), 72.
44. Mackie, 'The Function of Decorum at the Present Time', 157.
45. Wilde, *Earnest*, 288, lines 635–6.
46. Bankhead reportedly used the word 'ambisextrous' for shock value in conversation. The earliest reference to her use of it in print may be in Maurice Zolotow's *No People Like Show People* (London: Random House, 1951), 56. Joel Lobenthal's biography, *Tallulah!: The Life and Times of a Leading Lady* (London: HarperCollins, 2001), 96–7, notes how Bankhead employed wit to secure her reputation as a 'sexual adventuress'.
47. E. J. Fleming, *The Fixers: Eddie Mannix, Howard Strickling and the MGM Publicity Machine* (Jefferson, NC: McFarland, 2005), 110.
48. Madsen, *The Sewing Circle*, 114.
49. Schenkar, *Truly Wilde*, 23.
50. Madsen, *The Sewing Circle*, 14.
51. Oscar Wilde, *A Woman of No Importance*, in *The Importance of Being Earnest and Other Plays* (Oxford: Oxford University Press, 2008), 110, lines 444–7.
52. In *The Powers of Distance*, Anderson shows that Mrs Erlynne's defiant epigrammatic wit lifts her above her structural position as a fallen woman, although when faced with her daughter's situation in Act 2, a new note of melodrama and tragedy enters into her dialogue: Oscar Wilde, *Lady Windermere's Fan*, in *The Importance of Being Earnest and Other Plays* (Oxford: Oxford University Press, 2008), 34, lines 492–7.
53. Wilde, *Lady Windermere*, 54, lines 255–8.
54. Suzanne Rodriguez, *Wild Heart, A Life: Natalie Clifford Barney and the Decadence of Literary Paris* (London: Harper Collins, 2002), 31–2.
55. Natalie Clifford Barney, *Éparpillements* (Paris: La Coopérative, 2020), 39.
56. Barney, quoted in Jean Chalon, *Chère Natalie Barney: Portrait d'une séductrice* (Paris: Flammarion, 1992), 165.
57. Barney, *Chère Natalie Barney*, 165.
58. Barney, *Chère Natalie Barney*, 165.
59. Schenkar, *Truly Wilde*, 102–3.
60. Coward, quoted in Hoare, *Noël Coward*, 148.
61. Noël Coward, *Present Indicative* (London: Methuen Drama, 2007), 213.
62. Coward, *Present Indicative*, 189.
63. *The Pleasure Man* was reworked from her 1927 play *Drag* (written by West under the pen name of Jane Mast), which focused on a homosexual character.
64. Hext, 'Rethinking the Origins of Camp', 169.

65. Lillian Schlissel, 'Introduction', in *Three Plays by Mae West: Sex, The Drag and The Pleasure Man* (London: Routledge, 2013), 8.

66. Tanitch, *Oscar Wilde on Stage and Screen*, 374–5.

67. Schlissel, 'Introduction', 21.

68. 'He's divinely selfish; all amusing people are', Pawnie jokes in the opening scene of *The Vortex*: in Noël Coward, *Collected Plays: One* (London: Methuen, 1999), 76. Likewise, in *The Green Bay Tree*, Dulcimer's Wildean quips include, 'When you hear anyone describe an experience as "marvellous," you can be sure that it has made no impression on them whatsoever.' See Mordaint Sharp, *The Green Bay Tree* (London: Oberon Books, 2014), 16.

69. Emily Wortis Leider, *Becoming Mae West* (Jackson: Da Capo Press, 2000), 22.

70. Leider, *Becoming Mae West*, 22.

71. Robertson, *Guilty Pleasures*, 33.

72. Wilde, *Lady Windermere*, 11, lines 148–9.

73. Gabler, *An Empire of Their Own*, 204.

74. Leider, *Becoming Mae West*, 251–2.

75. Leonard J. Leff and Jerold L. Simmons, *The Dame in the Kimono: Hollywood, Censorship, and the Production Code* (Lexington: University Press of Kentucky, 2001), 31–2.

76. Beaton, quoted in Leider, *Becoming Mae West*, 49.

77. Robert Forsythe, 'Mae West: A Treatise on Decay', *The New Masses* (9 October 1934): 29.

78. MacAdams, *Ben Hecht*, 7.

79. Jack Babuscio discusses Horton's screen persona alongside those of Bette Davis and Mae West, suggesting that their combination of irony, aestheticism, theatricality, and humour makes them exemplars of camp performance in Hollywood. See Babuscio, 'The Cinema of Camp (aka Camp and the Gay Sensibility)', in *Camp: Queer Aesthetics and the Performing Subject*, ed. Fabio Cleto (Edinburgh: Edinburgh University Press, 1999), 118–19.

80. Linda Constanzo Cahir, 'A Shared Impulse, 8.

81. Wilde, *No Importance*, 115, lines 112–14.

82. Susan J. Navarette, *The Shape of Fear: Horror and the Fin de Siècle Culture of Decadence* (Lexington: University Press of Kentucky, 1998), 40–1.

83. Oscar Wilde, 'The Critic as Artist', in Wilde, *The Soul of Man Under Socialism and Selected Critical Prose* (London: Penguin, 2001), 223.

84. Anderson, *The Powers of Distance*, 173.

85. Mackie discusses how this questioning of key moral terms operates in Wilde's comedies. See Mackie, 'The Function of Decorum at the Present Time', 146–7.

86. DiBattista, *Fast-Talking Dames*, 105.

87. DiBattista, *Fast-Talking Dames*, 106.

88. Hagar Wilde, 'Bringing Up Baby', *Collier's Weekly* (10 April 1937): 20–2.

89. Howard Hawks, interview with Peter Bogdanovich in *Who the Devil Made It?*, ed. Peter Bogdanovich (New York: Alfred A. Knopf, 1997), 84.
90. Mark Glancy, *Cary Grant: The Making of a Hollywood Legend* (New York: Oxford University Press, 2020), 35–51.
91. Glancy, *Cary Grant*, 108.
92. Kristine Brunovska Karnick and Henry Jenkins, 'Comedy and the Social World', in *Classical Hollywood Comedy*, ed. Karnick and Jenkins (New York: Routledge, 1995), 280. There is a pervasive rumour that the gay Cukor, a friend of Nazimova, was inspired by her all-gay cast in *Salome* to employ an all-gay cast for his adaptation of *Camille* (1936).
93. Wilde, *Earnest*, 258, line 209.
94. John Mason Brown, quoted in Tanitch, *Oscar Wilde on Stage and Screen*, 273.
95. *New York World Telegram*, quoted in Tanitch, *Oscar Wilde on Stage and Screen*, 109; Tanitch collects further examples too at 268–9, 273.

Chapter 7

1. It opened on 29 September 1936 and ran for six weeks. The British film, *Oscar Wilde* (Vantage Films, 1960), was based on the Stokes' play, and also starred Morley as Wilde.
2. Gregory William Mank, *Laird Cregar: A Hollywood Tragedy* (Jefferson, NC: McFarland, 2018), 47.
3. Leslie Stokes and Sewell Stokes, *Oscar Wilde: A Play* (New York: Random House, 1938), 115.
4. Mank, *Laird Cregar*, 48, 54–8.
5. Mank, *Laird Cregar*, 51.
6. Quoted in Mank, *Laird Cregar*, 54.
7. Quoted in Mank, *Laird Cregar*, 55.
8. In *Laird Cregar*, 57, Mank notes Barrymore's attendance at *Oscar Wilde*. For a discussion of the Barrymore family's relationship with Wilde, see Chapter 2.
9. Fredda Dudley, 'Atlas with a Grin, Laird Cregar', *Screenland* 44 no. 2 (December 1941): 81. Lantern: Media History Digital Library. https://shorturl.at/dGUX9
10. Quoted in Mank, *Laird Cregar*, 45.
11. [Anon.,] 'Review: Oscar Wilde and The Yellow Nineties', *The Atlantic* (May 1940). https://cdn.theatlantic.com/media/archives/1940/05/165-5/132469059.pdf
12. Laird Cregar, Basil Rathbone, and George Sanders were all under consideration for the role in 1943. However, the Feature Script Review shows that Cregar was already ruled out of the role at the time of his death. Sandy Roth, Office of War Information: Los Angeles Overseas Bureau, Motion Picture Division, 6 March 1944, OWI Script Reviews N–R; Margaret Herrick Library, LA.

13. Vito Russo, *The Celluloid Closet: Homosexuality in the Movies* (New York: Harper & Row, 1981), 68.

14. Russo, *The Celluloid Closet*, 63.

15. Benshoff, *Monsters in the Closet:*, 20–2.

16. Benshoff, *Monsters in the Closet*, 20.

17. Benshoff, *Monsters in the Closet*, 20.

18. Benshoff, *Monsters in the Closet*, 46. Thesiger essentially reprised this role in *Bride of Frankenstein* (1935).

19. Ernest Thesiger, *Practically True* (London: Heinemann, 1927), 87.

20. See Thesiger's assorted scrapbooks held at the University of Bristol Theatre Collection's Ernest Thesiger Archive: e.g. photos and a flyer for a 1903 production of *Earnest* at the Imperial Theatre, London, in EFT/1/Box 1 [n.p.]; photo and flyer of a 1911 production of *Lady Windermere* at the St James's Theatre in EFT/3; scrapbooked articles on his 1930 production of *Lady Windermere*, in which he also starred as Dumby. The rights were granted gratis by Vyvyan Holland, in EFT/4, 79–87.

21. Philip Hoare, *Wilde's Last Stand: Scandal, Decadence and Conspiracy during the Great War* (London: Duckworth Overlook, 1997), 10–11.

22. Wilde, *Lady Windermere's Fan*, 51, lines 137–8.

23. Benshoff, *Monsters in the Closet*, 33–4.

24. David M. Earle, *Re-Covering Modernism: Pulps, Paperbacks, and the Prejudice of Form* (Farnham: Ashgate, 2009), 75–6.

25. Benshoff, *Monsters in the Closet*, 65.

26. See discussion in Chapter 1.

27. Benshoff, *Monsters in the Closet*, 65.

28. Dianne F. Sadoff, *Victorian Vogue: British Novels Onscreen* (Minneapolis: University of Minnesota Press, 2010), 224.

29. James Naremore, *More Than Night: Film Noir in Its Contexts*, 53.

30. Richard Dyer, 'Homosexuality in Film Noir', *Jump Cut* 16 (1977) https://www.ejumpcut.org/archive/onlinessays/JC16folder/HomosexFilmNoir.html; Steve Neale, ' "I Can't Tell Anymore Whether You're Lying": *Double Indemnity*, *Human Desire* and the Narratology of *Femmes Fatales*', in *The Femme Fatale: Images, Histories, Contexts*, ed. Helen Hansen and Catherine O'Rawe (London: Palgrave, 2010), 187.

31. William Hare, *Early Film Noir: Greed, Lust and Murder Hollywood Style* (Jefferson, NC: McFarland, 2010), 110.

32. Vera Caspary, *Laura* (London: Vintage, 2012), 6.

33. See Robert Tanitch, *Oscar Wilde on Stage and Screen* (London: Methuen, 1999), 273.

34. Wilde, *Earnest*, 257, line 166.

35. Wilde, *Earnest*, 258, lines 203–5.

36. Wilde, *Earnest*, 255, lines 81–111.

37. It is widely accepted that Faulkner was the principal writer of this adaptation, with assistance from Leigh Bracket on the first drafts, and later edits provided by Jules Furthman. It must be acknowledged though that there is only circumstantial evidence for this view.

38. John I. Irwin, *Unless the Threat of Death Is Behind Them: Hard-Boiled Fiction and Film Noir* (Baltimore: Johns Hopkins University Press, 2006), 41–6.

39. William Faulkner, Leigh Brackett, and Jules Furthman, *The Big Sleep* [Draft Screenplay, 1944], last accessed 17 January 2023, https://www.dailyscript.com/scripts/Big_Sleep.pdf, 3–4, 7.

40. Raymond Chandler, *The Big Sleep*, in Chandler, *The Big Sleep and Other Novels* (London: Penguin, 2000), 1–164, at 6.

41. Catherine Maxwell, *Scents and Sensibility: Perfume in Victorian Literary Culture* (Oxford: Oxford University Press, 2017), 182–3. See e.g. Theodore Wratislaw's collection *Orchids: Poems* (London: Leonard Smithers, 1896).

42. Wilde, *Dorian Gray*, 189, 200.

43. William Faulkner, *Absalom, Absalom!* (London: Vintage, 2005), 97. Faulkner's early Beardsley-style illustrations are indicative that the 'dominant sensibility' of his early poetic and dramatic work was defined by Verlaine, Swinburne, and Wilde. For a full discussion, see Daniel Joseph Singal, *William Faulkner: The Making of a Modernist* (Chapel Hill: University of North Carolina Press, 1997): 48–9.

44. For a full discussion, see Len Gutkin, 'The Dandified Dick: Hardboiled Noir and the Wildean Epigram', *ELH* 81 no. 4 (Winter 2014), 1299–1326, at 1299–1301. Project Muse. 10.1353/elh.2014.0043

45. See Faulkner, Brackett, and Furthman, *The Big Sleep* [Draft Screenplay], 6; Chandler, *The Big Sleep*, 8.

46. Gutkin, 'The Dandified Dick', 1313.

47. David Thompson, *The Big Sleep* (London: BFI, 1997), 54–5.

48. Gutkin, 'The Dandified Dick', 1301.

49. Gutkin, 'The Dandified Dick', 1301.

50. Gutkin, 'The Dandified Dick', 1316.

51. Gutkin. 'The Dandified Dick', 1303–4.

52. Kristin Mahoney, *Literature and the Politics of Post-Victorian Decadence* (Cambridge: Cambridge University Press, 2015), 30.

53. Andrew Spicer, *Film Noir* (Harlow: Pearson, 2002), 7.

54. Thompson, *The Big Sleep*, 64.

55. Naremore, *More Than Night*, 42–51.

56. Drawing on Lee Edelman's *No Future: Queer Theory and the Death Drive* (Durham, NC: Duke University Press, 2004), Vincent Sherry explores the concept of decadent temporality in *Modernism and the Reinvention of Decadence* (New York: Cambridge University Press, 2014), 25–6.

57. Dorothy B. Jones, 'The Hollywood War Film, 1942–1944', *Hollywood Quarterly* 1 no. 1 (October 1945), 1–19, at 1–6. Jstor. https://doi.org/10.2307/1209583

58. *The Canterville Ghost* [exhibition poster], *The Exhibitor* 32 no. 10 (19 July 1944), 2, https://archive.org/details/exhibitorjunnov132jaye/page/n536/mode/1up?view=theater.

59. Lubitsch originally wanted to cast Colman in the male lead of *Design for Living*, having directed him previously in *Lady Windermere*.

60. Susan Felleman, *Botticelli in Hollywood: The Films of Albert Lewin* (Woodbridge, CT: Twayne Publishers, 1997), 15.

61. Chris Cagle uses the term 'prestige realist melodrama': that is, a film adapted from a canonical novel and most often removed from New Deal politics. See Cagle, *Sociology on Film: Post-War Hollywood's Prestige Commodity* (New Brunswick, NJ: Rutgers University Press, 2017), 128.

62. Steve Neale, 'Technicolor', in *Color: The Film Reader*, ed. Angela Dalle Vacche and Brian Price (Abingdon: Routledge, 2006), 13–23, at 18.

63. Albert Lewin, *The Picture*, 20 April 1943, Turner/MGM Scripts 2268-f.P-546, Margaret Herrick Library, Beverly Hills. The full original title has been struck through and the film retitled.

64. [Anon.,] 'Dorian Gray . . . Heavy for Masses', *Box Office Digest* 16, no. 13 (28 February 1945), https://archive.org/details/boxofficedigest100nati_2/page/n53/mode/2up?view=theater 12.

65. Quoted in Felleman, *Botticelli in Hollywood*, 45.

66. Russo, *The Celluloid Closet*, 64.

67. Neal Gabler, *An Empire of Their Own: How the Jews Invented Hollywood* (London: Doubleday, 1988), 211.

68. Russo, *The Celluloid Closet*, 62–3.

69. Lewin, *The Picture*, 20 April 1943, 3–4.

70. Felleman, *Botticelli in Hollywood*, 51–2.

71. Albert Lewin, [Untitled essay,] in *The Real Tinsel*, ed. Bernard Rosenberg and Harry Silverstein (London: Collier-Macmillan Ltd, 1970), 100–24, at 118.

72. Lewin, *The Picture*, 20 April 1943 [unpaginated].

73. Albert Lewin, *The Picture of Dorian Gray: Composite Script*, 1945, 117, Turner/MGM Scripts 2268-f.P 546, Margaret Herrick Library, Beverly Hills. Like Wilde, Lewin evokes the painting mainly by its effects on those looking at it: 'It is a study in decay, degeneracy, and disintegration—sinister and frightening', he notes in the script here, adding that 'The colors have grown dim and dusty and morose'.

74. Felleman, *Botticelli in Hollywood*, 51–2.

75. Felleman, *Botticelli in Hollywood*, 45.

76. Adrian Singleton quotes the following lines: 'But grim to see is the gallows-tree, | ... | And, green or dry, a man must die | Before it bears its fruit!' See *The Ballad*

of Reading Gaol, in *The Annotated Prison Writings of Oscar Wilde*, ed. Nicholas Frankel (Cambridge, MA: Harvard University Press, 2018), 329.

77. See Nicholas Christopher, *Somewhere in the Night: Film Noir and the American City* (New York: Free Press, 1997), 4–6.
78. Wilde, *Dorian Gray*, 181.
79. Wilde, *Dorian Gray*, 144.
80. Wilde, *Dorian Gray*, 150.
81. Lewin, *The Picture*, 20 April 1943, 114.
82. Alain Silver and James Ursini, *The Noir Style* (Woodstock, NY: The Overlook Press, 1999), 38–9.
83. This dialogue does not open the scene in Wilde's novel. See Wilde, *Dorian Gray*, 177.
84. Wilde, *Dorian Gray*, 177.
85. Lewin, *The Picture*, 20 April 1943, 27.
86. Lewin, *The Picture*, 20 April 1943, 71.
87. Lewin, *The Picture*, 20 April 1943, 92.
88. Lewin, *The Picture,* 20 April 1943, 62.
89. Lewin, *The Picture of Dorian Gray*, 5 November 1943, 163.
90. Lewin, *The Picture of Dorian Gray*, 5 November 1943, 152.
91. Sturgis, *Oscar Wilde: A Life*, 386–7.
92. Ellmann, *Oscar Wilde*, 314.
93. Nicholas Frankel, 'Textual Introduction', in *The Uncensored Picture of Dorian Gray*, ed. Frankel (Cambridge, MA: Belknap Press, 2011), 34.
94. Wilde, *Dorian Gray*, 147.
95. Douglas Kerr, *Conan Doyle: Writing, Profession, and Practice* (Oxford: Oxford University Press, 2013), 24.
96. Wilde, *Dorian Gray*, 189–92.
97. [Anon.,] '*Dorian Gray* is Artistic Horror "Kitty O'Day": A Whodunnit Fun Dish', *Hollywood Reporter* (26 February 1926): 2. Kitty O'Day was a female detective character played by Jean Parker in *Detective Kitty O'Day* (1944) and *Adventures of Kitty O'Day* (1945). https://archive.org/details/hollywoodnitelif01holl/page/n157/mode/2up?view=theater
98. Vincente Minnelli, *I Remember It Well* (New York: Doubleday, 1974), 143.
99. *The Man in Half Moon Street* was remade as *The Man Who Could Cheat Death* (1959) by Hammer Horror, set in 1890, or beginning in 1890.
100. Stephen Rebello, *Alfred Hitchcock and the Making of Psycho* (London: Debner Books, 1990), 126–7.

Conclusion

1. Wilde, 'Phrases and Philosophies', 1205.
2. The most notable exception is Rupert Everett's film *The Happy Prince* (2018).

Select Works Cited

Archive Sources

New York Public Library, New York

Van Vechten, Carl. Letters. Carl Van Vechten Papers, 1833–1965
Van Vechten, Carl. Daybooks. Carl Van Vechten Papers, 1833–1965

Margaret Herrick Library, Beverly Hills

Lewin, Albert. *The Picture*. 20 April 1943. Turner/MGM Scripts 2268-f.P-546.
Lewin, Albert. *The Picture of Dorian Gray: Composite Script*, 5 November 1943. Turner/MGM Scripts 2268-f.P-546.
Mathis, June, and Alla Nazimova. 'Aphrodite'. Undated [1920]. 13-f.91, 1.
Roth, Sandy. Office of War Information: Los Angeles Overseas Bureau, Motion Picture Division, 6 March 1944. OWI Script Reviews N–R.

Bodleian Library, Oxford

MSS 7018/1, 7018/2, 7018/3, 7018/4: specific items cited individually in notes. Papers of Robert Ross and Vyvyan Holland relating to the Literary Estate of Oscar Wilde.

University of Bristol Theatre Collection, Bristol

Thesiger, Ernest. Assorted Scrapbooks. Thesiger Archive.

Printed Matter and Online Resources

Abel, Richard. *Americanizing the Movies and 'Movie-Mad' Audiences, 1910–1914*. Berkeley and Los Angeles: University of California Press, 2006.
Allen, Richard. *Hitchcock's Romantic Irony*. New York: Columbia University Press, 2007.
Anderson, Addell Austin. 'The Ethiopian Art Theatre'. *Theatre Survey* 33 (November 1992): 132–43.

Anderson, Amanda. *The Powers of Distance: Cosmopolitanism and the Cultivation of Detachment*. Princeton: Princeton University Press, 2001.

Anderson, Margaret C. 'Our First Year'. *The Little Review* 1, no. 11 (February 1915): 1–6. Modernist Journals Project.

Anderson, Margaret C. 'A Real Magazine'. *The Little Review* 3, no. 5 (August 1916): 1–2. Modernist Journals Project.

Anger, Kenneth. 'Diva of Decadence: Salomé (1922)'. In *Unseen Cinema: Early American Avant-Garde Film, 1893–1941*, edited by Bruce Charles Posner, 93–7. New York: Black Thistle Press/Anthology Film Archives, 2001.

Anger, Kenneth. *Hollywood Babylon*. New York: Dell Publishing, 1975.

Anon. [Roberts, Ed.] *The Sins of Hollywood: An Exposé of Movie Vice!* Los Angeles: Hollywood Publishing Co., 1922.

Arlen, Michael. *The Green Hat*. London: The Boydell Press, 1984.

Babuscio, Jack. 'The Cinema of Camp (aka Camp and the Gay Sensibility)'. In *Camp: Queer Aesthetics and the Performing Subject*, edited by Fabio Cleto, 117–35. Edinburgh: Edinburgh University Press, 1999.

Bakst, Léon. 'Tailpiece for Salome'. *Mir iskusska* [*World of Art*] 5, no. 5 (1901): 287.

Bakst, Léon. 'List of Pictures'. *Mir iskusska*[*World of Art*] 7, no. 2 (1902): 109.

Bangs, John Kendrick. *Mrs Raffles, Being the Adventures of an Amateur Crackswoman*. New York: Harper & Brothers, 1905.

Bankhead, Tallulah. *Tallulah: My Autobiography*. Jackson: University of Mississippi Press, 2004.

Bara, Theda. 'The Curse on the Moving Picture Actress'. The Forum (July 1919): 83–93. The Unz Review. shorturl.at/cfIT3

Barkan, Elliot Robert. *Immigrants in American History: Arrival, Adaptation, and Integration*. Santa Barbara, CA: ABC Clio, 2013.

Barlow, S. L. M. 'The Movies—An Arraignment'. The Forum (January 1922): 37–41. The Unz Review. https://www.unz.com/print/Forum-1922jan-00037.

Barney, Natalie Clifford. *Éparpillements*. Paris: La Coopérative, 2020.

Barrios, Richard. *Screened Out: Playing Gay in Hollywood from Edison to Stonewall*. London: Routledge, 2003.

Barton, Ralph. 'A Tuesday Night at the Cocoanut Grove'. Vanity Fair (June 1927): 62–3.

Baudelaire, Charles. 'The Painter of Modern Life'. In *The Painter of Modern Life and Other Essays*, translated and edited by Jonathan Mayne, 1–42. London: Phaidon, 2006.

Baxter, John. *Von Sternberg*. Lexington: University of Kentucky Press, 2010.

Beardsley, Aubrey. 'Aubrey Beardsley illustrations for Salome by Oscar Wilde'. Accessed 26 January 2023. British Library Online. https://imagesonline.bl.uk/search/?searchQuery=beardsley+.

Beckson, Karl, ed. *Oscar Wilde: The Critical Heritage*. London: Routledge, 1974.

Benjamin, Walter. *Charles Baudelaire: A Lyric Poet in the Era of High Capital*, translated by Harry Zohn. London: Verso, 1997.

Benshoff, Harry M. *Monsters in the Closet: Homosexuality and the Horror Film*. Manchester: Manchester University, 1997.

Berlin, Irving. 'Sadie Salome, Go Home!' 1909. Sadie Salome.com, last accessed 17 January 2023. http://sadiesalome.com/about.html?KeepThis=true.

Bershtein, Evgenii. '"Next to Christ": Oscar Wilde in Russian Modernism'. In *The Reception of Oscar Wilde in Europe*, edited by Stefano Evangelista, 285–300. London: Continuum, 2010.

Blythe, Ronald. *The Pleasures of Diaries: Four Centuries of Private Writing*. London: Pantheon, 1989.

Brands, H. W. *The Reckless Decade: America in the 1890s*. Chicago: University of Chicago Press, 2002.

Braudy, Leo. *The Hollywood Sign: Fantasy and Reality of an American Icon*. New Haven: Yale University Press, 2011.

Bridgwater, Patrick. *Anglo-German Interactions in the Literature of the 1890s*. Oxford: Legenda, 1999.

Brooks, Louise. *Lulu in Hollywood: Expanded Edition*. Minneapolis: University of Minneapolis Press, 2000.

Brown, Daniel. 'Wilde and Wilder'. *PMLA* 119, no. 5 (October 2004): 1216–30. Jstor. https://www.jstor.org/stable/25486118

Brown, Justine. *Hollywood Utopia*. Vancouver: New Star Books 2002.

Brown, Liz. *Twilight Man: Love and Ruin in the Shadows of the Clark Empire*. London: Penguin, 2021.

Brown, Melanie Ann. 'Five-Cent Culture at the "University in Print": Radical Ideology and the Marketplace in E. Haldeman-Julius's Little Blue Books, 1919–1929'. PhD thesis, University of Minnesota, 2006.

Buchanan, Judith. '*The Picture of Dorian Gray* (1915)'. Video commentary, last accessed 19 January 2023. https://vimeo.com/ondemand/thanhouserloc.

Burnett, William R. *Little Caesar*. New York: The Dial Press, 1929.

Butters, Ronald R. 'Cary Grant and the Emergence of Gay Homosexual'. *Dictionaries: Journal of the Dictionary Society of North America* 19 (1998): 188–204.

Cagle, Chris. *Sociology on Film: Post-War Hollywood's Prestige Commodity*. New Brunswick, NJ: Rutgers University Press, 2017.

Cahir, Linda Costanzo. 'A Shared Impulse: The Significance of Language in Oscar Wilde's and Ernst Lubitsch's "Lady Windermere's Fan"'. *Literature/Film Quarterly* 19, no. 1 (1991): 7–11. ProQuest. https://shorturl.at/nCIQ6

Canby, Henry Seidel. *Our House*. New York: The Macmillan Company, 1919.

The Canterville Ghost [exhibition poster]. The Exhibitor 32, no. 10 (19 July 1944), 2. https://archive.org/details/exhibitorjunnov132jaye/page/n536/mode/1up?view=theater

Carroll, John Daly. 'The False Burton Combs'. December 1922. Public Library UK. Last accessed 17 January 2023. http://public-library.uk/ebooks/34/20.pdf.

Caserio, Robert L. 'Queer Modernism'. In *The Oxford Handbook of Modernisms*, edited by Peter Brooker, Andrzej Gąsiorek, Deborah Longworth, and Andrew Thacker, 199–221. Oxford: Oxford University Press, 2010.

Chalon, Jean. *Chère Natalie Barney: Portrait d'une séductrice*. Paris: Flammarion, 1992.

Chandler, Raymond. *The Big Sleep and Other Novels*. London: Penguin, 2000.

Chandler, Raymond. *The Simple Art of Murder*. London: Vintage, 1988.

The Chap-Book. Magazine edited by Herbert Stuart Stone. Chicago: 1894–8.

Chauncey, George. *Gay New York: Gender, Urban Culture, and the Makings of the Gay Male World, 1890–1940*. New York: Basic Books, 1995.

Christopher, Nicholas. *Somewhere in the Night: Film Noir and the American City*. New York: Free Press, 1997.

Chronicling America: Historic American Newspapers. Last modified 2023, last accessed 30 July 2023. https://chroniclingamerica.loc.gov/

Clayton, Alex. *The Body in Hollywood Slapstick*. Jefferson, NC: McFarland, 2007.

Conley, Timothy K. 'Beardsley and Faulkner'. *Journal of Modern Literature* 5, no. 3 (September 1976): 339–56.

Conried, Heirich. 'Opera Wars, 1903–1908: Parsifal, Salome, and the Manhattan Opera Company'. In *Grand Opera: The Story of the Met*, edited by Charles Affron and Mirella Jona Affron, 53–75. Oakland: University of California Press, 2014.

Cook, Pam. 'Picturing Natacha Rambova: Design and Celebrity Performance in the 1920s'. *Screening the Past* 40 (September 2015). http://www.screeningthepast. com/2015/08/picturing-natacha-rambova-design-and-celebrityperformance-in-the-1920s/.

Cooper, John. 'The Lecture Tour of North America: A Flagship Project'. Oscar Wilde in America. Last modified 2022, last accessed 17 January 2023. https://www. oscarwildeinamerica.org/lectures-1882/lecture-intro.html

Coward, Noël. *Present Indicative*. London: Methuen Drama, 2007.

Coward, Noël. *The Vortex*, in *Collected Plays: One*. London: Methuen, 1999.

Crafton, Donald. *The Talkies: America's Transition to Sound, 1926–1931*. Volume IV of *History of the American Cinema*, edited by Charles Harpole. Berkeley and Los Angeles: University of California Press, 1999.

Cram, Ralph Adams. *The Decadent: Being the Gospel of Inaction*. Boston: Copeland & Day, 1894.

Crowell, Ellen. 'The Ugly Things of Salome'. In *Decadence in the Age of Modernism*, edited by Kate Hext and Alex Murray, 47–70. Baltimore: Johns Hopkins University Press, 2019.

Crump, James. *F. Holland Day: Suffering the Ideal*. Santa Fe: Twin Palms Publishers, 1995.

Cucullu, Lois. 'Wilde and Wilder Salomés: Modernizing the Nubile Princess from Sarah Bernhardt to Norma Desmond'. *Modernism/modernity* 18, no. 3 (September 2011): 495–524. Project Muse. https://doi.org/10.1353/mod.2011.0057

Danahay, Martin. 'Richard Mansfield, Jekyll and Hyde and the History of Special Effects'. *Nineteenth Century Theatre and Film* 39, no. 2 (Winter 2012): 54–72. Taylor & Francis Online. https://doi.org/10.7227/NCTF.39.2.4

Day, George Martin. *The Russians in Hollywood: A Study in Culture Conflict*. Los Angeles: University of Southern California Press, 1934.

de Acosta, Mercedes. *Moods*. New York: Moffat, Yard & Company, 1919.

Dean, Gabrielle. 'Cover Story: *The Smart Set*'s Clever Packaging, 1908–1923'. *Journal of Modern Periodical Studies* 4, no. 1 (2013): 1–29. Project Muse. muse.jhu.edu/article/524287

DiBattista, Maria. *Fast-Talking Dames*. New Haven: Princeton University Press, 2001.

Dierkes-Thrun, Petra. *Salome's Modernity: Oscar Wilde and the Aesthetics of Transgression*. Ann Arbor: University of Michigan Press, 2011.

Dietz, Howard. *Dancing in the Dark: An Autobiography*. New York: Bantam Books, 1976.

Dovzhyk, Sasha. 'Aubrey Beardsley in the Russian "World of Art"'. *British Art Studies* 18 (November 2020): 1–42. https://doi.org/10.17658/issn.2058-5462/issue-18/sdovzhyk

Dowson, Ernest. *Collected Poems*. Edited by R. K. R. Thornton. Birmingham: University of Birmingham Press, 2004.

Doyle, Arthur Conan. *The Sign of Four*. London: Penguin, 2001.

du Maurier, George. *Trilby*. Oxford: Oxford University Press, 2009.

Richard Dyer, 'Homosexuality in Film Noir', *Jump Cut* 16 (1977): https://www.ejumpcut.org/archive/onlinessays/JC16folder/HomosexFilmNoir.html

Earle, David M. *Re-Covering Modernism: Pulps, Paperbacks, and the Prejudice of Form*. Farnham: Ashgate, 2009.

Edelman, Lee. *No Future: Queer Theory and the Death Drive*. Durham, NC: Duke University Press, 2004.

Eliot, T. S. 'The Lesson of Baudelaire'. *Tyro: A Review of the Arts of Painting, Sculpture, and Design* 1 (Spring 1921): 4.

Eliot, T. S. *The Waste Land: A Facsimile and Transcript*. Edited by Valerie Eliot. London: Faber & Faber, 2011.

Ellmann, Richard. *Oscar Wilde*. London: Vintage, 1988.

Elsaesser, Thomas. 'The Dandy in Hitchcock'. *The MacGuffin* 14 (1994): 15–21.

Eltis, Sos. *Revisiting Wilde: Society and Subversion in the Plays of Oscar Wilde*. Oxford: Oxford University Press, 1996.

Evangelista, Stefano. 'Introduction: Oscar Wilde—European by Sympathy'. In *The Reception of Oscar Wilde in Europe*, edited by Evangelista, 1–19. London: Continuum, 2010.

Eyman, Scott. *Ernst Lubitsch: Laughter in Paradise*. New York: Simon and Schuster, 1993.

Faulkner, William. *Absalom, Absalom!* London: Vintage, 2005.

Faulkner, William, Leigh Brackett, and Jules Furthman. The Big Sleep [Draft Screenplay, 1944]. Last accessed 17 January 2023. https://www.dailyscript.com/scripts/Big_Sleep.pdf

Felleman, Susan. *Botticelli in Hollywood: The Films of Albert Lewin*. Woodbridge, CT: Twayne Publishers, 1997.

Fischer, Lucy, *Cinema by Design: Art Nouveau, Modernism, and Film History*. New York: Columbia University Press, 2017.

Fitzgerald, Edward. *Rubaiyat of Omar Khayyam*. London: Collins, 1926.

Fitzgerald, F. Scott. *The Last Tycoon*. London: Penguin, 2001.

Fitzgerald, F. Scott. *This Side of Paradise*. London: Penguin, 2000.

Fleming, E. J. *The Fixers: Eddie Mannix, Howard Strickling and the MGM Publicity Machine*. Jefferson, NC: McFarland, 2005.

Fletcher, Ifan Kyrle. *Ronald Firbank: A Memoir*. London: Duckworth, 1930.

Forsythe, Robert. 'Mae West: A Treatise on Decay'. The New Masses (9 October 1934): 29.

Foster, Paul. 'Kingdom of Shadows: Fin-de-Siècle Gothic and Early Cinema'. In *MonstrousMedia/Spectral Subjects: Imaging Gothic Fictions from the Nineteenth Century to the Present*, edited by Fred Botting and Catherine Spooner, 29–41. Manchester: Manchester University Press, 2015.

Frankel, Nicholas. *Oscar Wilde: The Unrepentant Years*. Cambridge, MA: Harvard University Press, 2017.

Frankel, Nicholas. 'Textual Introduction'. In *The Uncensored Picture of Dorian Gray*, edited by Frankel, 35–53. Cambridge, MA: Belknap Press, 2011.

Freedman, Jonathan. *The Jewish Decadence: Jews and the Aesthetics of Modernity*. Chicago: University of Chicago Press, 2021.

Freedman, Jonathan. *Professions of Taste: Henry James, British Aestheticism, and Commodity Culture*. Stanford, CA: Stanford University Press, 1990.

Fronc, Jennifer. *Monitoring the Movies: The Fight Over Censorship in Early Twentieth Century America*. Austin: University of Texas Press, 2017.

Gabler, Neal. *An Empire of Their Own: How the Jews Invented Hollywood*. London: Doubleday, 1988.

Gautier, Théophile. *Mademoiselle du Maupin*. Translated by Helen Constantine. London: Penguin, 2005.

Gibson, Preston. *The Turning Point*. New York, Samuel French Ltd, 1910.

Gilbert, Eliot L. '"Tumult of Images": Wilde, Beardsley, and "Salome"'. Victorian Studies 26, no. 2 (Winter 1983): 133–59. Jstor. https://www.jstor.org/stable/3827003

Gilbert, Nora. *Better Left Unsaid: Victorian Novels, Hays Code Films, and the Benefits of Censorship*. Stanford, CA: Stanford University Press, 2013.

Gilbert, W. S., and Arthur Sullivan. *Patience; or Bunthorne's Bride*. London: Chappell & Co., 1910.

Giovacchini, Saverio. *Hollywood Modernism: Film and Politics in the Age of the New Deal*. Philadelphia: Temple University Press, 2011.

Girdwood, Megan. *Modernism and the Choreographic Imagination: Salome's Dance after 1890*. Edinburgh: Edinburgh University Press, 2021. https://doi-org.uoelibrary.idm.oclc.org/10.1515/9781474481649.

Glancy, Mark. *Cary Grant: The Making of a Hollywood Legend*. New York: Oxford University Press, 2020.

Golding, Alan. 'The Little Review (1915–1929)'. In *The Oxford Critical and Cultural History of Modernist Magazines*, Volume II: *North America 1894–1960*, edited by Peter Brooker and Andrew Thacker, 61–84. Oxford: Oxford University Press, 2012.

Gorbach, Julien. *The Notorious Ben Hecht: Iconoclastic Writer and Militant Zionist*. West Lafayette, IN: Purdue University Press, 2019.

Gosling, Jessica. ' "Things Worldly and Things Spiritual": Huysmans's *À rebours* and the House at Fontenay'. In *Decadence and the Senses*, edited by Jane Desmarais and Alice Condé, 66–82. Oxford: Legenda, 2017.

Greene, Graham. *Brighton* Rock. London: Vintage, 2004.

Grieveson, Lee. *Policing Cinema: Movies and Censorship in Early-Twentieth-Century America*. Berkeley and Los Angeles: University of California Press, 2004.

Griffith, David Wark. 'The Rise and Fall of Free Speech in America'. In *The Griffith Project*, Volume 11: *Selected Writings of D. W. Griffith: Indexes and Corrections to Volumes 1–10*, edited by Paolo Cherchi Usai, 137–70. London: BFI, 2007.

Guiralt, Carmen. 'Self-Censorship in Hollywood During the Silent Era: *A Woman of Affairs* (1928) by Clarence Brown'. *Film History* 28, no. 2 (2016): 81–113. Jstor. https://doi.org/10.2979/filmhistory.28.2.04

Gutkin, Len. 'The Dandified Dick: Hardboiled Noir and the Wildean Epigram'. *ELH* 81, no. 4 (Winter 2014): 1299–1326. Project Muse. 10.1353/elh.2014.0043

Hall, Radclyffe. *The Well of Loneliness*. London: Penguin, 2015.

Hall, Sheldon, and Steve Neale. *Epics, Spectacles, and Blockbusters*. Detroit: Wayne State University Press, 2010.

Hallett, Hilary A. *Go West, Young Women! The Rise of Early Hollywood*. Berkeley and Los Angeles: University of California Press, 2013.

Hamilton, Sharon. 'American Manners: *The Smart Set* (1900–1929); *American Parade* (1929)'. In *The Oxford Critical and Cultural History of Modernist Magazines*, Volume II: *North America 1894–1960*, edited by Peter Brooker and Andrew Thacker, 224–48. Oxford: Oxford University Press, 2012.

Hammett, Dashiell. 'The Road Home'. Public Library UK. Last accessed 17 January 2023. http://public-library.uk/ebooks/82/82.pdf

Hanson, Ellis. 'Salome, Simile, *Symboliste*'. In *Decadent Poetics: Literature and Form at the British Fin de Siècle*, edited by Jason David Hall and Alex Murray, 141–62. Basingstoke: Palgrave, 2013.

Hare, William. *Early Film Noir: Greed, Lust and Murder Hollywood Style*. Jefferson, NC: McFarland, 2010.

Harris, Frank. *Oscar Wilde, His Life and Confessions*. New York: Brentano, 1916.

Hawks, Howard. 'Interview with Peter Bogdanovich'. In *Who the Devil Made It?*, edited by Peter Bogdanovich. New York: Alfred A. Knopf, 1997.

Hawthorne, Melanie C. ' "Comment Peut-on Être Homosexuel?": Multinational (In)Corporation and the Frenchness of *Salomé*'. In *Perennial Decay: On the Aesthetics and Politics of Decadence*, edited by Liz Constable, Dennis Denisoff, and Matthew Potolsky, 159–82. Philadelphia: University of Pennsylvania Press, 1999.

Hecht, Ben. *1001 Afternoons in Chicago*. Chicago: Covici-McGee, 1922.

Hecht, Ben. 'The Bomb Thrower'. *The Little Review* 7, no. 3 (September 1920): 18–23. Modernist Journals Project.

Hecht, Ben. *Child of the Century: The Autobiography of Ben Hecht*. New York: Signet Books, 1954.

Hecht, Ben. 'The Devil Slayer'. *The Smart Set*, 53, no. 1 (September 1917): 123–8. Modernist Journals Project.

Hecht, Ben. *Erik Dorn*. New York: G. P. Putnam's Sons, 1921.

Hecht, Ben. *Fantazius Mallare: A Mysterious Oath*. Chicago: Covici-McGee, 1922.

Hecht, Ben. *The Florentine Dagger*. London: George Harrap & Co Ltd, 1924.

Hecht, Ben. *Gaily, Gaily*. London: Elek Books, 1963.

Hecht, Ben. *Gargoyles*. New York: Boni and Liveright, 1922.

Hecht, Ben. *Humpty Dumpty*. New York: Boni & Liveright, 1924.

Hecht, Ben. *The Kingdom of Evil: A Continuation of the Journal of Fantazius Mallare*. New York: Pascal Covici, 1924.

Hecht, Ben. 'Lust'. *The Little Review* 5, no. 2 (June 1918): 14–20. Modernist Journals Project.

Hecht, Ben. 'Nocturne'. *The Little Review* 5, no. 1 (May 1918): 45–52. Modernist Journals Project.

Hecht, Ben. 'The Sermon from the Depths'. *The Little Review* 2, no. 3 (May 1915), 40. Modernist Journals Project.

Ben Hecht, 'The Reader Critic'. *The Little Review* 2, no. 9 (December 1915): 42. Modernist Journal Project.

Hefner, Brooks E. *The Word on the Streets: The American Language of Vernacular Modernism*. Charlottesville: University of Virginia Press, 2017.

Hergesheimer, Joseph. *Wild Oranges*. New York: Grosset & Dunlap, 1918.

Hext, Kate. 'Decadence on the Silent Screen: Stannard, Coward, Hitchcock, and Wilde'. *Volupté* 2, no. 2, special issue: *Decadence and Cinema* (Winter 2019): 21–45. https://doi.org/10.25602/GOLD.v.v2i2.1339.g1460

Hext, Kate. 'Making Decadence New: Carl Van Vechten's Cinematic Fiction'. In *Decadence: A Literary History*, edited by Alex Murray, 361–76. Cambridge: Cambridge University Press, 2020.

Hext, Kate. 'Rethinking the Origins of Camp: The Queer Correspondence of Carl Van Vechten and Ronald Firbank'. *Modernism/modernity* 27, no. 1 (January 2020): 165–83. Project Muse. https://doi.org/10.1353/mod.2020.0007

Hext, Kate. 'Victorians in the Closet: Oscar Wilde's Monstrous Hollywood Legacy'. *Victorian Literature and Culture* 49, no. 4, special issue: *The Scales of Decadence* (Autumn 2021): 711–29. https://doi.org/10.1017/S1060150320000303 Cambridge Core.

Hoare, Philip. *Noël Coward: A Biography*. London: Sinclair-Stevenson, 1995.

Hoare, Philip. *Wilde's Last Stand: Scandal and Conspiracy during the Great War*. London: Duckworth Overlook, 1997.

Hoffenstein, Samuel. *Life Sings a Song*. New York: Wilmarth Publishing Company, 1916.

Hoffman, Adina. *Ben Hecht: Fighting Words, Moving Pictures*. New Haven: Yale University Press, 2019.

Hornung, E. W. *Raffles: The Amateur Cracksman*. London: Penguin, 2003.

Huysmans, Joris-Karl. *Against Nature [À rebours]*. Translated by Robert Baldick. London: Penguin, 2003.

Huysmans, Joris-Karl. *The Damned [Là-bas]*. Translated by Terry Hale. London: Penguin, 2001.

Huysmans, Joris-Karl. *En Route*. Translated by W. Fleming. Sawtry: Dedalus Editions, 2002.

Huysmans, Joris-Karl. 'Preface Written Twenty Years After the Novel'. Translated by Patrick McGuiness. In Huysmans, *Against Nature*, translated by Robert Baldick, 290–309. London: Penguin, 2003.

Irwin, John I. *Unless the Threat of Death Is Behind Them: Hard-Boiled Fiction and Film Noir*. Baltimore: Johns Hopkins University Press, 2006.

Jackson, Holbrook. *The Eighteen Nineties: A Review of Art and Ideas at the Close of the Nineteenth Century*. London: Grant Richards, 1922.

Jacobs, Lea. *The Decline of Sentiment: American Film in the 1920s*. Berkeley and Los Angeles: University of California Press, 2008.

James, David E. 'Hollywood Extras: One Tradition of "Avant-Garde" Film in Los Angeles'. In *Unseen Cinema: Early American Avant-Garde Film, 1893–1941*, edited by Bruce Charles Posner, 44–52. New York: Black Thistle Press/Anthology Film Archives, 2001.

James, Henry. *Letters*, Volume III: *1883–1895*. Edited by Leon Edel. London: Macmillan, 1981.

James, Henry. *The Spoils of Poynton*. London: Penguin, 2006.

Janes, Dominic. *Oscar Wilde Prefigured: Queer Fashioning and British Caricature, 1750–1900*. Chicago: University of Chicago Press, 2016.

Johnson, Shirley Everton. *The Cult of the Purple Rose*. Boston: Richard G. Badger, 1902.

Jones, D. Michael. 'E. W. Hornung's Raffles and the Aesthetic Movement: The Rhetoric of Romance Masculinity'. *English Literature in Transition, 1880–1920* 59, no. 1 (2016): 44–66. Project Muse. muse.jhu.edu/article/603457.

Jones, Dorothy B. 'The Hollywood War Film, 1942–1944'. *Hollywood Quarterly* 1, no. 1 (October 1945): 1–19. Jstor. https://doi.org/10.2307/1209583

Joyce, Simon. 'Sexual Politics and the Aesthetics of Crime: Oscar Wilde in the Nineties'. *ELH* 69, no. 2 (Summer 2022): 501–23. Jstor. https://www.jstor.org/stable/30032029

Karnick, Kristine Brunovska, and Henry Jenkins. 'Comedy and the Social World'. In *Classical Hollywood Comedy*, edited by Karnick and Jenkins, 265–82. New York: Routledge, 1995.

Keil, Charlie. '1913: Movies and the Beginning of a New Era'. In *American Cinema of the 1910s: Themes and Variations*, edited by Keil and Ben Singer, 92–114. New Brunswick, NJ: Rutgers University Press, 2009.

Keil, Charlie. 'The Movies: The Transitional Era'. In *American Literature in Transition, 1910–1920*, edited by Mark Van Wienan, 312–26. Cambridge: Cambridge University Press, 2018.

Keil, Charlie, and Ben Singer. 'Introduction: Movies and the 1910s'. In *American Cinema of the 1910s: Themes and Variations*, edited by Charlie Keil and Ben Singer, 1–25. New Brunswick, NJ: Rutgers University Press, 2009.

Kellner, Bruce. *The Last Dandy: Ralph Barton, American Artist, 1891–1931*. Columbia: University of Missouri Press, 1991.

Kelly, Katherine E. 'Pandemic and Performance: Ibsen and the Outbreak of Modernism', *South Central Review* 25, no. 1, special issue: *Staging Modernism* (Spring 2008): 12–35.

Kennedy, Charles A. 'When Cairo Met Main Street: Little Egypt, Salome Dancers, and the World's Fairs of 1893 and 1904'. In *Music and Culture in America, 1861–1918*, edited by Michael Saffle, 271–328. New York: Garland, 1998.

Kerr, Douglas. *Conan Doyle: Writing, Profession, and Practice*. Oxford: Oxford University Press, 2013.

Kimmel, Michael. *Manhood in America: A Cultural History*. Oxford: Oxford University Press, 2011.

King, Rob. '1914: Movies and Cultural Hierarchy'. In *American Cinema of the 1910s: Themes and Variations*, edited by Charlie Keil and Ben Singer, 115–38. New Brunswick, NJ: Rutgers University Press, 2009.

Kohlmayer, Rainer, and Lucia Kramer. '*Bunbury* in Germany: Alive and Kicking'. In *The Reception of Oscar Wilde in Europe*, edited by Stefano Evangelista, 189–202. London: Continuum, 2010.

Kotsilibas-Davis, James. *Good Times, Great Times: The Odyssey of Maurice Barrymore*. New York: Doubleday, 1977.

Kovalova, Anna. '"The Picture of Dorian Gray" Painted by Meyerhold'. *Studies in Russian and Soviet Cinema* 13, no. 1 (January 2019): 59–90. Taylor & Francis Online. https://doi.org/10.1080/17503132.2019.1556429

Lahr, John. *Coward the Playwright*. Berkeley and Los Angeles: University of California Press, 2002.

Lambert, Gavin. *Nazimova: A Biography*. Lexington: University Press of Kentucky, 2021.

Lantern: Media History Digital Library. Last modified 2022, last accessed 17 January 2023. https://lantern.mediahist.org/

Lee, Laura. *Oscar's Ghost: The Battle for Oscar Wilde's Legacy*. Stroud, Gloucester: Amberley Publishing, 2017.

Leff, Leonard J., and Jerold L. Simmons. *The Dame in the Kimono: Hollywood, Censorship, and the Production Code*. Lexington: University Press of Kentucky, 2001.

Le Gallienne, Richard. 'The Coming Back of Oscar Wilde'. *Munsey's Magazine* 66, no. 2 (March 1919): 261–268.

Leider, Emily Wortis. *Becoming Mae West*. Jackson: Da Capo Press, 2000.

Levin, Joanna. *Bohemia in America, 1858–1920*. Stanford, CA: Stanford University Press, 2010.

Levy, Emanuel. *Vincente Minnelli: Hollywood's Dark Dreamer*. New York: St Martin's Press, 2009.

Lewin, Albert. [Untitled essay.] In *The Real Tinsel*, edited by Bernard Rosenberg and Harry Silverstein, 100–24. London: Collier-Macmillan Ltd, 1970.

Lewis, Lloyd, and Henry Justin Smith. *Oscar Wilde Discovers America [1882]*. New York: Harcourt Brace, 1936.

The Little Review. Journal edited by Margaret C. Anderson. Chicago, San Francisco, and New York: 1914–22. Modernist Journals Project.

Lobenthal, Joel. *Tallulah!: The Life and Times of a Leading Lady*. London: HarperCollins, 2001.

Loos, Anita. *Gentlemen Prefer Blondes*. New York: Liveright, 2014.

Louÿs, Pierre. *Aphrodite*. Translated by Lewis Galantière. New York: Modern Library, 1933.

Lubitsch, Ernst. 'Lubitsch Talks of Epigrams on Screen'. The New York Herald, New York Tribune (27 December 1925): 3.

MacAdams, William. *Ben Hecht: The Man Behind the Legend*. New York: Charles Scribner's Sons, 1990.

McCormack, Jerusha. 'Wilde's Dublin, Dublin's Wilde'. In *Oscar Wilde in Context*, edited by Kerry Powell and Peter Raby, 17–27. Cambridge: Cambridge University Press, 2013.

McCormick, Richard W. 'Transnational Jewish Comedy: Sex and Politics in the Films of Ernst Lubitsch—From Berlin to Hollywood'. In *Three-Way Street: Jews, Germans, and the Transnational*, edited by Jay Howard Geller and Leslie Morris, 169–96. Ann Arbor: University of Michigan Press, 2016.

Machen, Arthur. *The Hill of Dreams*. Aberystwyth: Library of Wales, 2017.

Machen, Arthur, and Montgomery Evans. *Arthur Machen and Montgomery Evans: Letters of a Literary Friendship, 1923–1947*. Edited by Sue Strong Hassler and Donald M. Hassler. Kent, OH: Kent State University, 1994.

Mackie, Gregory. 'Aubrey Beardsley, H. S. Nichols, and the Decadent Archive'. *Volupté: Interdisciplinary Journal of Decadence Studies* 3, no. 1 (2020): 49–74. https://doi.org/10.25602/GOLD.v.v3i1.1403.g1517

Mackie, Gregory. *Beautiful Untrue Things: Forging Oscar Wilde's Extraordinary Afterlife*. Toronto: University of Toronto Press, 2019.

Mackie, Gregory. 'The Function of Decorum at the Present Time: Manners, Moral Language, and Modernity in "an 'Oscar Wilde Play"'. *Modern Drama* 52, no. 2 (Summer 2009): 145–67. Project Muse. https://doi.org/10.1353/mdr.0.0099

McLellan, Diana. *The Girls: Sappho Goes to Hollywood*. London: Robson Books, 2001.

MacLeod, Kirsten. 'Making It New, Old School: Carl Van Vechten and Decadent Modernism'. *Symbiosis* 16 (2012): 209–24.

Madsen, Axel. *The Sewing Circle: Hollywood's Greatest Secret; Female Stars Who Loved Other Women*. London: Robson Books, 1998.

Mahoney, Kristin. *Literature and the Politics of Post-Victorian Decadence*. Cambridge: Cambridge University Press, 2015.

Malik, Shushma. 'The Criminal Emperors of Ancient Rome and Wilde'. In *Oscar Wilde and Classical Antiquity*, edited by Kathleen Riley, Alastair J. L. Blanchard, and Iarla Manny, 305–20. Oxford: Oxford University Press, 2018.

Mank, Gregory William. *Laird Cregar: A Hollywood Tragedy*. Jefferson, NC: McFarland, 2018.

Mao, Douglas. 'The Naughtiness of the Avant-Garde: Donald Evans, Claire Marie, and *Tender Buttons*'. In *Decadence in the Age of Modernism*, edited by Kate Hext and Alex Murray, 197–228. Baltimore: Johns Hopkins University Press, 2019.

Mappen, Marc. *Prohibition Gangsters: The Rise and Fall of a Bad Generation*. New Brunswick, NJ: Rutgers University Press, 2013.

Matich, Olga. *Erotic Utopia: The Decadent Imagination in Russia's Fin de Siècle*. Madison: University of Wisconsin Press, 2005.

Matich, Olga. 'The White Emigration Goes Hollywood'. *Russian Review* 64, no. 2 (April 2005): 187–380. https://doi.org/10.1111/j.1467-9434.2005.00357.x.

Maxwell, Catherine. 'Carnal Flowers, Charnel Flowers: Perfume in the Decadent Literary Imagination'. In *Decadence and the Senses*, edited by Jane Desmarais and Alice Condé, 32–50. Oxford: Legenda, 2017.

Maxwell, Catherine. *Scents and Sensibility: Perfume in Victorian Literary Culture*. Oxford: Oxford University Press, 2017.

May, Larry. *Screening Out the Past: The Birth of Mass Culture and the Motion Picture Industry*. Chicago: University of Chicago Press, 1983.

Mencken, H. L. 'Introduction'. In *Essays by James Huneker*. New York: Scribner's, 1929.

Mencken, H. L. *A Little Book in C Major*. New York: John Lane, 1916.

Mencken, H. L. 'Portrait of a Tragic Comedian'. *The Smart Set* 50, no. 1 (September 1916): 280–4. Modernist Magazines Project.

Mendelssohn, Michèle. *Henry James, Oscar Wilde, and Aesthetic Culture*. Edinburgh: Edinburgh University Press, 2007.

Mendelssohn, Michèle. *Making Oscar Wilde*. Oxford: Oxford University Press, 2018.

Merritt, Gregg. *Room 1219: The Life of Fatty Arbuckle, the Mysterious Death of Virginia Rappe, and the Scandal that Changed Hollywood*. Chicago: Chicago Review Press, 2016.

Merritt, Russell. 'Rescued from a Perilous Nest: D. W. Griffith's Escape from Theatre into Film'. *Cinema Journal* 21, no. 1 (Autumn 1981): 2–30. Jstor. https://www.jstor.org/stable/1225002

Meyerhold, Vsevolod. *The Picture of Dorian Gray* (1915). Edited and translated by Anna Kovalova and Ekaterina Ivanenko, *Studies in Russian and Soviet Cinema* 13, no. 1 (January 2019): 91–105. Taylor & Francis Online. https://doi.org/10.1080/17503132.2019.1557407

Minnelli, Vincente. *Casanova's Memoirs*. Edited by Joseph Monet. London: W. H. Allen, 1953.

Minnelli, Vincente. *I Remember it Well*. New York: Doubleday, 1974.

Misler, Nicoletta. 'Seven Steps, Seven Veils: Salomé in Russia'. *Experiment* 17 (2011): 155–84. Research Gate. https://doi.org/10.1163/221173011X611888

M'lle New York. Periodical edited by James Huneker and Vance Thompson. New York: 1895–8. New York Public Library.

Moeller-Sally, Betsy F. 'Oscar Wilde and the Culture of Russian Modernism'. *SEEJ* 34, no. 4 (1990): 459–72. Jstor. https://doi.org/10.2307/308194

Morris, Jerry. 'Julius Hopp and the Progressive Stage Society 1904–1906'. *My Sentimental Library*, 30 March 2020. Last accessed 17 January 2023, https://blog.mysentimentallibrary.com/2020/03/.

Morris, Michael. *Madam Valentino: The Many Lives of Natacha Rambova*. New York: Abbeville Press, 1991.

Morris Jr, Roy. *Declaring His Genius: Oscar Wilde in North America*. Cambridge, MA: Harvard University Press, 2013.

Munby, Jonathan. *Public Enemies, Public Heroes: Screening the Gangster from Little Caesar to Touch of Evil*. Chicago: University of Chicago Press, 1999.

Musser, Charles. *Before the Nickelodeon: Edwin S. Porter and the Edison Manu-facturing Company.* Berkeley and Los Angeles: University of California Press, 1991.

Musser, Charles. 'The Hidden and Unspeakable: On Theatrical Culture, Oscar Wilde, and Ernst Lubitsch's *Lady Windermere's Fan*'. *Film Studies* 4, no. 1 (Summer 2004): 12–47. https://doi.org/10.7227/FS.4.2.

Naremore, James. *The Films of Vincente Minnelli.* Cambridge: Cambridge University Press, 1993.

Naremore, James. *More Than Night: Film Noir in Its Contexts.* Berkeley and Los Angeles: University of California Press, 1998.

Nassar, Christopher S. 'Oscar Wilde's "Lord Arthur Savile's Crime" and *The Picture of Dorian Gray*: Point Counterpoint'. *ANQ: A Quarterly Journal of Short Articles, Notes and Reviews* 27, no. 3 (2014): 137–43.

Nathan, George Jean. 'The Popular Play'. *The Smart Set* (June 1918): 131–7. Mod-ernist Journals Project.

Navarette, Susan J. *The Shape of Fear: Horror and the Fin de Siècle Culture of Decadence.* Lexington: University Press of Kentucky, 1998.

Neale, Steve. ' "I Can't Tell Anymore Whether You're Lying": *Double Indemnity, Human Desire* and the Narratology of *Femmes Fatales*'. In *The Femme Fatale: Images, Histories, Contexts,* edited by Helen Hansen and Catherine O'Rawe, 187–98. London: Palgrave, 2010.

Neale, Steve. 'Technicolor'. In *Color: The Film Reader,* edited by Angela Dalle Vacche and Brian Price, 13–23. Abingdon: Routledge, 2006.

Nichols, H. S. *Fifty Drawings by Aubrey Beardsley.* New York: H. S. Nichols, 1920.

Nietzsche, Friedrich. *Twilight of the Idols.* Translated by Richard Polt. Cambridge, MA: Hackett, 1997.

Norton, Allen. *The Convolvulus.* New York: Claire Marie Press, 1914.

Nunokawa, Jeff. 'The Importance of Being Bored: The Dividends of Ennui in *The Picture of Dorian Gray*'. *Studies in the Novel* 28, no. 3, special issue: *Queerer than Fiction* (Fall 1996): 357–71.

O'Brien, Lee. 'Wilde Words: The Aesthetics of Crime and the Play of Genre in E. W. Hornung's Raffles Stories'. *English Studies* 96, no. 6 (2015): 654–69. Ingenta Connect. https://doi.org/10.1080/0013838X.2015.1045731

Pagello, Federico. 'A. J. Raffles and Arsène Lupin in Literature, Theatre, and Film: On the Transnational Adaptations of Popular Fiction (1905–1930)'. *Adaptation* 6, no. 3 (March 2013): 268–82. Oxford Academic. https://doi.org/10.1093/adaptation/apt002

Parker, Dorothy. 'On Oscar Wilde'. *Life* (2 June 1927): 13.

Pater, Walter. *Appreciations with an Essay on Style.* Evanston, IL: Northwestern University Press, 1987.

Pater, Walter. 'Denys L'Auxerrois'. In *Imaginary Portraits.* London: Modern Human-ities Research Association, 2014.

Pater, Walter. *Duke Carl of Rosenmold: An Imaginary Portrait.* Boston: Copeland & Day, 1897.

Pater, Walter. *Marius the Epicurean.* Oxford: Oxford University Press, 1986.

Pater, Walter. *Miscellaneous Studies*. London: Macmillan, 1928.

Pater, Walter. 'A Novel by Mr. Oscar Wilde'. The Bookman (November 1891): 59–60.

Pater, Walter. 'Poems by William Morris'. *Westminster Review* 34.2 (October 1868), 300–12.

Pater, Walter. *Studies in the History of the Renaissance*. Oxford: Oxford University Press, 1998.

Pater, Walter. 'A Study of Dionysus'. In *Greek Studies: A Series of Essays*. London: Macmillan, 1895.

Pierce, David. *The Survival of American Silent Feature Films: 1912–1929*. Washington DC: Library of Congress and Council on Library and Information Resources, 2013. Last accessed 19 January 2023. https://www.loc.gov/programs/static/national-film-preservation-board/documents/pub158.final_version_sept_2013.pdf

Proctor, Ben. *William Randolph Hearst: The Later Years, 1911–1951*. New York: Oxford University Press, 2007.

Pure, Simon. 'The Londoner'. *The Bookman* (September 1919): 39–44.

Ratner-Rosenhagen, Jennifer. *American Nietzsche: A History of an Icon and His Ideas*. Chicago: University of Chicago Press, 2012.

Rebello, Stephen. *Alfred Hitchcock and the Making of Psycho*. London: Debner Books, 1990.

Robertson, Pamela. *Guilty Pleasures: Feminist Camp from Mae West to Madonna*. Durham, NC: Duke University Press, 1996.

Robinson, Frank M., and Lawrence Davidson. *Pulp Culture: The Art of Fiction Magazines*. Portland, OR: Collectors Press, 1998.

Robinson, Harlow. *Russians in Hollywood, Hollywood's Russians: Biography of an Image*. Boston: Northeastern University Press, 2007.

Roditi, Edouard. *Oscar Wilde*. New York: New Directions Books, 1947.

Rodriguez, Suzanne. *Wild Heart, A Life: Natalie Clifford Barney and the Decadence of Literary Paris*. London: Harper Collins, 2002.

Rosenberg, Emily S. *Spreading the American Dream: American Economic and Cultural Expansion, 1890–1945*. New York: Hill and Wang, 2011.

Rothstein, Mervyn. 'David Hyde Pierce Reimagines *The Importance of Being Earnest*, With a "Mob" Twist'. *Playbill* (25 June 2012), last accessed 17 January 2023. https://www.playbill.com/article/david-hyde-pierce-reimagines-the-importance-of-being-earnest-with-a-mob-twist-com-195055

Russo, Vito. *The Celluloid Closet: Homosexuality in the Movies*. New York: Harper & Row, 1981.

Ruth, David E. *Inventing the Public Enemy: The Gangster in American Culture, 1918–1934*. London: University of Chicago Press, 1996.

Rutherford, Annabel. 'The Triumph of the Veiled Dance: The Influence of Oscar Wilde and Aubrey Beardsley on Serge Diaghilev's Creation of the Ballets Russes'. *Dance Research: The Journal of the Society for Dance Research* 27, no. 1 (Summer 2009): 93–107. Jstor. https://www.jstor.org/stable/40264008

Sadoff, Dianne F. *Victorian Vogue: British Novels Onscreen*. Minneapolis: University of Minnesota Press, 2010.

Saint-Amour, Paul K. *The Copywrights: Intellectual Property and the Literary Imagination*. Ithaca, NY: Cornell University Press, 2003.

Sammells, Neil. 'Pulp Fictions: Oscar Wilde and Quentin Tarantino'. *Irish Studies Review* 3, no. 11 (Summer 1995): 39–45. Taylor & Francis Online. https://doi.org/10.1080/09670889508455492

Schanke, Robert A. *Shattered Applause: The Lives of Eva Le Gallienne*. Carbondale: Southern Illinois University Press, 2010.

Schenkar, Joan. *Truly Wilde: The Unsettling Story of Dolly Wilde, Oscar's Unusual Niece*. Cambridge: Da Capo Press, 2000.

Schlissel, Lillian. 'Introduction'. In *Three Plays by Mae West: Sex, The Drag and The Pleasure Man*, 1–30. London: Routledge, 2013.

Sedgwick, Eve Kosofsky. *Epistemologies of the Closet*. Berkeley and Los Angeles: University of California Press, 2008.

Sharp, Mordaint. *The Green Bay Tree*. London: Oberon Books, 2014.

Sheehy, Helen. *Eva Le Gallienne: A Biography*. New York: Alfred A. Knopf, 1996.

Sherry, Vincent. *Modernism and the Reinvention of Decadence*. Cambridge: Cambridge University Press, 2014.

Showalter, Elaine. *Sexual Anarchy: Gender and Culture at the Fin de Siècle*. London: Virago, 1992.

Silver, Alain, and James Ursini. *The Noir Style*. Woodstock, NY: The Overlook Press, 1999.

Sinfield, Alan. *The Wilde Century: Effeminacy, Oscar Wilde and the Queer Moment*. London: Cassell, 1994.

Singal, Daniel Joseph. *William Faulkner: The Making of a Modernist*. Chapel Hill: University of North Carolina Press, 1997.

Singer, Ben. 'Griffith's Moral Profile'. In *A Companion to D. W. Griffith*, edited by Charlie Keil, 34–73. London: Wiley, 2017.

Slide, Anthony. *Silent Topics: Essays on Undocumented Areas of Silent Film*. London: Scarecrow Press, 2004.

Spicer, Andrew. *Film Noir*. Harlow: Pearson, 2002.

Spillane, Joseph F. 'The Road to the Harrison Narcotics Act: Drugs and Their Control, 1875–1918'. In *Federal Drug Control: The Evolution of Policy and Practice*, edited by Jonathon Erlen and Joseph F. Spillane, 1–24. New York: Pharmaceutical Products Press, 2004.

Stamp, Shelley. 'Women and the Silent Screen'. In *The Wiley-Blackwell History of American Film*, Volume I: *Origins to 1928*, edited by Cynthia Lucia, Roy Grundmann, and Art Simon, 1–26. London: Wiley-Blackwell, 2012. onlinelibrary.wiley.com.

Stein, Gertrude. *Tender Buttons*. New York: Claire Marie Press, 1914.

Stokes, Leslie, and Sewell Stokes, *Oscar Wilde: A Play*. New York: Random House, 1938.

Stoloff, Sam. 'Normalizing Stars: Roscoe "Fatty" Arbuckle and Hollywood Consolidation'. In *American Silent Film: Discovering Marginalized Voices*, edited by Gregg Bachman and Thomas J. Slater, 148–75. Carbondale, IL: Southern Illinois University Press, 2002.

Stone, Jonathan. 'The Journal as Archive: *Vesy* and the Russian Reader's Encounter with Decadence'. *Volupté* 3, no. 1 (Summer 2020): 75–91. https://doi.org/10. 25602/GOLD.v.v3i1.1404.g1518

Sturgis, Matthew. *Oscar Wilde: A Life*. London: Head of Zeus, 2018.

Swaab, Peter. *Bringing Up Baby*. London: BFI, 2010.

Symons, Arthur. 'Bertha'. *The Little Review* 4, no. 11 (March 1918): 51–3. Modernist Journals Project.

Symons, Arthur. 'The Decadent Movement in Literature'. Harper's Monthly Magazine (November 1893): 858–67.

Symons, Arthur. 'A Prelude to Life'. In *The Memoirs of Arthur Symons: Life and Art in the 1890s*, edited by Karl Beckson, 6–24. London: Pennsylvania State University Press, 1977.

Symons, Arthur. *Spiritual Adventures in Paris*. Cambridge: Modern Humanities Research Association, 2017.

Symons, Arthur. *Wanderings*. London: J. M. Dent and Sons Ltd, 1931.

Tanitch, Robert. *Oscar Wilde on Stage and Screen*. London: Methuen, 1999.

Thesiger, Ernest. *Practically True*. London: Heinemann, 1927.

Thompson, David. *The Big Sleep*. London: BFI, 1997.

Thompson, Kristin. *Herr Lubitsch Goes to Hollywood: German and American Film after World War I*. Amsterdam: Amsterdam University Press, 2005.

Thompson, Kristin. 'Lubitsch, Acting and Silent Romantic Comedy'. *Film History* 13, no. 4, special issue: *Before Screwball* (2001): 390–408. Jstor. https://www.jstor.org/stable/3815457

Trail, Armitage. *Scarface*. London: Bloomsbury, 2005.

[Unsigned.] *Teleny, or The Reverse of the Medal*. N.p.: Gay Erotica Classic, 2013.

[Unsigned review.] '*Dorian Gray* . . . Heavy for Masses'. *Box Office Digest* 16, no. 13 (28 February 1945), 12. Archive.org. https://archive.org/details/boxofficedigest100nati_2/page/n53/mode/2up?view=theater.

Vanderham, Paul. *James Joyce and Censorship: The Trials of Ulysses*. London: Macmillan, 1998.

Van Dine, S. S. *The Benson Murder Case*. New York: Felony & Mayhem, 2018.

Van Vechten, Carl. 'Hollywood Parties'. *Vanity Fair* 28, no. 4 (June 1927): 47, 86, 90.

Van Vechten, Carl. *In the Garret*. New York: Knopf, 1920.

Van Vechten, Carl. *Peter Whiffle: His Life and Works*. New York: Knopf, 1922.

Van Vechten, Carl. 'Ronald Firbank'. In Van Vechten, *Excavations: A Book of Advocacies*, 170–6. New York: Alfred A. Knopf, 1926.

Van Vechten, Carl. *Spider Boy: A Scenario for a Moving Picture* (New York: Alfred A. Knopf, 1928).

Viereck, George Sylvester. *The House of the Vampire*. New York: Cornell University Press, 2010.

Vilain, Robert. 'Tragedy and the Apostle of Beauty: The Early Literary Reception of Oscar Wilde in Germany and Austria'. In *The Reception of Oscar Wilde in Europe*, edited by Stefano Evangelista, 173–88. London: Bloomsbury Academic, 2010.

Wainscott, Ronald H. *The Emergence of Modern American Theater, 1914–1929*. New Haven: Yale University Press, 1997.

Waymouth, Nigel. Interview with Kate Hext, 15 August 2015, London.

Weir, David. 'Alla Nazimova's *Salomé*: Shot-by-Shot'. *Volupté: Interdisciplinary Journal of Decadence Studies* 2, no. 2 (Winter 2019): 178–246. https://doi.org/10.25602/GOLD.v.v2i2.1348.g1467

Weir, David. *Decadence and the Making of Modernism*. Amherst: University of Massachusetts Press, 1995.

Weir, David. *Decadent Culture in the United States: Art and Literature against the American Grain, 1890–1926* (Albany, NY: State University of New York Press, 2007).

White, Edward. *The Tastemaker: Carl Van Vechten and the Birth of Modern America*. New York: Farrar, Straus and Giroux, 2014.

White, Patricia. 'Nazimova's Veils: *Salome* at the Intersection of Film Histories'. In *A Feminist Reader in Early Cinema*, edited by Jennifer M. Bean and Diane Negra, 60–88. Durham, NC: Duke University Press, 2002.

Wilde, Hagar. 'Bringing Up Baby'. Collier's Weekly (10 April 1937): 20–2.

Wilde, Oscar. '*The Ballad of Reading Gaol*'. In *The Annotated Prison Writings of Oscar Wilde*, edited by Nicholas Frankel, 317–71. Cambridge, MA: Harvard University Press, 2018.

Wilde, Oscar. *The Complete Letters of Oscar Wilde*. Edited by Merlin Holland and Rupert Hart-Davis. London: Fourth Estate, 2000.

Wilde, Oscar. *De Profundis*. In *The Annotated Prison Writings of Oscar Wilde*, edited by Nicholas Frankel, 53–291. Cambridge, MA: Harvard University Press, 2018.

Wilde, Oscar. 'The English Renaissance of Art'. In *Essays and Lectures*, edited by Robert Ross, 111–55. London: Methuen & Co, 1908.

Wilde, Oscar. 'House Decoration'. In *Essays and Lectures*, edited by Robert Ross, 157–71. London: Methuen & Co, 1908.

Wilde, Oscar. *The Importance of Being Earnest and Other Plays*. Oxford: Oxford University Press, 2008.

Wilde, Oscar. 'Lord Arthur Savile's Crime'. In *The Complete Short Stories*, 3–32. Oxford: Oxford University Press, 2010.

Wilde, Oscar. *Oscar Wilde in America: The Interviews*. Edited by Matthew Hofer and Gary Scharnhorst. Champaign: University of Illinois Press, 2010.

Wilde, Oscar. 'Phrases and Philosophies for the Use of the Young'. In *Complete Works of Oscar Wilde*, 1205–6. London: Book Club Associates, 1976.

Wilde, Oscar. *The Picture of Dorian Gray*. Oxford: Oxford University Press, 1998.

Wilde, Oscar. *Salome*. Boston: Copeland & Day, 1894.

Wilde, Oscar. *The Soul of Man Under Socialism and Selected Critical Prose*. London: Penguin, 2001.

Wilson, Edmund. *The Shores of Light: A Literary Chronicle of the Twenties and Thirties*. New York: Farrar, Straus and Young, 1952.

Winwar, Frances. *Oscar Wilde and the Yellow 'Nineties*. New York: Harper & Brothers, 1940.

Wratislaw, Theodore. *Orchids: Poems*. London: Leonard Smithers, 1896.

Yeats, W. B. *The Collected Works of W. B. Yeats*. Edited by Douglas Archibald and William O'Donnell. New York: Scribner, 1999.

The Yellow Book. Periodical edited by Henry Harland and Aubrey Beardsley. London: 1894–7. Lantern: Media History Digital Library. Last accessed 17 January 2023. https://lantern.mediahist.org/.

Zolotow, Maurice. *No People Like Show People*. London: Random House, 1951.

Selected Filmography

Adventures of Kitty O'Day, directed by William Beaudine. Monogram, 1945.
Angels with Dirty Faces, directed by Michael Curtiz. Warner Brothers, 1938.
Arsenic and Old Lace, directed by Frank Capra. Warner Brothers, 1944.
The Awful Truth, directed by Leo McCarey. Columbia Pictures, 1937.
Az élet királya, directed by Alfréd Deésy. Hungary, 1917.
Baffles, Gentleman Burglar, directed by Henry Lehrman. Keystone, 1914.
Ben-Hur, directed by Fred Niblo. MGM, 1925.
The Big Sleep, directed by Howard Hawks. Warner Brothers, 1946.
Das Bildnis des Dorian Gray, directed by Richard Oswald. Germany, 1917; lost.
The Black Cat, directed by Edgar G. Ulmer. Universal, 1934.
The Blonde Venus, directed by Josef von Sternberg. Paramount, 1932.
Bride of Frankenstein, directed by James Whale. Universal, 1935.
The Bridge, directed by Charles Vidor. Independent, 1929.
Bringing Up Baby, directed by Howard Hawks. RKO, 1938.
Bulldog Drummond, directed by F. Richard Jones. Goldwyn, 1929.
The Burglar and the Lady, directed by Herbert Blanché. Sun Photoplay, 1914; lost.
Cabiria, directed by Giovanni Pastrone. Italy, 1914.
Camille, directed by Ray C. Smallwood. Metro, 1921.
The Canterville Ghost, directed by Jules Dassin. MGM, 1944.
Citizen Kane, directed by Orson Welles. RKO, 1941.
Cleopatra, directed by J. Gordon Edwards. Fox, 1917.
The Cook, directed by Roscoe Arbuckle. Paramount, 1918.
Cover Girl, directed by Charles Vidor. Columbia, 1944.
The Cricket on the Hearth, directed by D. W. Griffith. Biograph, 1909.
Crime Without Passion, directed by Ben Hecht and Charles MacArthur. Paramount,1934.
Crossed Wires, directed by Frederick Sullivan. Thanhouser, 1915.
Daughters of the Rich, directed by Louis J. Gasnier. Preferred Pictures, 1923.
David Copperfield, directed by Theodore Marston and George Nichols. Thanhouser, 1911.
The Days of Wine and Roses, directed by John Frankenheimer. CBS, 1958.
Days of Wine and Roses, directed by Blake Edwards. Warner Brothers, 1962.
Design for Living, directed by Ernst Lubitsch. Paramount, 1933.
Detective Kitty O'Day, directed by William Beaudine. Monogram, 1944.
The Devil is a Woman, directed by Josef von Sternberg. Paramount, 1935.
Dr Jekyll and Mr Hyde, directed by Lucius Henderson. Thanhouser, 1912.
Dr Jekyll and Mr Hyde, directed by Herbert Brenon. IMP, 1913.
Dr Jekyll and Mr Hyde, directed by John S. Robertson. Paramount, 1920.

Dr Jekyll and Mr Hyde, directed by Rouben Mamoulian. Paramount, 1931.

A Doll's House, directed by Maurice Tourneur. UA, 1922; lost.

Dorian Grays Portræt, directed by Axel Strom. Denmark, 1910; lost.

A Double Life, directed by George Cukor. Universal, 1947.

Dracula, directed by Tod Browning and Karl Freund. Universal, 1931.

DuBarry was a Lady, directed by Roy Del Ruth. MGM, 1943.

Duck Soup, directed by Leo McCarey. Paramount, 1933.

The Evidence of the Film, directed by Edwin Thanhouser and Lawrence Marston. Thanhouser, 1913.

The Extra Girl, directed by F. Richard Jones. Sennett, 1923.

The Fan, directed by Otto Preminger. Twentieth Century Fox, 1949.

Flesh and Fantasy, directed by Julien Duvivier. MGM, 1943.

The Florentine Dagger, directed by Robert Florey. Warner Brothers, 1935.

A Florentine Tragedy, directed by J. Farrell MacDonald. Powers Photoplays, 1913.

Foolish Wives, directed by Erich von Stroheim. Universal, 1922.

Forbidden Fruit, directed by Cecil B. DeMille. Paramount, 1921.

The Four Horsemen of the Apocalypse, directed by Rex Ingram. Metro, 1921.

Friends and Lovers, directed by Victor Schertzinger. RKO, 1931.

The Front Page, directed by Lewis Milstone. RKO, 1931.

Gods and Monsters, directed by Bill Condon. Lions Gate Films, 1998.

Gone with the Wind, directed by Victor Fleming. MGM, 1939.

The Greatest Show on Earth, directed by Cecile B. DeMille. Paramount, 1952.

Hangover Square, directed by John Brahm. Twentieth Century Fox, 1945.

The Happy Prince, directed by Rupert Everett. Independent, 2018.

Hollywood: A Celebration of the American Silent Film, directed by Kevin Brownlow and David Gill. Thames Television, London, 1980.

An Ideal Husband, directed by Alexander Korda. Lion Film Productions, 1947.

If You Had a Wife Like This, director unknown. Production unknown, c.1908.

I'm No Angel, directed by Wesley Ruggles. Paramount, 1933.

The Importance of Being Earnest, directed by Anthony Asquith. General Film Producers, 1952.

In Hollywood with Potash and Perlmutter, directed by Alfred E. Green. Goldwyn, 1924.

Intolerance, directed by D. W. Griffith. D. W. Griffith, 1916.

It Happened One Night, directed by Frank Capra. Columbia, 1934.

It's a Wonderful Life, directed by Frank Capra. RKO, 1946.

I Wake Up Screaming, directed by H. Bruce Humberstone. Twentieth Century Fox, 1941.

The Jazz Singer, directed by Alan Crosland. Warner Brothers, 1927.

Kildare of Storm, directed by Harry L. Franklin. Metro, 1918.

King of Kings, directed by Cecil B. DeMille. DeMille Productions, 1927.

Kiss Me Kate, directed by George Sidney. MGM, 1953.

Kiss of Death, directed by Henry Hathaway. Twentieth Century Fox, 1947.

The Lady Eve, directed by Preston Sturgis. Paramount, 1941.

Lady Windermere's Fan, directed by Fred Paul. Ideal Films Co., 1916.

Lady Windermere's Fan, directed by Ernst Lubitsch. Warner Brothers, 1925.

The Last Man on Earth, directed by John G. Blytone. Fox, 1924.

The Last Moment, directed by Paul Fejos. Zakoro, 1928.

Laura, directed by Otto Preminger. Twentieth Century Fox, 1944.

The Life and Death of 9413—A Hollywood Extra, directed by Slavko Vorkapich and Robert Florey. FBO Picture, 1928.

Little Caesar, directed by Mervyn LeRoy. Warner Brothers, 1931.

The Lodger, directed by John Brahm. Twentieth Century Fox, 1944.

Lullaby, directed by Boris Deutsch. Independent, 1929.

Mad Love, directed by Karl Freund. MGM, 1935.

Madame DuBarry, directed by Ernst Lubitsch. Germany, 1919.

Male and Female, directed by Cecil B. DeMille. Paramount, 1919.

The Man in Half Moon Street, directed by Ralph Murphy. Paramount, 1945.

The Man Who Could Cheat Death, directed by Terence Fisher. Hammer, 1959.

Manhatta, directed by Charles Sheeler and Paul Strand. Production unknown, 1921.

Manhattan Melodrama, directed by W. S. Van Dyke. MGM, 1934.

Manslaughter, directed by Cecil B. DeMille. Paramount, 1922.

The Marriage Circle, directed by Ernst Lubitsch. Warner Brothers, 1924.

Merton of the Movies, directed by James Cruze. Adolph Zukor and Jesse Lasky,1924.

Mildred Pierce, directed by Michael Curtiz. Warner Brothers, 1945.

Miss Fatty's Seaside Lovers, directed by Roscoe Arbuckle. Keystone, 1915.

A Modern Salome, directed by Léonce Perret. Hope Hampton Productions, 1920; lost.

The Musketeers of Pig Alley, directed by D. W. Griffith. General Film Company, 1912.

My Little Chickadee, directed by Edward F. Cline. Universal, 1940.

My Man Godfrey, directed by Gregory La Cava. Universal, 1936.

Now, Voyager, directed by Irving Rapper. Warner Brothers, 1942.

The Old Dark House, directed by James Whale. Universal, 1932.

One Hour with You directed by Ernst Lubitsch. Paramount,1932.

The Outlaw, directed by Howard Hughes. RKO, 1943.

The Palister Case, directed by William Parke. Goldwyn, 1920.

The Picture of Dorian Gray, directed by Edwin Thanhouser. Thanhouser, 1915.

The Picture of Dorian Gray, director unknown. Browne Films, 1916; lost.

The Picture of Dorian Gray, directed by Albert Lewin. MGM, 1945.

Portret Doriana Greia, directed by Vsevolod Meyerhold. Russia, 1915; lost.

Psycho, directed by Alfred Hitchcock. Paramount, 1960.

The Public Enemy, directed by William A. Wellman. Warner Brothers, 1931.

Queen Christina, directed by Rouben Mamoulian. MGM, 1933.

Quo Vadis?, directed by Enrico Guazzoni. Italy, 1913.

Raffles, directed by Gilbert M. Anderson. Vitagraph, 1905.

Raffles, directed by George Fitzmaurice. UA, 1930.

Raffles, the Amateur Cracksman, directed by George Irving. Hyclass,1917.

Raffles, the Amateur Cracksman, directed by King Baggot. Universal, 1925.

Raffles the Dog, director unknown. Edison, 1905; lost.

The Red Lantern, directed by Albert Capellani. Metro, 1919.

The Roaring Twenties, directed by Raoul Walsh. Warner Brothers, 1939.

Robin Hood [released first as *Douglas Fairbanks in Robin Hood*], directed by Allan Dwan. UA, 1922.

Romeo and Juliet, directed by J. Gordon Edwards. Fox, 1916; lost.

Romeo and Juliet, directed by John W. Noble and Francis X. Bushman. Metro, 1916; lost.

Rosita, directed by Ernst Lubitsch. UA, 1923.

The Rug Maker's Daughter, directed by Oscar Apfel. Bosworth, 1915; lost.

Salome, directed by J. Gordon Edwards. Fox, 1918; lost.

Salome, directed by Charles Bryant. Nazimova Pictures, 1922.

Salome Craze, director unknown. Phoenix Film Company, 1909; lost.

Salome; or, The Dance of the Seven Veils, director unknown. Vitagraph, 1908; lost.

The Saloon Dance, director unknown. Production unknown, *c.*1908; lost.

The Salvation Hunters, directed by Josef von Sternberg. UA, 1925.

Scarface, directed by Howard Hawks. UA, 1932.

The Scoundrel, directed by Ben Hecht and Charles MacArthur. Paramount, 1935.

The Sea Hawk, directed by Frank Lloyd. Frank Lloyd Productions, 1924.

The Secret Life of Dorian Gray, directed by Massimo Dallamano. Constantin Films, 1970.

Small Town Idol, directed by Mack Sennett. Associated Producers, 1921.

The Society Raffles, director unknown. American Mutoscope and Biograph, 1905; lost.

The Soul of the Cypress, directed by Dudley Murphy. Production unknown, 1920.

Sunset Boulevard, directed by Billy Wilder. Paramount, 1950.

Suspense, directed by Lois Weber. Rex, 1913.

Suspicion, directed by Alfred Hitchcock. RKO, 1941.

Svengali, directed by Archi Mayo. Warner Brothers, 1931.

The Tell-Tale Heart, directed by Charles Klein and Leon Shamroy. Independent, 1928.

The Ten Commandments, directed by Cecil B. DeMille. Famous-Players Lasky 1923.

Trouble in Paradise, directed by Ernst Lubitsch. Paramount, 1932.

Twentieth Century, directed by Howard Hawks. Columbia,1934.

Underworld, directed by Josef von Sternberg. Paramount, 1927.

An Unseen Enemy, directed by D. W. Griffith. Biograph, 1912.

Wild Oranges, directed by King Vidor. Goldwyn, 1924.

The Woman and the Puppet, directed by Reginald Barker. Goldwyn, 1920.

A Woman of No Importance, directed by Denison Clift. Ideal Films Co., 1921.

A Woman of Paris, directed by Charlie Chaplin. UA, 1923.

A Woman of the World, directed by Mal St Clair. Famous-Players Lasky, 1925.

The Women, directed by George Cukor. MGM, 1939.

Wuthering Heights, directed by William Wyler. Goldwyn Pictures, 1939.

Ziegfeld Follies, directed by Vincente Minnelli et al. MGM, 1946.

Acknowledgements

Like most books, *Wilde in the Dream Factory* was thought out and written among various life upheavals. The figures on its pages have been great company to me over the years. If my words about them and their time has moments of enjoyment for the reader too, this is entirely due to my luck in finding myself in a supportive, encouraging university with friends and colleagues who value research for its own sake, or as close to it as is possible to get in the English higher education system. I owe a debt of gratitude to the University of Exeter and successive Deans and Associate Deans for funding research travel and leave, and consistently assuring me that I should write the book I wanted to write, rather than making do with a book that would be ready in time for the REF. I'd also like to thank my dear friends in the Department of English and Creative Writing. In particular, Regenia Gagnier, Jo Gill, Jason Hall, Fiona Handyside, Sam North, Vike Plock, Angelique Richardson, and Chris Stokes, as well as my students, whose enthusiasm for Wilde and film has kept up my own when necessary.

I began thinking about Wilde and cinema in 2010. My family have been kind enough to share in my seemingly random interests for this and that film or concept, and not to mind my habitual distractions as I've worked these out. I'm grateful to my boys Rufus and Laurence for their enthusiasm about 'Mummy's book' and Rufus's help in taking the screenshots of movies that appear throughout it. It is dedicated to Rufus with thanks for his emotional intelligence and technical know-how, as well as his entirely independent determination to read *Salome* at the age of 10.

Throughout, my mum, Claire, has been a kind, thoughtful, and dedicated grandmother-looker-after, giving me the kind of thought-space that is rare for mothers of small children. Conferences, symposia, seminars, and supervisions have been essential to develop this story about Wilde and the movies. Thanks to those who have invited me to speak about what I'm working on, asked questions, suggested leads, put me straight, and picked up conversations in the bar. Of these, Joseph Bristow, Dennis Denisoff, Nick Freeman, Steve Neale, Charlie Page, Kathleen Riley, Darcy Sullivan, Margaret Stetz, and Carolyn Williams have provided especially invaluable suggestions and inspiration. Many more have kindly taken time to reply to my emails and I'd like to thank Shelley Stamp and Gregory Willam Mank, in particular, for their guidance. I am grateful to the Margaret Herrick Library in Beverley Hills, the Bodleian Library in Oxford, the New York Public Library, and the University of Bristol Theatre Collection for their help, and to Merlin Holland and Edward M. Burns for permissions to quote unpublished material from the Papers of Robert Ross and Vyvyan Holland relating to the Literary Estate of Oscar Wilde and the Carl Van Vechten Papers, respectively. At Oxford University Press, Eleanor Collins, Jacqueline

Norton, and Emma Varley really understood the concept of this book and my enthusiasm for it from the start and have been patient with the speed at which it has been written. Rowena Anketell has been a patient and astute copyeditor. My thanks to Roopa Nelson for her calm and diligent work on the proofs. (Any errors that remain are my fault.)

Sharing and discussing ideas with friends has been the most enjoyable part of putting this study together. Beci Carver, Sasha Dvornyk, Peter Evans, Sarah Parker, Neil Sammells, Jon Stone, and Jeremy Treglown have provided generous comments on draft chapters. Like the very best people, their astute intellectual insights have been accompanied by common sense, great kindness, and a sense of fun. Without Peter this book would not have been started. My sincere thanks to him for telling me I must write about films in 2008 and helping me believe I could.

With particular gratitude and pleasure I'd like to thank my co-conspirators in Wilde and all things decadent, Kristin Mahoney and Alex Murray. Their humour, commiserations, and distractions, as well as detailed suggestions on drafts over the years, have made this monograph feel like a lark we're all on together, as, in a way, it has been. Long may we find more larks together.

And finally, Aidan Foster-Carter has been my unwavering support from the moment I began sketching ideas till the final manuscript submission. His devotion to our family and pragmatism in 'returning to the immediate' while my head is on the West Coast mean more than any words can say.

Index

Note: Tables and figures are indicated by an italic *t* and *f* following the page number.